The Second United States
Sharpshooters in
the Civil War

The Second United States Sharpshooters in the Civil War

A History and Roster

GERALD L. EARLEY

McFarland & Company, Inc., Publishers
Jefferson, North Carolina

The present work is a reprint of the illustrated case bound edition of The Second United States Sharpshooters in the Civil War: A History and Roster, *first published in 2009 by McFarland.*

Library of Congress Cataloguing-in-Publication Data

Earley, Gerald L.
The Second United States Sharpshooters in the Civil War : a history and roster / Gerald L. Earley.
p.   cm.
Includes bibliographical references and index.

ISBN 978-0-7864-9546-7 (softcover : acid free paper) ∞
ISBN 978-0-7864-5302-3 (ebook)

1. United States. Army. Sharpshooters Regiment, 2nd (1861–1865) 2. United States—History—Civil War, 1861–1865—Regimental histories. 3. United States—History—Civil War, 1861–1865—Campaigns. 4. Berdan, Hiram, ca. 1823–1893. 5. United States. Army. Sharpshooters Regiments, 2nd (1861–1865)—Registers. 6. United States—History—Civil War, 1861–1865—Registers. I. Title.
E492.7.E37   2014   973.7'6—dc22   2009003333

British Library cataloguing data are available

© 2009 Gerald L. Earley. All rights reserved

No part of this book may be reproduced or transmitted in any form or by any means, electronic or mechanical, including photocopying or recording, or by any information storage and retrieval system, without permission in writing from the publisher.

On the cover: in the forefront, Colonel Hiram Berdan; in the background, men from Company F, 2nd U.S.S.S.

Manufactured in the United States of America

*McFarland & Company, Inc., Publishers
Box 611, Jefferson, North Carolina 28640
www.mcfarlandpub.com*

To Clara Jones Featheringill

Table of Contents

Preface — 1

1 — Elite and Unique: The Genesis of Berdan's Sharpshooters — 5
2 — Berdan's Camp of Instruction: Training and Turmoil — 16
3 — At the Bloody Point of Lincoln's Sword — 33
4 — A Continual Wasting Effect — 45
5 — "There Was Bloody Work Done" — 70
6 — The Most Dismal and Despondent Days — 93
7 — At Their Best: Chancellorsville — 106
8 — "Turning the Tide": Gettysburg — 116
9 — The Feckless Campaigns — 135
10 — With Ulysses in the Wilderness — 151
11 — A Plethora of War: Spotsylvania to Cold Harbor — 165
12 — Winning the Hard Way: Petersburg — 184

Epilogue — 198
Appendix: Roster — 207
Chapter Notes — 227
Bibliography — 237
Index — 241

Preface

Several years ago I traveled to Richmond, Virginia, to visit some of the numerous battlefields and Civil War sites in that area. At Cold Harbor I wanted to examine the Confederate works on the south portion of the field where the Federal II Corps had been badly mangled on June 3, 1864. Unfortunately little of the battlefield is owned by the National Park Service, and the area I wanted to visit was apparently owned by an African American farmer. Following a map, I drove down a narrow, dusty lane to the farmer's house; there the farmer's son offered to lead me on foot to the place I wanted to see.

As we walked among the weathered, overgrown remnants of the Confederate works, I remarked that it was here that a Union corps had been shattered — it was perhaps the most terrible killing field of the war. The farmer's son replied matter-of-factly that the Yankees never could fight anyhow.

His perception that "Yankees never could fight anyhow" is by no means unique in the South today. At the outbreak of the Civil War this perception of Yankee martial inferiority was widespread even in the North. In the New England states, the home of the original Yankees, many people felt an intellectual superiority to their Southern counterparts. The New England states undoubtedly had a better educated population and a more developed industrial economy than the South as a whole. However, those in a position to judge military matters believed that in terms of infantry and cavalry the South held a decided edge.

There were valid reasons for the New Englanders' concerns about their ability to wage war with the South. To a large extent the Yankees understood that cultural and geographical differences had shaped each region's pool of potential soldiers. A thick volume would be required to properly address the cultural differences between the regions, one founded by the Puritan and the other by the Cavalier. Succinctly, while the Yankees were confident that their Navy and artillery were superior, they also believed that their ground forces, especially in terms of marksmanship, were not equal to what the South could bring to the field.

Because of this perception of potential Southern superiority in the infantry arm, concerned Northerners urged the country's premier marksman, Hiram Berdan, to form a regiment or corps of expert riflemen to bolster the Federal Army. While Berdan was not a military man, he was well known for his shooting prowess and was acquainted with many other talented shooters. Thus, Berdan was a natural choice to recruit a body of men equal or superior in marksmanship to anything the South had to offer.

This is the story of *the* quintessential pan–Yankee ground unit in the Civil War, the 2nd U.S. Sharpshooters. There was only one other true pan–Yankee regiment in the Civil War, the 1st U.S. Sharpshooters. These two regiments, recruited through the efforts of Hiram Berdan, were known as Berdan's Sharpshooters. Originally Berdan had intended to recruit companies of expert marksmen in each loyal state. In practice, however, the companies that formed Berdan's Sharpshooters were mainly recruited in the region of the upper North known as greater New England: that is, the region settled by Yankees as they moved westward and then dominated by Yankee culture. Of Berdan's two regiments, the 2nd U.S. Sharpshooters was clearly the most thoroughly Yankee. The 1st U.S. Sharpshooters, for one thing, had one full company originally recruited entirely from Swiss and German immigrants.

Expert marksmen, or sharpshooters, have long been a subject of fascination for Americans. In the late nineteenth century, sharpshooters captivated audiences throughout the country in traveling Wild West shows. My own maternal grandmother was proud to say that her father, Sergeant William Jones, was a sharpshooter in the Eleventh Kentucky Infantry during the Civil War. Years after her death, I learned that her father's regiment had been armed with New Model 1859 Sharps Rifles, the same weapon issued to Berdan's Sharpshooters. This was indeed a distinction, as very few infantry units carried Sharps Rifles during the war.

While there were several other sharpshooter units in the Federal and Confederate armies, Berdan's Sharpshooters were the most renowned, perhaps the standard by which all the others should be judged. The aforementioned Sharps Rifle, already famous because of the use of Sharps Carbines in "Bleeding Kansas" during the 1850s, was the best weapon available for sharpshooting at the onset of the war. It is a testament to the influence of Berdan and his men that they were able to demand and then receive specially manufactured Sharps Rifles to be carried in the field. The Sharps Rifles themselves no doubt contributed to the fame of Berdan's marksmen.

Unfortunately, the potential of the 2nd U.S. Sharpshooters was never fully realized because of extreme attrition early in the war. Nearly one year passed before the 2nd experienced heavy combat, and in that time the regiment, already two companies under strength, was severely reduced by disease and by injuries resulting from a train accident. The regiment was largely composed of men with above average abilities and intelligence, many of whom quickly became disillusioned by the realities of war and left the regiment when opportunities arose.

There were discipline and attitude problems especially evident in the 2nd U. S. Sharpshooters. Again, this was a true Yankee unit with a healthy dose of self-respect from a region renowned for its equalitarian ideals. Nevertheless, the 2nd compiled an impressive combat record and earned the enduring respect of its enemies. In so doing the 2nd proved that the "Yankees couldn't fight" adage is a misapprehension. The regiment fought in all of the battles involving the Army of the Potomac from 2nd Bull Run to Petersburg, providing valuable service and inflicting heavy losses on the enemy. However, the most telling aspect of its story is that, when left alone by the army brass, it fought with the methods and tactics favored in the wars fought in the following century. It would not be an exaggeration to say that this regiment was ahead of its time.

I have made no effort to edit quoted material for this book, and there is no interpolation of *sic* in application to quotes. Editing of quotations sometimes distracts the reader and potentially, though unintentionally, can alter the meaning of the quoted material. All quotations are verbatim. Brackets are used in quotes when an explanation or further detail is suggested.

In preparing and researching this book I received indispensable assistance that I wish to acknowledge. First, I want to thank my wife Myrna for her support, encouragement, and companionship during the long treks to distant battlefields. The following National Parks Service staffers were especially helpful in providing research materials: John Heiser, Gettysburg National Military Park; Ted Alexander, Antietam National Battlefield; John A. Reid, Manassas National Battlefield; Donald C. Pfanz, Fredericksburg and Spotsylvania National Military Park; Robert E.L. Krick, Richmond National Battlefield; Jeffrey L. Patrick, librarian at Wilson's Creek National Battlefield; and Steve Muckala, a volunteer staffer at that library.

Janice Frye of the Chancellorsville National Battlefield Visitor Center was very gracious in assisting me while I photographed an original Berdan Sharps Rifle there. The staff at Chancellorsville was very knowledgeable and was of great help in pointing out troop movements and locations pertaining to the battles of Chancellorsville, Mine Run, the Wilderness and Spotsylvania.

1

Elite and Unique: The Genesis of Berdan's Sharpshooters

Colonel Emory F. Best of the 23rd Georgia Infantry was living the nightmare military commanders have dreaded since the dawn of time. He and his men were trapped by the enemy with seemingly only three options: run, surrender or die. The colonel knew that utilizing a suppressing or covering fire was impracticable, so making an orderly retreat seemed improbable. He was facing an enemy that had exhibited almost uncanny marksmanship and running would render his men vulnerable to it.

It seemed to Best as if his men were being pursued by an entire brigade of Federals, perhaps four regiments. A high volume of accurate fire had forced his regiment to take cover in an unfinished railroad bed that sliced through a forest. Over the embankment on his front, Best could see flashes of flame and billowing white smoke from the edge of the dark green forest about 300 yards distant. To the rear was another 150 to 250 yards of cleared ground from the railroad bed to the other edge of timber. The railroad bed at this point cut slightly into the terrain, enough to shelter all of Best's men.

Time was running out on the Georgians. Federals dressed in unusual dark green uniforms had crept around the flanks, and soon they could enfilade the railroad cut. Best knew that an enemy sweep around the rear would cut off any hope of retreat. One of the trapped men later wrote about the incident, explaining that for the Georgians the only chance was to climb over the railroad embankment and run or be taken captive. "It was very plain," he wrote, "that we had done all that we could do."[1]

Colonel Best had been ordered to hold the Federals back while General "Stonewall" Jackson made his famous flank march to attack Howard's Corps at Chancellorsville. The 23rd Georgia was to hold a position until Jackson's artillery and wagon train cleared a nearby road and then join the flanking march. In protecting Jackson's trains, the 23rd Georgia had been cut off from the rest of the Confederate army. Now the colonel yelled out to his men to make their escape any way they could. He and about twenty nearby men bolted out of the railroad cut and sped across the cleared space, escaping into the timber beyond.

When others tried to follow, the Federals opened with an accurate fire. The bullets, though fired from nearly 300 yards distance, struck all around the Georgians, raising telltale plumes of dust, forcing the men back to the shelter of the cut. Seeing that their colonel was gone and their escape route was swept by enemy fire, the Georgians hunkered down in the cut for a few minutes until one of them waved a white cloth to signal surrender.

It was some minutes before the careful Federals emerged to take the Georgians prisoner. The green-clad Federals had to negotiate the wide clearing while covering the huddled Confederates. But before long nearly 300 men, most of the 23rd Georgia Infantry, marched out of the railroad cut and into the Federal lines.

As the Confederates soon learned, it was not a large Federal brigade that cornered the 23rd Georgia but only two under-strength regiments. In fact only about 100 Federals had actually pinned down the Confederates in front of the railroad cut while the remainder of the two regiments worked the flanks and beyond.[2] These were, however, not ordinary Federals. They belonged to the "crack unit" of the Army of the Potomac, Berdan's Sharpshooters.[3]

What the two Federal sharpshooting regiments accomplished in capturing the 23rd Georgia brings to mind Corporal Alvin York's feat in the Argonne Forest during World War I, though on a larger scale. York used his shooting skills to coerce 132 Germans into surrendering.[4] Moving through wooded terrain, York utilized cover and stealth to approach the Germans and then exceptional marksmanship to subdue them. For his valor York received the Medal of Honor and became a national hero. Berdan's Sharpshooters, like the famous York, utilized accurate fire from concealment to disorient and demoralize the 23rd Georgia. Colonel Best did not know that he was facing only 100 Federals on his front, or he likely would have avoided the loss of most of his regiment.

It was shortly after the attack on Fort Sumter in the spring of 1861 that events necessitated a call for special men to accompany the thousands already rushing to arms to save the Union. On April 15, 1861, President Lincoln called for 75,000 militiamen to serve for ninety days to suppress a growing Southern rebellion.[5] Reaction to the president's call was immediate, with nearly every loyal state mustering infantry regiments to serve for three months. Two states, Ohio and Pennsylvania, actually raised over twenty of these temporary infantry units.[6] Within days, however, it became clear that these troops would not suffice.

Three days after Lincoln's first call for troops, the U.S. Armory at Harpers Ferry, Virginia, was occupied by Virginia militia commanded by Captain Turner Ashby.[7] In less than a month the eleven-state Confederacy was complete, with Missouri, Kentucky and Maryland also in danger of leaving the Union. Throughout the South, Federal property was being seized; the Confederate government was quickly consolidating power and recruiting a large army.

President Lincoln's original token call for troops had precipitated events that now required him to create an army capable of fighting a prolonged war. On May 3, 1861, Lincoln issued another call that eventually raised over 700,000 men, 657,868 of them for three years of service.[8] Shortly afterwards the country began to hear from Hiram Berdan, a wealthy inventor who just happened to be perhaps the best marksman in the country. Berdan would play a vital role in selecting special men from the hundreds of thousands rushing to arms to save the Union.

Just before the extraordinary recruiting frenzy that swept the North in answer to Lincoln's call, an article appeared in the *New York Times* on May 1, 1861. The article was addressed to the new recruits, and it was filled with well-intentioned advice about drill, uniforms, etc. However, the crux of the article was about marksmanship, a subject of great concern with the prospect of war looming:

> Especially should attention be paid to sharp-shooting.... At the South, skill in sharp-shooting is almost universal. At the North it is extremely uncommon. If our raw recruits ... will consume every hour in target practice, they will be able to give a better account of themselves.[9]

Soon after this *Times* article appeared, Hiram Berdan was leading an effort to assemble a regiment composed entirely of expert marksmen. Perhaps the idea of gathering an entire regiment of crack shots was pressed upon Berdan for the very reason mentioned in the *Times*, as is indicated by the words of William Y.W. Ripley. Ripley, who eventually served as the lieutenant colonel of Berdan's first regiment, made the following observation after the war:

> Very soon after the outbreak of the war for the Union ... it became painfully apparent that, however inferior the rank and file of the Confederate armies were in point of education and general intelligence to the men who composed the armies of the Union, however imperfect and rude their equipment and material, man for man they were the superiors of their northern antagonists in the use of arms.... Indeed, there were in many regiments in the northern armies men who had never even fired a gun of any description at the time of their enlistment.
>
> On the other hand, there were known to be scattered throughout the loyal states, a great number of men who had made rifle shooting a study, and who, by practice on the target ground and at the country shooting matches, had gained a skill equal to that of the men of the South in any kind of shooting, and in long range practice a much greater degree of excellency.[10]

Ripley's observation about the superiority of Southern infantry was later echoed by General Henry Hunt, chief of artillery for the Army of the Potomac. According to General Hunt, "The South had at the beginning of the war the better material for infantry and cavalry," but the North had better personnel for artillery. He continued, "No country furnishes better men for the artillery proper than our Northern, and particularly our New England, states."[11]

Although Hiram Berdan started his search for crack shots about the time of President Lincoln's call for three-year volunteers, the concept of expert riflemen serving in the field of battle as sharpshooters was older than the nation itself. Americans were used for flank rifle companies during the French and Indian War, years before the Revolution.[12] They were chosen for their reputation as skilled marksmen.

During the Revolutionary War, General Washington recognized the value of expert riflemen, and he authorized ten companies of riflemen for his army. "The choice of riflemen attested to the belief that specialists in the use of this new weapon would be a valuable adjunct to the musketry of New England."[13] There were numerous examples of American rifle-fire devastating the British. At Saratoga, for instance, riflemen continually harassed British outposts from a distance beyond musket range. Also at that battle, Tim Murphy, an American sharpshooter, "picked off" British general Simon Fraser.[14] And at Kings Mountain, a force of American sharpshooters annihilated 1,100 Redcoats while losing only "28 killed and 62 wounded."[15]

Americans during the colonial and frontier years excelled at rifle production, making rifles second to none in utility and accuracy. Frontiersmen made good use of these weapons for hunting and Indian fighting. With a wealth of shooting experience from life in the vast, wild forests, Americans were renowned for their rifles and their marksmanship. Indeed, British general George Hanger, who was familiar with European armies and their rifle units, said that in his expert opinion "the American rifle was the best in the world and the American marksman the best shot."[16]

The significance of sharpshooting and the tradition of American marksmanship were well known at the outset of the Civil War. However, there is some controversy over exactly who originated the idea of forming the first true regiments of American sharpshooters. In one of the first newspaper articles relating Hiram Berdan to a regiment of sharpshooters, Berdan indicated that the effort to raise sharpshooters was underway before his involvement:

> FIFTH AVENUE HOTEL NEW YORK, May 30, 1861.
> To the Sharp-Shooters in the Loyal States:
>
> Gentlemen: Many of you are undoubtedly aware that an effort is making to get up a regiment to be composed entirely of first-class rifle shots at long distances, and that in consequence of my having myself done something in this way of rifle shooting, suggestions have been made in the public press that I should aid in this effort. I am, moreover, receiving almost daily applications, by letter and in person, to the same effect, and I see so clearly the great importance of the object in view, that I do not feel at liberty to refrain from doing what I can to further it.
>
> With this view I propose that all such gentlemen that have made themselves good shots at long distances, who are willing to place their skill in this way at the service of our country, in this her great struggle, should send their names to me, with an affidavit, showing the best shooting they have done at two hundred yards, or more.
>
> As soon as the necessary arrangements are made for equipment, &c, notice will be given to all those whose applications are approved.
>
> No application will be considered in which the average of ten consecutive shots exceeds five inches from the centre of target to the centre of the ball at two hundred yards.
>
> The prodigious efficiency of detachments of such Sharp-Shooters, armed with our Northern Patent Target Rifles, needs only to be alluded to to be recognized at once by all who have any knowledge of this subject.
>
> Need I add one word to enforce the duty of our amateur target-shots to make their peculiar skill useful to our country at this time of trial? That skill — the offspring of a mainly Northern sport — can be converted into a powerful military instrument so readily, I feel confident the subject need only to be suggested to insure its being fully and promptly attended to.
>
> Very respectfully, your obedient servant,
> H. Berdan.[17]

This article demonstrates that Hiram Berdan had been approached to lead an effort to recruit the best long-range shooters from the "Loyal States" for a regiment to defend the Union. Berdan mentioned that the press had suggested that he "aid in this effort." He gave no indication that it was his idea, but it is clear that he was already involved in the recruiting effort in May 1861.

Hiram Berdan was an obvious choice to form a sharpshooter regiment. Born in Phelps, New York, on September 6, 1824, of Huguenot descent, Berdan was a bright, inventive, and accomplished man.[18] As a boy Berdan moved to Plymouth, Michigan, where he grew up living a frontier farm life. As a youth he studied engineering at Hobart College in Geneva, New York. Soon after college Berdan began a career as an inventor, which proved a success by earning him considerable wealth. From his boyhood days Berdan had excelled in shooting, and by the 1850s he was known as an elite marksman. Indeed, it was reported that Berdan had made "the best rifle shot on record, so far as can be ascertained" for that time period.[19]

While it is impossible to say, Berdan's Huguenot ancestry perhaps influenced his character and behavior. The Huguenots were a Calvinist sect that fled religious persecution in France to Holland, Ireland and on to America. As Calvinists, Huguenots were similar in many ways to the Puritans, America's primordial Yankees. French nobles made up the majority of the first Huguenots, and a sort of aristocratic air characterized the sect. Believing themselves to be God's chosen people, the Huguenots were taught that their life's work was a calling; thus, their success in life's work was God's blessing and a sign of His favor. Another attribute of this sect was a proclivity to dictate to others how they should live, perhaps derived from their sense of special status as a chosen people.[20]

One thing is for certain: Hiram Berdan's subsequent record as a military officer proved that he was much more concerned with success through advancement in rank than with reputation for bravery. Time and again he would prove by his actions that for him the ultimate measurement of his worth was how well his efforts prospered. He apparently did not especially concern himself with ideals or virtues; success and personal advancement superseded such concerns in his moral universe.

By early June, Berdan had begun to formulate plans for the use of his special regiment. However, it was the usual custom during the Civil War for governors to appoint the colonels of volunteer regiments. Since Berdan was gathering men from several states, he had to tender his regiment and his services to the national government. He soon traveled to Washington for this purpose, and on June 13, 1861, he met with President Abraham Lincoln and also Secretary of War Simon Cameron to introduce his plans to the government.[21] He was immediately referred to General-in-Chief Winfield Scott. The following day General Scott had a letter sent to Berdan informing him that he was "very favorably impressed," and that he believed that Berdan's sharpshooter regiment would be of "great value and could be advantageously employed by him in the public service."[22]

Berdan very quickly received authorization to proceed with his efforts to raise his sharpshooter regiment as a United States volunteer unit. He returned to New York and set to work trying to obtain recruits from every loyal state. An article appearing in the *New York Times* on June 28, 1861, mentioned Berdan's efforts: "W.S. Rowland of New York, who was appointed to see the Governors of the Western States, to urge them each to furnish one company of sharpshooters for Col. Berdan's regiment, says he has been successful in every application as yet."[23]

The summer of 1861, when Berdan sought volunteers for his regiment, was easily the most productive recruiting period of the war. Throughout the country men were looking for opportunities to serve. In some cases men left their native states to serve in regiments being raised in neighboring states. There were many cases where regiments were quickly filled in districts and no further recruiting was ongoing. Groups of men would then apply to other states for an opportunity to enlist. Men from Illinois, for example, served in Missouri and even Kansas regiments.

Recruiting officers could afford to be very selective in July 1861. One excellent example is the case of Elisha Hunt Rhodes, who tried to enlist as a private in the 2nd Rhode Island Infantry. Acting as a clerk signing up volunteers for that regiment, Rhodes was much better educated than the average Civil War soldier. Nevertheless, Rhodes was nearly rejected by the surgeon examining the recruits. Only after convincing the colonel to overrule the surgeon did Rhodes manage to enlist as a private. He later became the colonel of the very regiment that nearly rejected him as a private.[24]

On Wednesday, July 17, 1861, the *New York Times* printed a detailed article about the proper use of sharpshooters. During the early war period this newspaper often published articles about war-related topics of special interest, such as ironclad warships, fortifications, etc. This article is of particular interest because it addresses the European method of using sharpshooters. The purpose of this article was to "consider by light of European practice, and the experience of our own troops upon the frontier: the form in which a valuable arm of the service can be made most effective."

> Shall the Sharp-shooters be formed into regiments, according to the plan of Mr. Berdan, or into companies? Shall any particular weapon be universally adopted, or shall each rifleman be allowed to choose his own weapon? Should the weapons be provided with bayonets, or should the bearer be reserved for service that does not require the use of that supplementary weapon?
>
> Consulting European usage.... The French Sharp-shooter undergoes a systematic course of instruction in the use of his piece. ... his eye is brought to calculate by practice distances with the greatest accuracy; and he is otherwise instructed on every point that may enable him to do the greatest possible execution at the greatest possible distance.

The article continued by discussing the use of sharpshooters in the Swiss Army and in Austria and making suggestions for the use of sharpshooters in the Federal Army. On the subject of bayonets, sharpshooters "should be devoted to sharp-shooting and nothing else." Berdan's idea of regiments of sharpshooters was rejected; they should, according to the article, "be formed into companies, or even smaller bodies, and have their position on the wings of the regiments, and not be consolidated into regiments."[25]

As mentioned previously, there is some evidence that Hiram Berdan was not actually the first to suggest a regiment of sharpshooters for the Federal army. Towards the end of July 1861, a Swiss immigrant and soldier of fortune, Caspar Trepp, offered a company of Swiss and German marksmen for Berdan's regiment. These men became the first company mustered into service as U.S. Sharpshooters. Rudolph Aschmann served as a captain in this company during the war. He had the following take on this subject: "So it was a Swiss, my unforgettable friend and patron C. Trepp, who later was to shed his blood on the battlefield at Mine Run, who became the founder and organizer of a system of sharpshooters. In July 1861 he called attention to the establishment of such a corps, describing in some newspapers its usefulness and advantages, and offered to organize one if men of influence could take care of the matter and effect the government's sanction."[26]

Perhaps because of Berdan's wartime record and reputation, some historians have accepted this account by Aschmann as fact. One could infer, from the *Times* article above, that Caspar Trepp might have in fact suggested European sharpshooter methods to the press. However, Berdan was mentioned in the press in May 1861 as the man recruiting a regiment of sharpshooters. Aschmann and this July *Times* article dates Trepp's involvement considerably after Berdan's, at least two months. Aschmann may have truly believed that Trepp founded and organized the U.S. Sharpshooters in July 1861. However, most if not all period accounts credit Berdan as the founder of the sharpshooters, and the newspapers in 1861, having no obvious reason to ignore Trepp, coined the name Berdan's Sharpshooters.

During that summer of 1861, as Hiram Berdan and his agents worked to gather qualified men, the prevailing trend of the war worsened drastically. It was becoming clear by August that the conflict would be lasting, bloody and arduous. After the Battle of Bull Run on July 21, 1861, the Federal army retreated into Washington, and a lengthy lull in the fighting ensued in the Eastern Theater. This situation allowed Berdan time to organize and train his regiment. Since his men were not immediately needed for a campaign, Berdan was able to continue his recruiting efforts, and he apparently attempted to reach into every Northern state and even the border states of Kentucky and Missouri.

On August 7, 1861, Berdan was again the subject of an article in the *New York Times*. This time Berdan was given full credit for the concept of the U.S. Sharpshooters. The article noted that Berdan was a "first-class rifle shot" who during travels in the North and West had acquainted himself with "so many good rifle shots that it occurred to him to raise a regiment" of sharpshooters for the war. This detailed article mentioned recruiting efforts, uniforms, and weapons for his regiment:

> Through the agency of Mr. W.S. Rowland, no less than thirteen states have already signified their intention to furnish companies, while Francis P. Blair, Jr., in Missouri, and other gentlemen in Kentucky have each signified their intention of raising companies, so that in all there will be fifteen companies, outside of New-York, of 100 men each.... This work is now in progress and the rendezvous is at Weehawken.... During their stay at Weehawken the men will be instructed in the peculiar drill and signals of their corps — quite different from the drill of any other regiment in the country. The first company mustered into the service was a company of Swiss Sharp-shooters, who were sworn into the service last Friday. They are under the command of Caspar Trepp....
>
> The uniform of the Sharp-shooters will be green in summer and gray at other seasons, to assimilate as nearly as possible the colors of nature. They ridicule the idea of Zouave and Havelock uniforms, as affording too splendid a target for marksmen. They will be armed with the most Improved Springfield rifle, with a plain silver pin sight at the muzzle, and ... the globe sight at the breech.... It was at first

intended to arm them with the Northern target rifle, but it was found that there were not enough in the country....

The design of the Colonel is to have the regiment detached in squads on the field of battle to do duty in picking off officers and gunners on the European plan, by which they take the risk of being cut off by cavalry, or executed, as they certainly would be, if taken.[27]

Berdan's conception of his sharpshooters and of their role evolved through several phases during this organization period. His plans for arms, uniforms and methods of operation seemed to constantly change as the realities of war demanded. At one point in September, Berdan decided he wanted to test all of his recruits and select the best 100 men for special sniping duties. Those special men would then form a separate company. This concept, along with probably many others, never fully materialized.[28]

The recruiting canvass for Berdan's Sharpshooters continued through the summer and fall of 1861. Berdan seemed determined to create as large a command for himself as possible. In some ways the recruitment process was similar to most volunteer regiments. A captain was appointed to find qualified men and to get them signed onto the muster rolls. However, in many if not most volunteer regiments the men from each company were from one county or region of a state. In some cases Berdan was able to find enough men in one city or region to form a company, but in several cases his agents had to recruit statewide. In Company D, 2nd U.S. Sharpshooters, for instance, men were selected from numerous towns in Maine.

News of Berdan's effort to raise his sharpshooter regiment received good press coverage in the portion of the North called greater New England: that is, the areas settled by the New Englanders.[29] This region was composed of the original New England states, western and upper New York, upper Pennsylvania, Michigan, Wisconsin and Minnesota. It is significant that these were the only states that eventually furnished companies for Berdan's Sharpshooters, with the exception of Connecticut and Rhode Island. Although Berdan sent W.S. Rowland to recruit in the West, his efforts were unsuccessful except in the states mentioned above.

The region where Berdan recruited successfully (with the exception of New York City and Albany) was the most thoroughly Yankee cultural region of the nation. This region was settled by the "Puritan diaspora" from England. The word "Yankee" represented a "distinct new culture" introduced by Cromwell's allies who left England for America. The word possibly derived from "Jan Kaes, or John Cheese, the name given to the New England settlers by the seventeenth-century Dutch."[30] The name "Yankee" also could have been a "mistranscription of the Algonquin way of pronouncing 'English,' or perhaps 'Anglais.'"[31]

Again, Yankee culture descended from the Puritan culture planted at Plymouth Rock, and this Yankee culture was distinctly different from the remainder of the Northern states and the South. The original Yankees patterned their lives on a religious system; the Old South was dominated by the culture of the original Tidewater aristocracy of Virginia patterned "on a social system."[32] Other sections of the nation, such as the Ohio Valley and the lower portion of the Northwest Territory, for instance, were settled by mixtures of other ethnic and cultural groups: the Scots-Irish, Pennsylvania Dutch, and frontiersmen from the upper South. During and since the Civil War every Federal soldier has been called a Yankee. This, of course, is a misnomer, because the true Yankees were the inhabitants of greater New England. Federal soldiers from West Virginia, Kentucky and Missouri were called Yankees. Obviously, they were no more Yankee than Confederates from Virginia or North Carolina. Berdan's Sharpshooters, on the other hand, were Yankees in the truest sense.

Yankees were a cliché to the inhabitants of the rest of the country, with a well-known stereotype before the Civil War. They were known as sharp dealers: Yankee traders. They were innovative and world famous for their inventions, thus the term Yankee ingenuity. They were believed by some to be avaricious; one English author called them "money-getting roundheads."[33] But the most important Yankee trait, in terms of this story, was their egalitarianism — their belief in and insistence on a "consensual social contract."[34]

On September 28, 1861, Hiram Berdan notified the War Department that his first regiment was fully recruited and that he was organizing his second regiment.[35] Berdan employed various methods for finding his sharpshooters. Advertisements and articles in newspapers praised Berdan's efforts and implied that his sharpshooters would be the finest troops in the service. This alone generated great interest in Berdan's regiment. In addition, broadsides and posters in public places called for sharpshooters to meet at prearranged locations to apply for acceptance in the regiment. Berdan also sent agents to seek and test recruits. Every effort was made to imply that this was an elite unit: only the best would be chosen.

An article from a Vermont newspaper, the *Rutland Daily Herald*, dated August 10, 1861, is an excellent example of the favorable press coverage Berdan received during his recruiting phase. The article described a shooting exhibition Berdan apparently held at Weehawken. He shot at a target of Jefferson Davis at slightly over 200 yards, hitting the cheek, forehead, eye, etc., with each of seven shots. Berdan then asked where to place his eighth shot and was told to hit the nose. Of course, Berdan then shot the target in the nose and repeated the same feat twice more. Next some of Berdan's recruits took a turn. Out of forty-eight men who fired, all but four shots were classed as mortal hits. Berdan finished with the following comments about his recruits:

> These are picked men. I cannot tell how many kegs of powder we have wasted in getting them. They are artists. If you wished to get up a concert, would you engage hod-carriers to make music? This war with the rebels is simply a grand concert, and we are going to teach Davis, Beauregard and Company to appreciate *Hail Columbia* and *Yankee Doodle*.[36]

Two days later, in the same newspaper, a call was published for a Vermont company of sharpshooters to join Berdan's regiment. In a separate column, the following "inducements for joining this arm of the service" were listed:

1. Each Company of the Regiment will be the pet Company of the state, and the Regiment itself will be the *corps de esprit* of the army.

2. The service admits of less personal restraint and more freedom of individual action, and of course better opportunities for individual distinction.
3. The men will not be especially exposed to the dangers and hazards of the battlefield.
4. The uniform will be selected with particular references to its appearance, convenience, and durability.
5. Each man may choose his rifle and side arms.
6. The service rendered in the war will be the highest degree effective.
7. Arms will be furnished or paid for by the government ... the prospect of [pay] being increased by voluntary contributions.
8. The Regiment being composed of a company from each State, there will exist a constant and commendable emulation, tending to add greatly to the efficiency and renown of the several commands.[37]

Yet another newspaper article lauded Berdan's regiment as "the crack corps of the army," whose "special mission ... is to pick off the officers of the rebel army." The article continued: "The thanks of the people of the loyal states are due to Mr. Berdan for this addition of so important an arm to the military services in this, the hour of peril."[38]

Berdan's inducements to volunteers varied as the recruitment process played out. However, one factor remained constant. Each applicant was required to pass a shooting test before being accepted into the sharpshooters. In fact, it became a stipulation by the army's General Order 149 on October 2, 1862: "No person shall be mustered into the service ... as a member of the sharpshooters unless ... he had in five consecutive shots, at 200 yards at rest, made a string not over twenty-five inches, or the same string offhand at 100 yards."[39]

The recruits were required to qualify with open sights. Such shooting with Civil War–era black powder rifles required a very steady hand and excellent eyesight. The allowance was about five inches per shot from the center of the target to the center of the bullet hole for a total string of twenty-five inches. Today with modern scope-mounted rifles, this level of marksmanship would not qualify for police S.W.A.T. service. Sergeant Scott Brunow, a former police sniper of the Wichita, Kansas, Police Department, indicated that a hit within a two-inch bull is required for S.W.A.T. applicants at 200 yards. Police snipers require an even greater level of accuracy, and probably only thirty percent of the better marksmen qualify. However, the applicants in Berdan's day probably had greater natural shooting ability, as much greater skill was needed when using black powder rifles versus ballistically superior modern rifles with scopes.

The companies destined to form the 2nd U.S. Sharpshooters arrived at the Camp of Instruction in Washington, D.C., separately. Company A arrived in Washington on October 10, 1861, after four days of travel from Minnesota. This company would have been Company F of the 1st U.S. Sharpshooters, "but owning to the fine appearance of the company it was made Company A of a new regiment."[40] Some of the problems that would afflict the entire regiment were already evident when Company E left West Randolph, Vermont, in late November 1861. The men departed "in high glee. But owning to sickness and dissatisfaction but ninety-six men went forward."[41]

Colonel Henry A.V. Post, an acquaintance of Hiram Berdan, took command of the 2nd U.S. Sharpshooters. While most Civil War infantry regiments had ten companies, this regiment was composed of only eight, because two Massachusetts sharpshooter companies originally raised for Berdan transferred to Massachusetts infantry units. The 2nd U.S. Sharpshooters organized as follows[42]:

Company	State	Commanding Officer
A	Minnesota	Captain Francis Peteler
B	Michigan	Captain Andrew Stuart
C	Pennsylvania	Captain John Dewey
D	Maine	Captain James Fessenden
E	Vermont	Captain Homer Stoughton
F	New Hampshire	Captain Henry Caldwell
G	New Hampshire	Captain Wm. McPherson
H	Vermont	Captain Gilbert Hart

As already noted and as seen above, the entire 2nd U.S. Sharpshooters hailed from Yankeedom. A study of Army muster rolls revealed that three-fourths of the two million Federal soldiers who served in the Civil War were born in America.[43] The percentage of foreigners varied in Federal regiments: some units, like the Irish Brigade, were almost entirely manned by foreigners. Four-fifths of the regiments in the famous Iron Brigade hailed from Yankeedom, but only a "small majority of the men in the regiments were native-born Americans."[44] Conversely, the vast majority of the original recruits for the 2nd U.S. Sharpshooters were born in the United States. For instance, Company A showed only seven foreign-born original recruits, less than seven percent of the total. Scattered throughout the regiment were a few men from Canada, Ireland, England and Germany, but far fewer than represented in an average Federal regiment. Company F was almost entirely New Hampshire–born, and Company G, also from New Hampshire, had only two foreign-born original members.[45]

In late fall of 1861 the 2nd gathered at Berdan's Camp of Instruction in Washington to prepare for war. By early January 1862 most recruits had reported to camp. Anxious for a turn at the rebels and to make their mark in the war, few if any of the men deserted on the journey there. They anticipated a life of daring, high risk and perhaps some distinction. These men rightly considered themselves elite and unique, "a superior set of men, intellectually as well as physically," and as capable a set of marksmen as could be gathered.[46]

2

Berdan's Camp of Instruction: Training and Turmoil

As the neophyte soldiers of the 2nd U.S. Sharpshooters (2nd U.S.S.S.) arrived for training at a camp less than two miles from Capitol Hill, the atmosphere that greeted them was as dismal and dreary as the winter itself. The individual companies had departed their home states with great anticipation and justifiable sanguinity. Destiny would make them the most important and popular regiment in the Army, of that they had been repeatedly assured. But the unforeseen harsh realities and disillusionments of Berdan's Camp of Instruction would critically test their resolve and shove them to the brink of chaos during that bleak first winter of the war. These elite recruits with their Yankee mindset would soon chafe at the Army's bureaucratic pragmatism.

Hiram Berdan had been training recruits for his first sharpshooter regiment for months before most of the companies destined to become the 2nd U.S.S.S. arrived in Washington. During that period Berdan made an odious name for himself with the men of his first regiment. When Company F of the new regiment arrived at the Camp of Instruction from New Hampshire, the New Hampshire company from Berdan's first regiment escorted them to the camp. One of the newcomers was taken aback by the attitude of the men from Berdan's camp. He remembered their doleful report "of the meanness of Colonel Berdan," and how the soldiers railed against Berdan, denouncing him as a fraud, liar and imposter who failed to keep any of his promises. The initials U.S.S.S. on their hats, they said, stood for "Unfortunate Soldiers Sadly Sold" rather than their service branch designation as United States Sharpshooters. The newcomer professed that he had never seen "a more indignant company of men."[1] The gloomy aura permeating these trainees was not an anomaly: it was a true indication of the morale in Berdan's camp. Conditions would only worsen as the winter wore on.

Like a good many of the men leading volunteer regiments during the Civil War, Berdan was not a military man by training or nature. Berdan had quickly encountered challenges as an army colonel that he had never imagined. There were endless particulars to attend, particulars unique to his command. Such vexatious and complicated details could not have been anticipated. Unfortunately for his sharpshooters, Berdan apparently failed to communicate with honesty and tact to garner cooperation from the ranks as required by an effective leader.

Colonel Berdan was handicapped by personality traits that would have weakened any soldier's leadership potential. He was perceptively vain and egocentric. His foppery and inflated self-importance generated loathing in the ranks. A perception of dishonesty and lack of moral and physical courage tainted his reputation during and after his military service. Still worse was his proclivity to engender acrimony and division within his command — he had loyal supporters whom he relied upon to offset a host of bitter enemies. But in fairness to Berdan, he was a very good manager who surmounted great obstacles in fulfilling his role of organizing and outfitting his regiments. Few if any others could have accomplished what Berdan did for his command in the early days of the Civil War, his deficiencies notwithstanding.

Berdan had envisioned and sold his concept of sharpshooting regiments as a separate branch of the Army. He and his men considered themselves as separate from the infantry as from the cavalry or the engineers. Therefore, he had many distinct particulars to consider such as uniforms, tactics, arms, and equipment that would differ from infantry units. Much had been decided during the early days of recruiting, such as the choice of green uniforms with leather leggings rather than standard issue dark blue uniforms of the Federal Army. But the question of how to arm his men proved perhaps the most demanding and troublesome.

It was soon apparent that the heavy target rifles with which Berdan had intended to arm his sharpshooters were not only impractical for field use but also impossible to obtain in large numbers. He desperately needed an alternative weapon to fit the special requirements of sharpshooting. Arms dealers, inventors and manufacturers from all over the North and Europe had descended on Berdan's camp hoping to obtain a contract to arm his now famous sharpshooters.[2] But Berdan's marksmen already had a favorite of their own: the Sharps New Model 1859 Military Rifle.

One of Berdan's recruits from Company C, 1st U.S. Sharpshooters, Truman Head, a.k.a. California Joe, had purchased his own Sharps Rifle to use in the war. At first, Head was leery of the Sharps because it wasn't a true target rifle, but after a day's use he was delighted with its accuracy. Apparently Private Head's rifle impressed the men in camp, for after examining it they made the Sharps their rifle of choice. Unlike the muzzleloading target rifles, the Sharps utilized a vertically sliding breech block activated by a lever to expose the breech for loading. A special priming system using flat disc primers that fed automatically as the hammer fell allowed the rifle to fire even faster. The Sharps could also be fired by

Colonel Hiram Berdan, the man credited with organizing the 1st and 2nd U.S. Sharpshooters (Library of Congress Civil War Collection).

using a standard percussion cap.³ Private Head's Sharps was much lighter and handier than the target rifles and far superior for skirmishing use. It could quickly and easily be loaded even by a prone shooter and could be fired three times faster than a muzzleloader. The Sharps had superior sights and was simply much more accurate than the standard issue rifle musket beyond 200 yards.

Berdan was initially unsuccessful in obtaining the Sharps Rifles wanted by his sharpshooters from the Ordnance Department. Instead, he was offered new Springfield Rifle Muskets by the conservative chief of ordnance, General James Wolfe Ripley. The sixty-seven-year-old ordnance chief opposed the use of breechloaders for ground troops. Ripley proved adamant in his opposition. Convinced that the new breechloaders were a "great evil," he was determined to retain use of the muzzleloading weapons of his generation, notwithstanding Berdan's request for Sharps Rifles.⁴ General-in-Chief Winfield Scott backed Ripley, believing the Sharps Rifles would ruin Berdan's regiments.

At first Berdan was inclined to accept the Springfield muzzleloaders. He had no object in challenging the chief of ordnance. Also, the Sharps Rifles his men expected were special-order weapons yet to be manufactured for sharpshooter use and thus unobtainable for months, even if authorized. In late 1861 the demand for rifled arms of any kind greatly exceeded supply. Scores of Federal regiments, especially in the West, were being armed with outdated smoothbore muskets. The shortage of rifled infantry arms forced the government to purchase thousands of foreign muskets and rifles, many of dubious quality. Any regiment receiving Springfield Rifle Muskets would count itself very fortunate.⁵ Under the circumstances, Berdan probably felt compelled to accept the arms from Springfield with slight alterations.

Nevertheless, Berdan's men were opposed to the Springfields, even though the new rifled guns were usually going to elite units or regiments with special political connections. The sharpshooters understandably expected to be armed with the Sharps since it was the best arm available for their use and also their weapon of choice. In fact, many recruits believed that the rifle had been promised as a condition of their enlistment. Unfortunately, by rejecting all other arms, the sharpshooters created a situation that would render proper marksmanship training an impossibility during their entire training period.

Meanwhile, most of Berdan's two regiments remained unarmed. Some target rifles were in camp but too few to arm more than a company or two. With his men firmly in favor of Sharps Rifles, Berdan concentrated his efforts on obtaining these and abandoned efforts to get his men to accept Springfields. As early as October 22, 1861, a letter from Berdan appears in the regimental record book addressed to Secretary of War Cameron and requesting Sharps Rifles for his regiments. Berdan wrote that the Sharps Rifle was the "most suitable weapon" for his sharpshooters. He stated that "ordinary weapons" like the Springfields "would make my men but little better than the common infantry." He concluded by stating, "The men as well as myself feel that with these weapons we can not only make a name for ourselves but be of vast service to the country."⁶

2 — Berdan's Camp of Instruction

Berdan must have realized that General Ripley would never acquiesce to his request for the desired Sharps Rifles; the letter to Secretary Cameron was just a step in what was to be a protracted struggle with Ripley. Unfortunately for Berdan, the sharpshooters were expecting to be armed with the Sharps Rifles quickly, and the men began to suspect Berdan of subterfuge and deception because the rifles were not forthcoming. Consequently Berdan was placed in the quandary of facing resentment from the sharpshooters and disdain from the Ordnance Department, and it would require all his persuasive skill and an innate guileful disposition to find the means of obtaining the Sharps breechloaders for his men.

The long delay in obtaining rifles for the sharpshooters created a worst-case scenario with regard to target practice. The recruits had anticipated spending most of the instruction period honing their shooting skills. However, with perhaps only one rifle available for every ten men and factoring in the time required for muzzleloading target practice, it is unlikely that the 2nd received even a fraction of the range training needed and expected.

In fact, the record of the daily routine for the 2nd U.S.S.S. at the Camp of Instruction does not even mention target practice. The following is the daily routine as written in the Regimental Record Book[7]:

6.30	A.M.	Reveille
7.00	"	Breakfast
8.00	"	First Call Guard Mounting
8.15	"	Guard Mounting
8.45	"	Sick Call
9.00	"	First Call for Drill
9.15	"	Drill
11.30	"	Recall
12.00	M	Dinner
1.00	P.M.	First Call for Drill
1.15	"	Drill
3.00	"	Recall
3.45	"	First Call for Parade
4.00	"	Retreat
5.30	"	Supper
8.30	"	Tattoo
8.45	"	Taps

Despite the insistence of Berdan and his men that the sharpshooters were not infantry, much of the routine at the Camp of Instruction was similar to that of any Federal infantry regiment. Expecting to spend their days target shooting, the recruits were disillusioned to discover that their time would be devoted to drill and ordinary soldierly duties such as guard duty, manual of arms and close order marching. And perhaps most unsettling to the sharpshooters was the required instruction in bayonet drill; they had not signed up with Berdan to charge the rebels and fight at close quarters.

However, one form of drill practiced and perfected by the recruits, skirmish drill, suited the recruits' purpose and expectations. Fortunately, skirmish drill did not require a rifle. A sharpshooter described it as "an open order drill" used to deploy the regiment for sharpshooting work.[8] During drill the men learned to change formation upon the order to deploy by separating into files and separating again into two ranks with five paces between each man. When thus deployed, the 2nd could form a line nearly one mile long. Because no one voice could carry the length of the line, the men were taught to listen for bugle calls. These bugle calls announced a number of evolutions including orders to advance, commence firing, cease firing, march by the flank, assume prone position, halt, and nearly every order necessary move and command the regiment.[9]

In a letter dated January 27, 1862, a sharpshooter described his experience during a skirmish drill in wooded terrain rather than the open field as described above. He mentioned that the men were trained to run for cover behind the nearest tree or to hug the ground to escape enemy fire.[10] This type of training was a complete departure from usual stand-up infantry tactics of that time. The sharpshooters were repeatedly drilled in skirmishing tactics during the Camp of Instruction to ingrain an instinct to utilize any available cover at the appearance of an enemy. This drill as much as anything would separate the sharpshooters from ordinary infantry in perception as well as in practice during the war.

By January 1862 Berdan had made strides in his effort to outflank Chief of Ordnance Ripley and obtain an order for the Sharps Rifles he desperately needed. According to Captain Charles Stevens of the 1st U.S.S.S., Berdan gained the support of President Lincoln during a target shooting exhibition. After Berdan made an impossible shot, hitting a life-sized figure in the eye at 600 yards, the president, who attended the exhibition, promised to help. "Colonel, come down to-morrow," Lincoln said as he was leaving, "and I will give you the order for the breech-loaders."[11] The president's intervention on behalf of the sharpshooters proved decisive in overruling General Ripley and facilitating the procurement of Sharps Rifles for the sharpshooters.

General Ripley, through Ordnance Department bureaucracy, wielded immense influence over arms procurement contracts. In his battle with Ripley, Berdan resorted to crafty subterfuge to overcome Ripley's obstinate resistance to his request for breechloaders. Berdan knew that Colonel R.B. Marcy, chief of staff for Army of the Potomac commander General George B. McClellan, was personally acquainted with Samuel Colt of the Colt Firearms Company. Colonel Marcy had been an advocate of Colt Revolving Rifles, recommending them for U.S. Army issue since 1859. Berdan quickly seized the opportunity to gain General McClellan's endorsement for breechloaders by employing Colonel Marcy as an ally, an ally with influence on the supply and authorization aspects of Berdan's problem.[12]

During the period of this dispute, Samuel Colt gambled that Berdan would win and had a quantity of his revolving rifles manufactured for the sharpshooters to be immediately available should a procurement order be obtained. Of this Berdan was informed by a Colt agent. The Sharps breechloaders, on the other hand, were unavailable under any circumstances for months. Berdan, it seems, decided to seek authorization for the available Colt Revolving Rifles first, anticipating that obtaining any breechloader would enable him to eventually get the Sharps breechloaders he really wanted. By means of his association with Colonel Marcy, Berdan received General McClellan's endorsement for the Colt order. With President Lincoln and General

2 — Berdan's Camp of Instruction

McClellan supporting Berdan's request for Colt breechloaders, General Ripley was maneuvered into compliance with Berdan's request. On January 27, 1862, Berdan got the opportunity he craved — Colt Revolving Rifles were ordered by the Ordnance Department for his sharpshooters.[13]

The Colt breechloaders, having previously been readied and shipped to Washington, were immediately available for issue to the sharpshooters. Now Berdan had breechloaders for his sharpshooters, not just breechloaders but five-shot repeating breechloaders. One can imagine what Ripley thought of this development. The old general disapproved of breechloaders in the first place because he was intensely concerned about ammunition wastage. The Colt guns potentially would result in even greater expenditure of ammunition than single-shot breechloaders like the Sharps Rifle. Berdan took advantage of this circumstance by demanding Sharps Rifles for his regiments. General Ripley apparently preferred single shot breechloaders to the Colt repeaters, because he immediately acquiesced and ordered 1,000 Sharps Rifles on the same day the Colt guns were issued.[14]

In the midst of the strife over the Sharps order, Berdan was reported to have tested the Spencer Repeating Rifle for his troops. A newspaper article reported that General

The author at the West Point Museum. The Sharps Rifle on display, serial no. 56745, is the only known example having a direct provenance to Berdan's Sharpshooters.

McClellan had requested Spencer Rifles for Berdan and further reported that the "expensive weapons will not be given to any other corps."[15] The Spencer was somewhat similar in appearance to the Sharps; however, it was a seven-shot repeating breechloader, something Ripley no doubt would have thoroughly despised. Berdan did not at that time attempt to obtain Spencer Rifles in any case. The sharpshooters had already expressed their preference for the Sharps, and Spencer Rifles would not soon be available in quantity anyway.

Meanwhile, the sharpshooters had become increasingly restive in camp because of the long delay in obtaining arms. In many accounts the sharpshooters were disappointed with their training and felt their progress and efficiency as soldiers trailed expectations. Although the sharpshooters' regimental historian never mentioned it, too many sharpshooters viewed Berdan with contempt, considering him and his entire sharpshooter concept (in their own words) a humbug. Many were seeking an opportunity to transfer to other home state regiments or to exit the Army entirely.

A letter from a sharpshooter to the editor of a Vermont newspaper describing the situation at Berdan's camp indicates the frustration and growing agitation as the months passed without arms:

> ...I am sorry to announce that the high expectations of efficiency entertained by the public have not yet been realized. You well know under what promises we left the State, that rifles were in readiness for us and that we should soon see the enemy. Instead of this not a company has received its rifles, although months have elapsed since their arrival, and it is now rumored that guns of an inferior quality are to be furnished us. This is the only thing of which we can complain, for our rations are good, and skirmishing in the morning and battalion drill in the afternoon fully occupy our time.... And perhaps it is better that we remain inactive for a time provided we are not idle, but the men are becoming disheartened, for those death dealing tubes with which we were to meet the southern foe are yet wanting, to give us confidence.
>
> Now, Mr. Editor, I wish to ask if this is right; is it right that thirteen hundred men, men of superior intelligence, who have left situations both lucrative and honorable should remain without arms. Can the government afford to sustain men unarmed who are capable of using effectively the most deadly weapon known in civilized warfare, the long range rifle.... Had a few heavy rifles been in action but a short time since, it might have saved the slaughter of the Massachusets regiment and the death of the gallant Baker. [This refers to the Battle of Ball's Bluff.] It was to meet similar necessities that Berdan's Sharpshooters were enlisted, and is this design now to be frustrated by the delay of the War Department?
>
> Should not Congress take up this matter as concerning not a few regiments but the whole country? Many in our own State suppose that we are ready to take the field but let them be undeceived and know that unless energetic measures are adopted by men in authority we may remain for some time yet unable to face the enemy. P.[16]

Most of the onus for the poor morale rested on Berdan and fairly so. He was ultimately responsible for the inflated expectations that had induced the men to follow him to war. As tension mounted in camp, Berdan and his officers failed to communicate to the men their efforts to obtain the Sharps Rifles. Also Berdan inaptly failed to take into account the type of soldiers he had recruited. Instead he expected them to blandly accept the situation without complaint.

These New Englanders and denizens of Yankeedom resented Berdan's domineering, flippant leadership. Historically, Yankees had always cherished egalitarianism, valuing a consensual, mutually beneficial society. During the Revolutionary War, Southerners were appalled by instances of low-status tradesmen commanding New England militia units. Cobblers elected as officers, for example, actually mended the shoes of the wealthier gentlemen soldiers they commanded in battle.[17] Natives of a region renowned for town hall meetings, public education, and activism, the sharpshooters were a natural foil for Berdan's methods. Although Berdan was a thoroughly respectable marksman, his leadership did not inspire the men. To them he was a lame peacock, and in all likelihood the sharpshooters would have voted him out of the colonelcy, had the opportunity arisen.

The escalating tension climaxed on January 28 when the newly arrived Colt Revolving Rifles were to be issued to the 2nd U.S.S.S. The men almost universally disapproved of the Colts, and they had steadfastly refused to be armed with anything except Sharps Rifles. A rumor spread quickly through the camp that Berdan and his officers would soon force the sharpshooters to accept the Colts. Another rumor had it that Berdan was to receive a paid commission from the Colt Company should the regiment be issued the unwanted arms.[18]

Soon after it was announced that the Colt guns were to be issued, the mood of the regiment grew ugly and a riot nearly ensued. Men gathered in the company streets and began to yell epithets and catcalls directed at Colonel Berdan. An effigy of the colonel appeared as a target for the sharpshooters' spleen, and for a time it appeared that a mutiny was in the making. Berdan was so shaken by the mob that he took measures to protect himself by arming the Swiss and German company from his first regiment and posting them "around his headquarters to protect him from the rest of the command."[19]

It was an excruciating dilemma for Berdan and his fellow officers. Having bested General Ripley in obtaining breechloaders for his regiments, Berdan now could not convince his men to accept them. Adding further humiliation, the sharpshooters resorted to political maneuvering to thwart Berdan's efforts. Not only did the men write letters to their home state political representatives, in at least one case, and probably others, a sharpshooter was sent to Capitol Hill to personally petition a U.S. senator for assistance to thwart the issue of Colt guns.

The son of Maine senator William Pitt Fessenden, James Fessenden, was the captain of Company D, 2nd U.S.S.S. The men from his company vehemently resisted accepting the revolving rifles. Private Llewellyn Buck of Company D "slipped through the camp guard" and made his way to Senator Fessenden's office shortly after Berdan introduced the revolving rifles to the regiment.[20] Buck was himself an excellent example of the overall high intellectual character of the 2nd U.S.S.S. Although he enlisted as a private and never served as a commissioned officer, he became a physician and a highly esteemed citizen of his community as a civilian following the war.[21] He reported to his captain's father the conditions in camp: that is, the men were being forcibly required to accept the revolving rifles. Men who refused the Colts were subjected to threats by officers and in some cases were being arrested and confined.

Senator Fessenden took up the sharpshooters' cause with the secretary of war and General McClellan. McClellan personally assured Private Buck that the men would have Sharps Rifles as soon as they could be manufactured and recommended that the men accept the Colts for the time being. This recommendation, reported by Buck when he returned to camp, helped ease the contention and encourage the men to take the revolving rifles.[22]

The case of Private Buck was not unique; there were other documented examples of petitions or appeals to congressmen and politicians. An officer close to Colonel Berdan believed the political appeals emboldened the men to resist orders with which they disagreed or disliked. He considered the 2nd to be "in a state of chronic mutiny." The political petitioning, he wrote, enabled the privates to have "influence" through politicians to countermand even the orders of commanding generals. "What sort of discipline is that?" he asked.[23]

An example of the officers' efforts to quell dissent in camp and establish discipline is found in the court-martial of Corporal Wilber Howard as written in the regimental record book:

> Charge 3rd Conduct prejudicial to good order and military discipline.
> Specification — In this that the said Wilber Howard Clerk in the Commissary Dept 2nd Regt. Berdans U.S.S.S did in camp call Col. H. Berdan 1st Regt. U.S.S.S. a "— old liar and a — old fool and did say that he Col. H. Berdan had no commission; had fooled the men and was trying to put all the money he could in his own pocket" or words and figures to the same effect. This at Camp Instruction Washington D.C. on or about the 31st day of January 1862.[24]

The twenty-three-year-old corporal was found guilty, but he completed his enlistment with the sharpshooters and reenlisted, serving until the regiment was disbanded. Howard was possibly the only one who actually stood official court-martial for speaking out during the defiant period involving the revolving rifles. However, many men were detained, and Colonel Post went as far as to threaten men who refused the Colts with being "shot by a regiment of regulars."[25]

Dissatisfaction and acrimony were not constrained to the enlisted ranks of Berdan's Sharpshooters. With such an assemblage of talent, egos inevitably clashed, even among the most committed. The frustration in camp no doubt bred conflicts on a personal level. Leaders in continual close contact with Berdan, weary of constant turmoil and of Berdan himself, took the option available only to officers — resigning, as illustrated by this letter from Captain Caspar Trepp to Colonel Berdan:

> Col
> In tendering to you my resignation of this date, it is due you that I have been compelled to take this course entirely in consequence of want of confidence in Major W.S. Rowland as a military man and as a gentleman.
> It is also due you that I should say, that I insinuated to some of the Line Officers that the Col must be equally bad to have such a man as Major with him. It was at

an excited moment and without the least knowledge or belief that you had ever been guilty of anything unbecoming an officer and a gentleman, and I ask you to accept a full and heartfull apology....[26]

In this particular case, Berdan and Trepp were allies against Major Rowland. It was Rowland who canvassed the western states for Berdan in search of qualified recruits in 1861. Without Rowland, Berdan probably wouldn't have found sufficient men to form his regiments. Once in camp, however, Rowland apparently proved of little value, and he soon turned against Berdan. An endorsement to Trepp's letter explains Berdan's response: "I did not accept Capt. Trepp's resignation as I had already given Maj. Rowland his alternative to resign or be court-martialled. He preferred to resign which settled the difficulty."[27]

While Berdan did not here accept Trepp's resignation, he probably later wished that he had. The two became principals in a number of bitter disputes, bringing charges one against the other until Berdan left the army and Trepp was killed in action.

By early February most camp rumors had run their course, including one that Congress would disband the sharpshooters. The men began to accept their fate regarding the Colts, which they called "revolving candle moulds" and "pepperbox guns."[28] Assurances from General McClellan that Sharps Rifles would soon replace the revolving rifles had a soothing effect in camp. The revolving rifles were test-fired and found to be serviceable, but still not what the men wanted.

There is little documentation concerning target practice for the 2nd U.S.S.S. other than the mention of shooting matches and target shooting. Berdan's Sharpshooters no doubt had more press coverage of their target practice than any other regiment, perhaps all other regiments combined. Dignitaries ranging from the president to foreign nobility often visited Berdan's camp during shooting exhibitions and target practice. Newspaper correspondents from all over the East scribbled accounts of these events, increasing the notoriety of Berdan and his men.

When President Lincoln visited at target practice, he sometimes would take up a rifle to try his skill at shooting. One sharpshooter mentioned that "Abraham Lincoln handled the rifle like a veteran marksman, in a highly successful manner, to the great delight of the many soldiers and civilians surrounding." The president was once heard to say, "Boys, this reminds me of old-time shooting."[29]

Another sharpshooter had a more somber account of seeing the president at target practice:

> President Lincoln would go over with Secretary Stanton every few days to watch us at drill and target practice.... President Lincoln was very fond of watching the target practice, and rarely paid us a visit without firing a few rounds himself. He was an excellent shot, too.
>
> Our favorite target at that time was the life-size figure of a Zouave, his uniform painted in gaudy color, the distance ranging from two hundred yards to six hundred yards. On one occasion our range instructor had prepared a target. It was painted to represent a man in civilian's attire and labeled in big, plain letters "Jeff Davis." This target was to be run up when the President's time came to fire.

Mr. Lincoln stepped up, selected his rifle, and indicated his readiness to fire. Then with the rifle half raised he looked full at the target for the first time.

"We want to see you take a crack at that, Mr. President," said the instructor.

Mr. Lincoln lowered his rifle and turned from the target to the instructor. He didn't say a word. He simply looked at him with an expression full of surprise, of disappointment, and of sorrow. Then he laid his rifle down gently and went a little way off from the group, walking up and down by himself with folded arms and bowed head for several minutes. After a time he came back and fired several shots at the regular target — that unlucky new one had vanished — but he was unusually silent and soon went away.[30]

While much was written about the sharpshooters at target practice, very little was recorded concerning the method of instruction Berdan used to teach his marksmen. European armies had instituted schools of musketry with the increased use of rifled arms dating from the 1840s. The French and English utilized a scientific method of range estimation in training riflemen. Precise range estimation was the single most important factor in long-range marksmanship during the Civil War era. The United States Army did not establish a school of musketry prior to the Civil War. European training methods were known to the Army, but no official school for long-range target practice was in effect for American riflemen.[31]

Just how well schooled the sharpshooters were in range estimation is difficult to determine. Without a doubt there were many expert shooters in Berdan's camp, but many of these men had practiced target shooting on a range where the distance to the target was prearranged and known to the shooter. Others were hunters, and this group probably had the greatest experience in judging distance. It is fairly easy to train shooters the art of judging distance, with ample practice. From accounts of Berdan's Camp of Instruction, the men fired at targets on a firing range at predetermined distances. A true systematic course of training in range estimation was quite possibly not implemented in Berdan's camp.

All Civil War–era black powder firearms fired bullets at a relatively low velocity. The standard Civil War–era rifle musket fired a 510-grain bullet with a 60-grain powder charge, producing a muzzle velocity of 963 feet per second. A modern infantry rifle fires a bullet at over three times that velocity. The World War II .30-06 bullet weighed a little over a third of a Civil War .58 caliber elongated ball. Because Civil War firearms used heavy bullets fired at a slow velocity, the trajectory was very high, a rainbow trajectory. As a comparison, a Civil War rifle musket sighted for 300 yards had a trajectory of forty-three inches, while a World War II .30-06 had a trajectory of just over seven inches. The .30-06 drops as little as fifty inches from the line of sight at 500 yards, while a .58 Springfield drops hundreds of inches at the same distance. A slower bullet velocity results in a higher trajectory, because the slower a bullet travels, the faster it falls.[32]

The high or rainbow trajectory of Civil War–era firearms made accurate range estimation essential. Rifle sights had to be adjusted according to distance with very little margin for error. For instance, if a soldier correctly sighted at a target 500 yards distant, the bullet would rise completely over every man-sized obstacle between the ranges of 100 to 400 yards. At 300 yards the bullet would rise 150 inches over the target, meaning that even a mounted man would not be struck in the line of fire.[33]

Berdan's Sharpshooters were subject to the same limitations resulting from the rainbow trajectory of black powder firearms. As an example, if a sharpshooter overestimated the distance of his target at 540 yards by thirty yards, he would completely miss a man-sized target, even if his aim were perfect. A comparatively small margin of error existed for all distances beyond 150 yards, but at long range the distance estimation had to be nearly exact. To hit a man between the head and feet at 600 yards, the rifle sights had to be precisely set to a space within sixty yards of the actual distance of the target.[34]

A brass stadia sight was in use during the Civil War to aid riflemen in determining the range of a target. By holding the apparatus at the exact length of its attached chain, the shooter adjusted a sliding aperture until the target filled the viewing area. He could then read the range on a scale lined on the edge of the sight.[35] This instrument was probably available in limited numbers, however.

To make matters worse for marksmanship training, Berdan's men practiced with heavy-barreled target rifles rather than the Sharps Rifles they would eventually be issued. The target rifles, with their thick barrels, could hold a much greater powder charge than the Sharps. The greater powder charge increased bullet velocity, resulting in improved downrange trajectory over the Sharps Rifle. Some Sharps ammunition contained as much as sixty-five grains of powder, but "the maximum possible charge is 65 to 70 grains." This is because the breech of a Sharps Rifle could not contain more than seventy grains of powder.[36] It was impossible for Berdan's men to acclimate themselves to the weapon they would eventually use in combat, because the target rifles were simply not ballistically equivalent to the Sharps.

The winter weather also disadvantaged the 2nd U.S.S.S. versus Berdan's other regiment in terms of rifle practice. The 1st U.S.S.S. had arrived in camp during the late summer and autumn when the weather was more agreeable for target practice. But the most pernicious aspect of winter was its attendant sickness, which also affected the 2nd at nearly double the rate of the other sharpshooter regiment.

Measles struck the 2nd very hard during that first winter of the war. It is likely that the 2nd suffered more severely from camp diseases such as mumps, measles,

A modern military cartridge and a fired Civil War .52 caliber Sharps bullet. Note the linen cartridge impression on the comparatively enormous Sharps bullet.

dysentery, and typhoid than the 1st U.S.S.S. because of the more rural origin of its recruits. Regiments composed of soldiers from the countryside suffered much worse from common camp diseases than those recruited predominantly from cities. Army doctors agreed that urban dwellers were more accustomed to crowded, unsanitary conditions and therefore had greater immunity. Diseases such as measles were spread more widely in cities; the city bred recruits were much more likely to have already been infected as children and thus had immunity.[37] The Swiss-German company of Berdan's first regiment thought that their diet of boiled meat, soups and vegetables, as opposed to the fried food diet of the Americans, accounted for their better health in camp.[38] However, the foreign company, like two others from the 1st U.S.S.S., was from New York, and these men were more likely to have been exposed to crowed conditions and childhood diseases than the New Hampshire, Minnesota, Vermont and Western Pennsylvania men of the 2nd U.S.S.S.

The report of surgeon C.S. Tripler, medical director of the Army of the Potomac, substantiates the fact that troops from the less populated states suffered the worst from sickness. He noted that Vermont regiments in Brooks's Brigade had the highest ratio of sick men in that army.

Tripler reported that the sharpshooters were suffering severely from measles and that their camp was "in a bad sanitary condition" and "badly located." He noted that the camp should be moved because "its drainage is bad." Measles in Berdan's sharpshooters, as was often the case during the Civil War, weakened the men and brought on "severe lung complications."[39] The disease was sometimes fatal by itself, but just as often men developed complications from measles that became chronic, leading to eventual disability.

The muster and descriptive rolls of the 2nd U.S.S.S. are replete with remarks indicating men discharged for disability during the first year of the war and entries for men who died of disease also during this period. On February 6, 1862, a tally listed 132 men out of 720, or 18.3 percent of the men in the 2nd U.S.S.S., as sick.[40] Men who developed chronic conditions from camp illnesses usually had three choices eventually. According to a Federal lieutenant, the chronically ill could "resign, obtain a leave of absence, or die."[41] In the case of enlisted men, a chronically ill soldier could go to the regimental surgeon and request a discharge for disability, or, if he could afford to pay his way home, he could obtain a leave of absence to recover. The rolls of the 2nd began to diminish rapidly during the spring of 1862; the trend would continue with irreplaceable men leaving because of disenchantment, their disease providing the means of escape.

While the 2nd U.S.S.S. had commendably few desertions during the war, a relatively large number of men left the regiment by disability or transfer for such an elite organization. One should bear in mind that the regiment had a universal reputation as being composed of recruits with above average intelligence. An Army major remarked to Colonel Post after the men were paid for the first time in January 1862, "Colonel, you have one thing of which you should be proud; you have a regiment of almost eight hundred men, and every man steps up and signs the pay-roll himself. I do not believe such a thing ever happened before in the worlds history of war."⁴² A large portion of the sharpshooters also left successful civilian situations to enlist, which, perhaps, helps account for the comparatively high losses from disability, men who chose discharge rather than medical leave or perseverance.

As the winter waned and the weather warmed, the remaining fit men anticipated the season for active campaigning, anxious to leave behind the boredom of camp routine. Still dissatisfied with the Colt Repeating Rifles, the sharpshooters remained impatient to receive the promised Sharps breechloaders. Private Darius Starr of Company F complained in a letter to his mother about the unwanted Colt repeaters: "They were tried the other day and not more than one ball in forty hit a target six feet by ten, at a distance of 600 yards, but one man in the regt who had a target rifle on the ground, fired and his first shot went not more than eight inches from the centre of the target." Starr, like most of the sharpshooters, held Berdan responsible for the long delay in obtaining proper rifles. "They say that Berdan + Barnum are going into partnership," he wrote, "and I believe they would make a good pair, for one is as big a humbug as the other."⁴³

Berdan felt the stress and disappointment from the long delay in obtaining the favored Sharps breechloaders. The newspapers now continually called for a move against the rebel capital; a loud call of "On to Richmond" echoed throughout the North. The colonel anticipated that McClellan would soon have to go on the offensive, and he intended to see his sharpshooters take a prominent role in the upcoming campaign. On March 6, 1862, Colonel Berdan vented his frustration in a direct letter to J.C. Palmer, the president of the Sharps Manufacturing Company and the man who had failed to keep his promise to deliver the arms quickly.⁴⁴

> My Dear Sir,
> You wrote me on the 28th of Jany. that you would deliver here 1000 guns in 20 to 25 days and this in answer to a dispatch in which I was particular to ask you not to deceive me as to the time the guns would be delivered. Instead of receiving the guns as promised I received a note from you on the 24th ult. stating that the first 250 guns would be delivered in a few days, and the balance in lots of 400 per week, if you were not disappointed about bayonets (^of which I understood you to say when here that you had some 6000 all ready). Ten days have now elapsed and no guns yet. It is unnecessary to say that neither my men or myself are willing to put up quietly any longer with these promises and delays, especially when we are informed at the Ordnance Department that no order for carbines was in any way to interfere with these guns being made at once. I now learn at the Dept. that you have not only delivered many hundred carbines since you received this order, but have written a letter to the Department promising many hundreds more before the guns for my Corps are delivered. I strongly suspect that you are employing a large portion of your force on carbines which you distinctly promised me you would not do.
> You told me here that if you receive the order, you would put your entire force on my guns, and work night and day until they were completed. The order would have allowed you to do this, and I shall be glad to learn that my fears are unfounded, and that the first thousand at least will be forthcoming. Such must be the case, if you expect the Govt. to take the guns for my Corps if I have anything to say about

it, for I am determined that both my regiments shall be in the forward movement, and if we have to take the Colt's guns we will most likely keep them.

Now my dear sir, I must ask you to give me by return mail the exact times if possible when the 250 will be here, and when the balance of the first thousand will be here, that we may be able to decide what course the interest of the service demands.

Very Respfy.
H. Berdan
Col. Comdg. U.S.S.S.

From this letter it is obvious that Berdan was determined to take the field with McClellan's army without the rifles he had promised to his men. The Colt guns were only grudgingly being accepted as temporary replacements for the promised Sharps Rifles. This letter was a bluff to induce Palmer to hurry his delivery of the ordered guns. However, Berdan had made a decision to take his sharpshooters into combat without indoctrination for the very weapon he and his command expected to rely upon in battle.

Berdan's second in command, Lt. Colonel William Y.W. Ripley, recognized the limitations imposed by conditions in Berdan's camp. He was concerned that the men were not ready in terms of discipline and perhaps also training. On March 18, 1862, Ripley wrote to his wife about his concern that the sharpshooters were to accompany McClellan's army on the offensive: "I do not like the move at all this sending troops into the field with out preparation is all wrong. the Country Expects so much of the Sharp Shooters that we Can not afford to take the field ... but Col Berdan thinks differently + has overruled me. The Dept would never have ord the Regt ford unless Berdan had offered it as ready for service."[45] The next day Ripley admitted in another letter to his wife that he wished that he had never heard of the U.S. Sharpshooters.[46]

The rank and file, on the other hand, were probably as ready to leave Washington and the Camp of Instruction for the war as Berdan was himself. One young sharpshooter wrote to his mother about the expected move into Virginia, saying that he did not enlist to play and that the rebels would give in after one good battle.[47] This same soldier had been wavering in his commitment to the Army since his arrival in Washington. He had received letters from friends and relatives urging him to stay the course and not to desert. Nothing is as demoralizing to the volunteer as the thought of wasting his life, far from home and opportunity, passing time in idleness and pointless monotony.

One of the ninety-day volunteer regiments from the previous summer, by comparison, had become so disillusioned by camp life around Washington that when the time came for battle, the men refused to fight, their enlistment having expired on the day of the Battle of First Bull Run. The regiment had marched out of Washington with that first advance on Manassas, but when the commanding general asked these men to extend so that they could take part in the battle, they refused and left for home.[48] In many ways the men of Berdan's Sharpshooters had more of which to complain than those ninety-day men of 1861 who left the war at that crucial time, but unlike the ninety-day volunteers, their enlistment was far from over.

Berdan's men had volunteered for a specific type of duty. It was dangerous and arduous duty. They had rightfully expected the government to properly arm and train them for their special place in the Army. A letter from a sharpshooter provides an insight into the self-image of the average soldier in Berdan's regiments: "...we have in this regt a set of men who do not look up to anybody, and in fact most of the boys are fit to take command of a regiment, and they all know they are a more intelligent set of men than the officers of most regiments.... I had rather be a private in this regiment than an officer in any other in the service."[49]

Soldiers from other units in both armies, Federal and Confederate, were less likely to take umbrage than Berdan's Yankees. A soldier from the non–Yankee butternut cultural region of Ohio wrote, "It is true that I won't make much money by going to war. I did not volunteer for that purpose.... I think it my duty to fight for my country, liberty, the Union.... I am willing to face the cannonballs for 13 dollars a month for my country and liberty."[50] The sharpshooters were perhaps just as committed to these same causes as the Ohio soldier, but their expectations for their service differed. Berdan's recruits expected and demanded a level of cooperation from the government commensurate with the talents they brought to the service. Their New England heritage of egalitarianism and activism, their higher general intelligence, made the sharpshooters less accommodating, less trusting, and less willing to accept deficiency.

One writer commented that Berdan's Sharpshooters were exceptional not for being ahead of their time but for being an example of what good training produces.[51] It is true that compared to the average Civil War infantry regiment the sharpshooters were exceptionally well trained. Berdan had over six months to train his first regiment and nearly three months to work with most of the 2nd U.S.S.S. Obviously, the first regiment was the better trained of the two. But on the field of battle the 2nd performed as well or better than the 1st U.S.S.S. It was not Berdan's training that made the sharpshooters famous.

Even a cursory examination of Berdan's Camp of Instruction reveals serious deficiencies. The natural place to assign blame is the leadership. Here the most serious flaws were glaring. Berdan and his officers did not inspire the men; instead they presented a contentious spectacle of infighting and intrigue. Berdan himself made the egregious mistake of promising more to his recruits than he could deliver. He compounded his mistake by underestimating the sharpshooters' intelligence; thus, his vigorous efforts to procure the Sharps Rifles for his men largely went unnoticed at the time. In the end the sharpshooters never received proper familiarization training for the rifles they eventually used in combat throughout the war. Overall Berdan's training camp at Washington was nearly as destructive as it was instructive; too many valuable and irreplaceable men were lost to death, disability and disillusionment.

"Sharpshooters, like fiddlers, are born and not made."[52] This observation by Confederate general A.P. Hill applied to Berdan's men as much as any. Good sharpshooters were more than simply excellent marksmen. The innate capacity to react intelligently at the point of combat while acting as an individual, to instinctively utilize any available cover and, most importantly, to preserve presence of mind under fire characterized the effective sharpshooter.[53] The wartime record of Berdan's Sharpshooters proves that many fulfilled their potential. While better overall training would have improved the regiment's readiness, effective battlefield performance ultimately depended upon the quality of the men themselves. Berdan had the pick of the North in 1861; it is a shame that so much natural talent was wasted by the inadequacies of the Federal leadership, especially that first year of the war.

As spring neared and the weather warmed, Berdan's Green Coats prepared to leave camp for the move against Richmond. A sharpshooter from Company D noted in his diary on March 18 that the anticipated marching orders had arrived during dress parade. Most of the men, he wrote, were ready to leave, though obviously some would rather have gone home.[54] So the best from Yankeedom, green in garb as well as experience, readied to sally forth for honor and country, unaware of the vicissitudes and grim trials that lay in store across the Potomac.

3

At the Bloody Point of Lincoln's Sword

At 10 A.M. on March 19, 1862, a long drum roll sounded, directing the sharpshooters to assemble and prepare to break camp; the drums signified the end of preparation and the onset of the ordeal of war. None of them, officer or enlisted, had an inkling of the unrelenting peril fated in the woods and fields of Old Virginia, soon to be their destination. These were the boys of '61, and while Bull Run had taught a hard lesson that the war would be bloody and arduous, the newspapers and opinion makers still anticipated a successful move against Richmond, and soon. The popular and inspiring "Young Napoleon," George B. McClellan, would lead the way.

Throughout the winter months of 1861–1862, Federal forces made significant gains against the rebellion. The U.S. Navy implemented a blockade of Southern ports that only grew stronger and more effective as the war continued. Western Virginia was placed under Federal control, becoming a resource for Federal recruitment and later a new Union state. All along the Southern coast the Army and Navy cooperated to capture forts and establish coastal footholds. Operations to gain control of the Mississippi River were well underway, and soon only two rebel citadels, at Port Hudson, Louisiana, and Vicksburg, Mississippi, would remain to threaten Federal transport on that river. On February 16, 1862, forces under General U.S. Grant captured Fort Donelson in northern Tennessee, with Grant issuing his famous "unconditional surrender" ultimatum. Grant's success effectively cleared Kentucky of Confederate influence and opened Tennessee for direct invasion. Soon Nashville and much of that state would be under Federal occupation.

While Federal progress gained momentum elsewhere, the principal eastern army, the Army of the Potomac, remained inert within the Washington defenses. Major General George B. McClellan had superseded the aging Mexican War hero Brevet Lieutenant General Winfield Scott as general-in-chief on November 1, 1861. By mid-winter General McClellan, or "Little Mac" as he was also known because of his stumpy appearance, was being constantly goaded by the press and the administration to take the offensive in northern Virginia.

Born in Pennsylvania in 1826, McClellan was a West Point graduate and distinguished Mexican War veteran. In 1857 he resigned from the Army for a career in railroad engineering. He quickly progressed to president of the Ohio and Mississippi Railroad Eastern Division. After the attack on Fort Sumter he returned to the Army as a major general of Ohio volunteers, and after a few minor victories in western Virginia he seemed as qualified for high command as any officer in the North. During his prewar railroad career he was acquainted with Abraham Lincoln, but as a conservative Democrat he was by no means a political ally of the future president.

Like Hiram Berdan, McClellan was an excellent organizer and planner, but he was as conservative in his military strategy as he was in his political orientation. President Lincoln soon realized that the general was not eager to please his Republican bosses; McClellan would not take the president or the cabinet into his confidence. With little, if any, idea of McClellan's plans, the president issued General War Order Number One on January 27, 1862, directing the Army and Navy to take the offensive on February 22. Little Mac, however, did in fact have a plan for an offensive into Virginia, and on February 3 "he submitted a lengthy paper defending his strategy," saying he would stake his life and reputation on his plan. The plan called for an amphibious landing on the Rappahannock River to avoid an overland campaign from Washington. McClellan envisioned a march from the Rappahannock directly to Richmond, bypassing Confederate forces in northern Virginia.[1]

President Lincoln was unwilling to fully accept McClellan's plan to bypass the enemy in northern Virginia. The president was equally or perhaps even more concerned with protecting Washington than with capturing the rebel capital. Over a series of meetings with the general, Lincoln demanded that sufficient forces be kept in place to protect Washington. Eventually McClellan and the president came to an agreement providing forces to defend Washington and to move against Richmond simultaneously. Forces defending Washington would eventually be organized into departments as follows: in western Virginia, the Mountain Department; in the Shenandoah Valley region, the Department of the Shenandoah; and in northern Virginia, the Department of the Rappahannock. McClellan would take the bulk of the Army of the Potomac for his campaign against Richmond.

But before McClellan could initiate his amphibious campaign, the Confederates withdrew several miles to below the Rappahannock River. McClellan immediately advanced from Washington to engage the retreating rebels. As McClellan moved south with much of the Army of the Potomac, the two sharpshooter regiments remained unarmed and unattached at the Camp of Instruction. It was perhaps the sharpshooters' intransigence regarding arms that kept them out of this movement.

McClellan and his army marched to the Centerville and Manassas area and found that the enemy had retreated, burning bridges as they moved south. Lacking the grit for an inevitable series of bloody battles that would coincide with an overland move against Richmond, McClellan decided on a second amphibious option for a campaign against the enemy capital. He would sail with his army to Fortress Monroe and attack up the Virginia Peninsula rather than attempt a crossing of the Rappahannock.

In early March, President Lincoln directed that the Army of the Potomac's numerous divisions be reorganized into a corps system. The portion of the army to be under McClellan's direction consisted of four corps: the I Corps commanded by Major General Irvin McDowell, the II Corps commanded by Major General Edwin V. Sumner, the III Corps commanded by Brigadier General Samuel Heintzelman, and the IV Corps commanded by Brigadier General Erasmus D. Keyes. This realignment of McClellan's army was part of the president's effort to secure Washington and provide troops for the campaign against Richmond. By summer two more army corps would be created, the

V and VI. During a three-month interval from March to June there would be an almost constant shifting of regiments from one organization to another to adjust to the realignment.[2]

General McClellan returned to Washington and quickly received approval for his plan to attack via the Virginia Peninsula. The newly formed II, III and IV Corps gathered for transport, and on March 17 the first divisions of McClellan's invasion force embarked at Alexandria for the voyage to Fortress Monroe. McClellan held back McDowell's I Corps, to which the 2nd U.S.S.S. was attached, intending to utilize these troops as a dependable reserve to be sent into the fight where most needed.[3]

So it was that when the 2nd broke camp on March 19, many, having no knowledge of McClellan's intention to hold them as a reserve, thought the regiment would march to Alexandria and embark with McClellan's army for the voyage to Fortress Monroe. The regiment marched out of camp as part of the newly created I Corps of the Army of the Potomac, assigned to General C.C. Augur's 1st Brigade of King's Division. Colonel Stoughton later recalled that "Battery B, Fourth U.S. Artillery, Capt. John Gibbon commanding," and cavalry commanded by future general Judson Kilpatrick were with the 2nd at that time, to show how the sharpshooters were "surrounded at the outset."[4] Gibbon, of course, later commanded the famous Iron Brigade and the XXIV Corps. The 2nd crossed the Potomac over Long Bridge and followed the Alexandria Pike before turning away from the river. It was soon obvious that the rumors about embarking with the invasion force were false.

Berdan's 1st U.S.S.S. followed the next day across the Potomac and soon embarked with the invasion force as part of the III Corps. Thus, Berdan's Sharpshooters were immediately separated upon breaking training camp. But the two regiments were forever linked and before long would be reunited; ultimately the 1st would be absorbed into the 2nd U.S.S.S. Each regiment would serve its entire term in the Eastern Theater. The 2nd would be assigned briefly to Pope's Army of Virginia, but both regiments belonged to the Army of the Potomac.

Civil War historian Jeffery D. Wert astutely noted that while the Army of the Potomac remains "America's most star-crossed army," it also remains the one army most closely associated with an American president.[5] It was Lincoln's army. He was always with this army from its inception, as he was with the sharpshooters themselves. He was there to visit this army in camp, at reviews and parades, at Antietam after America's bloodiest day, and he eulogized its dead famously at Gettysburg. The Army of the Potomac was the metaphorical, though very personal, weapon Lincoln employed to attack his counterparts in Richmond. Now Lincoln and his army are inextricably joined in the memory of the soldiers' descendants through thousands of anecdotes passed down from generation to generation. Many years after the war, as the martyred "Old Abe" was increasingly revered, the old soldiers gained stature just for having seen the great man; this and their ultimate victory over Lee's famous army helped make these veterans the most celebrated in our nation's history.

Berdan's Sharpshooters were created for a special purpose: to be the point-men of an army, Lincoln's army. It was their destiny to serve at the bloody point of Lincoln's sword. It was their duty to lead the way into the fight, finding the enemy and punishing him before the main assault followed. The Green Coats would be the vanguard of Lincoln's army; surpassing their conceptual role as snipers and scouts, they would function as the piercing point of this weapon Lincoln repeatedly thrust at Richmond.

That first march across the Potomac was a very hard lesson for the fledgling soldiers, one few would ever forget. As was almost always the case with raw troops, the sharpshooters carefully stuffed their knapsacks with, in their estimation, only the most essential articles. They packed their overcoat, dress uniform, blanket, extra shoes, shaving kit, extra uniforms, eating utensils, writing materials, sewing kit, rubber blanket, and underwear, and with the heavy knapsack was carried the usual accouterments and their ten-and-a-half-pound Colt "pepperbox gun." It was a ponderous burden for even a leisurely stroll.

Just marching through Washington's environs quickly initiated the sharpshooters to the extreme trial of the march. The columns of soldiers carried loads exceeding sixty pounds as they moved through the city with frequent stops, intermittently standing in ranks while waiting for the march to resume. During the frequent halts the men could not rest, and the constant standing, stopping and starting while under a heavy load very quickly drained even the fittest men. As the hours and miles slowly passed, the march assumed the effect of torture, inflicting pain and fatigue so severe that many faltered and most began to fear they would not endure the day. As they soon learned, an army march was exceedingly more difficult than a lone hike of the same distance bearing the same load.

A few hours into the march the men began to straggle and lag behind. They started jettisoning superfluous items, and as the march progressed more things were discarded. The streets and roads along the route were strewn with new overcoats, blankets, knapsacks and all sorts of impedimenta. Like a ship's storm-tossed crew casting away ballast and cargo to stay afloat, the flagging columns cast their heretofore valuable gear aside for survival's sake.

With time the men learned how to prepare for the march. They would learn that certain items like their overcoats had to be borne on the march, regardless of the difficulty. Many would suffer later for their inexperience. Throughout the Civil War new regiments reacted to the torture of the march in much the same manner. Even when new regiments later in the war were advised by experienced veteran comrades and officers, the results were much the same. New soldiers had to learn to cope with the hardships of soldiering by the hard school of personal experience.[6]

At day's end the column halted near Fort Ward, just outside the District of Columbia near Alexandria, Virginia. The march was likely a distance of less than fourteen miles, but the effect was not soon forgotten. With blistered feet and aching backs the sharpshooters went into camp in a cleared wood, without tents for shelter — except for the officers. That place was apparently called "Camp Williams" by the sharpshooters, and there they remained until April 4.[7]

On that day McDowell's I Corps was merged into the newly created Department of the Rappahannock, with McDowell remaining in command. The 2nd U.S.S.S. was assigned to the 1st brigade of King's Division, Department of the Rappahannock. Defending Washington was the mission of McDowell's new department, which was assigned to cover the area east of the Blue Ridge, south from Washington between the Potomac and the Patuxent.[8] McDowell intended to establish his headquarters on the Rappahannock at Fredericksburg; thus, on the 4th the sharpshooters started south again.

Leaving camp at about 3:30 P.M., the regiment marched about six miles and camped for the night. On the 5th the march resumed at 7 A.M. and continued for about eighteen miles. That night the men slept in abandoned rebel huts, very grateful for a night spent off the cold hard ground. At about noon on the 6th the column continued southward. The journey led the sharpshooters through Fairfax Courthouse, a town which Private William Greene of Company G said was nearly in ruins and all but uninhabited by whites.[9] The march continued through Centerville and on to Bristoe Station.

At Centerville, an area heavily fortified by the Confederates, the regiment "encountered the formidable wooden guns left by the rebels."[10] These were called "Quaker guns"

One of the Confederate Quaker guns fashioned from a log to deceive the Federals at Centerville, Virginia, in 1862. Library of Congress Civil War Collection.

by the press, a large log carved to resemble a cannon barrel and painted black. The retreating Confederates had left the fake cannon in their fortifications to delay McClellan's advance in early march. One sharpshooter noted that he visited an abandoned battery and examined the guns up close before realizing that they were made of wood. He also noted that as he marched over the Bull Run battlefield he saw many Confederate graves, but he saw little else indicating that a great battle had happened there.[11]

The regiment remained in camp at Bristoe Station until April 15. During that stay some of the men wandered to the nearby Bull Run battlefield. One sharpshooter mentioned in a letter that the men of the 14th Brooklyn, also called the 84th N.Y.V., a regiment brigaded with and camped near the sharpshooters, were incensed to find the unburied body of a comrade who had been killed during the battle the previous July. One of the New Yorkers, forced to retreat with the rest of the army, had left his dead brother beside a tree on the day of the battle. He hiked out of camp and found his brother's decomposed body in the same spot, identified by its clothing.[12]

With so many enemy graves located around the sharpshooters' camp, some men from Company A decided to check for relics at a gravesite. They chose a promising grave that was separated from a group of enlisted Confederates' graves. Anticipating relics from an officer's burial, the Minnesotans opened the grave. The disappointed grave robbers found no sword or worthwhile artifact to reward their labors.[13] Such disregard of respect for the enemy dead was commonplace during the Civil War, ranging from rifling the pockets and removing shoes and clothing from the dead, to improper burial. The battlefield dead were often thrown in a jumbled mass into a common trench without regard to identification. At New Market, Virginia, dead Federals were piled into a shallow depression and covered with a thin layer of soil by the victorious Confederates. In uncommon cases, involving irregular troops, there were even instances of savage mutilation of enemy dead.

Rainy, miserable weather kept the sharpshooters and McDowell's other troops bogged down for days during the stay at Bristoe Station. The rain turned to heavy snow that punished the ill-equipped soldiers with dangerous exposure, accumulating to over a foot soon after the sharpshooters arrived. Afterwards the skies cleared and the snow quickly melted, transforming the Virginia soil into a muddy quagmire that a sharpshooter noted was "some less than three feet deep."[14] That was enough to render the roads impassable, and supplies and rations did not reach Bristoe Station for days. An officer in a neighboring regiment complained that the heavy rain made his boots so wet that they would not fit, forcing him to stay in his tent until his boots dried.[15] The enlisted sharpshooters were not so fortunate as to have even a tent, so the men were forced to find shelter anywhere and any way they could. Many men had discarded their heavy overcoats during the march, making the suffering from exposure all the more severe. When the rain and snow broke, the men set to work erecting crude log huts using their rubber blankets for a roof, and probably more than a few "shebangs" or rough brush harbors were erected to shelter campfires and gathering areas.

But the sharpshooters were almost immediately employed as foragers after making camp at that place. Withdrawing Confederates had destroyed mountains of supplies and rations, but the surrounding farms were well stocked with sheep, hogs and cattle. William Greene of Company G wrote to his mother about the bountiful supply of chickens, turkeys, pigs and so forth brought in by the foragers. He remarked that the sharpshooters were "living first-rate" on confiscated rebel property.[16] General McClellan was none too keen on having his soldiers seize the property of Virginia's civilians, but he was far away and the sharpshooters weren't going to pass on farm-fresh rations. In any case there was little choice if the men were going to eat, as supplies of rations were held up by the impassable muddy roads.

While the 2nd endured the pouring rain and immobilizing mud in northern Virginia, Berdan and his 1st U.S.S.S. were engaging the rebels at Yorktown and quickly becoming famous for it. On March 24 the 1st disembarked from a transport at Hampton on the Virginia Peninsula. By April 5 the regiment was in action at Yorktown with McClellan's expeditionary army. The nation's attention was centered on McClellan's campaign, and Northern news correspondents found Berdan's green-clad riflemen a subject of special interest. In fact, no other unit during that campaign garnered as much press coverage as the 1st U.S.S.S.[17]

On April 12, 1862, a *New York Times* front-page headline read "Exploits of Berdan's Sharpshooters." This and numerous other articles exaggerated the prowess of the sharpshooters to an extent that even strained credulity. For instance, the *Times* article stated that a rebel "hand above the parapet becomes an instant mark for half-a-dozen rifles, which at a thousand yards distance rarely fail to hit their mark."[18] Such a shot with period rifles was obviously impossible for Colonel Berdan himself, not to mention a "half-a-dozen rifles" instantly and simultaneously hitting "their mark."

One yarn published in a newspaper told of a detachment from the 1st U.S.S.S. that fired into sandbags to drive sand into the muzzle of a rebel cannon. According to the tale, the sharpshooters kept up the sand-spraying shots until the cannon became fouled; and when the cannon fired after several shots, it exploded and blew the barrel to smithereens. Other articles had it that California Joe, the old sharpshooter mentioned previously who bought his own Sharps Rifle, shot a rebel dead at two miles' distance on his *first* shot. The Confederates did, however, have a healthy respect for Berdan's Sharpshooters on the Peninsula.[19]

Remarkably enough, the sharpshooters camping in the mud at Bristoe Station saw some of these inflated stories in newspapers that incredibly always found their way to camps regardless of the weather. On April 12, William Greene mentioned the record of the 1st at Yorktown in a letter to his mother. He remarked that the 2nd would soon have as good or better a name for itself, because he had heard while in Washington that the 2nd was the better of the two sharpshooter regiments.[20] His confident expression was no doubt widely shared, and the men were anxious to prove themselves in battle. Like many others who had rushed to the flag in 1861 and were yet to see combat, many of the sharpshooters feared that the war would end before they could experience battle.

On the 15th the sharpshooters left their log shanties behind and moved south again, marching about six miles to Catlett's Station on the same Orange and Alexandria Railroad. The regiment remained at Catlett's for only a couple of days. There General McDowell held brigade drill. It was the first time that the 2nd U.S.S.S. had been drilled in brigade tactics, having spent the winter in training independently. The sharpshooters were thrown out in the advance as skirmishers in a mock attack, the role for which they had been created. Seeing themselves as special troops, the sharpshooters expected the infantry to be responsible for the main assault or bayonet charge. Since the time of General George Washington, rifle units had been utilized to strike from a distance, avoiding close encounters with the enemy. The sharpshooters envisioned their role as specialists for targeting enemy officers, enemy artillerymen and opposing marksmen. Throughout the war they would feel misused when ordered to attack as infantry.

During this period while McDowell's troops struggled to reach Fredericksburg, General McClellan was anxious for reinforcements, and he wanted some of McDowell's troops in particular. On April 6, McClellan telegraphed the president from Yorktown asking specifically for General William Franklin's division from McDowell's department. McClellan wrote, "The enemy is strong in my front, & I have a most serious task before me, in the fulfillment of which I need all the aid the Government can give me. I again repeat the urgent request that Genl Franklin & his division may be restored to my command." That same day McClellan telegraphed General Franklin telling him that he had "twice urgently telegraphed the Presdt requesting that you & your Division might be restored to my command. Do all you can to accomplish it. Heaven knows I need you here."[21] The embattled McClellan wanted Franklin because he sensed opposition and resistance from his corps commanders, and he felt he could rely on General Franklin for complete cooperation.

On April 11 McClellan was granted the use of Franklin's Division from McDowell's department. Interestingly, one of the sharpshooters noted in a letter home that he had seen Franklin's troops moving north through the camp on their way to join McClellan's army.[22] The fact that a private in King's Division knew the destination of Franklin's entire division on the day it moved illustrates that intelligence and communications moved at a much greater pace than what one would expect for that time. If a private could discover this intelligence, no doubt the Confederates could do the same.

Despite General McClellan's constant calls for reinforcement, President Lincoln was unwilling to release the balance of McDowell's troops from their mission to protect Washington. The plan called for McDowell to advance to Fredericksburg on the Rappahannock River. There his troops could defend against an enemy thrust at Washington or go on the offensive by marching to join McClellan at Richmond. Poor weather conditions had slowed McDowell's movement south. By the time the sharpshooters reached Catlett's, the roads were drying, and General Augur's Brigade was launched on the 17th with a view of gaining a Federal bridgehead at Fredericksburg. The object of Augur's movement was to capture three bridges over the Rappahannock before a small Confederate holding force could burn them.

Augur's Brigade consisted of three two-year New York infantry regiments, the 22nd, 24th and 30th; the 84th New York Infantry (14th Brooklyn); and the 2nd U.S.S.S. The sharpshooters marched out of Catlett's Station with Augur's New Yorkers on the morning of April 17. Augur was a career Army officer, a West Point graduate and a veteran of the Mexican War. He was a capable officer with experience on the frontier before the Civil War. In 1861 he was serving as commandant of cadets at West Point. Promoted to brigadier general of volunteers on November 12, 1861, he was assigned as brigade commander with the new I Corps; this movement to Fredericksburg was his first active field service of the war.[23]

The sharpshooters and New Yorkers were pushed hard on the march to Falmouth, a small hamlet just north of the river and across from Fredericksburg. Twice the sharpshooters stopped on the march after dark, thinking they would be allowed to camp for the night. During one of the breaks a messenger from the front was killed as he tried to ride through the sharpshooters' picket line. Oliver Jones and Willard Wheaton of Company A reported that they had killed the man, whom they thought was a rebel. The unfortunate messenger apparently thought he had ridden into an enemy position and fired at the pickets. Lt. Colonel Peteler went to the scene and found that the dead man carried a message from Augur "for the sharpshooters to advance."[24] It was determined that although the rider was hit five times by the pickets, there was no misconduct involved because the messenger mistakenly acted hostile by drawing his weapon and trying to ride over the sharpshooters.

After the accidental shooting the sharpshooters pressed on with Augur's Brigade, marching all night on the dark road through woods and clearings, crossing several streams. As the column neared Falmouth they encountered a barricade the enemy had constructed of rails and logs at the edge of a wood to thwart the advance. The accompanying Harris Cavalry led by Judson Kilpatrick, later of fame as commander of the "Kill Cavalry," charged this barricade twice without success. The Confederates manned the position with at least four infantry companies from the 40th Virginia Infantry and the 9th Virginia Cavalry deployed on the right and left of the barricade; it was too much for Kilpatrick and the cavalry, which lost seven killed and sixteen wounded, with several horses killed.[25]

About two hours after the cavalry clash, the 2nd reached the barricade as the morning sun rose over the horizon. The Confederates had pulled back into the woods, retreating towards Falmouth. Here the sharpshooters for the first time saw up close the true horror of war as the column passed the barricade. Dead cavalrymen lay along the road in pools of their own blood. A wounded cavalryman lay with his bowels exposed outside of his bloody blouse. It was a daunting and sickening scene for the uninitiated sharpshooters to endure, knowing well that the same fate might await them in the woods just ahead.[26]

At the edge of the wood the sharpshooters deployed as skirmishers, their first experience at practicing their favorite drill in actual combat. Soon after the skirmishers stepped into the timber, one of General Augur's scouts "persisted in going with the skirmishers, but insisted in going ahead of the line some 75 paces in the road."[27] Lt. Colonel Peteler warned the scout to stay with the line so as not to be mistaken for the enemy. Peteler's warning went unheeded, and soon the scout was out ahead of the sharpshooters. The rebels were known to be in the woods, and as the scout attempted to return to the line, a sharpshooter fired his Colt Rifle from far on the right. The shot, fired from about 400 yards' distance, struck the hapless scout in the leg, fracturing the bone. General Augur mentioned this incident in his report of the skirmish by noting, "I regret to add that our valuable scout (Britton) was severely wounded in the leg."[28]

It was an inauspicious beginning for the untested sharpshooters. So far they had killed one ally and severely wounded another by mistake. At first it appeared that the 2nd was too anxious to shoot, but upon examination it was clear that in both cases the sharpshooters were not at fault.

The Confederates fell back through the woods to Falmouth. Rebel bullets buzzed and whizzed around the advancing sharpshooters, but apparently no one was hit. To the sharpshooters, however, it was a harrowing experience facing enemy fire for the first time.

As the Federals reached Falmouth, the Confederates had already burned two bridges and the third was afire. A rebel battery across the Rappahannock fired shells at the 2nd as the men came into sight above the river. The shells screeched overhead, their fuses hissing, and exploded near enough for the sharpshooters to hear the peculiar whizzing sound of the broken shell pieces flying through the air. Captain John Gibbon deployed a section of his Battery B, 4th U.S. Artillery to return fire, and soon the Confederates abandoned the fight. A portion of the bridge was saved by the cavalry, which rode down to put out the fire as the Confederates scattered.

The action around Falmouth was probably costlier in casualties for the Federals than the Confederates. However, one of the sharpshooters remembered that squads of Confederates were rounded up after the firing ceased, having been cut off on the north side of the river.[29] The post-action report of Confederate Brigadier General Charles Field might have underreported the missing; he listed his losses as only four killed and wounded and ten captured.[30] All Federal casualties were to the cavalry, most occurring at the barricade along the road to Falmouth.

Although the Confederates managed to destroy the bridges over the Rappahannock, the reconnaissance was a success overall. McDowell was finally in position to occupy Fredericksburg, his preferred headquarters location. The damaged bridges were no major obstacle; the Federals could span the river easily and soon did. The expedition resulted in acclaim for Augur's Brigade, as noted by Lt. Colonel Francis Peteler: "From the rapid advance and prompt action of Auger's brigade, it was called the 'Iron Brigade,' the first of that name in the Army of the Potomac."[31] The Iron Brigade better known to history was composed of the 2nd, 6th and 7th Wisconsin infantry regiments, the 19th Indiana and the 24th Michigan, commanded by General John Gibbon. However, it is a fact that Augur's Brigade to which the 2nd belonged "was the original Iron Brigade, and that Gibbon's Brigade was not known by that title until after Antietam, at which time it was so designated by a war correspondent, who was apparently unaware of his lack of originality."[32]

While this first hostile fire endured by the 2nd at Falmouth did not really amount to much, it was sufficient to introduce the novice soldiers to the realities of combat. The grotesque, bloody, gunshot corpses, and the whizzing incoming bullets and artillery shells, were as real as they were unpleasant. It was a comparatively soft introduction, but the forthcoming sequel promised something much worse. One sharpshooter remembered that some of the men who before had been so anxious for a turn at the rebels apparently lost their fervor after the skirmish. He noted that the effect of the little skirmish was to "take all of the fight out of them," and these demoralized men very quickly found ways of getting discharged before facing enemy fire again.[33]

From the very beginning at Berdan's Camp in Washington, the sharpshooters had lost men to sickness and disability at an unacceptable rate. Obviously many men left out of dissatisfaction, and now, others were seeking discharge out of fear. The 2nd U.S.S.S. was by no means unique in this attrition; its losses were probably higher than many other regiments but not the highest. One might look to discipline, or lack of it, as the chief reason for this type of loss, as indicated by the postwar remarks of a Federal general:

> ...a thorough administration and discipline enables a government to put sixty per cent of the troops ... in the front rank with muskets in their hands ... while in fact from the lack of it we were able to put only about thirty per cent of the troops in line of battle.... Living is better than dying, health better than sickness, thrift better than squalor. Therefore, order is better than disorder; for order is essential to all these things, and discipline alone makes order possible.[34]

A study of World War II American combat soldiers found that only about fifteen percent of the men would actually take aim at the enemy in a fire fight. The overwhelming majority of American soldiers did not want to kill. This probably was not the case at close quarters when a man's life was threatened if he did not kill. But the results of the study indicated that only a small percentage of combat soldiers actually sought to kill the enemy on a continual basis.[35] Likewise, only a percentage of Civil War soldiers could truly be counted upon to perform effectively in combat. The type of service required by the sharpshooters would naturally result in nonperformance by a percentage of those on the rolls. Although the 2nd U.S.S.S. was an elite unit with hand-picked men, many of the original recruits were not cut out to be killers.

The relative ease of exiting the Army during the first years of the Civil War no doubt accounts, at least in part, for the large number of losses due to discharge in the sharpshooters. Men who were especially squeamish about killing no doubt also sought means to transfer or obtain a discharge after Falmouth. Increasingly now, the men who remained were the committed, the ones who could be depended upon to fight and stick around to finish the fight.

So the 2nd U.S.S.S. had made a successful debut in its first active campaign of the war. In fact the sharpshooters earned very high praise for their performance in support of Battery B at Falmouth. Captain Stewart of that battery remarked that he "never felt so much relieved by any troops" as when the sharpshooters came up in support. He also added, "I must say that their firing was the most accurate I ever saw up to that time," and that the green-clad marksmen kept enemy sharpshooters at bay quite thoroughly.[36] The regiment was fortunate not to suffer any casualties while accomplishing its first mission successfully. During this first month of actual field service the men had experienced the ordeal of the march and the hardship of field camping in miserable weather. They were quickly adjusting, hardening and toughening for the life they would lead for the remainder of their service. They still awaited their special-order Sharps Rifles, and at Falmouth they would wait for events to take shape in northern Virginia to determine whether they would join the "On to Richmond" campaign.

4

A Continual Wasting Effect

Over a month passed while the 2nd camped at Falmouth and remained in the Fredericksburg vicinity. Before long the Rappahannock was spanned to enable McDowell's troops to occupy the town and march south to join McClellan's army. But instead of joining McClellan on the Peninsula, the sharpshooters would be detained in northern Virginia as insurance against an enemy threat to Washington. In the months during McClellan's campaign to capture Richmond, the 2nd would be involved in an enervating series of movements and marches orchestrated in response to Confederate operations in the Shenandoah Valley. During the frustrating months from May to August of 1862, the sharpshooters and King's Division atrophied significantly without achieving a compensatory success. The summer of 1862 had a continual wasting effect on Berdan's Sharpshooters; week by week men disappeared from the rolls from death and disability, irreplaceable men. Yet by late summer nothing would be gained of significance, and they and the rest of Lincoln's army would be forced back into the Washington vicinity, where the campaign had begun in March. Much blood and treasure were sadly wasted by McClellan's overly conservative methods. Instead of ending the war that summer as Little Mac had pledged, his leadership instead effectively removed the Federal threat to Richmond, and it would be two years before the Federals would again reach the environs of the Confederate capital in force.

For the first few days after reaching Falmouth the Sharpshooters worked to secure their position on the north bank of the Rappahannock. Patrols went out checking for lurking rebels, duty later known as "mopping up." Guard stations, picket posts and provost headquarters were set up, and the routine duties of occupation were soon in effect. Augur's Brigade was out in advance of McDowell's force. It was hostile territory, rebel country, and prudence dictated that due caution be observed.

Just a few days later, on the 23rd, reinforcements arrived in the form of Cutler's Brigade. The crowding in of more blue-clad Northerners did not sit well with the locals. Some residents had already fled. The newly arrived soldiers marched into Falmouth to find "nearly every white woman" crying and the slave population rejoicing.[1] McDowell now had enough men in place to secure Falmouth and to move across the Rappahannock. On the 30th McDowell was authorized to occupy Fredericksburg, and within a few days he sent troops across the newly completed bridge to take charge of the town.

Soon the sharpshooters settled into routine at Falmouth and drilling resumed. Tents were finally issued to the men and a standard camp with streets was laid out. The fortunate ones had little to do except occasional guard duty and drill. Some went swim-

Men from Company F, 2nd U.S.S.S. This photograph was probably taken near Falmouth before June 1862 while the regiment was still armed with Colt Revolving Rifles. Some, not all, of the men were identified as follows: Sgt. Horace Caldwell, Privates Amos Abbott, Charles Applin, William Beard, Cyrus Farnum, Isaac Farnum, Leonard Spead and William Spead. U.S. Army Military History Institute.

ming in the Rappahannock or visited Fredericksburg looking for something to buy. The regiment was paid for the previous two months by May, but the prices were high in Fredericksburg.[2] The sharpshooters found it difficult to purchase anything in the town, because the local merchants wanted only Confederate bills.[3] Fredericksburg would suffer severely a few months later when McClellan was set aside and a hard war policy prevailed.

While McDowell waited for instructions at Fredericksburg, the Confederates abandoned Yorktown on May 3 and began a retreat towards Richmond. President Lincoln, Secretary of War Stanton and Secretary of the Treasury Chase departed Washington on May 5 to travel to the Peninsula for a meeting with General McClellan. On May 9 the president, concerned with mounting evidence of poor cooperation among McClellan's senior subordinates, sent a letter to the general. Lincoln mentioned that McClellan reportedly had "no consultation or communication" with three of his corps commanders. He noted that McClellan was said to only communicate with Generals Porter and Franklin, and he wanted to know if McClellan could afford to set his "foot upon the necks" of the other three corps commanders all at once.[4] In addition to alienating his senior commanders, McClellan was bedeviling the president with his overcautious management of the campaign. He constantly overestimated Confederate strength and repeatedly called for reinforcements, McDowell's troops in particular. During the month of May the president would continually look for an opportunity to send McDowell's troops and the 2nd to reinforce McClellan's army on the Peninsula, hoping to embolden Little Mac and provide the impetus for his success.

Berdan's other regiment had performed well at Yorktown and on the Peninsula, and the regiment continued to be lauded in the Northern press while the 2nd was barely even noticed along the Rappahannock. A late April newspaper article praised the first regiment's "California Joe," or "Old California" as he was also known. Joe was one of the oldest of Berdan's Sharpshooters and was a favorite of the press. As mentioned previously, he carried his own privately purchased Sharps Rifle, and according to the article he had distinguished himself with "his unerring skill with the rifle, every shot bringing down a foe." Truman Head or "California Joe" used the type of rifle ordered by Berdan to arm his two regiments, and the article noted that he was "delighted with the accuracy of fire."[5]

On May 7, 1862, at Yorktown, the first of the special-order, double-set-trigger Sharps Model 1859 Military Rifles were finally received by Berdan. This was the first shipment composed of the first 600 rifles manufactured for the sharpshooters between April 11 and April 23. The balance of the 2,000 rifles were finished in increments of 500 and completed on May 24.[6] Of course the first guns went to Berdan and the 1st U.S.S.S. fighting on the Peninsula, but Sharps Rifles would soon be on their way to Falmouth to arm the 2nd and replace the unwanted "pepperbox" Colt Revolving Rifles.

With McClellan's army finally making progress toward Richmond, McDowell was directed to proceed overland to reinforce McClellan on May 17. Secretary Stanton directed McDowell to move as soon as General Shield's division joined him at Falmouth.[7] But when Shield's troops showed up at Falmouth they were in such poor condition that McDowell delayed in order to reequip and supply them. Shield's men had seen hard service in the Shenandoah Valley against Jackson; their uniforms were in tatters and the men were showing the effects of poor rations and hardship.

On May 23, President Lincoln traveled from Washington to Fredericksburg to confer with General McDowell. The president had informed McClellan on the 21st that he would soon send McDowell overland to reinforce him, saying that a march would get the troops to him faster than a voyage by boats.[8] Lincoln apparently wanted to review McDowell's troops before sending them off to Richmond, and the 2nd crossed the river to take part in the review. Private Greene of Company G decided he did not care enough about seeing the president to bother; instead, he stayed in camp to write a letter.[9] Most of the men had already seen Lincoln more than once at camp in Washington, so probably more than a few chose to loaf rather than take part in the review, if allowed.

The next morning found the 2nd on the march south of Fredericksburg with McDowell's troops "intending to join McClellan."[10] President Lincoln left McDowell's headquarters after dark on the 23rd. By the evening of the 24th, as the sharpshooters toiled on the march, the president wired McClellan to inform him: "I have been compelled to suspend Gen. McDowell's movement to join you."[11] This, of course, meant that the sharpshooters, who had already marched fifteen weary miles, would have to turn back.

President Lincoln's decision to "suspend" the reinforcement of McClellan was exactly what the Confederates intended to achieve with forces in the Shenandoah Valley. General Robert E. Lee was aware that should McDowell march south from Fredericksburg, Richmond would be threatened by a "powerful Federal pincer" movement. Lee wanted forces in the Shenandoah Valley under General Thomas "Stonewall" Jackson to prevent Federal reinforcements from combining under McDowell at Fredericksburg.[12] When General Shield's division marched to Falmouth, the remaining Federal troops in the valley under General Banks were vulnerable to an attack by Jackson's forces. On the 24th, Banks was driven out of Front Royal, and the Confederates pursued him to Winchester. There on the following day Banks was put to flight by Jackson.

The Federal defeat at Winchester alarmed the president, and he turned to McDowell to deal with Jackson. The president wanted McDowell to send troops to trap Jackson's force near Harpers Ferry. He noted that McDowell could provide "very valuable, and very honorable service ... to cut them off." Lincoln feared that Washington could be threatened, so much so that he wired McClellan: "I think the time is near when you must either attack Richmond or give up the job and come to the defence of Washington."[13]

On the evening of May 24, President Lincoln directed McDowell to suspend "for the present the movement on Richmond." He ordered McDowell to send 20,000 troops towards the Shenandoah Valley with a view of capturing the rebel valley forces under Jackson and Ewell. Though disappointed and uncertain of the propriety of the orders, McDowell immediately complied. He ordered King's Division to halt the march south from Fredericksburg, and he ordered Shield's Division to return to the Shenandoah Valley.[14]

The sharpshooters went into camp near the widow Alstead's, about eight miles south of Fredericksburg, to await instructions from McDowell concerning the return march to Fredericksburg and on to the Shenandoah Valley. There the regiment remained until the morning of the 29th. News that the long-awaited Sharps Rifles would be issued at Falmouth reached the men on the 28th, somewhat relieving the fatigue of the march on the following day. The 29th dawned pleasantly, but the day proved very hot. As the regiment neared Fredericksburg, the 2nd left the brigade column heading for the depot at Falmouth, anxiously anticipating their first look at the prized Sharps Rifles.[15]

The battle Hiram Berdan waged with General Ripley and J.C. Palmer to obtain the much-desired Sharps breechloaders was finally crowned with success at the Falmouth depot on May 29. On that day the men at least got the opportunity to examine their brand-new rifles. The sharpshooters' custom-built rifles were indeed handsome pieces. Besides having double-set triggers for smooth firing, each had blued barrels and case-hardened metal parts including barrel bands, patchbox, butt plate, lever, lock and hammer. The case-hardened parts showed variegated colors of blue, gray and brown. Blued

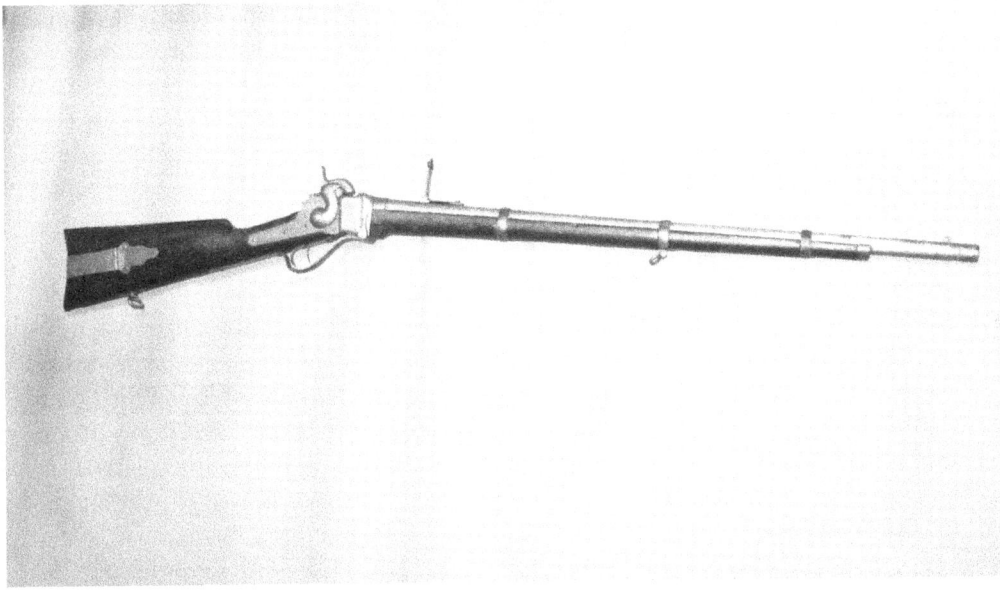

Berdan Sharps Rifle, serial no. 55066, on display at Chancellorsville National Battlefield Museum.

barrels did not flash in sunlight as did the bright steel barrels of standard issue rifle muskets. Some of the rifles were apparently even fitted with high-grade burled walnut stocks intended for high-quality sporting rifles, perhaps as a result of pressure on Palmer to speedily complete the contract.[16] Initially these arms excelled standard infantry arms in appearance as well as utility, but hard use would quickly obliterate the superior finish. Some wartime photographs of Berdan's Sharpshooters holding their breechloaders show weapons with bright barrels and shiny metal parts, all original finish completely polished away.

Rear sights on the Sharps Rifles were designed to flip up and adjust for various ranges from 100 to beyond 700 yards. Since 1859 the standard issue American rifle musket employed a flip-up notched rear sight designed for only three distances: 100, 300, and 500 yards. This simplified design was suited for laying down curtains of fire by volleys adjusted for the rainbow trajectory of standard ammunition. It was not well suited for accurate individual shooting. At distances of over 300 yards the Sharps Rifle proved much more accurate and precise than the Springfield Rifle Musket. Muzzleloading rifles had one rarely utilized advantage over the Sharps, however. A much greater powder charge could be loaded into rifle muskets and muzzleloading target rifles. Breechloaders were designed to hold a limited charge in the breech, while muzzleloaders could accept any charge that the barrel was designed to withstand without bursting. One example of extending effective range of muzzleloaders in combat occurred during the 1864 battle at Winchester, Virginia. There a Federal infantry regiment silenced a Confederate battery at long range by doubling the powder charge in their Springfields.[17]

Although the new rifles had been shipped to Falmouth for issue to the 2nd, ammunition did not arrive with them.[18] The first shipment of Sharps Rifles Berdan received at Yorktown also arrived without ammunition. Berdan got his ammunition within one day, but the 2nd was on the march and urgently needed; consequently, the new rifles were left at Falmouth. It would be over two weeks before the 2nd U.S.S.S. would be issued the new rifles with ammunition.[19]

Retaining the Colt Rifles, the 2nd rejoined their brigade on the march about five miles north of Falmouth.[20] As part of King's Division, the sharpshooters were urgently needed for Lincoln's plan to trap "Stonewall" Jackson in the Shenandoah Valley. General McDowell informed one of his subordinates on the 29th concerning the destination of the sharpshooters: "The question now seems to be one of legs — whether we can get to Jackson and Ewell before they can get away.... I have ordered King's division to Cattlett's, thence to Warrenton and to White Plains...."[21] The men were thusly pushed hard to reach Catlett's. On the 30th the sharpshooters marched through a steamy afternoon rain that soon turned the dirt roads to mud. The march proved so grueling that the 6th Wisconsin of King's Division had 150 men fall out along the roadside.[22]

On the 31st General McDowell ordered King to load his division on trains at Catlett's Station, telling King to "Let no time be lost in getting the men on the cars...." The sharpshooters and the 14th Brooklyn were apparently the first to be loaded on cars at Catlett's. King informed McDowell that the sharpshooters were aboard and that the other regiments would be loaded up "as fast as they arrive." Gibbon's Brigade would bring up the rear.[23] By afternoon the sharpshooters' train steamed into Manassas Junction. There the train stopped until after darkness set in.[24]

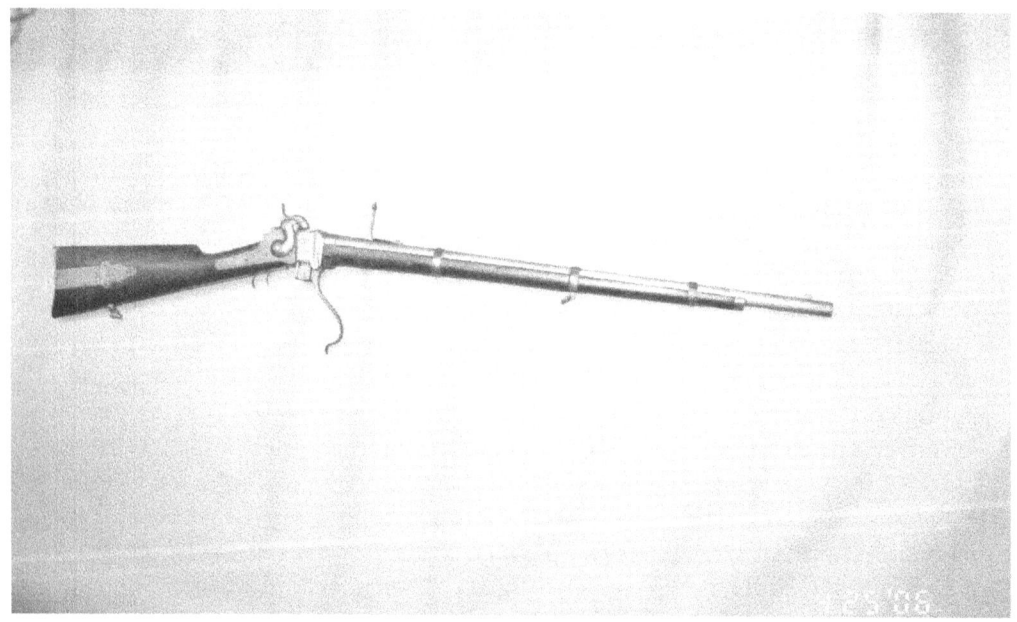

The Chancellorsville Berdan Sharps with the lever down and the breechblock exposed.

General McDowell had advised King as to the particulars of his train transport before the sharpshooters and 14th Brooklyn departed Catlett's. He told King that nine trains would be involved in the movement. He cautioned King to "let the train move off as the railroad dispatcher may indicate, so as to avoid collisions." He mentioned that other Federals had been fired at along the route from Catlett's to Thoroughfare Gap and that the grades were steep enough that it could "be necessary for the men to leave the train whilst they are ascending."[25] Apparently a freight train carried the sharpshooters from Manassas Junction. One sharpshooter mentioned that some of the cars were of the platform type without a roof or covering.[26]

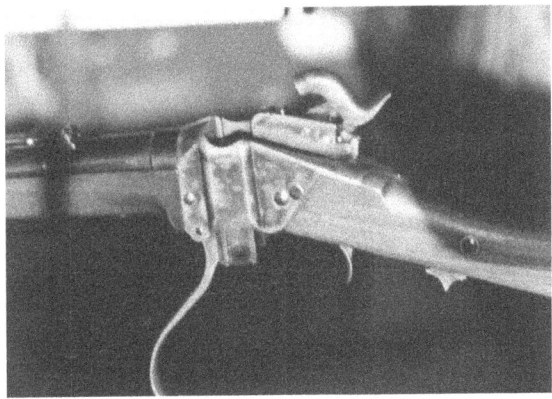

An original Sharps Military Rifle in factory-new condition showing the case-colored lock, lever, hammer and breechblock and blued barrel. Rifles issued to the sharpshooters usually quickly lost all of their original finish.

Sometime after midnight in the predawn darkness of June 1, 1862, after passing through Thoroughfare Gap, the train carrying the sharpshooters stalled on a hillside near White Plains. Just as General McDowell had cautioned, the engine could not pull the cars up the grade. Before the sharpshooters could be awakened and ordered to detrain, another train now transporting the 14th Brooklyn plowed into the rear car of the stalled train. Apparently the signal light on rear car of the sharpshooters' train had gone out, and the following train, accelerating to negotiate the steep hillside, collided with the darkened, motionless train.[27]

According to an account by a sharpshooter present during the accident, the rear car struck in the collision was a platform car occupied by Company A. Most of the men on the platform car jumped off and escaped injury. But the struck platform car slammed into the next car, a boxcar occupied by Company E, crushing the walls and injuring many men. In front of the smashed boxcar was another platform car carrying Company C, and this car was forced through yet another boxcar packed with men from Company D. Sanford Bartlett of Company D was killed instantly, smashed by a wheel from one of the colliding cars. Nearly every man in Company D was injured to some extent.[28]

Most of the injured were riding in the smashed boxcars, men from Companies D and E. The remaining uninjured sharpshooters, riding in undamaged cars, jumped off the train to rescue their comrades trapped in the splintered boxcars. Bartlett was apparently the only man killed in the accident, but forty-four others were injured.[29] Some men suffered bone fractures and head injuries. The injured were later transported to Rector Station to receive medical attention. After sunrise, damaged equipment and arms were salvaged from the battered cars. A few Colt Rifles were found with twisted barrels from the impact of the collision.[30] The unfortunate Bartlett was sewn into blankets as a makeshift coffin and buried on a slight rise near the train track.[31]

After several hours the regiment again boarded cars for the trip to Front Royal. But before the train reached that place, General McDowell learned of the escape of Jackson's troops from the planned effort to entrap them. King was ordered to immediately stop the movement of his division. The sharpshooters learned that they were not needed for the pursuit of Jackson, and found themselves again on a train headed the opposite direction, toward Manassas Junction. Near Haymarket the sharpshooters were ordered off the train to set up a temporary camp. General McDowell explained the logic for the temporary stop at Haymarket: "The difficulty just now of supplying troops at this point and beyond has caused me to concentrate King's division near Thoroughfare Gap."[32]

Two days later the sharpshooters were on the march again to return to Falmouth. Having started for Richmond in late May, the regiment had spent the past ten days rushing pell-mell from one destination to another. The return trip to Falmouth proved extremely fatiguing. During one stretch of the trip, the sharpshooters marched twenty-six miles in ten hours. The temperatures soared and combined with humidity from recent heavy rains; one sharpshooter complained that it was the hottest day he had ever seen. He noted that "quite a number" fell out and died, and the color bearer of the 30th New York Infantry fell dead as he was marching in the column.[33]

By June 15 the sharpshooters were back at their previous camp at Falmouth. Stonewall Jackson had held his own in the Shenandoah Valley and had managed to keep McDowell's troops from joining McClellan for the campaign against Richmond. Jackson remained in the valley until June 17, but he was no further threat to Washington. Consequently, General McDowell sent George McCall's division of Pennsylvania Reserves to reinforce McClellan. Nevertheless, Jackson apparently remained enough of a concern to induce the president to retain King's Division at Fredericksburg throughout the month of June.

On June 16, 1862, the 2nd U.S.S.S. finally was issued new Sharps Model 1859 Military Rifles, exchanging the used Colt guns for them. The regiment was also issued new accoutrements for the new arms. From all accounts the men were highly pleased with the change and were more than happy to turn in the Colt Revolving Rifles. One sharpshooter opined that a Sharps was worth more than all the Colt guns ever made.[34]

During the Civil War the government purchased 4,600 Colt Revolving Rifles for issue to Federal troops. Since both sharpshooter regiments were originally issued revolving rifles, approximately 2,600 were purchased for other units. At least twenty Federal cavalry regiments were armed at least in part with the revolving rifles, as were twenty-seven infantry regiments.[35] With so many Federal units showing revolving rifles on ordnance returns, it is probable that the guns exchanged by the sharpshooters were returned to service elsewhere and quite soon after the exchange.

While there is little to indicate that the sharpshooters systematically trained in target practice with the new Sharps Rifles while at Falmouth, some officers and men evidently practiced with their new rifles within days of getting them. One sharpshooter mentioned setting up targets at 500 and 600 yards. He had no complaints and indicated that the rifle was quite accurate. Like the men from Berdan's other regiment, the 2nd was well pleased with the new rifles.[36]

Once again camped at Falmouth, the sharpshooters settled into an uneasy routine while General McDowell and the president studied developments in McClellan's campaign and awaited Confederate General Jackson's next move. Stalled in a quasi-war zone, the sharpshooters were unable to properly train or drill, having to be always at the ready to take up their traps and head for the scene of the fighting. It was not so for Berdan's other regiment, the 1st U.S.S.S.

Most of the fame ascribed to Berdan's Sharpshooters was initiated by the 1st U.S.S.S. on the Peninsula and during the Seven Days' Battles around Richmond in the spring and summer of 1862, while the 2nd U.S.S.S. remained sidelined in northern Virginia. Berdan's other men were often mentioned in newspaper articles describing their value as snipers and marksmen. As the campaign wore on, the 1st Sharpshooters were less of a novelty and were mentioned in fewer articles. At Gaines's Mill and again at Malvern Hill, Berdan's men fought in advance of the main battle line to punish the enemy with precision shooting from a skirmish line. While Berdan's men did excellent service in battles around Richmond, not that much praise was given them in the reports of their senior commanders.

Pvt. J.C. Paige of Company F, 1st U.S.S.S. posing with a cocked Berdan Sharps and wearing a belt with full accoutrements. U.S. Army Military History Institute.

During the Civil War most units that received high praise were usually recognized for two salient reasons: standing their ground under great pressure, and driving the enemy from a defensive position. This was not the sort of work the sharpshooters were recruited and trained for. General Porter, who commanded Berdan and his 1st U.S.S.S. during the Seven Days' battles, put his assessment of the concept of sharpshooters in unmitigated candor following McClellan's failed campaign. According to Porter, the sharpshooters lacked training as infantry, had no confidence in their officers or themselves in the presence of the enemy, and were not properly armed to face the enemy at close quarters. Porter did not even regard Berdan's men as efficient as light infantry.[37]

It is quite understandable how General Porter came to his conclusion about the sharpshooters. Like many ranking Federal officers, he probably viewed Berdan's men as troublesome infantrymen that reportedly were above average marksmen. Apparently Ported did not believe that Berdan's men were reliable and could not be depended upon to stand fast under enemy pressure. Additionally, Berdan's leadership, courage and even his lucidity had come into serious question during the fighting around Richmond.

By the end of the Seven Days' battles, Berdan's reputation was being frequently assailed. A letter written to the *Penn Yan Chronicle* in October of 1862 detailed Berdan's flaws and serves as an excellent indication of why his leadership reflected badly upon the sharpshooters. The letter alleged that Berdan lacked "military knowledge enough to conduct either a dress parade, or inspection." The following are some excerpts from the unsigned letter:

> In the winter of '61 and '62, it became known in camp that Col. Berdan intended to take the field in person as Colonel. This caused a universal feeling of gloom and discontent. The men said, and they reasoned correctly, "Of what use is it that we are the best drilled regiment in the service, if we are to have a Colonel utterly incompetent even to review his own regiment."

At the Battle of Hanover Courthouse:

> Col. Berdan divided his regiment in two equal parts, sending the first into the woods under Lieut. Col. Ripley, and the second to follow under command of Capt Hastings. When the regiment reached the woods where the rebels were posted, Col. Berdan left, and rode back up the road, where he remained until the end of the battle.

At the Battle of Mechanicsville:

> After leaving the regiment in the hands of the Adjutant to go alone into the great battle of Mechanicsville, Col. Berdan returned to camp, where he found the Quartermaster ... and a few stragglers. He immediately ordered the lights to be extinguished and retired to his tent. Col. Ripley overtook the regiment before it reached Mechanicsville and led it gallantly through.

At the Battle of Gaines's Mill:

> He went to the front, posted the men, and retired. This was two hours before the action commenced. The Colonel was not seen again that day on the battlefield. He was heard of away in the rear trying to rally stragglers, where he became so excited as to shoot an artillery horse with his revolver, and then he endeavored to persuade the Lieutenant that it was a shell that hit the horse.... The Colonel first said he went to the rear for ammunition; afterwards he did not press that reason, for any intelligent Sergeant could have obtained the ammunition, which by the way was not needed.... He dwelt strongly upon what he did at the rear, without first explaining how he came to be there, when his regiment was in the very front.

At the Battle of Malvern Hill:

> Col. Berdan posted his regiment in the very front, and then retired as usual to the rear, and did not come near the battlefield again that day. His excuse was, that he was trying to get some fresh beef for his men. The men were indeed hungry, but they had no time then to eat, and the rawest recruit needs not to be told that the Colonel's place is with his men in their hour of deadly peril.... Lieut. Col. Ripley ... said; "Berdan shoves us to the front to be killed for his glory. He dare not accompany his regiment into battle. He sends us to the very front, and the more we fight,— the more of us who are killed,— the greater is his glory, and he always in the rear."[38]

By the late summer of 1862, Hiram Berdan's reputation had sunk to a new low. Not only was he widely regarded as dishonest and self-serving, he was now considered incompetent and cowardly. His leadership could not help but have a debilitating effect upon the sharpshooters as a whole. In the following months his association with both regiments of sharpshooters, for the most part, would serve only one useful purpose: as an advocate to maximize attention to the sharpshooters' accomplishments. As always, Berdan was a bright, capable administrator; however, he was not morally and mentally qualified to lead men into combat.

At Falmouth the 2nd spent the month of June awaiting developments to determine their next move. General King took measures to seek intelligence about enemy activity through spies and cavalry operations while the sharpshooters remained idle. By late June, McClellan had lost the initiative, drawing his army toward the James River in a series of retrograde movements.

With McClellan's campaign unraveling and the series of Federal setbacks in the Shenandoah Valley, President Lincoln decided to reorganize forces in northern Virginia and bring in a successful general from the Western Theater to command them. On June 26 the president consolidated the Mountain Department, Department of the Shenandoah and the Department of the Rappahannock into one force named the Army of Virginia.[39] To command the newly formed army, the president appointed Major General John Pope. The freshly appointed commander had compiled a record of success in operations on the Mississippi River, helping clear Confederate forces on the river north of Memphis. The president needed a capable general to organize the scattered forces in northern Virginia, with a view of eventually combining with McClellan to crush Lee's army near Richmond.

Now assigned to the 1st Brigade, 1st Division of the III Corps, Army of Virginia, the sharpshooters passed the month of June at Falmouth. Meanwhile, General McClellan continued his retreat to Harrison's Landing on the James River, southeast of Richmond. The landing McClellan chose for his final defensive position was located near Berkeley Plantation, the ancestral home of the 9th president, William Henry Harrison. By the first week of July, McClellan was still in position to seriously threaten Richmond. General Pope was working to organize his new army in northern Virginia. Pope would soon be able to move against Richmond from the north while McClellan could resume the offensive from the east along the James. In fact, the Confederate Army had been badly handled and severely punished at Malvern Hill on July 1. At least one Federal corps commander believed that McClellan could resume the offensive after that battle, and other senior commanders believed that the army should remain near Richmond.[40]

So the first three weeks of July passed with McClellan waiting for reinforcements at Harrison's Landing. By the third week of July, General Lee had decided that he could risk a movement against Pope's forces north of Richmond, and General Jackson was sent to the Gordonsville area. Jackson's movement was reported to Pope on July 21, prompting Pope to order a reconnaissance to investigate the report.[41] On July 24, General King directed Brigadier General John Gibbon to "use diligent efforts to ascertain what Confederate forces are at Orange Court House and Gordonsville."[42] Gibbon was directed to make a reconnaissance with a force of cavalry, infantry, artillery and some sharpshooters. Companies A and C of the 2nd accompanied Gibbon under command of Lt. Colonel Peteler, departing Falmouth with Gibbon on the 24th.

The two companies of sharpshooters, about sixty men in total, accompanied Gibbon's column on the afternoon of July 24. According to Gibbon's report, he had reached the vicinity of Orange Courthouse on the morning of the 26th. About five miles from the courthouse, Gibbon left his main force and pushed ahead with one infantry regiment (apparently the 2nd Wisconsin), two artillery pieces, some cavalry and the sharpshooters. After skirmishing with enemy cavalry, Gibbon received intelligence, possibly from a spy or scout, that Jackson's force was located six miles away at Liberty Mills. He estimated Jackson's strength at about 30,000.[43] This was a considerable overestimate; Jackson probably had fewer than 20,000.[44]

Having succeeded in his mission, Gibbon ordered a withdrawal. According to Gibbon, the rebel cavalry "made a dash at our rear guard, but was easily repulsed, with the loss of 1 prisoner, who was brought in, and reports 5 of his people wounded in the morning skirmish."[45] According to a sharpshooter who heard Lt. Colonel Peteler's account of the fight, the sharpshooters did all the firing at the enemy cavalry. The sharpshooter mentioned that five rebels were killed. The captured man was thrown from his saddle after his horse was struck and was then taken prisoner. Afterwards the sharpshooters acted as rear guard for the withdrawal.[46] Gibbon concluded his report by mentioning that he returned to Falmouth on the 27th and that the sharpshooters "were conspicuous during the march for their well-filled ranks, losing very few men by straggling, although the weather was very warm and the marching on the way out rapid."[47]

The military situation confronting President Lincoln during the summer of 1862 required him to seek a professional to oversee the entire Federal war effort. McClellan had held the job until the commencement of the Peninsular Campaign, leaving the position vacant. So on July 11, 1862, the president appointed Major General Henry "Old Brains" Halleck to the office of Commander-in-Chief of the Federal Army, to coordinate all Army operations. Halleck was a West Point graduate and veteran of the Mexican War. He had a widely held reputation for high intellect and had a successful record as a commander in the Western Theater. While the president appointed Halleck with the hope of finding a capable military advisor and strategist, the general proved to be a first-rate administrator but little else of value. Halleck himself indicated that he did not want the position: "I did everything in my power to avoid coming to Washington; but after declining several invitations from the President I received the order ... which left me no option."[48]

After assuming command Halleck failed to spur McClellan into action against Richmond and failed to initiate an offensive by coordinating the Federal forces in Virginia. By early August the president had determined that McClellan's campaign would not succeed; he directed General Halleck to order the withdrawal of McClellan's Army from Harrison's Landing with a view of reinforcing Pope's Army of Virginia. The focus of the war shifted from the James to northern Virginia. The 2nd U.S.S.S., after nearly one year of service, would finally be in position to render significant service at the seat of war.

In late July, Brigadier General John Porter Hatch assumed command of the 1st Brigade, to which the 2nd U.S.S.S. was attached. The new brigade commander was a West Point graduate, class of 1845. As a young second lieutenant he served gallantly with the mounted rifles during the Mexican War. He remained in the Army, serving at various obscure outposts in the West until the outbreak of the Civil War. In 1861 he was brought east and soon promoted to brigadier general of volunteers. His performance as a cavalry commander prior to his assignment to the sharpshooters' brigade was undistinguished.[49] Hatch would soon lead the 2nd into its first major battle. As brigade commander Hatch would at least demonstrate a modicum of appreciation for the role of his sharpshooters and utilize them as skirmishers rather than ordinary infantry in battle.

One week after the 2nd returned from the Orange Courthouse reconnaissance, on August 3, President Lincoln directed Halleck to order the evacuation of McClellan's forces at Harrison's Landing. Lincoln was concerned that McClellan's Army would be vulnerable to attack should McClellan withdraw from his strong position at Harrison's Landing. In fact Lincoln had met with McClellan's corps commanders to determine if a withdrawal from the Peninsula were possible.[50] By August 3, part of Lee's Army under Stonewall Jackson had been sent north, as was validated by Gibbon's reconnaissance. With McClellan preparing to withdraw from Harrison's Landing, it became imperative for Pope's forces to prevent the return of Jackson's Confederates to Lee at Richmond. In effect, the withdrawal of McClellan placed the Federals in a dilemma; it made McClellan and Pope both vulnerable to defeat in the event that Lee could concentrate his entire army for an attack.

To prevent the Confederates from concentrating forces against McClellan during the withdrawal, Pope stepped up his pressure against the rebel force at Gordonsville. On August 5, he sent Gibbon's Brigade on a raid out of Falmouth in the direction of Frederick's Hall Station on the Virginia Central Railroad south of Fredericksburg.[51] Also on that day the 2nd marched across the Rappahannock on a reconnaissance to Guiney Station, south of Fredericksburg a few miles. While Gibbon's force attempted a raid on the railroad, the sharpshooters "took part in more or less skirmishing" against Jeb Stuart's cavalry near Guiney.[52] When the rebel cavalry moved off, the sharpshooters continued their reconnaissance in a westerly direction, marching to Spotsylvania Courthouse.

By the evening of August 7 the sharpshooters were back in Falmouth. The reconnaissance accomplished little and cost the regiment three men captured, including Sergeant Samuel Murry of Company F.[53] Gibbon's Brigade, having marched much farther in the extreme heat, lost fifty-nine men who had straggled during their long trek. The lesson learned on this operation: "to straggle was to be lost."[54]

Pope's efforts to detain Jackson's Confederates during early August proved unnecessary. General Lee soon discovered McClellan's intention to evacuate Harrison's Landing, and he very quickly decided to concentrate as much force as possible to attack Pope in northern Virginia. Jackson, instead of marching south to reunite with Lee's troops around Richmond, went on the offensive against Pope's scattered forces near Culpeper. On August 9, Jackson with 22,000 troops collided with Federal Major General Nathaniel Banks's 12,000 at Cedar Mountain, a few miles south of Culpeper.[55]

The outnumbered Federals put up a tough fight but were driven from the field. General Pope quickly sought to concentrate his scattered army to face Jackson's victorious rebels. On August 10, the 2nd U.S.S.S. accompanied King's Division on a hurried march north from Falmouth to reinforce the Federals at Cedar Mountain. King was ordered to leave his wagons under guard and to push forward day and night to reach Cedar Mountain as soon as possible.[56] Pope was now concerned that he, not McClellan, was endangered by a concentration of Confederate forces. From Cedar Mountain on the morning of August 11, Pope mentioned his concern to General-in-Chief Halleck: "...I am satisfied that one-third of the enemy's whole force is here, and more will be arriving unless McClellan will keep them busy and uneasy at Richmond.... Please make McClellan do something to prevent re-enforcements being sent here."[57]

The sharpshooters arrived at Cedar Mountain too late to take part in the battle. Expecting to be sent into their first large-scale combat at first light, the sharpshooters instead awoke to find that Jackson "had skedadled" and they "were not needed."[58] History records that both sides claimed victory at Cedar Mountain, but Jackson withdrew and Pope did not follow. As a result, the sharpshooters camped near the Cedar Mountain battlefield until August 19, while Pope assessed the situation and awaited reinforcements from McClellan.

By August 19 Pope had learned that Lee was concentrating his army north of the Rapidan River, seriously threatening Pope but virtually ignoring McClellan. Pope drew back and concentrated his forces north of the Rappahannock River between Sulphur Springs and Kelley's Ford.[59] The 2nd U.S.S.S. marched away from Cedar Mountain on the 19th, crossing the Rappahannock and taking a position near Rappahannock Station by the 20th.

Meanwhile General Lee probed several fords and crossings of the Rappahannock. On August 21 the sharpshooters were involved in one of the rebel attempts to get across the river. Near Rappahannock Station on the 21st, four companies of sharpshooters were ordered by General Hatch to investigate reports of rebel cavalry and artillery present on the Federal side of the river. Lt. Colonel Peteler led the four companies, forming a skirmish line on the undulating terrain near the river. On the last swell of ground near the river, Peteler detected swirling dust stirred up by the enemy cavalry.

Peteler brought up his reserve companies commanded by Captain Caldwell and placed them in position to fire in support of his skirmish line. As he positioned the reserve, Peteler was nearly hit by enemy fire. Peteler's skirmishers opened fire on the rebels and drove them back across the river. One of the sharpshooters wounded the enemy commander's horse, which then bolted into the skirmish line. The wounded horse toppled into a ditch, trapping the rebel commander beneath it. Sergeant Major Shoup and two others helped the enemy captain from under the horse and took him prisoner.

The rebel captain strenuously objected to being taken prisoner by enlisted men and asked for an officer. Lt. Colonel Peteler soon appeared and questioned the prisoner. Apparently getting little useful information from the captured officer, other than that he was a captain in Stuart's cavalry, Peteler ordered the prisoner sent to the rear under the escort of two privates. Confederate artillery positioned across the river opened on the sharpshooters before the captain could be sent to the rear, forcing him to endure the shelling along with the sharpshooters. While the dignified rebel captain sheltered from the shellfire, another rebel cavalryman surrendered to the sharpshooters and further humiliated the captain by telling the sharpshooters that he had been seeking a chance to surrender "for a long time."[60]

On the following day the sharpshooters again skirmished with the enemy. Corporal Warren Stevens of Company H was reported as killed in action on this day.[61] Again on the 23rd the regiment was called out to prevent a Confederate crossing of the river near Rappahannock Station. On this day the 2nd was pinned between the contending artillery of both armies, "120 pieces of artillery doing their best" to destroy each other.[62] The shelling began at daylight amid thick smoke and fog, rendering it impossible for the sharpshooters to pick targets across the river. With no works or shelters present, the men lay in a pine grove behind a small hill for five hours while shells shrieked overhead and exploded in the treetops.

It was the most trying day the men had experienced to date in the war and one of the fiercest artillery duels seen by any troops in the war. Shattered and splintered pine limbs cascaded down on the immobile sharpshooters for hours until the men were covered with pine needles, bark and limbs. Sharpshooters supporting a Rhode Island battery witnessed perhaps the most horrifying sight of the day. A rebel shell exploded directly over the back of Sergeant Preston Cooper of the Minnesota company, tearing away the flesh from the small of his back, "and for nine months thereafter he couldn't lie on his back." The sergeant was lost to the sharpshooters for good, later being transferred to the Invalid Corps. Two corporals positioned behind the sergeant were killed by the same exploding shell, and three other men were wounded.[63]

Nearby the sharpshooters, a man in the 24th New York Infantry, brigaded with the sharpshooters, was beheaded by a shell as he peered through the sheltering brush. Some of the sharpshooters no doubt later saw the New Yorker's body with his head detached in the grass, "nose, eyes, moustache, chin and everything perfect ... the eyes wide open and staring at the men as they lay in the ranks."[64]

Some of the other wounded sharpshooters never returned to the regiment after Rappahannock Station. Corporal William T. Collins of Company A lost his leg to a wound there. Sylvester Hadley of Company F, also wounded at Rappahannock Station, was discharged for disability on November 18, 1862.[65] The action at Rappahannock Station was particularly wasteful because the sharpshooters were unable to get at their enemies across the river. The intensity of the bombardment forced the men to stay in place, hoping not to be spotted by the enemy artillerymen.

By August 26 General Lee had determined to pass around the Federal defensive line on the Rappahannock by sending his army on a circuit to the northwest. Lee left the assignment of holding the south bank of the river to General R.H. Anderson. Anderson's division, supported by Stephen D. Lee's artillery battalion, held defensive positions across the river from McDowell's Federals to mask the Confederate movement. McDowell was directed to seek a crossing of the river for a possible strike against Lee, but when he encountered Anderson's force he decided to assume a defensive posture at Sulphur Springs, upriver from Rappahannock Station.[66] McDowell probed the rebel positions at Sulphur Springs on the 26th with Patrick's Brigade from King's Division. The 2nd was on the march to the springs to support McDowell's reconnaissance when an aide from McDowell galloped up and ordered the sharpshooters to double-quick it to the front. Upon reaching the springs the sharpshooters deployed as skirmishers along the river bank.

A soldier from Gibbon's brigade remembered the scene at the springs:

> A company of Berdan Sharpshooters occupied the hotel, firing at the enemy across the river. From a small hole through the side of the hotel I had a good view of the country across the river and to the right of where we were. There was a growth of willows on both banks, which were occupied by the advance-skirmishers of the two armies — King's Division on our side and Anderson's Division, of the Confederate army, on the other, composed mostly of Georgia troops.[67]

The sharpshooters along the river bank also quickly went to work finding targets on the opposite side: "...in 10 minutes after taking position the rebel lines on the opposite side of the Rappahannock were entirely silenced. The enemy found good rifles in front of them, and men who knew how to handle them, and they hunted their holes."

Nevertheless, the two senior officers of the regiment had a close call near the hotel. Colonel Post and Lt. Colonel Peteler were standing in front of the hotel's board fence while Peteler sniped at a rebel hiding behind a fence across the river. Peteler was capping his rifle when a shot from across the river passed between the two and struck the fence just behind them. A puff of white smoke revealed that the shot had come from about 500 yards to the right and from behind a pile of rails. It was an expert shot by the rebel, but almost instantly his hiding place was peppered by Sharps bullets fired by sharpshooters in retaliation.[68]

Sniping and skirmishing continued until nightfall with several outbursts of Confederate artillery fire directed at the sharpshooters. Towards evening some Confederates appeared near a burned bridge under a flag of truce, ostensibly to discuss a prisoner and to request a cease-fire to bury their dead. When the firing stopped, the rebel skirmishers along the river bank scrambled from their cover and ran behind a nearby hill to escape the sharpshooters' fire.[69]

Anderson's Confederates withdrew after dark, ending the desultory action. The skirmishing at Sulphur Springs did absolutely nothing to aid the Federals, but it allowed the Confederates to withdraw from the Rappahannock line undisturbed. By the following day General Lee had completely bypassed the defensive line along the Rappahannock; he was moving his army to strike Pope's Federals on more favorable ground.

Private Daniel Willis of Company H was killed in action at Sulphur Springs, shot through the head.[70] He was the only casualty resulting from enemy fire. The six days of skirmishing along the Rappahannock had proved costly to the sharpshooters. Four men were killed and at least seven wounded. Apparently artillery fire did most of the damage.

Although the long-range confrontation along the Rappahannock amounted to nothing more than a footnote in the Bull Run campaign, it provided the sharpshooters with an opportunity to perform their unique role in actual combat. A sharpshooter from Company G expressed in a letter what many others also no doubt felt: that along the Rappahannock he had finally "had a chance to do what I have always been anxious to do — sight my rifle on a rebel."[71] At Sulphur Springs the 2nd U.S.S.S. had demonstrated its effectiveness as a special force with a unique mission. The regiment had been called upon to deal with enemy marksmen and had effectively overpowered them. One sharpshooter from Company D admitted that the rebels forced his comrades to take caution, but it was the rebels who were silenced and who requested a truce to escape the sharpshooters' accurate fire.[72]

While the sharpshooters skirmished at Sulphur Springs, General Pope guessed the location of Stonewall Jackson's wing of the rebel army. He ordered his strung-out army to concentrate at Gainesville, just west of the Bull Run battlefield. Pope had sufficient information to indicate that General Lee had divided his army, and he determined to crush Jackson's half of that army near Manassas. McDowell was directed to follow General Franz Sigel's First Corps from Sulphur Springs to Gainesville on the following day, August 27.[73]

The 2nd remained at Sulphur Springs until noon on the 27th, then followed King's division on the road to Gainesville. That night the regiment camped near Buckland, a short distance west of Gainesville. General King was ailing, perhaps from epilepsy, and his worsening illness would result in his departure from command of the division. Within two days King would be superseded by the sharpshooters' brigade commander, Brigadier General John Hatch. Command of the brigade would devolve upon Colonel Timothy Sullivan of the 24th New York. King's performance, perhaps affected by his illness, would have a weighty impact on the outcome of Pope's plan to deal with Jackson.

On the following day General Pope's efforts to concentrate his forces against Jackson met with much greater difficulty than he could have imagined. First, he could not pitch into Jackson because he did not know exactly where to find him. Other disconcerting news reached Pope. He learned that the right wing of Lee's army, under General James Longstreet, was approaching from the west, enroute to reinforce Jackson. In face of these developments, Pope had to make an immediate decision. He could split his army to prevent a juncture of Jackson and Longstreet, or he could concentrate most of his force against Jackson in hopes of destroying half of Lee's army before it could be combined. Pope decided on the latter: he would look for Jackson and attack him, hoping to finish the job before Longstreet could intervene.[74]

Most of August 28 was consumed in waiting to locate Jackson's whereabouts. Although Pope was certain that he would find Jackson at Manassas Junction, when Federals arrived there the Confederates had vanished. The wily Jackson had hidden his

25,000-man army wing on a wooded ridge just north of a hamlet called Groveton near the First Bull Run battlefield. An unfinished railroad grade cut through the woods, providing a strong fortified position for the Confederates. Behind the railroad construction the crest of the ridge provided a good location for artillery to enfilade an approaching enemy. Without even erecting fieldworks on the ridge, Jackson had a very secure position to hold off the Federals.[75]

Throughout that frustrating day Pope sought to locate Jackson's force, knowing that the remainder of Lee's army approached and would soon be in position to allow Lee to take the offensive. The 2nd had started for Manassas early that morning, but by afternoon the regiment rested with King's division in a wood near Gainesville. Although the sharpshooters did not know it, they were very near to the quarry Pope so desperately sought.

Finally that afternoon Pope thought he had located Jackson near Centerville, a few miles to the east of Gainesville. He ordered McDowell to hurry towards Centerville immediately. King's Federals moved from the woods onto the Warrenton Turnpike with Hatch's Brigade in the lead. Behind came Gibbon's, Doubleday's and Patrick's brigades, in that order.[76]

Jackson spotted King's troops on the turnpike and, knowing that the rest of Lee's army was within supporting distance, he decided to attack. Jackson sent six brigades out from his hiding place to attack the unsuspecting Federals. Hatch threw out the 2nd U.S.S.S. in a skirmish line as soon as Jackson's move was discovered. Gibbon also moved north from the turnpike to investigate rebel activity near the Brawner farmhouse. Before Gibbon engaged the rebels, Colonel Post "sent Adjutant Parmelee back to Gen. Hatch warning him that the rebels were in line of battle on our left." With this information Hatch could have immediately gone to assist Gibbon. But Hatch "refused to believe it ... saying there were no rebels anywhere near there, and took no heed of the Sharpshooter's report."[77]

Gibbon, of course, never received a report from the sharpshooters about the large rebel line emerging from the woods towards his brigade. He formed his brigade into a line of battle and stood his ground, facing nearly three times his number.[78] One of the sharpshooters from Company D noted in his diary for August 28 that it was 5 P.M. when the rebels were found. He mentioned that soon afterwards a terrific musketry was heard coming from the sharpshooters' left.[79] It was the noise from Gibbon's fight at the nearby Brawner Farm. Gibbon engaged in a fierce stand-up fight with six rebel brigades in the fading late afternoon light until darkness put an end to it. Only troops from Doubleday's brigade arrived in time to assist Gibbon's outnumbered regiments.

Hatch moved his brigade back toward the sound of the fighting, but he arrived too late to take part in the fight. Years after the war a former sharpshooter wrote that during this action the skirmishers from the 2nd had seen the rebels and had done their duty. He remarked, "The Sharpshooters were ahead and saw the enemy — that's what they were out there for. It was not very long thereafter, before it got to be understood that the Sharpshooters' report from the extreme front, was to be depended on."[80]

After the fighting sputtered out in darkness, Gibbon rode back to find General

King. His brigade had put up an inspiring fight but had suffered heavy casualties, and Gibbon was angered that King had failed to support him. The ailing division commander tried to mollify Gibbon and turned the discussion to the next course of action.

The other brigade commanders joined in the discussion, and all agreed that King's division was heavily outnumbered and would have to withdraw from Jackson's front. King had orders to march to Centerville, but he now knew that Jackson was not there as General Pope had believed. Gibbon felt that the road to Centerville might be strongly held by the enemy anyway and advised King to pull back to Manassas rather than attempting to reach Centerville. Darkness having set in, the safest solution was to follow Gibbon's plan; King penned a message to General McDowell advising him that he had found Jackson's force, his position was untenable and he was withdrawing southward to Manassas.[81]

General King's withdrawal flustered Pope and has since been criticized by historians. King was in position along the turnpike to prevent Longstreet from joining Jackson, and with timely reinforcement King could have made things difficult for the Confederates. However, John Hennessy in his study of the Second Battle of Manassas concluded that King made a reasonable decision. To remain would have likely resulted only in having his division crushed by the Confederates the following morning.[82] Hennessy's studied assessment indicates that the outcome of the campaign would not have been significantly altered had King held his ground on the night of August 28.

Thus King withdrew in the direction of Manassas, marching south through the darkness until safely out of Jackson's reach. To this point the 2nd U.S.S.S. had yet to see or participate in a large-scale battle. On the following day that would change; the regiment would be initiated in the terrifying and traumatic experience of combat by the thousands.

On the morning of August 29 Pope remained confident that he could and would whip Jackson. Though disappointed with King's withdrawal, he adjusted his strategy to fit his view of the tactical situation. Pope decided upon a plan to use McDowell's Corps in conjunction with Porter's V Corps to create a pincer movement against Jackson. He ordered McDowell to march to Gainesville to prevent a Confederate retreat while the balance of his army attacked Jackson's line along the unfinished railroad. General King was too ill to continue leading his division under the strain of battle. He turned over command of the first division to Brigadier General John Hatch that morning.[83]

Yet again, as so often occurred during this campaign, Pope's plan went awry. When McDowell started toward Gainesville he found rebels in force blocking his march. By 1 P.M. Longstreet had arrived from his circuitous route to reinforce Jackson; his force deployed on Jackson's right, south of the Warrenton Turnpike. McDowell abandoned his march to Gainesville and instead moved north on the Sudley Road to join Pope's main force on the battlefield at the junction of Sudley Road and Warrenton Turnpike. Hence the 2nd U.S.S.S. spent the night of the 28th and much of the 29th avoiding a fight with the enemy.[84]

Still hoping to crush Jackson and claim the distinction of whipping that famous general, Pope ordered assaults on Jackson's line throughout the day on August 29. Pope seemingly ignored the fact that Longstreet had arrived to reinforce Jackson and focused all of his efforts against Jackson. Unfortunately for the Federals, Pope's attacks on the 29th were made without sufficient strength and support to succeed. He struck Jackson's center with only two regiments, hit his left with only five and then attacked the center again in the afternoon with three regiments. None of these attacks were supported, although each temporarily broke Jackson's line.[85]

By evening Pope was convinced that his minor push against Jackson had been successful to the extent of causing Jackson to retreat. Towards sunset Pope directed General McDowell to push westward on the Warrenton Turnpike to scatter the supposedly withdrawing Confederates. McDowell selected Hatch's division; informing Hatch that the enemy was retreating, he urged him to hurry his advance down the pike to disconcert the retreating enemy.[86]

General Hatch gave his description of the advance as follows:

> I was ordered by General McDowell in person (who was at the time stationed near the stone house, on the turnpike from Centerville to Gainesville) to move the division on the Gainesville road in pursuit of the enemy, who, he informed me, were retreating.... I proceeded with all the speed possible, hoping by harassing the enemy's rear to turn their retreat into a rout.
>
> After marching about three-quarters of a mile the Second Regiment of U.S. Sharpshooters was deployed to the front as skirmishers, the column continuing up the road in support. The advance almost immediately became warmly engaged on the left of the road.[87]

The 2nd was thus properly employed by Hatch to find the enemy position in advance of the division. Half of the regiment deployed south of the pike, commanded by Colonel Post, and the other half deployed north of the pike with Lt. Colonel Peteler. The following account describes the sharpshooters' role in the subsequent fighting:

> ...the sharpshooters, who had made the last mile of the advance at double-quick, were halted with the brigade, and placed in line in the pike, on the slope of a slight hollow, beyond the opposite ridge of which was the enemy's line. While the rest of the brigade was forming on their left, four companies of the sharpshooters were sent to the right of the pike, while the other four, among which were the Vermont companies, advanced to the top of the hill to hold the road, which the enemy threatened from the right. Taking a position behind a rail fence which bordered the road, they saw a line of the enemy advancing across the field and opened upon it, at short range, a deliberate and effective fire, which quickly scattered it. Soon bullets began to come from another direction, and they saw in the gathering twilight a compact line of men formed across the pike, with a standard in the centre. The sharpshooters now divided their attention between this body and the force still lurking beyond the fence. The flag of the regiment on the pike went down under their fire, was then raised, and again disappeared as the line over which it floated crumbled and fell back. Meantime the rest of the brigade had fallen back and the sharpshooters must go too or be surrounded. The word was accordingly passed from man to man and they went back through the hollow to some high ground beyond. Half an hour's desultory firing followed from the opposing lines, and then the fighting ceased in the darkness and the brigade held the second ridge.[88]

What the 2nd met at the top of the hollow along the Warrenton Pike was Confederate General John B. Hood's division; four regiments from Law's brigade sent by Longstreet to probe the Federals collided with the sharpshooters along the pike. According to Private Henry Richards of Company F, "Most of our regiment ran back down the road."[89] The rebels followed on their heels and slammed into Sullivan's Brigade as nightfall darkened the woods along the pike. A vicious, disordered fight ensued in the twilight. Muzzle flashes provoked volleys from opposing sides; like lightning, the flash of flame from scores of muskets provided the only means of identifying the enemy.

According to a postwar account of the fighting, the 2nd remained along the pike "alone and deserted until long after dark when they succeeded in getting away, Company A having six men captured along with the second lieutenant, James E. Doughty."[90] During the three days of fighting at Second Bull Run, the 2nd U.S.S.S. suffered forty-two casualties, most of them on the 29th: four killed, sixteen wounded and twenty-two missing.[91] All four of the sharpshooters killed at Bull Run were shot during the fighting along the pike on the 29th; these were Charles Jacobs and Francis Storrs of Company A, Charles Keith of Company E and Benjamin Graham of Company G.[92]

Colonel Post, unlike Colonel Berdan, enhanced his reputation for gallantry during the fighting on the 29th. During the melee in the woods the color bearer of the 24th New York inadvertently walked right into the 18th Georgia and was stripped of his flag. Colonel Post noticed some rebels carrying a Union flag off the field as the fighting was sputtering out. The colonel, "on seeing it going off the field in the possession of only a few men, galloped hard after them, caught the flag-staff and wrenched it from the man, then wheeled and put the spurs to his horse, which was a good Union horse as she gave her heels to one of the Johnnies, sending him sprawling out, astonishing the others so, that the colonel came off with the flag."[93] This was no mean feat by Post. Unfortunately for the sharpshooters, Colonel Berdan would never demonstrate such valor on the battlefield and would provide little in the way of an example to the men.

The fighting on the 29th fizzled out after nightfall, and Hatch's troops fell back behind Patrick's brigade to regroup and camp for the night. Hatch's division had been roughly handled and suffered significant casualties, but very little was gained from the fracas. Pope remained convinced that the Confederates were going to retreat. Somehow he ignored the fact that Longstreet's men had repulsed Hatch. His attention remained focused on crushing Stonewall Jackson; ignoring all else, he would concentrate on attacking Jackson in the morning.

Pope's plan for August 30 called for General Porter's V Corps to repeat the push westward along the Warrenton Turnpike with Hatch's division in support.[94] It was a tailor-made plan to produce a decisive Confederate victory. Pope had made practically no allowance to deal with the half of Lee's army positioned south of the Warrenton Turnpike.

On the morning of the 30th Jackson had indeed not retreated; instead, he still held the same strong line along the unfinished railroad embankment. Still, Porter had his orders, so he adjusted his lines and prepared to attack. It was nearly 4 P.M. before Porter deployed his lines and sent them forward for the attack. Hatch was ordered to place his division to the right of Porter's front and attack in conjunction with Porter. It was a daunting task facing the Federals. The attacking lines would have to pass through Groveton Woods, cross the fence-lined Groveton-Sudley Road, and then rush across nearly 600 yards of artillery-swept ground to reach the Confederate lines. Jackson's men were sheltered along the railroad embankment, enabled to take deliberate aim at the approaching Federals.[95]

Hatch moved his division from the Warrenton Turnpike "to the woods in which Porter's men lay, and then clumsily moved into position on Porter's right." As he had done during the previous fighting, Hatch sent out the 2nd U.S.S.S. as skirmishers in front of his division. The green-clad sharpshooters linked up with the 25th New York of Robert's brigade, also deployed as skirmishers, on their left. Behind the sharpshooters, at the edge of Groveton Woods, Sullivan's brigade was arrayed in two lines with the 24th and 30th New York in front and the 14th Brooklyn and 22nd New York behind. Farther in the rear were Patrick's and Gibbon's brigades.[96]

The 1st U.S.S.S. was deployed to the left and front of the 25th New York and soon advanced to a stream bed in the open field. There the 1st sheltered in the stream bed and exchanged fire with the Confederate infantry protected by the railroad embankment at the place known as "Deep Cut." Major Edwin Gilbert of the 25th New York described the situation faced by his men and the 2nd U.S.S.S. on August 30:

> We had advanced but a short distance into the woods when we met the enemy's skirmishers. We drove them back until the left of our line of skirmishers came to an open field.... A severe fire continued to pick off our men. We advanced by degrees, but very slowly ... the Second Regiment sharpshooters, consisting of a little more than 100 men, arrived. I directed where they should join our line on the right. Just as they were put in position I heard, away to our left, a rushing of men.[97]

What the major heard above the din of battle was the rustle of hundreds of Sullivan's men rushing through the trees on their way to attack Jackson's line, making no effort to conceal their approach. The 2nd U.S.S.S. moved into the open field to support Sullivan's attack, but the sharpshooters did not accompany the attackers beyond the middle of the field. Instead, the sharpshooters spread out in the same stream bed sheltering Berdan's other regiment, but farther to the west of Deep Cut. Confederate artillery swept the field, battering the attacking Federals. Sullivan's 24th and 30th New York somehow managed to push across the killing field and almost reached the railroad embankment before turning back.

Along came the 14th Brooklyn, whose men had sworn to get revenge against the rebels, moving on the attack to the right of the sharpshooters. Major Gilbert noted: "As soon as the Fourteenth had arrived at a position some 15 or 20 paces in rear of our skirmishers, they received the flanking fire that had annoyed our skirmishers. They immediately broke, but were rallied again."[98] The 14th Brooklyn, accompanied by the 22nd New York, made it to the creek bed near the sharpshooters; once there, the 14th "broke and fled."[99]

At the railroad embankment Major Andrew Barney of the 24th New York rode his white horse along the railroad grade, waving his sword to defy the rebels. Some of the enemy soldiers were so impressed with his gallantry that they called to their comrades to spare the major, yelling, "Don't kill him!"[100] Within moments, however, Barney fell from his horse riddled with bullets, a symbol of the futility of the entire assault. More Confederate artillery joined in the fusillade blasting the Federals in the open field, and then Hatch's men fell back to Groveton Woods. Porter's attack also disintegrated and recoiled from the Deep Cut area.

A sharpshooter from the nearby 1st U.S.S.S. described the unsuccessful Federal attack from his perspective to the left of the 2nd that afternoon:

> We lay in the ditch until three or four o'clock, and then our column charged ... what a sight it was! What a slaughter in our ranks! Shot, shell, grape, canister, and musket balls filled the air.... It was a badly managed attack from the beginning; our artillery was back too far and did not reply only once and awhile to theirs.[101]

On the following day a Confederate chaplain walked through the area occupied by the sharpshooters and wrote of his observations. He was appalled at the sight of Yankees mutilated and mangled by the Confederate artillery, some with faces shot away, others with bowels exposed. By that time the corpses were bloated and many were blackened and decomposed beyond recognition.[102] The fighting around the railroad deep cut would long be remembered, even by the Confederates, as an awful slaughter — one of the most uneven fights of the entire war.

As Porter's and Hatch's troops fell back to Groveton Woods, Confederate General Longstreet launched his 30,000 fresh troops against the unprepared Federals south of the Warrenton Turnpike. Longstreet's attack was immediately successful, sweeping away Federal resistance and creating an unanticipated crisis for Pope. For the remainder of the day the Federals would be forced to scramble to avoid annihilation.

Before dark, Jackson took the offensive against the Federals north of the pike; the 2nd U.S.S.S. along with Hatch's Division held their ground against Jackson on a ridge east of the Dogan House. Supported by artillery, Hatch's troops twice repulsed the Confederates, but the Federals to the right gave way and Longstreet threatened from south of the pike.[103] The 2nd U.S.S.S. "stood their ground with their cannonade, until there was danger of being out-flanked and captured, and then only by the most strenuous effort did they get away."[104] A sharpshooter from Company F remembered that the regiment manned a rail fence at dusk until the enemy flanked them on the left. As the sharpshooters fell back, they found that they were isolated and Confederates were already in force between them and the rest of the Federal army.[105]

Like the sharpshooters, Pope's army escaped only through strenuous effort. A stand by the Federals at Henry House Hill slowed Longstreet until the bulk of the army could retreat under the cover of darkness. The night also covered the retreating sharpshooters who crossed Bull Run and joined Hatch's troops at Centerville Heights, a short distance east of the battlefield.

The outcome of the battle was immediately controversial and has remained so ever since. General Pope quickly laid the blame for his defeat upon Fitz-John Porter, commander of the V Corps. Pope eventually succeeded in having Porter court-martialed and dismissed from the army for failing to follow orders during the battle. Others obviously shared Pope's opinion. Years after the war a sharpshooter offered his opinion: "Had Porter, when he was sent to the left to intercept Longstreet, fought him there, as he did in the afternoon, there would have been a different tale told of second Bull Run. I believe that on the start Pope had the best of the fight, and had Porter carried out Pope's order Pope would have whipped Lee's army in detail."[106] President Lincoln himself felt that Pope had been victimized by senior officers who failed to fully support the general during the campaign. He believed that General McClellan had actually hoped that Pope would be defeated so that he could look good by comparison.[107]

Regardless of the outcome of the battle, the 2nd U.S.S.S. had performed well during the campaign. Lt. Colonel Homer Stoughton wrote of this campaign years after the war, noting that the men under his command "were under fire every day from August 23." He explained that the sharpshooters performed many important functions and acts of valor that went unrecorded: "It is hard at this moment to enumerate the deeds of special daring performed by these men, often called upon to go and find troublesome Rebel sharpshooters, and invariably with a good account...."[108] From all indications the regiment stood its first real trial of combat well.

Nevertheless, the 2nd was barely mentioned in the reports of senior officers for their contribution in the battle. This would often be the case during the war. The type of service rendered by the sharpshooters did not generate much attention at the division and corps level. General McDowell mentioned Colonel Post and his sharpshooters in his report for Second Bull Run without much detail: "Colonel Post, commanding Second Sharpshooters, a valuable regiment, much exposed, and which rendered most excellent service, is deserving of especial mention for his conduct, amongst others, in the battle of the 30th." McDowell also noted that the division to which the 2nd belonged was "one of the finest, best-drilled, best-disciplined bodies of troops in the service...."[109]

Having regrouped somewhat, Pope started his army for Washington on September 1. General Lee, hoping to further damage Pope's force, sent Stonewall Jackson swinging north in an attempt to block Pope's retreat. Pope reacted to the threat by sending troops to intercept Jackson. At a place called Chantilly, named for a country mansion, Federal Generals Phil Kearny and Isaac Stevens were killed as Pope's troops attempted to drive off Jackson.[110] On the morning of September 2, the 2nd U.S.S.S. formed a skirmish line at the scene of the fighting, but no casualties were recorded. Soon the regiment resumed the march to Fairfax, through Falls Church and towards Alexandria. The campaign begun by McClellan in March to capture Richmond ended now six months later where it began, a complete failure.

Although the 2nd U.S.S.S. had not participated in the Peninsular Campaign and its numerous battles, the effect of the summer's operations was devastating. Of the more than 700 men on the rolls in January, "when the first roll was called near Alexandria, September 2nd, 127 answered their names."[111] A great many were either already discharged for disability or soon would be. The regiment would remain a shell of its former self, despite recruiting efforts during the war.

Having set out nearly six months earlier from Alexandria to capture the enemy's capital, the sharpshooters found themselves back where they had started, now with the bulk of the regiment gone forever. Years after the war one sharpshooter remembered of this day that he had mulled over the cost of the summer with "all the toils, deaths and suffering," and with stoical understatement noted that he was "a little downhearted."[112]

5

"There Was Bloody Work Done"

As Pope's beleaguered and beaten army neared Washington, President Lincoln mulled over the command dilemma created by the defeat of both his eastern armies. The huge combined forces of the Army of Virginia and Army of the Potomac were demoralized by defeat and rife with turmoil. Pope was unpopular with the men in the ranks, but worse yet the general faced intrigue, hostility and an obvious lack of cooperation from the Army of the Potomac. With news of the Federal defeat at Manassas, President Lincoln realized that a change of command was incumbent. On September 2, 1862, the president met with General McClellan in Washington to offer him command of the Army of the Potomac and Pope's Army of Virginia, the two armies to be again merged into the Army of the Potomac. Halleck would remain as general-in-chief.[1]

President Lincoln's decision to turn once again to George B. McClellan was made with great reluctance out of unavoidable necessity. Within days of Pope's defeat, intelligence revealed that Lee was not going to stay in Virginia; he would invade Maryland and perhaps approach Washington from the northwest. In the Western Theater, General Braxton Bragg prepared to march on Kentucky, apparently as part of a Confederate move to invade Ohio. With an unprecedented double threat of invasion, the president could not afford to leisurely address the command problems plaguing his eastern army. Additionally, dozens of newly recruited regiments raised during Lincoln's summer call for new volunteers had arrived and were to be absorbed by the Army of the Potomac. In McClellan the president had a general with a proven record of efficiency in discipline, a talent for reorganization and also a leader who would immediately shore up the army's morale.

In September of 1862 Lincoln really had no one else he could count on to take charge of the Army of the Potomac on such short notice. The general-in-chief, Halleck, had shown no capacity to lead an army aggressively. While there were several generals with a proven combat record available, such as Joseph Hooker and Winfield S. Hancock, none of these officers had experience at the army command level. Perhaps the deciding factor favoring McClellan was his popularity with the soldiers of the Army of the Potomac. Despite his inadequacies, "Little Mac" instilled confidence in the Army of Potomac, and confidence was sorely needed after the debacle at Bull Run.

General Robert E. Lee's decision to invade Maryland and points north was sound and reasoned, even when viewed with the benefit of hindsight. Opportunities far outweighed risks associated with invasion. By invading Pennsylvania the Confederates could obtain provender for Lee's army and its animals while allowing time for the autumn harvest in Virginia to escape Federal confiscation. Political considerations favoring invasion were substantial. Among those Northerners already opposed to war, a rebel invasion would heighten stridency and strengthen politicians already speaking out to end the war. More importantly yet, a Confederate success on Northern soil would go far in encouraging foreign powers to formally recognize the Confederate government. The only real risk facing Lee concerned the condition of his army. After a summer of severe and bloody fighting, the Army of Northern Virginia was tired, worn and ill equipped.[2] And General Lee would soon learn that taking the offensive into enemy territory exceeded his army's capabilities. Campaigning and fighting on the enemy's soil, just as playing a sport on the opponent's home field, greatly increases the odds against success.

Within a few days of accepting command, General McClellan began marching his army out of Washington to intercept the enemy in Maryland. McClellan took the bulk of a restructured army, six corps or about 84,000 men, with him into Maryland, leaving behind two corps commanded by generals Samuel Heintzelman and Franz Sigel to man the Washington defenses.[3] On September 8, 1862, the 2nd U.S.S.S. once again crossed the Potomac River via Long Bridge to campaign against Lee's veterans. By September 12, as McClellan's troops reached Frederick, Maryland, the reorganization of the Army of the Potomac became official. The Federal Army of Virginia was officially discontinued, merged into the Army of the Potomac. Troops from the Army of Virginia's III Corps were transferred into the recreated I Corps of the Army of the Potomac to be commanded by Major General Joseph Hooker. The 2nd U.S.S.S. now belonged to the First Brigade of the First Division of the I Corps, Army of the Potomac.[4] In effect, the 2nd U.S.S.S. had the honor of being at the head of Lincoln's army, on paper, the first of the first. The sharpshooters could take pride in their command assignment.

On September 13, General McClellan was handed the opportunity of a lifetime in the form of a written copy of General Lee's Special Order No. 191. Two soldiers from the 27th Indiana found the document wrapped around three cigars, lying in a meadow outside of Frederick. The authenticity of the document was very quickly revealed. In short, the document was a copy of Lee's marching orders. The paper detailed Lee's plans for his operations in Maryland. Lee was basically dividing his army into four parts. Half of the army under General Longstreet would wait just west of South Mountain near Boonsboro while the other half, divided into three parts, assailed the Federal garrison at Harpers Ferry. Lee's order further directed, "The commands of Generals Jackson, McLaws, and Walker, after accomplishing the objects for which they have been detached, will join the main body of the army at Boonsborough or Hagerstown." It was a risky move by the Confederates, yet typical of General Lee, and it afforded McClellan with a very feasible opportunity to crush Longstreet's half of the Confederate army before Lee could react.[5] McClellan could shift his focus to Harpers Ferry after dealing with Longstreet's heavily outnumbered force.

Unfortunately for the Federals, General McClellan wasted much of this opportunity by delaying his movement against the vulnerable Confederates. As was his usual misfortune, McClellan overestimated the size of Lee's army and thus proceeded with excessive caution. On September 13, McClellan's available force of nearly 87,000 men almost doubled the strength of Lee's entire invading force.[6] Instead of moving immediately to engage Longstreet's overextended force, McClellan delayed to plan and make preparations. McClellan's sluggishness allowed time for Lee to discover own his vulnerability, and he would immediately take measures to save his army.

In fairness to General McClellan, the Army of the Potomac was an unwieldy weapon throughout the entire term of its service. No commander of this army during the war was able to match the speed and alacrity of Lee's army, or for that matter, the Federal armies operating in the Western Theater. Thus, it is impossible to know whether McClellan could have struck a decisive blow against Longstreet even if he had attempted to move with alacrity on September 13, 1862.

By evening of September 13, McClellan had determined his plan of battle and had sent instructions to his corps commanders. Major General Jesse L. Reno would lead the IX Corp in advance followed by Hooker's I Corps. Major General Edwin Sumner's II Corps, the XII Corps commanded by Brigadier General Alpheus Williams, and a division of regular infantry commanded by Brigadier General George Sykes would follow. All troops were to remain in camp near Frederick until dawn of the 14th. McClellan's plan of battle was to march these corps west from Frederick to attack Longstreet near Boonsboro, Maryland.[7] The federals would follow the National Road from Frederick, crossing over Catoctin Mountain and through Turner's Gap at South Mountain to reach Boonsboro and the valley beyond these mountains. In an effort to relieve the Federal garrison at Harpers Ferry, McClellan directed Major General William Franklin, commanding the VI Corps, to march through Crampton's Gap and pass through South Mountain south of the National Road and nearer to Harpers Ferry. South Mountain presented a formidable obstacle, a high ridge with heights exceeding 1,500 feet stretching fifty miles north from near Harpers Ferry into Pennsylvania. The terrain at South Mountain is rough and rocky, with thickly wooded ravines and steep slopes; the thick vegetation alone would make maneuver difficult for an attacking army.

On the evening of the 13th General Lee was informed that the Federals were moving west from Frederick and camping in large numbers near Middletown, within a short march of South Mountain. Lee sent orders for General Daniel H. Hill to defend the passes at South Mountain, and he directed Longstreet to march to support Hill at Turner's Gap. Lee would take advantage of natural barrier of South Mountain to stall McClellan until his army could be reunited.[8]

Reno's IX Corps troops were the first to reach the eastern approach to Turner's Gap at South Mountain on the morning of September 14. As Brigadier General Jacob Cox neared the pass on the National Road he decided to lead his Kanawha IX Corps division of 3,000 Ohio and West Virginia troops on a flanking maneuver via an alternate road, the Old Sharpsburg Road, through Fox's Gap just south of the main pass at Turner's Gap. Cox hoped to outflank the defenders at Turner's Gap and open the passage for the rest of McClellan's approaching corps.[9]

By 9 A.M. Cox began his push to capture Fox's Gap, outnumbering the defenders by more than two to one. Following about two hours of fierce fighting, Cox held Fox's Gap and prepared to move north to secure the main gap at the National Road. Confederate General Hill was in desperate trouble, but somehow he managed to slow the Federals until a fresh brigade arrived from Boonsboro to check Cox's advance. As Hill's reinforcements arrived, Cox stopped his advance to await reinforcements from the oncoming IX Corps. There was a lull in the fighting for several hours during which Hill received further reinforcements and ended McClellan's opportunity to easily pass over South Mountain.[10]

It was well past noon before the 2nd U.S.S.S. arrived at the base of South Mountain with Hatch's I Corps division. By then Hill had sufficient troops on hand to defend Turner's Gap and Fox's Gap. While fighting raged around Fox's Gap between Reno's IX Corps and newly arrived Confederates, Brigadier General Robert E. Rodes's brigade of Alabamians took defensive positions north of Turner's Gap. It would now require a desperate and bloody fight to clear South Mountain. Had McClellan pushed rapidly through Turner's Gap with two of his corps on the morning of September 14, his army would have moved into the Boonsboro vicinity without serious opposition. While McClellan had anticipated an easy passage across South Mountain, by late morning he was aware that the Confederates were defending the passes. His deliberate, even sluggish movement from Frederick enabled General Hill to hold South Mountain all day on the 14th.

Sometime after 4 P.M. the Federal I Corps was in position to attack at South Mountain, turning off the National Road onto the Old Hagerstown Road in an effort to outflank Turner's Gap from the north. In his report General McClellan explained the alignment of Hooker's three divisions for the attack: "Meade was then directed to advance his division to the right of the road, so as to outflank them ... while Hatch was directed to take with his division the crest on the left of the Old Hagerstown Road, Ricketts' division being held in reserve." McClellan noted that the terrain on the mountainside was "of the most difficult character for the movement of troops ... being very steep and rocky, and obstructed by stone walls and timber."[11]

The 2nd U.S.S.S. was attached to the first brigade of Hatch's First Division. Command of the brigade had devolved upon Colonel Walter Phelps of the 22nd New York, a prewar lumber merchant.[12] General Hatch sent forward his third brigade commanded by Brigadier General Marsena R. Patrick, deploying Patrick's 21st New York and 35th New York regiments as skirmishers. According to Hatch, "The remainder of Patrick's brigade was moved to the front, as a support for the two regiments deployed as skirmishers." The 21st New York had been ordered to move up towards the crest of the mountain through a ravine; however, the New Yorkers instead "moved up the mountain in front of the division." To fill the gap created by the 21st New York, "the Second U.S. Sharpshooters, Colonel Post, were detached from the First Brigade, and proceeded up the ravine to the point indicated." The remainder of Phelps's Brigade and Hatch's second brigade followed Patrick's regiments up the mountainside.[13] Gibbon's Forth Brigade was given the daunting assignment of attacking Turner's Gap straight on, using the National Highway as an approach.

Detached from their infantry brigade, the 2nd U.S.S.S. fought at South Mountain independently as skirmishers, in their element, as they had been instructed. The sharpshooters moved cautiously up the steep, rocky, overgrown mountainside, watching for enemy skirmishers and seeking targets of opportunity. A sharpshooter from Company D wrote in his diary about fighting that day. He mentioned hiding behind a rock to snipe at a "Jackass gun" or mountain howitzer as it fired at the nearby 13th Pennsylvania Bucktails and then moving into the lines of the 21st New York.[14]

Interestingly, the Pennsylvania Bucktails fought as sharpshooters at South Mountain with great success against Confederate skirmishers from Rodes's brigade. These Bucktails had just recently managed to "appropriate" Sharps Rifles from Colonel Berdan's personal hoard. Of course Berdan demanded the return of his spare rifles, but the custom-made Sharps would remain with the Pennsylvanians.[15] Going into the fight with Colonel Berdan's rifles, the Bucktails received credit for decimating Rodes's skirmish line in advance of the I Corps attack. So successful were the Bucktails that General Rodes, apparently having learned the value of sharpshooters, later organized his own battalion of sharpshooters for picketing and skirmishing.[16] James Matthews, of Company D, U.S.S.S., took note of the good work accomplished by the Bucktails against Rodes. According to Matthews, the Pennsylvanians "did fight the rebels well."[17]

Hatch's troops followed the sharpshooters slowly up the ravine and engaged the Confederates along a fence lining a cornfield. Although Hatch was severely wounded, his division prevailed after a fierce shootout along the fence, and Rodes's Alabamians gave way. During this action atop the ravine, the 2nd U.S.S.S. was the first unit to carry the crest of the mountain. The 2nd got credit for capturing several rebels and two mountain howitzers atop South Mountain, and William Humphrey of Company E mentioned counting twenty-seven enemy dead lying behind "the brush fence" after the Confederates withdrew.[18]

Brigadier General Abner Doubleday, of baseball fame, replaced Hatch in command of the First Division after Hatch was hit. At dusk the division pushed on in an effort to capture Turner's Gap and ran into General James Longstreet with three small brigades of rebel reinforcements. Longstreet's weary and outnumbered men were driven back, but the fighting fizzled out after nightfall.[19] A good portion of McClellan's attacking troops were scattered over the dark forest of South Mountain and would await dawn to locate their regiments.

While McClellan's attacks had not completely driven the Confederates off South Mountain, Lee realized that his army was imperiled and a retreat from South Mountain was in order. Franklin's VI Corps had driven off the light defending force at Crampton's Gap, about six miles south of the main battlefield. The door was now open for Franklin to march south to relieve the besieged garrison at Harpers Ferry. Franklin's command totaled 19,500 men; combined with nearly 13,000 Federals at Harpers Ferry, they represented a force sufficient to ensure that Lee would remain isolated and Jackson would be outnumbered at Harpers Ferry.[20] At first light on September 15, Federal probes at Turner's Gap revealed that the Confederates were gone. Lee had abandoned South Mountain.

Colonel Post apparently never submitted a report for his regiment's part in the fighting at South Mountain, and few specifics were mentioned in the reports of the brigade, division and corps commanders concerning the 2nd. General Hatch mentioned that he did not receive a report from Colonel Post; however, Hatch had heard good things about the sharpshooters: they "came early into action and rendered very important service during the day."[21] Clearly the 2nd was in its element and functioning in its capacity on the steep and heavily wooded slopes at South Mountain. A look at the casualties among the participating brigades indicates that the 2nd was not involved at the point of the heaviest fighting. The 2nd fought between the two regiments of Patrick's brigade sent up the mountain as skirmishers. Patrick's entire brigade suffered only twenty-three casualties, and the 2nd had only two men wounded during the entire battle. The 13th Pennsylvania Bucktails, however, suffered fifty casualties including eleven killed while fighting in the same manner as the sharpshooters.[22] The 2nd did not fight as part of Phelps's brigade, being detached, so the report for this brigade does not pertain to the sharpshooters. From all indications the 2nd U.S.S.S. fought well at South Mountain; the capture of several rebels and two howitzers, not to mention Lieutenant Humphrey's body count, at the cost of two wounded speaks well of its contribution at South Mountain.

General McClellan's performance at South Mountain was much the same as any fight he presided over, except that he was more involved on the battlefield than usual. The one point seldom mentioned, but of paramount importance to the men who followed the general, is that yet again forces commanded by "Little Mac" inflicted heavier losses on the rebels than they sustained. During the Seven Days' Battles around Richmond, McClellan's army inflicted significantly higher casualties on Lee's army, especially when comparing those killed and wounded. The final tally of Federal casualties at South Mountain included 325 killed, 1,403 wounded, and 85 missing.[23] Confederate losses, which were very likely underreported, totaled 2,700.[24] Considering that the Federals were on the attack in difficult terrain, the disparity in casualties is noteworthy. McClellan's approach and reaction to the evolving battle left much to be desired, but at the point of combat superior force and firepower were brought to bear. McClellan's cautious approach again limited casualties but failed to deliver decisive results.

On the morning of September 15, McClellan followed the path of Lee's retreating army through Turner's Gap into the valley beyond. As the sharpshooters passed through the gap many wounded and dead were lying about along the road. James Matthews of Company D followed along, looking for the regiment. He had lost contact with his company during the skirmishing on the eastern slope of the mountain and had spent the night with a few others from the regiment waiting for first light to find his company. Matthews noted in his diary entry for the 15th that a colonel was spotted with five gunshot wounds and another rebel officer was a "perfect sieve" with many shots having passed through his torso.[25] James S. Kent of Company F and a few of his comrades went out after breakfast to investigate a report of a squad of rebels lurking nearby. Kent reported that he and the others "got them, nine in all. Some of them were inclined to show fight, but when they found Sharpe's rifles bearing on them they concluded to surrender."[26]

During their descent from Turner's Gap the sharpshooters were afforded an opportunity to take in a truly splendid panorama. The view from the western slope of South Mountain is magnificent, stretching for at least twenty miles on a clear day. Local residents so esteemed the view that a tower was erected near Turner's Gap and dedicated to President George Washington. The tower, constructed of stone and mortar with a spiral stairway leading to the top, stands today as it did during the fighting at South Mountain. From the western slope the valley stretches for miles, its patchwork crop fields of greens and browns contrasting to the dark, bluish, heavily forested ridges and peaks of distant mountains.

At the western base of the mountain the sharpshooters passed through friendly Boonsboro, residents lining the road to welcome McClellan's army, waving flags and shouting encouragement. Turning to the left on the outskirts of town, the regiment marched southwest to Keedysville, heading for Sharpsburg where Lee's retreating army was said to be waiting.

For George B. McClellan and the Union cause September 15, 1862, was the ultimate day of lost opportunity. Just beyond Keedysville, across Antietam Creek, were General Lee and approximately 15,000 Confederates.[27] To be sure, Lee had placed his artillery and infantry expertly to take advantage of every feature of the terrain, ensuring that any assault by the Federals would be costly. But Lee was simply bluffing. The Federals overwhelmingly outmatched what Lee had available along Antietam Creek; and had McClellan pushed ahead, Lee would have been forced to hurry across the Potomac for any hope of escape. It is impossible to know just how this scenario would have played out, but a timely attack by McClellan on the 15th, with the Potomac at Lee's back, should have enabled the Federals to crush Lee and then run a severely outnumbered Jackson to ground.

As it was, General McClellan dawdled away his greatest opportunity. His report submitted on October 15, 1862, written well after the fact with ample time to account for and mitigate his shortcomings, mentioned that he "hoped to come up with the enemy during the 15th in sufficient force to beat them again and drive them into the river." He went on to explain that upon finally reaching the front he found "but two divisions," and "it was too late to attack that day."[28] By afternoon McClellan had abandoned hope of rescuing the garrison at Harpers Ferry and had ordered his army concentrated at Sharpsburg to attack Lee. That being the case, it was all the more reason to immediately attack Lee before Jackson could reach the battlefield. Instead of making a late afternoon attack, McClellan examined Lee's troop dispositions and set about assigning bivouacs and battery locations.

At 7 A.M. on September 16, McClellan telegraphed General-in-Chief Halleck to inform Halleck that dense fog had prevented him from "doing more to ascertain" whether Lee was still in battle array across Antietam Creek.[29] McClellan waited for the fog to clear and then set about devising a battle plan, rather than simply pitching into an enemy he knew was badly outnumbered. By afternoon, after studying the terrain and evaluating the opposition, he determined to "make the main attack upon the enemy's left — at least to create a diversion in favor of the main attack, with the hope of something more by assailing the enemy's right — and, as soon as one or both of the flank movements were fully successful, to attack the center with any reserve I might then have on hand."[30] McClellan would send the I Corps and the XII Corps north of Sharpsburg for the attack on Lee's left. The II Corps and other troops would be in position to hit Lee's center, and the IX Corps was assigned the task of "assailing the enemy's right," at the Lower Bridge southeast of Sharpsburg. The afternoon was spent perfecting his arrangements for what would now be the next day's battle.

Around 4 P.M. the I Corps crossed Antietam Creek near the Upper Bridge, just east of Keedysville. Brigadier General Meade took his Third Division across the bridge, followed by the First Division, now commanded by Brigadier General Abner Doubleday, which crossed at a ford below the bridge. Brigadier General James Ricketts's Second Division crossed over Upper Bridge, bringing up the rear.[31] The 2nd splashed across Antietam Creek and deployed as skirmishers in response to shots fired by rebel sharpshooters or pickets. Sergeant Edwin H. Chadwick of Company F described the brief action that ensued after the regiment deployed. "We advanced through the open field about half a mile and discovered the position of the rebel pickets when we were called back. Had some sharp firing one of our men being mortally wounded. After being recalled our brigade [Phelps's] was moved forward and took a position near the right of our line of battle."[32] Another sharpshooter from Company D noted that after the bullets came "whistling among us," at the ford, the sharpshooters deployed to "find the fellows who had been so bold" as to fire at a regiment of sharpshooters. Washington Tucker of Company D was shot during the skirmish and carried to the rear. He died that night.[33]

It was after nightfall when the sharpshooters arrived at their bivouac near the Hagerstown Pike on the farm of Joseph Poffenburger. Just to their south was a wooded area that history would name the North Woods and below that the Miller farm and cornfield. Two other wooded areas grew on opposite sides of the pike, the West Wood below and west of the Miller place, and across the Miller farm ground was the East Wood, now occupied by Federals. Soon after dark it began to rain; the weary sharpshooters sheltered as best they could with rubber blankets or whatever was on hand. The rebels were close, too close to make camp comfortable, so the men lay on the ground with their Sharps Rifles. One sharpshooter wrote: "That night we laid on our arms within a hundred rods of the rebel lines."[34] General Robert E. Lee knew the whereabouts of Hooker's I Corps and he shifted and rearranged his troops to meet it, setting the stage for perhaps the fiercest shootout of the entire Civil war.

General Joseph Hooker was determined to attack at first light on the 17th, and that he did, posting Doubleday's First Division on his right and Ricketts's Second Division on the left. Meade's Third Division backed up the advance. According to Hooker, "My object was to gain the high ground nearly three-quarters of a mile in advance of me, and which commanded the position taken by the enemy on his retreat from South Mountain."[35]

Awaiting Hooker's attack was Stonewall Jackson with his old division, now commanded by Brigadier General John R. Jones, and Ewell's division, commanded on this day by Brigadier General Alexander Lawton. The Confederates were arrayed from their left to right facing Hooker's Corps as follows: Jones's Brigade and the Stonewall Brigade near the West Woods north of the Dunker Church, across the Hagerstown Pike left to right were Lawton's Brigade, Trimble's Brigade and men from D.H. Hill's Division. Hays's Brigade backed up Lawton, and just south of the Dunker church were the brigades of Taliaferro, Starke, Hood and Law. To the west of the Miller Farm on elevated ground were Major General J.E.B. Stuart's cavalry with several batteries positioned to enfilade Hooker's attack down the Hagerstown Pike. Brigadier General Jubal Early's Brigade supported the artillery east of the Hagerstown Pike. Over 9,000 Confederates and a heavy concentration of well-positioned artillery faced Hooker's Corps at dawn on the 17th.[36]

From his First Division, Hooker sent forward perhaps the hardest fighting brigade in the Army of the Potomac, Gibbon's Fourth Brigade, now known as the Iron Brigade, to lead the attack down the Hagerstown Pike. Rebel batteries opened on Gibbon's men as they moved down the Pike, causing several casualties. Near the Miller farmhouse rebel pickets fired into the advancing Federals, but soon Gibbon's boys drove them off and the brigade passed the farm buildings and fences, pushing southward towards Hooker's objective.[37] From here Hooker could see masses of rebels in Miller's Cornfield, just to the south of the farmhouse, as he described in his report: "...I discovered that a heavy force of the enemy had taken possession of a corn-field ... in my immediate front, and from the sun's rays falling on their bayonets ... could see that the field was filled with the enemy." Hooker gave orders for his artillery to go into battery on the west side of the pike across from the Miller farmhouse, "and to open with canister at once."[38]

The sharpshooters were rudely awakened by an artillery barrage at their bivouac at first light on the 17th. A sharpshooter described situation as the officers called for the men to fall in: "The men were slow and cross but soon a shell or shot came among the N.H. [New Hampshire] boys cut the throat of two horses, struck the ground, bounded over our heads. Then there was lively work falling in."[39] Sergeant Chadwick of Company F also mentioned the unnerving artillery barrage: "Shot and shell flew around us in a way that is not very agreeable when you can not tell but that the next one may burst at your feet and send you into eternity."[40]

After forming up, the 2nd U.S.S.S. followed Gibbon's Brigade through the North Woods and past the Miller farm buildings and orchard to the edge of Miller's Cornfield. There the regiment was "deployed in line of battle" with the right of the regiment even with the Hagerstown Pike.[41] At this point in time, approximately 6:10 A.M., General Gibbon had sent two of his regiments to the west of the pike to meet a Confederate advance from the West Woods, and the remainder of his brigade (most of the 6th Wisconsin and the 2nd Wisconsin) were moving into the Miller Cornfield. A section of Battery B, 4th U.S. Artillery commanded by Lieutenant James Stewart "careened across the pike" and unlimbered near the Miller barn amid the farmer's haystacks.[42] Duryea's First Brigade of Ricketts's Division had moved into Miller's Cornfield along the southeastern edge near the East Woods.

Dawn of September 17, 1862, marked a moment of departure for the 2nd U.S.S.S.

5 — "There Was Bloody Work Done" 79

The Miller farmhouse. The sharpshooters passed this structure during their advance into Miller's Cornfield. Library of Congress Civil War Collection.

To this point the regiment, or some part of it, had been in action perhaps nine times. Never had the regiment been sent into a fight as infantry in line of battle. The sharpshooters did not consider themselves infantrymen. To them the infantry was a separate branch of the Army, and they belonged to a small, elite, specialized branch of the service, just like the engineers. From their perspective sharpshooters should be devoted to scouting, skirmishing and sniping — and not stand-up fighting or charging enemy lines. Their job was to cooperate with the infantry where needed as expert marksmen, picking off enemy artillerymen, officers and artillery horses. It is quite probable that the vast majority of them did not feel that the regiment should ever be in a position to use a bayonet. To this point in the war the regiment had been used as and considered as riflemen, for the purpose of striking the enemy with accurate, well-directed fire. Dawn of America's bloodiest day marked a departure from this convention.

As the 2nd neared Miller's Cornfield, Gibbon's Iron Brigade ran into a maelstrom of rebel fire. The famous Confederate Stonewall Brigade, commanded by Colonel Andrew Grigsby, lashed the front and flank of Gibbon's exposed Wisconsin regiments from the west side of the pike, across from the Cornfield. The 6th Wisconsin's commander sent a runner to General Gibbon asking for support. Gibbon reacted by ordering two of his regiments on the left to charge towards the West Woods, and he requested reinforcements from his division commander, General Doubleday.[43]

Colonel Walter Phelps, leading the First Brigade, to which the 2nd belonged, had been ordered personally by General Hooker to follow Gibbon's regiments into the Miller Cornfield. According to Phelps, he was instructed to move "into a corn-field, to form line of battle and support Gibbon's brigade."[44] Little did Phelps or his regiment of sharpshooters know that they were about to enter one of the truly horrendous killing fields of the Civil War, or for that matter any war. Noted Civil War historian James McPherson wrote of the Miller Cornfield, "Many cornfields were the scene of fighting during the Civil War, but this one was ever after known as *the* Cornfield."[45] And hard-fighting Confederate combat commander John B. Hood described the fighting in this section of the battlefield as "the most terrible clash of arms, by far, that has occurred during the war."

As the sharpshooters approached the Cornfield, an order was shouted to "down fence." William Humphrey of Company E thought the order was to lie down, which he immediately did. Instantly a "shell took off one mans leg," and the next man behind Humphrey "was wounded by a minnie ball through right shoulder." The order to tear down the fence was repeated, and instantly the rails were flying "like so many sticks of wood." Colonel Phelps sent the sharpshooters well into the field and halted them about twenty-five yards behind Gibbon's Wisconsin troops. The sharpshooters were near the pike at the edge of the field when Phelps ordered the men to lie down in the tall corn to wait until he was ready to move up in support of Gibbon. Humphrey estimated that the men lay prone for about fifteen minutes while rebel bullets and an occasional shell flew overhead.[46]

Colonel Phelps observed that the enemy had an advantage in position and could fire into the flank of his brigade, so he ordered the sharpshooters to advance alongside the two regiments of Gibbon's Brigade. The following is from the colonel's post-action report:

> Having ascertained that the enemy line was formed with their left advanced, making a crotchet, and that they were in position to partially enfilade our lines, I ordered the Second U.S. Sharpshooters, Colonel Post, to move to the right and front, advancing his left, and to engage the enemy at that point. I immediately advised General Doubleday (in command of the division) of the enemy's position in front, on my right, and of the disposition of the Second U.S. Sharpshooters. General Doubleday approved the movement, and ordered the brigade to their right while the Sharpshooters were engaging them. The remainder of this brigade still held its position in the rear of Gibbon's line.
>
> The effect of the engagement between the Sharpshooters and the enemy was to draw a very heavy-fire from their advanced line.... The loss of the Second U.S. Sharpshooters at this point was severe.[47]

Exactly what happened as the sharpshooters wheeled out of the Cornfield is difficult to determine by study of post-action reports and eyewitness accounts. As eyewitness William Humphrey noted, "I have never read history yet where they had every thing

5 — "There Was Bloody Work Done" 81

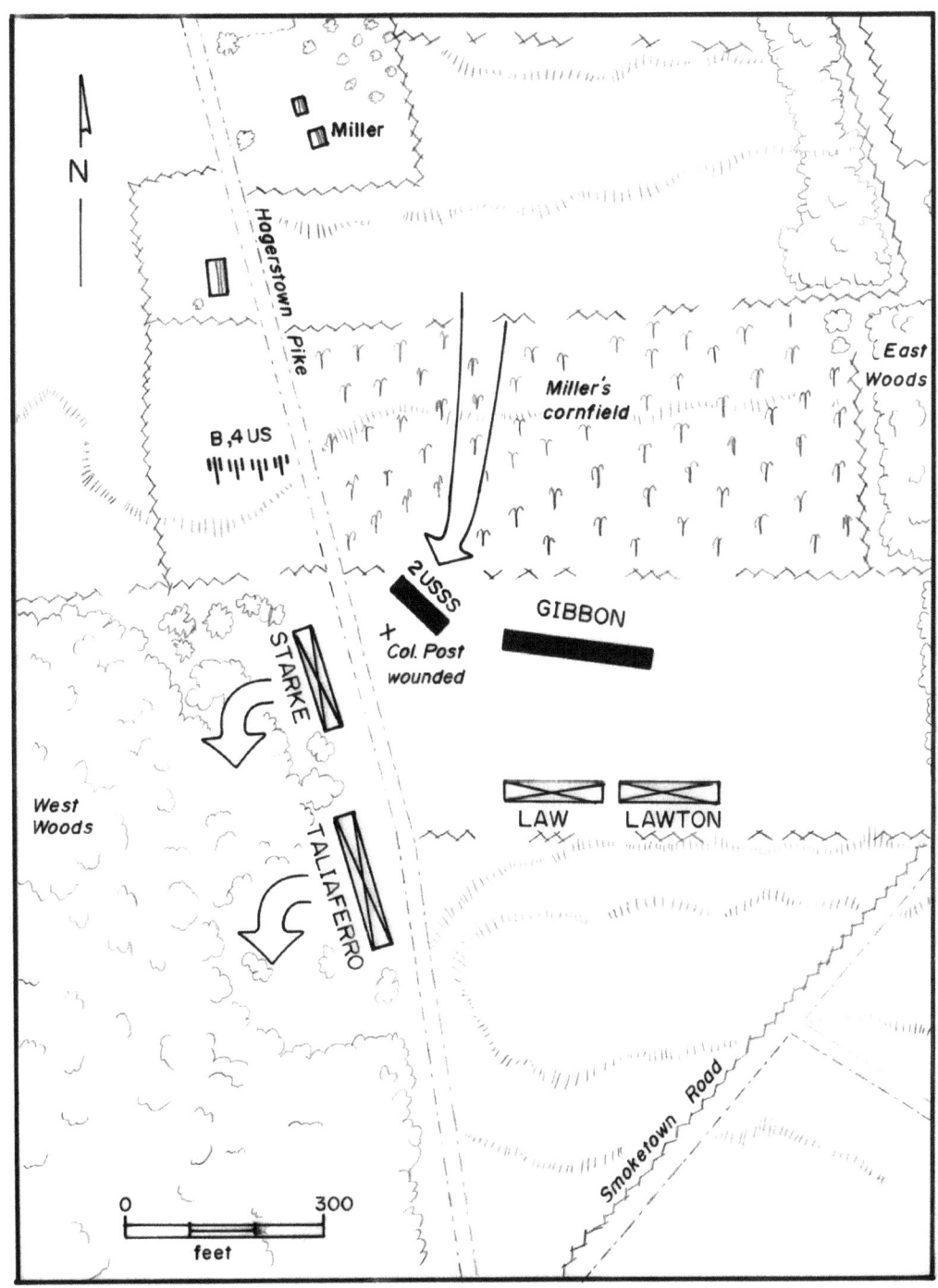

The Battle of Antietam, early morning, September 17, 1862. Map by John Heiser.

correct.... You must remember no to [two] men or 100 men can go to the Worlds Fair and come back and tell the same story of what they have seen, but that is no sign there is no such thing as the Worlds Fair."[48]

Just as the sharpshooters emerged from the Cornfield with a view of the happenings in the cleared fields to the south and west, a line of rebels stood up from behind a rail fence across the pike to fire at the advancing Yankees. These were probably men from the Stonewall Brigade and Jones's Brigade. Then the earth fairly shook as the sharpshooters opened fire and Stewart's cannon roared from the Miller barnyard. It was too much for the outnumbered Virginians, and they ran for cover in the shelter of the West Woods.[49]

Almost immediately after the sharpshooters emerged from the Cornfield and into the meadow beyond, Colonel Henry Post was wounded and he went to the rear. Once into the meadow Adjutant Lewis Parmelee "caught the colors and rushed ahead, saying, 'They are running, come on, boys!'"[50] Parmelee led the regiment well into the meadow, chasing the enemy, who "began to run leaving guns, knapsacks, and everything that impeded their progress on the ground beside their dead and wounded comrades."[51]

An apparently disoriented rebel color bearer approached the sharpshooters as his comrades were retreating. According to Humphrey the man carried a lone star flag, probably an old edition of the Confederate States banner featuring a single star, somewhat similar to the Texas flag. Humphrey noted, "It always looked to me as though the color barer went to advance but did not know all his Regt were dead, so he climbed the fence and came about ⅓ of the way ... [across] the ... meadow and was killed." William Kerr of Company A was advancing at the right of the regiment on the Hagerstown Pike when he spied the enemy color bearer. Kerr ran to the fence, took deliberate aim with his Sharps and killed the color bearer. Humphrey remembered that several sharpshooters went after the flag while exposed to enemy fire: "We sulked along the fence when Adjt. Parmilee [Parmelee] jumped up ran

Colonel Henry A.V. Post, commanding officer of the 2nd U.S. Sharpshooters, wounded at Antietam. Library of Congress Civil War Collection.

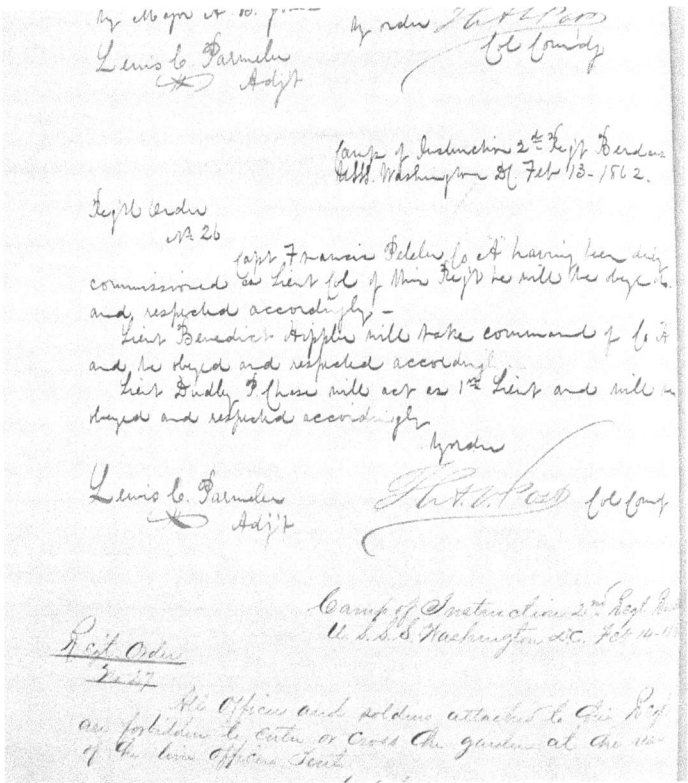

The signatures of Colonel Post and Adjutant Parmelee appear together on this Regimental Order #26 from the 2nd U.S. Sharpshooters record book.

down, picked up the flag but the staff was broken off near the colors ... he sticks his sword into the broken staff, raises the flag above his head and starts back to our lines...." The adjutant did not take more than a few steps before being struck by at least five rebel bullets, at least one in the chest. As the dying adjutant fell, Private Kerr, who had also rushed towards the flag with the others, picked up the lone star flag and brought it off the field.[52]

Two fresh enemy brigades, Taliaferro's and Starke's, emerged from the West Woods near the Dunker Church in an attempt to stem the Federal advance. Humphrey recalled the scene: "I remember after we had driven the enemy from our front, and the firing had slacked up some I hear our boys cry out look over the fence and there we saw the rebs comeing out of the wood going for Gibbons guns, so we went to putting our bullets after them when they turned back for the woods again."[53]

Another sharpshooter described shooting at Starke's Brigade after it emerged from the woods into an open field west of the Hagerstown Pike:

> I had a box of ammunition in my hand ready for them and placing it on the ground I dropped on one knee and began to load and fire. I always stood up when I fired so that I could take better aim. Sometimes I would have to wait a minute before

the smoke would roll away or a rebel would expose himself so that I could get a good chance at him. I always intended to have my rifle cover a man before I fired except once or twice when I was ordered to fire at the colors. While I was thus engaged poor Twombly [Private Robert Twombly of Company F], a New Hampshire boy, fell close beside me shot through the head. I had no time to observe others who were killed or wounded but he was so near that I could not help seeing him as I stooped to load.... We had to shoot through *two* rail fences before we could hit them. The rails were fairly riddled with balls.[54]

Brigadier General William E. Starke led the Confederate advance from the West Woods. Starke grabbed the Louisiana Tigers' flag and was directing his troops toward the pike when he was struck by three bullets "that sent him tumbling from his horse mortally wounded." Starke's Louisiana Brigade was "shattered" in the fight along the Hagerstown Pike, several companies in some Louisiana regiments were nearly wiped out and the 9th Louisiana was "almost destroyed." The Confederates lay dead in windrows along the rail fence, and the road was so thickly strewn with the slain that a path had to be cleared through the road by dragging "the bodies off it" after the battle.[55]

There is no doubt that the 2nd U.S.S.S. played a significant role in the heavy casualties suffered by the Confederates on both sides of the Hagerstown Pike south of the Cornfield. As Starke's and Taliaferro's men fell back, they were subjected to a punishing fire from the sharpshooters. One sharpshooter remembered seeing the dust fog out of the Confederates' uniforms as they were struck by bullets during their retreat: "...when they turned back for the woods as they done so the rebs stooped over and down to the ground as close as they could and our bullets would strike them in their but end and they would keel over and to see the dust fly out of their clothing made me laugh out...."[56] Sergeant Edwin Chadwick examined the field on the west side of the pike after the battle and counted "fifty-three dead rebels lying close to the fence ...

Adjutant Parmelee assuming a classic pose during his halcyon days before Antietam. Library of Congress Civil War Collection.

and there were twenty five or thirty more in the field beyond that we shot while they were running. As there were no other shooting at them I can safely say that the Sharp-Shooters as responsible for that part of the work."[57]

With the collapse of Jackson's brigades south of the Miller Cornfield, the sharpshooters followed the beaten rebels towards the Dunker Church, riding the crest of apparent victory. Humphrey indicated that the regiment advanced far enough to see the Smoketown Road, which branches off to the east of the church, and the battle-damaged walls of the whitewashed church. Here the sharpshooters were driven back by Hood's and Law's brigades of fresh troops. James Kent of Company G was preoccupied with firing and "saw nothing of a brigade of rebels coming down on our left till I heard a Lieut. sing out, 'Retreat boys, we are surrounded!'" Kent was so exhausted from the morning combat that he was hard-pressed to escape with the regiment. During the retreat towards the Cornfield, the regiment's color bearer was hit and dropped the flag. Kent "turned back into the storm and picked up the colors and the gun and brought them off in safety."[58]

The sharpshooters, Gibbon's two Wisconsin regiments and Phelps's handful of survivors, faced a wrathful storm of musket fire from Hood's Texans and Law's Brigade. Bullets zipped in such profusion around the sharpshooters that most were either hit or cut through the clothing and probably all had a near miss. Approximately 2,332 fresh troops, some of the best in Lee's army, swept the battle-weary Federals back into the

A monument erected for the Vermont companies of the 2nd U.S.S.S. at the southern edge of the Cornfield at Antietam. The regiment passed over this position during its morning advance.

Cornfield.⁵⁹ Falling back slowly, many sharpshooters continued to fire carefully aimed shots at the advancing Confederates, as described by Sergeant Chadwick: "I stopped and fired several times while going back, the enemy not being more than a dozen rods off. A bullet struck me, cutting through the strap of my haversack and stopping when it reached my belt."⁶⁰

As the jumbled and fought-out Federal regiments slid back into the now ragged Cornfield, Hood's rebels swarmed in after them. Several sharpshooters crossed the pike to support Battery B, rallying behind the colors. Others from the regiment joined a tangled mess of survivors from Phelps's Brigade and the Iron Brigade at the north end of the Cornfield. The gunners from Battery B "were afraid they would lose their guns, and wanted to limber up and be off," but the rallying sharpshooters "told them their guns should not be taken, and General Gibbon put in a double charge of grape and sighted the gun himself."⁶¹ Several sharpshooters witnessed the quite extraordinary sight of a general officer aiming a 12-pounder Napoleon like a common gunner. But Gibbon was growing desperate as artillerymen continued to fall and few horses remained to drag away the guns. Rebels firing at close range from the Cornfield, now "a hideous and disorganized mass of fire and crossfire," threatened to wipe out the remaining gunners and battery horses.⁶²

General Gibbon noticed that one of the brass Napoleons in Battery B was overshooting the enemy in the Cornfield, so he adjusted the elevating screw and the gun blasted a load of canister right on target. Gibbon's action made quite an impression on the sharpshooters, as at least three of them mentioned the effect of Gibbon's shot. Humphrey wrote:

> When Gibbon fired the first round of canister I saw the air well filled with hats, caps, every thing soldiers have. I saw an arm go 30 feet into the air and fall back again. It looked as though it had been torn off close up to the shoulder. It was just awful!⁶³

The effect of the close-range canister fire was stunning as the other cannons pounded the Cornfield. One sharpshooter saw a "whole windrow" of Hood's men lifted "twelve feet into the air," with "whole bodies, arms, legs and all sorts of fragments" blown above the corn. Shattered fence rails were blasted through the Confederate ranks with mangling effect.⁶⁴ The 1st Texas, one of Hood's best regiments, absorbed the brunt of the devastating canister fire.⁶⁵

Miller's Cornfield was now a gory, nauseating scene, sufficient to make even Charon recoil. The carnage made a lasting impression on General Hooker, who emphatically described the area in his post-action report: "Every stalk of corn in the northern and greater part of the field was cut as closely as could have been done with a knife, and the slain lay in rows precisely as they had stood in ranks a few moments before. It was never my fortune to witness a more bloody, dismal battle-field."⁶⁶

Finally, fresh units from Meade's Pennsylvania Reserve Division and the Federal XII Corps reached the Cornfield to take up the fight. Battery B limbered up and withdrew to its previous position north of the Miller farm. With many carrying empty cartridge boxes, the sharpshooters also pulled back to the north. Hooker's I Corps was

A modern-day view of the rail fence and field on the west side of the Hagerstown Pike where many Confederates fell to sharpshooter bullets.

shot up and fought out, done for the day. Hooker himself was carried from the field swooning from blood loss, having been shot in the foot. The general was unaware of his wound until, affected by shock, he nearly fell from his horse.

The unique green uniforms worn by the sharpshooters simplified the task of gathering up the regiment, and the scattered sharpshooters eventually fell in with what was left of Phelps's Brigade north of the Cornfield. Phelps formed the remnant of his brigade into line of battle "some 80 paces in rear of the corn-field" and stood ready until General Doubleday ordered him to fall back upon the rest of the First Division. Then, Phelps wrote, "I stacked arms and allowed the men to rest. This was about 1.30 P.M."[67]

Still the fighting raged through the Cornfield and into the West Woods, spreading like a conflagration that consumed men from both armies along the entire length of Lee's position. McClellan kept feeding divisions into the fight at different points on the field without ever concentrating sufficient force to collapse Lee's line. Although McClellan's attacks made progress, in each instance Lee was able to shift forces in time to save his army. The great fault of McClellan at Antietam, as is to be expected with his penchant for safety, was feeding his strength piecemeal into the fight. Burnside's attack on the Confederate right took too long to develop, enabling Lee to thwart McClellan's uncoordinated attacks north of Sharpsburg. Throughout the day much of the fighting was done at close range in the outdated stand-up fashion; the casualties were appalling. By the evening of September 17, 1862, an American record for casualties during a single day of combat was established that endures to this day. Nearly

23,000 total casualties were reported, including more than 3,600 killed. Nearly one in four men engaged in the fighting became a casualty.[68]

Even a cursory analysis of the 2nd U.S.S.S. at Antietam yields one obvious fact: the sharpshooters were a formidable weapon on the battlefield, capable of inflicting telling casualties even when under the most severe stress of combat. Homer Stoughton, who was promoted to major on the day of the battle, succinctly validated this with his remarks about the 2nd at Antietam: "...they did more damage to the enemy than any brigade in our front or to our right, we firing obliquely."[69] The heavy casualties suffered by Starke's and Taliaferro's brigades, fighting directly across the pike from the sharpshooters, strongly substantiate Stoughton's observation. Out of the approximately 500 engaged from Taliaferro's Brigade, twenty-eight were killed and 143 were wounded. Starke's Louisianans suffered even worse casualties: 274 killed and wounded.[70] As one of the sharpshooters summarized it, "There was bloody work done on that part of the field."[71]

At Antietam the 2nd U.S.S.S. suffered approximately a fifty percent casualty rate for those engaged in the battle. Out of approximately 130 men who actually went into action, thirteen were killed or died of wounds, fifty-one were wounded and two went missing, a total of sixty-six casualties.[72] Although the regiment may have numbered over 250 men present for duty, it is likely that only a little over half that number actually went into action on September 17, 1862. Some men were needed for details such as teamsters, stretcher bearers, and messengers, while others were incapacitated from various causes or found ways to escape being sent into combat.[73] Company F went into action at Antietam with only eight men, and Company G went in with only seventeen. According to Sergeant Chadwick of Company F, out of the eight men in action "one was killed and four wounded, while only one escaped without being hit." Company G was shot up nearly as badly with two killed and ten wounded out of seventeen "who went into battle."[74]

The Battle of Antietam did not destroy the 2nd U.S.S.S.; it might well have if the regiment had been at reasonable strength during the fighting. Berdan's Camp of Instruction, with its concurrent sickness and disillusionment, had exacted a great toll before the sharpshooters fired their first shot in anger. At Antietam, Phelps's Brigade of five veteran regiments including the sharpshooters took only 425 men into the battle, losing forty-three percent as casualties.[75] As a comparison, the brand-new 14th Connecticut Infantry went into the fight at Antietam with over 1,000 men in the ranks, well over twice the number in Phelps's entire atrophied brigade.[76] About two-thirds of the original recruits from the 2nd U.S.S.S. were not present at Antietam while the newly mustered 14th Connecticut showed up with a full regimental complement. The effects of hard service, sickness and disenchantment had reduced the sharpshooters worse than even the single bloodiest day of the war.

On the morning of September 18 both armies remained in their lines around Sharpsburg. Lee briefly considered attacking the Federal right near the West Woods, but, fortunately for the Confederates, he reconsidered. Two fresh divisions reinforced McClellan, about 14,000 men, giving the Federals a nearly 2 to 1 advantage in troop strength. Little Mac also had several thousand troops on hand that had yet to be engaged or had been only slightly engaged in the battle.[77] Still he did not attack. Having fought Lee in the Seven Days' Battles, McClellan should have realized that his opponent would certainly attack if at all possible, especially if he held a numerical advantage. Thus, as Lee remained on the defensive, there is nothing to account for McClellan's deference other than an apparent satisfaction in having thwarted Lee's invasion plans.

Towards evening Lee began withdrawing his army from the Sharpsburg area with a view of crossing the Potomac near Shepherdstown at Boteler's Ford. Lee's plan called for a retreat into the Shenandoah Valley, where he would have more room to maneuver and better positions for a defensive stand. Again McClellan had an opportunity to severely damage, possibly even destroy Lee's army if only he would take aggressive action. But Little Mac failed to close in on the vulnerable Confederates with their backs to the river, wasting perhaps the best single opportunity of the war to catch Lee at an utter disadvantage. McClellan did finally send a force that included the 1st U.S.S.S. to Boteler's Ford to follow the retreating Confederates, but it was too late to catch Lee crossing the river. The end result was a stinging setback for Porter's V Corps.

The 2nd U.S.S.S. remained in camp north of Sharpsburg on the battlefield. By September 19, two days after the battle, burial details were going out, and Sergeant Chadwick of Company F volunteered for that duty, hoping to find the adjutant's body and others whom he knew.[78] Words cannot adequately describe the absolutely horrible sights and smells on those Maryland fields in the heat of September. Many accounts mention the terrible odor of rotting dead horses and the bloated, blackened corpses lying about profusely. Photographs of the dead on the battlefield show the swollen bodies, many with pockets rifled and faces distorted, but these reveal only a partial indication of the true repugnance of the scene.

At least nine men from the 2nd U.S.S.S. were buried on the field at Antietam, including Adjutant Lewis C. Parmelee and Second Lieutenant John Thompson of Company G, who was shot through the head during the advance.[79] Apparently many of the killed were buried where they fell or in groups near where they fell. Since the battle was fought in Federal-controlled area rather than in Virginia or somewhere in the South, it is probable that more of the dead than usual were claimed by families and shipped home for reburial. That was the case with the remains of Adjutant Parmelee.

On the day Parmelee's body was recovered and buried, Regimental Quartermaster Benjamin Calef penned a letter to the adjutant's father to inform him. During the Civil War there was no formal governmental system for informing families of battle deaths. Often families resorted to checking casualty lists printed in newspapers. The more fortunate ones received letters from comrades of the victims.[80] Fortunately Calef's letter was preserved. The following excerpt from his letter to Parmelee's father provides an example of a comrade's casualty notification:

> To me is given the painful task of informing you that your son, Lewis C. Parmelee, was killed in the battle near this place on the morning of the 17th. He had been leading on the remnant of our little band after the Col. Was wounded, & had just succeeded in taking a rebel color, when he was struck by a ball in the arm & breast. He could not have lived but a short time. His body was recovered this morning &

interred near the field. The place will be marked so it maybe known where he lies. It was impossible to have it sent home as the army is moving & there are no facilities for doing so.

'Twere seeming mockery to offer our poor condolences in this your hour of affliction. Yet I would assure you, our deepest sympathies are yours, & we morn the loss of a true friend, good soldier, & brave man, who has fallen in nobly defending a nation's honor.

His effects will be cared for & sent to you at the earliest convenience.[81]

McClellan's army remained encamped near Sharpsburg for weeks after the battle while Lee's army bivouacked several miles south at Winchester, Virginia. No doubt General Lee anticipated that McClellan would remain inactive after such a sanguinary battle as Antietam, otherwise perhaps he would have withdrawn to a better defensive position. Each day McClellan waited at Sharpsburg saw Lee's army gain strength from returning stragglers and reinforcements. President Lincoln understood the importance of pressuring Lee immediately; McClellan, however, was in no rush to take the offensive.

Confederate dead photographed behind the fence along the Hagerstown Pike shortly after the Battle of Antietam. Library of Congress Civil War Collection.

President Lincoln had been awaiting a propitious time to announce his administration's plans to liberate all slaves held in the rebellious states. Antietam afforded the president with circumstances favorable for making his plans public. On September 22, 1862, Lincoln presented his preliminary Emancipation Proclamation to his cabinet. The terms of the proclamation were to go into effect on January 1, 1863. Lincoln's final version of the proclamation read in part: "...all persons held as slaves within any State or designated part of a State, the people whereof shall then be in rebellion against the United States, shall be then, thenceforth, and forever free; and the Executive Government of the United States, including the military and naval authority thereof, will recognize and maintain the freedom of such persons...."[82] Two days later the proclamation was released to the public. The entire essence of the war was transformed in a single day. It was now an abolition war to the cynical, a war for freedom to the idealistic, and a war of necessity to the pragmatic.

While President Lincoln was anxious for McClellan to press his advantage against Lee's army, even the common soldiers sensed that a great opportunity was being wasted. On the day after Lincoln released his proclamation to the public, a sharpshooter mused about the meaning of Antietam: "If it is only the beginning of the end, the country may be satisfied with the dearly bought victory, but if the advantage is not followed up as it should be, as I am a little fearful it was not, it may well complain that so much blood is spilled for nothing."[83]

In the immediate aftermath of the battle, McClellan "deluged" the government with demands for supplies and reinforcements. The government responded by designating twenty new infantry regiments to be sent to the Army of the Potomac. Wagonloads of supplies were forwarded to the army, which, in fairness, was in a state of need.[84] According to the sharpshooters' regimental historian, "While at this camp the soldiers were poorly supplied with clothing and rations, the latter causing much complaint, especially the wormy crackers."[85] McClellan mentioned the strained and undersupplied condition of his army while informing General-in-Chief Halleck that he "did not feel authorized to cross the river in pursuit of the retreating enemy," because doing so would "place that stream ... between this army and its base of supply."[86]

Growing increasingly frustrated, the president traveled to the battlefield on October 1 to visit the army and view the battlefield. McClellan sensed Lincoln's growing impatience. In a letter to his wife McClellan noted, "I incline to think that the real purpose of his visit is to push me into a premature advance into Virginia." In the weeks after Lincoln returned to Washington, McClellan would direct much of his correspondence to the president in explaining why the Army of the Potomac could not move to engage the Confederates. One member of Lincoln's cabinet complained, "All his official correspondence is with the President direct and no one else."[87]

By late October the president's tone in his correspondence with McClellan was bordering on blatant sarcasm. When McClellan forwarded a report to Halleck about the poor condition of cavalry mounts, Lincoln almost immediately shot back: "I have just read your dispatch about sore-tongued and fatigued horses. Will you pardon me for asking what the horses of your army have done since the battle of Antietam that fatigues anything?"⁸⁸ After the general replied with an explanation in defense of his cavalry corps, Lincoln answered with the following on October 27:

> To be told, after more than five weeks' total inaction of the army, and during which period we have sent to the army every fresh horse we possibly could, amounting in the whole to 7,918, that the cavalry horses were too much fatigued to move, presents a very cheerless, almost hopeless, prospect for the future, and it may have forced something of impatience in my dispatch. If not recruited and rested then, when could they ever be? I suppose the river is rising, and I am glad to believe you are crossing.⁸⁹

Finally on October 26 McClellan sent his reinforced army out of its camp, and, as Lincoln acknowledged, crossed the Potomac River over a pontoon bridge at Berlin, near Harpers Ferry. The sharpshooters broke camp near Sharpsburg on the 30th and also crossed the river at Berlin. All this activity was in response to President Lincoln's suggestion that McClellan should take the shorter path to Richmond and beat Lee and his army to that place. McClellan planned to concentrate his forces at Warrenton, Virginia, and that was the sharpshooters' immediate destination.

Whether he realized it or not, General McClellan was in a very precarious position with the president. Lincoln expected the army to move swiftly to gain an advantage on the Confederates. When Lee reacted and placed half of his army in McClellan's path at Culpeper Court House, Lincoln had seen enough. He concluded that McClellan had failed again. As Lincoln explained it to a member of his cabinet, "I said I would remove him if he let Lee's army get away from him, and I must do so. He has got the slows, Mr. Blair."⁹⁰

So the Army of the Potomac and the sharpshooters would have a new commander and, as a consequence of Lee's reaction, a new campaign strategy. History has judged George B. McClellan harshly for his overcautious command style and his questionable fortitude. But we will never know if Lincoln made the best decision in removing McClellan. From hindsight we know that two and a half more years and a very bloody series of battles were required to defeat Lee and his Army of Northern Virginia. Perhaps it is possible that, given time and resources, McClellan, regardless of his flaws, might have bled out Lee's army faster and at less cost than was the case under a series of other generals. The facts indicate that when McClellan was in command, the Army of the Potomac inflicted greater losses on the enemy in most battles than it sustained and never suffered unbalanced losses. We know that McClellan's soldiers wanted him to remain as their commander. Perhaps they sensed that Little Mac had given better attention to their well-being and cared more for their lives than could be expected from other generals.

As the sharpshooters marched towards Warrenton, they were entering a new, darker phase of the war. A popular general was being sent away, a new and uncertain commander would lead them through the vicissitudes of fighting Lee and his army. The mood of the army and the country darkened in reaction to Lincoln's emancipation policy and the ever-increasing cost of the war. Now the mettle of the army, and the nation, would be tested as never before or since.

6

The Most Dismal and Despondent Days

November 7, 1862, was a snowy day in northern Virginia. The unseasonable weather, emblematic of the dying year, presaged the end of an epoch for the Army of the Potomac. Two days previously President Abraham Lincoln had made provisions for relieving Major General George B. McClellan from command of the Army of the Potomac. By direction of Secretary of War Edwin Stanton, Brigadier General Catharinus Buckingham boarded a special train on the 7th and headed to army headquarters near Warrenton to personally deliver the news and orders to McClellan. Accompanying Buckingham was the man whom the president had selected to supersede McClellan: Major General Ambrose E. Burnside.[1] The popular general who had organized and prepared Lincoln's army for battle was now finished as a commander. Although the army had always fought well under Little Mac, it had not accomplished the president's objective — capturing Richmond. Lincoln was increasingly impatient; he expected and demanded progress in his effort to subdue the Confederate East. McClellan's insecure approach to warfare would no longer be tolerated.

With the benefit of hindsight the selection of Ambrose Burnside to command the Army of the Potomac seems improbable and ill-conceived. Burnside himself felt unqualified for such a demanding position and only agreed to accept his appointment because it would have otherwise gone to Major General Joseph Hooker, whom he loathed. Born in Liberty, Indiana, in 1824, Burnside graduated from West Point in 1847. His life experience and service before the Civil War was, for the most part, mundane. Probably his most noteworthy accomplishment was the design of a breech-loading carbine. He resigned from the army in 1853 to concentrate on producing and selling his invention, but the effort failed, leaving him on the brink of financial ruin. George McClellan, whom he had befriended at West Point, intervened to rescue Burnside by offering him a job with the Illinois Central Railroad.[2]

With the outbreak of hostilities in 1861, Burnside, who had been active in the Rhode Island Militia, took command the 1st Rhode Island Infantry. At First Bull Run he led a brigade of Rhode Island troops adequately and soon was given a command operating against the Confederates on the North Carolina coast. This was the most successful period of his service; his forces captured New Bern and thus provided a foothold for Federal forces on the Southern coast. He was rewarded with a promotion to Major General and command of the IX Corps, and hence his reputation began to tarnish.[3]

When Lincoln appointed Burnside in November 1862, there were two logical reasons for his selection. First, Burnside had done nothing to convince the president that he was incompetent. He had succeeded in North Carolina, but his performance at Antietam with the IX Corps, which was a good indication of his true command potential, was less than satisfactory. However, when viewed in light of the outcome of Antietam, his performance did not merit extreme criticism. Second, Burnside, being a close friend of McClellan, was not someone who would be viewed as a usurper by the army. He had an engaging personality, and his ascension to command would be less likely to create disharmony and dissention within the ranks. In short, Burnside was a logical choice to provide a smooth transition in separating the army from McClellan and his clique.[4]

The immediate reaction within the Army of the Potomac was "like a thunderclap" of "infernal outrage." Lincoln's recent controversial plan to emancipate slaves cast a political taint to the removal; McClellan as a Democrat was no source of support for Lincoln's new policy. The greatest opposition and grumbling came from the old regiments that had served under McClellan on the Peninsula.[5] A Massachusetts soldier exemplified the army's feelings in a letter to his family dated November 10, 1862. The soldier noted that the army was deflated, was complaining vociferously about the "Abolitionists," and many in the ranks were swearing not to fight under "any other general."[6] McClellan held his last review of the troops on November 10 and then left the Army of the Potomac for good.

But there was absolutely nothing to be done about the change of command, and the army was there to fight a rebellion, not to instigate yet another one. A soldier serving in the same division as the sharpshooters had the true mindset of the army. He told the home folks that the army would stand by the flag and would continue to fight the enemy regardless of who was in command.[7] Ultimately, especially among those from Yankeedom, the men would support Lincoln, knowing that they shared his goals.

General Burnside had devised a plan to hurry south from Warrenton, capture Fredericksburg, and then try to get to Richmond before Lee could intervene with his army. Burnside's campaign plan was haltingly accepted by the administration as well as his proposal to reorganize the Army of the Potomac into three "grand divisions." Under Burnside's new organizational scheme the 2nd U.S.S.S. remained in the I Corps, now assigned to the Left Grand Division commanded by Major General William B. Franklin. The VI Corps also answered to Franklin, as well as a cavalry brigade commanded by Brigadier General George Bayard. General Hooker left the I Corps to command the Center Grand Division, and Major General John Reynolds assumed command of the I Corps in his place. The other grand division of Burnside's scheme, the Right Grand Division, was commanded by Major General Edwin V. Sumner. The XI Corps was held in reserve and the XII Corps remained at Harpers Ferry to protect that place.[8]

It was mid–November when the sharpshooters stepped out from Warrenton as part of Burnside's Fredericksburg Campaign. The 2nd was not the same battered, depleted regiment that had camped near Sharpsburg after the Battle of Antietam. Following that battle the regiment's companies were so badly thinned that Major Stoughton, who had assumed command after Colonel Post was wounded, consolidated the regiment into three companies. It was not a popular move; the men would be answering to different officers, in some cases officers from different states. As one sharpshooter noted in his diary, "The boys can't see it."[9] On October 1, Company E had only thirteen men left for duty. But while the regiment camped near Sharpsburg, men who had been sick, wounded or on detached duty trickled in. Company E alone received thirty recruits on October 17.[10] At Warrenton others, including Sergeant Joseph Murray, who had been captured the previous August and apparently exchanged, returned to the regiment.[11] Despite the influx of recruits, the regiment would never again approach full strength, but it was no longer the skeletal remnant it had been the previous month.

By November 19, the sharpshooters had reached Falmouth once again. The previous day Colonel Post tendered his resignation in Washington. He had visited the regiment at Warrenton on the 9th and had traveled to Washington to try to get additional recruits "and new companies added."[12] The following is Colonel Henry Post's letter of resignation as recorded in the regimental record book:

> Washington November 18, 1862
>
> Fellow officers and soldiers of the Second Regiment of Sharp Shooters.
>
> Private considerations compelled me to resign my position as Colonel of this regiment. In taking care of you permit me to thank you all for the confidence you have placed in me and for prompt obedience to all orders. In endeavoring to do my duty in the many harassing difficulties peculiar to this organization, if you have thought me too severe, or unjust, I trust you will now harbor no ill feeling, but that you will attribute all now to the head and not the heart.
>
> I trust we shall meet again on the battle field; if not I wish to say to you all that when our troubles are over and when we have all retired to the walks of civil life, nothing will afford me more pleasure than to meet you, with whom I shall associate so many pleasant recollections.
>
> It is needless for me to say, do your duty in the future, as you have done in the past and honor and glory will crown your efforts. My prayers to a just God in heaven will be for you. Farewell, Farewell
>
> H.A.V. Post
> Late Col 2d U.S.S.S.[13]

Major Homer R. Stoughton of Randolph, Vermont, officially assumed command of the 2nd U.S.S.S. after Post's resignation. Lieutenant Colonel Francis Peteler had taken a leave of absence in August to return to Minnesota because of an Indian uprising in that, his home state. Peteler would never return to the sharpshooters, his resignation being accepted on June 23, 1863. The regiment was so under-strength that never again would a colonel command it. There were also a number of promotions from the ranks to replace officers who had resigned or had been killed in battle. Unlike the regular Army, volunteer regiments usually filled officer vacancies with sergeants or other enlisted men who demonstrated gallantry or leadership potential. The 2nd U.S.S.S. was replete with enlisted men as qualified or better qualified than the average Civil War army officer.

Rain pelted the army at Falmouth all day on the 18th and 19th and continued in northern Virginia for two more days. This routine occurrence of nature was enough to derail Burnside's campaign and hemlock Lincoln's latest hope to eliminate Lee and his army. Burnside would not risk crossing the Rappahannock by fords upstream from

Fredericksburg, especially with the risk of high water due to the rains. Instead, he waited at Falmouth for pontoons to arrive so that army engineers could span the river with a floating bridge. The pontoons arrived late, very late. When the pontoons finally did arrive, General Lee had positioned his army on the heights above Fredericksburg. The essence of Burnside's plan was to quickly skirt past Lee and his army on the way to Richmond, something now impossible.

The hapless Burnside should have called off the enterprise and tried a different tack. But the president had demonstrated through his dismissal of McClellan that he would not tolerate more excuses for endless delays. Burnside had substituted his own plan for the president's, and Fredericksburg was a major objective in his plan. Unfortunately for the Army of the Potomac, Burnside was not much for adaptation. He would wait on the north bank of the Rappahannock and seek an opportunity to strike Lee at Fredericksburg.

Days and then weeks passed while Burnside delayed his attack at Fredericksburg. Lee would have preferred to make a stand along the North Anna River farther south, but President Jefferson Davis had informed Lee that he wanted the Federals stopped at Fredericksburg. So Lee positioned his forces to defend Fredericksburg and the river fords in that region of the Rappahannock. At length Burnside decided to cross the river just below Fredericksburg and attack with Franklin's Grand Division. He expected to drive a wedge between the two defending corps of Lee's army and capture the heights above the town before Lee could react.[14]

Of course Burnside's plan had no chance of success against a master of defensive warfare like General Lee. The Confederates could observe every move by Burnside's forces and react accordingly with time to spare. Burnside was not crafty enough to devise an alternate plan with a better chance of success, so he convinced himself that his plan to split Lee's corps would succeed. He was perceptive enough to sense that any offensive move by his army would leave him in better standing with the president than further delay.

The truth is that President Lincoln wanted his army to attack Lee, period. Unlike McClellan, the president understood that the Union had a great advantage over the Confederacy in manpower and resources. Lincoln once remarked to a secretary that there was an "awful arithmetic" at work in the war. To Lincoln it was quite simple. If the two armies fought weekly with the same ratio of casualties produced thus far in the war, the Confederacy would soon be depleted and the Union would still have a mighty army left standing. When he could find a general who comprehended this fact, he believed, the war would soon be over.[15]

On December 9 the 2nd U.S.S.S. finally moved out its camp near Brooks Station, where the regiment had waited since November 26, and marched to a position near the river below Fredericksburg. Burnside had issued orders that morning for his division commanders to put their commands in readiness to cross the river, directing that each man should have three days of cooked rations and sixty rounds of ammunition. Franklin's Grand Division was to cross the Rappahannock on the two pontoon bridges spanning the river about one mile below Fredericksburg.[16]

Covered by artillery suppressing fire, the Federal engineers began constructing pontoon bridges before daylight on December 11, 1862. Two companies of the 18th Mississippi fired at the engineers from the opposite side of the river, wounding six men and hitting several pontoon boats. Federal batteries soon drove off the Mississippians, and when two other larger rebel forays appeared to fire on the bridge builders, the rebels were in each case "scattered in ludicrous confusion" by the Federal guns.[17] While this was taking place, the 2nd U.S.S.S. and the 10th Pennsylvania Reserves stood at ease on the river bank, probably as insurance against further incursions by rebel sharpshooters.[18]

Finally after 4 P.M. Burnside ordered General Franklin to send his grand division across the Rappahannock. After some delay Franklin had part of his VI Corp on the Fredericksburg side of the river. Before Franklin could cross all of his troops, an order arrived from Burnside directing him to leave only one brigade to hold the bridgehead during the night. So it was afternoon of the 12th before Franklin had his grand division across the river and in position to take the offensive, thirty-six hours after the engineers began laying the pontoon bridges.[19]

It is conceivable that Burnside's plan of attack could have succeeded had he moved with alacrity. Unfortunately for the Federals, he did not. After crossing the river during the morning of December 12, Burnside's two grand divisions remained idle throughout that day. The president had suggested to Burnside at the onset of the campaign that the general would have to move rapidly to succeed. Now at the crucial point of campaign, Burnside, apparently encumbered by the burden of command, reacted ploddingly. General Lee used the 12th to effectively prepare for Burnside's now obvious attack plan.

By the morning of December 13, Lee had his army positioned on the heights above the Rappahannock with Longstreet's Corps on the left just west of Fredericksburg and Jackson's Corps facing Franklin's Grand Division above the open plain west of the river. According to one historian, "Lee could hardly have wished for a more advantageous defensive position."[20]

Nevertheless, Burnside sent orders for Franklin to attack the hills above the Rappahannock. At about 8:30 A.M. Meade's and Gibbon's divisions from the I Corps moved to attack under the cover of a heavy fog. Doubleday's Division, including the 2nd U.S.S.S., stood by to guard against an attack by Stuart's cavalry on the extreme left. Around 10 A.M. the fog rapidly dissipated, and the Confederates had an unobstructed view of the advancing Federal divisions. Doubleday sent the 2nd U.S.S.S. to relieve Meade's troops about 1,200 yards beyond the Bernard House, then Doubleday's troops followed "for about half a mile, driving in the enemy's skirmishers."[21]

Franklin's attack, and for that matter Burnside's main attack, was composed of only the two divisions, Meade's and Gibbon's, from the I Corps. Franklin had Major General William F. "Baldy" Smith's VI Corp at hand to use in the attack and reserve troops from Hooker's Grand Division. Without these forces involved the attack against Jackson stood no chance.

Meanwhile Doubleday continued his advance parallel to the river. A wooded area extending from the river bank was held by Confederate cavalry and infantry and was supported by artillery placed within the main Confederate line. Inside the wood were masked batteries set in place by the Confederates to confront gunboats on the river. A heavy fire was erupting out of the wooded patch, which Doubleday believed was intended to disrupt his "farther progress." Doubleday called up Battery B, Fourth U.S. Artillery, to shell the woods as a precursor to an attack. Then Doubleday sent out the 2nd U.S.S.S. as skirmishers to lead an attack by Meredith's 7th Wisconsin and 24th Michigan.[22]

The sharpshooters moved across an open field under heavy fire from firing artillery posted elsewhere in the woods. One sharpshooter recalled that the case, shell and canister flew "very freely" during the advance. A high rail fence backed by a bank of earth provided shelter for the sharpshooters as they neared the wood, and the bugler sounded halt. Enemy artillery played upon the sheltering sharpshooters with terrifying effect for a few moments until Meredith's regiments caught up at the fence. Then the bugler sounded the advance. Combined artillery and musket fire swept the remaining seventy-five yards separating the sharpshooters from their objective; a sharpshooter remembered that if any man stood on his feet, the chances of being hit were "almost sure."[23]

At this point history provides another glimpse of the sharpshooters' disdain for the infantry charge. Many in the regiment obviously felt that charging enemy lines was work for ordinary infantry, and this is indicated by an anecdote from the 24th Michigan. It was recalled that when the Michiganders overtook the sharpshooters at the rail fence, the sharpshooters' commander ordered the infantrymen to "kick his men over the fence."[24] It proved unnecessary as the sharpshooters responded to the bugle call and rushed into the wood without a single casualty.

Once into the trees the Federals faced little opposition. Most of the rebels retreated out of the wood before the sharpshooters entered, and those who remained were quickly rounded up as prisoners, the sharpshooters capturing several men and horses. The Confederates had previously fortified the area to guard the river with several cannon in embrasures along the river bank. For some reason the guns were not sent to the rear by the Federals and were left in the wood until after the battle, otherwise the 2nd could have claimed credit for capturing several cannon.[25]

Meredith's Brigade pushed on through the wood and deployed to counter Confederate skirmishers. The sharpshooters moved through the wood utilizing skirmish drill to ensure that the place had been completely cleared of the enemy. Throughout the rest of the day the men remained in a skirmish line, lying on their arms in the wood as shells screamed over and through the trees. The men had experienced this kind of unnerving trial at Rappahannock Station the previous August. While this shelling was probably not as intense as what the regiment had seen on that August day, Major Rufus Dawes of Meredith's Brigade believed that it was the worst trial he ever experienced on the battlefield. Dawes mentioned that watching the nearby rebel cannon firing directly at his position, experiencing the concussion of the blast and the shower of spraying dirt from exploding shells, being unable to respond or even move away, was as unnerving as anything he had yet experienced.[26]

Nevertheless, the sharpshooters were very lucky on that 13th of December. Not a single man from the regiment was killed, and only one man was wounded during the entire battle.[27] On other portions of the field the Federals were wantonly sacrificed in the poorly managed battle. That afternoon thousands were shot down on the Federal right during ill-conceived assaults above Fredericksburg. A fortuitous placement on the left of the Federal line doubtlessly saved many sharpshooters that day. The regiment remained in the wood until dark and then pulled back to Doubleday's headquarters, again under heavy artillery bombardment all the way.

On the dreary night of the 13th, the sharpshooters were deployed at the front on picket. The men were close enough to the enemy to hear their muffled voices. No fires were allowed that night, and the men throughout the army suffered from the bitterly cold December night. Before dawn on the 14th the regiment was relieved and returned to Phelps's Brigade, boiling coffee for the first time in two days.

Sometime after breakfast on the 14th, as the men lay resting in line of battle on the open plain, the rebels rolled out a breech-loading Whitworth rifled cannon to send a few long-range shots at the massed Yankees. These cannon, like the sharpshooters' rifles, were designed for rapid, accurate long-range fire, and were probably the most accurate long-range field guns used during the Civil War. General Doubleday mentioned the incident in his report: "About 11 A.M. a Whitworth gun opened on us from the banks of the Massaponax, near the river, enfilading our lines along the Bowling Green road."[28] The Whitworth fired a hexagonal solid projectile, called a bolt, at the sharpshooters from a distance of approximately two miles.

Some of the sharpshooters noticed a white puff of smoke from far to the left, the distance being so great that no report was heard from the firing cannon. Seconds later a Whitworth bolt ploughed up dirt in front of the regiment and ricocheted away. Again the men saw the flash and smoke of the firing cannon. This time the shot "tore the knapsack from the back of ... George A. Clay, in Company E, sending the man's clothing, etc., 20 feet in the air...."[29] A third bolt passed overhead and struck a large oak post just behind the men. By now the sharpshooters were not amused; one man remembered the incident as so terrifying that he believed the men were ready to stampede.[30] At this point, according to General Doubleday, "Colonel Phelps skillfully evaded the danger by a partial change of front. Hall's battery replied to this gun, firing about 20 rounds, but most of the projectiles appeared to fall short."[31] A battery firing from across the river finally succeed in driving off the Whitworth, and the frightening ordeal ended for the sharpshooters.

Shortly after the Whitworth was withdrawn, the sharpshooters were ordered out to the picket line to counter Confederate sharpshooters. The sharpshooters continued their duty on the picket line until Burnside ordered his troops to recross the Rappahannock on the night of December 15. On their last day on the Fredericksburg bank of the river, the regiment was sent to a particularly troublesome section of the picket line. A line of infantry was firing at the Confederates so fiercely that it was feared that it would bring on a resumption of the battle. The sharpshooters were sent to suppress the enemy sharpshooters and pickets. With the intention of withdrawing after dark, the Federals did not want to risk an incursion or advance by enemy pickets.

The sharpshooters deployed among the infantrymen and soon had them cease firing. The Confederate pickets were at first "exposing themselves recklessly ... evidently suffering little from the infantry." Carefully choosing their targets, the sharpshooters soon nearly silenced the Confederate pickets. The Confederates called for a parley between the lines and explained that the sharpshooters' guns were too sharp for them. It was soon agreed that the Confederates would not fire again without giving notice. With the situation quieted down, the sharpshooters returned to their previous place on the picket line. Colonel William Rogers, commanding Doubleday's third brigade, praised the sharpshooters for their performance in his report for the battle: "Occupying the front for three days and nights, in the face of an active and wary foe, the responsibilities and duties of officers and men were of no light character, but they were assumed and performed with cheerfulness and alacrity.... I take pleasure also in testifying to the very efficient service rendered by the Second U.S. Sharpshooters, under Major Stoughton, of Colonel Phelps' brigade."[32]

After dark on the 15th Franklin's troops started their retreat across the Rappahannock over the same pontoon bridges constructed under such great duress a few days previously. By 4 A.M. the sharpshooters had made it across the bridge and were safely encamped.[33] The Federals didn't need to worry about the Confederates rushing across the pontoon bridges in pursuit, but the bridges were nonetheless cut loose and soon were swept away downstream. The withdrawal under the very noses of the Confederate pickets was a noteworthy accomplishment, one of the very few successes boasted by Burnside's forces at Fredericksburg.

While the hapless Burnside accepted complete responsibility for the debacle at Fredericksburg, within a few days he had determined to take another shot at Lee. This demonstrated a remarkable determination on his part, especially considering the difficulty of undertaking offensive operations with the onset of winter. On December 20 part of the army marched away from the heights across from Fredericksburg to move to a camp a dozen or so miles northeast. General Burnside's intention was to move the army across the Rappahannock on pontoon bridges at Banks Ford and U.S. Ford with a view of attacking Lee's army from behind the heights above Fredericksburg.[34]

Burnside ordered supplies for a ten-day operation on December 26 and directed each command to be prepared to march on a twelve-hour notice. Apparently Burnside at about this time decided to utilize the sharpshooters where needed most for true sharpshooting duties, because on December 28 the 2nd U.S.S.S. was moved from Phelps's brigade to an unattached status with a different corps. Just when Burnside was ready to commence his operation across the Rappahannock, he received a message from President Lincoln: "I have good reason for saying you must not make a general movement of the army without letting me know."[35] The general immediately informed the president that he would be in Washington the next day and would see him then. In brief, two generals from Burnside's army had met with Lincoln and informed him that Burnside's latest scheme would result in yet another, perhaps greater, defeat. It was for this reason that Burnside was directed not to move his army. Thus Burnside's plan to move across the Rappahannock was temporarily shelved.

Returning to his headquarters at Falmouth from Washington, Burnside continued to call for a movement across the Rappahannock, telling General-in-Chief Halleck, "I have no other plan of campaign for this winter and I am not disposed to go into winter quarters."[36] On January 7, Halleck finally agreed that an attempt should be made to cross the Rappahannock. The following day President Lincoln assented to Burnside's plan with the following message:

> I understand that General Halleck has sent you a letter of which this is a copy. I approve this letter. I deplore the want of concurrence in opinion with you by your general officers, but I do not see the remedy. Be cautious, and do not understand that the Government or country is driving you. I do not yet see how I could profit by changing the command of the Army of the Potomac, and if I did, I should not wish to do it by accepting the resignation of your commission. A. Lincoln[37]

Despite this authorization no movement was immediately forthcoming. Burnside set about making preparations for getting the operation underway. On January 14, 1863, Burnside gave orders for consolidating all of the sharpshooter units in the Army of the Potomac into a single command under Colonel Hiram Berdan. The 1st and 2nd U.S.S.S. would form a sharpshooter brigade, leaving their former brigade assignments according to Burnside's special order No. 14:

> IV. The regiments and companies of sharpshooters in this army will form a distinct arm of the service, and will be under the command of Colonel Berdan, as chief of sharpshooters, who will report directly to these headquarters. Detachments from this force will be sent from time to time to different grand divisions on detached service, to be used as sharpshooters.[38]

It is interesting that this order finally came about after the 2nd U.S.S.S. proved so effective at silencing Confederate picket firing on December 15. Something or someone perhaps convinced the general that Berdan's men were not simply infantrymen with a different designation, as were the Zouaves and chasseurs. Burnside's decision to implement a sharpshooter specialty was a step that, under a more capable leader, could have provided the Federal army with a distinct improvement. The Confederates did, in fact, develop sharpshooter battalions, and these proved very successful and valuable during the later part of the war. In Lee's Army of Northern Virginia sharpshooters "proved so efficient that rapidly every division was equipped with a corps. These soon became a necessary adjunct and a fixture throughout his [Lee's] entire army."[39]

As a result of Burnside's special order the 2nd "bade farewell to Phelps's brigade, which was paraded in its honor, and pitched its camp by the First regiment near Stoneman's Switch."[40] The regiment's winter camp at Stoneman's Switch was located along the railroad tracks a few miles northeast of Falmouth, situated on a hillside facing south.

On January 20, 1863, Burnside was ready to commence his operation across the Rappahannock. The general proclaimed to the troops that it was the propitious time to win a decisive victory against the rebellion, and then he sent his army out of its camps with vigor and optimism as a band played "Yankee Doodle." Berdan's sharpshooter brigade left Falmouth and marched to Bank's Ford, where, as noted, Burnside hoped to cross part his army. The sharpshooters spent that night in a wood concealed from enemy troops that were watching the ford.[41]

That night rain began to fall steadily and by morning was falling in torrents. It continued unabated for three more days. One can imagine the effect of a cold driving rain, blown by strong January winds, upon the troops making the march. But the effect that has been remembered ever since was the deep, paralyzing Virginia mud. Burnside's January offensive has since been known as the infamous "mud march." This event has been well documented in many Civil War histories because of its extremely demoralizing effect upon the army and the home front. In short, the Virginia roads turned to quagmires that trapped artillery and wagon trains. The roads were simply impassable; the heavy army traffic created a deep, slippery morass where the roads had been. Many an unfortunate soldier spent the three cold, miserable, rainy days trying to extricate draft animals and their vehicles from the clinging, seemingly bottomless mud. By the second day of the "march," General Burnside realized that the elements were against him and by the 22nd he had called the whole operation off, sending the army back to its camps north of Fredericksburg.

The sharpshooters returned to their camp at Stoneman's Switch by the 23rd. The Army of the Potomac would spend the rest of the winter in camps near Fredericksburg with a new army commander. Soon after the army returned to its camps, General Burnside traveled to Washington to meet with President Lincoln. At that meeting he informed the president that certain conditions had to be met or else he would resign from the Army. He wanted Generals Hooker, Brooks, and Newton dismissed from the Army. He also wanted Generals Franklin, W.F. Smith, Sturgis, Ferrero and Cochrane relieved from duty. Instead the president reassigned General Burnside to command of the Department of the Ohio. In his stead he appointed Major General Joseph Hooker to command of the Army of the Potomac.

While the sharpshooters camped that winter, the army and the North were experiencing the most dismal and despondent days of the war. Burnside's ineptitude dismayed an already grieving nation. All across the North the debacle at Fredericksburg was reported in the newspapers. Then came the ill-starred "mud march" orchestrated by Burnside. President Lincoln naturally suffered from guilt by association, having appointed the hapless general.

But the string of Federal military disappointments was not limited to the fighting south of Washington. On November 2, 1862, Major General Ulysses S. Grant had commenced his campaign to capture the main Confederate stronghold on the Mississippi River at Vicksburg, Mississippi. On December 29, General William Sherman, coordinating with Grant's campaign, attacked the Confederates at Chickasaw Bluffs near Vicksburg. Sherman was soundly defeated by a force less than half the size of his own, losing many times as many men as the Confederates. This action simply strengthened Lincoln's adversaries who were calling for a negotiated settlement to end the war.

Lincoln and the nation were embroiled with controversy over the Emancipation Proclamation, which the president prepared to sign and enforce on the first day of 1863. The immediate effect of the proclamation was to create division and intense disaffection in portions of the North. The resulting tension was so severe in the Midwest that for a time it was feared that the "North itself might become the scene of civil strife."[42] Many Federal soldiers, particularly in the West where a large portion of the troops had Southern roots, believed the president's move was unconstitutional. One historian noted that during that dismal winter, "a bitter and explicit disagreement about emancipation divided northern soldiers."[43] Lincoln was so concerned with disgruntlement in Ohio, Indiana and Illinois that in January 1863 he told Massachusetts Senator Charles Sumner that he feared potential rebellion in those states more than he feared Southern victory.[44]

As for the sharpshooters themselves there is little to indicate much dissatisfaction regarding Lincoln's decision to free the slaves. This is not to say that the sharpshooters did not share typical attitudes and perceptions of their day concerning the slaves themselves. But hailing from New England and Yankeedom, the men were accustomed to antislavery themes that had been shouted from pulpits, colleges, and town hall meetings throughout their entire lives. New Englanders in particular feared the southern "Slaveocracy" and had a history of abhorring servitude of any sort. Since the founding of the Republic, New Englanders had opposed wars to extend slavery, believing that slavery was incompatible with their social and economic structure. While elections in the Midwest tilted strongly against Lincoln's party after his emancipation policy became public, his party's losses in the Northeast "were minor to middling."[45] It would be safe to assume that most members of the 2nd U.S.S.S. would have sided with Lincoln in campfire arguments about emancipation.

The example of intrigues and infighting between Burnside and his fellow generals had its parallel within the sharpshooter organization. During the winter at Stoneman's Switch, turmoil and squabbling among the officers commenced almost immediately and intensified as the sharpshooters idled in camp. As one sharpshooter remembered, the officers "would find fault, often among themselves almost to an open quarrel."[46] As if to further heighten dissention, Berdan apparently carried on a personal vendetta against Lieutenant Colonel Caspar Trepp of his 1st U.S.S.S. By this stage of the war, Trepp appears to have simply wanted to walk away, having already submitted his resignation four times without acceptance. On January 25, 1863, shortly after the army's return from the "mud march," Berdan placed Trepp under arrest, preferring charges against Trepp that resulted in a court-martial.[47] Trepp was acquitted by the end of February, and in turn, Trepp filed charges of tampering with a witness against Colonel Berdan. Again the verdict was "not guilty."[48]

Berdan and Trepp were the two officers most important to the efficiency of the sharpshooter brigade, and both, the record shows, left much to be desired as leaders. While Trepp was perhaps the most capable and experienced officer available to the sharpshooters in terms of sharpshooting methods, he was too lax in enforcing discipline and military bearing during periods of inactivity. He would again be court-martialed in September 1863 for neglect of duty and failing to instruct his officers on picket duty. Trepp was found "not guilty" on the neglect charge but "guilty" on failure to instruct. He was sentenced to only a simple reprimand.[49] The "not guilty" verdicts in the court-martial proceedings only reinforced contempt for military discipline within the sharpshooter organization. Overall mediocre to poor leadership plagued these two otherwise elite regiments. The lack of dynamic and innovative leadership ultimately stunted the utility of Berdan's Sharpshooters. What the sharpshooter organization needed was an officer with tactical savvy and the flexibility to adjust and implement new methods as needs arose. Instead, the self-serving Berdan turned his attention to dealing with his adversaries. Sharpshooter Charles A. Stevens diplomatically mentioned the topic after the war: "They that handled the weapons that did the fighting, were silent lookers-on, wondering why their officers quarreled so. Was this setting a proper example?"[50]

While the two sharpshooter regiments idled in camp, some attempt was made to return to a routine that included drill when weather permitted and guard duty. The new recruits were especially in need of instruction, not having had the benefit of even basic instruction before arriving at the front. Two highlights of the winter encampment near Falmouth were the president's grand review on April 8, 1862, and the sharpshooters' regimental celebration held the following day.

Major General Joseph "Fighting Joe" Hooker, having replaced Burnside in command of the Army of the Potomac, staged a memorable grand review of his army for the president as a morale booster. The president, mounted on a bay horse, rode to the front and tipped his hat as each of the scores of regiments marched past. General Hooker had abandoned the grand division organizational system introduced by Burnside and reinstated the corps system. In March Berdan's Sharpshooter Brigade had been assigned to General Daniel Sickles' III Corps, so the 2nd U.S.S.S. went from the first of the first of the first, to the third of the third of the third: that is, the regiment now belonged to the 3rd Brigade of the 3rd Division of the III Corps. And thus the regiment passed in review with a new corps. The lengthy parade was one of the grandest spectacles of the war, and Hooker staged it on Falmouth heights in full view of the Confederates across the Rappahannock.[51]

The regimental celebration held on April 9 was apparently the brain child of Colonel Berdan, designed as a competition of target shooting and athletics. The events included off-hand shooting at 100 yards, shots from a treetop at 200 yards, a 100-, 200- and 400-yard dash, wrestling, long jumping and climbing a greased pole. Most of the prizes were won by the larger 1st U.S.S.S. The 200-yard target competition was won by Joseph Lamprey of Company F, 2nd U.S.S.S. Two men from the 1st U.S.S.S. tied for first place in the 200-yard dash at 28.5 seconds; not an especially fast time by modern standards, but taking the footwear and course conditions into consideration, it probably was good on that day. Berdan, who had just recently returned from an absence for a minor wound received at 2nd Bull Run, and at thirty-eight years of age, incredibly won the long jump competition. Berdan had produced a good idea to boost morale and break the boredom of camp routine, and it was successful in that the men of both regiments fully enjoyed the day.[52]

By mid–April, with warmer weather and fine spring days, the sharpshooters sensed that another campaign was in the offing. Morale in the army had improved somewhat since the forlorn days of mid–December. In Tennessee, Federal Major General William Rosecrans had won a narrow but hard-fought victory by blunting Confederate attacks from December 31, 1862, until January 2, 1863, near Murfreesboro. The battle eased some of the pressure on Lincoln, as he acknowledged to General Rosecrans: "I can never forget, whilst I remember anything, that you gave us a hard-earned victory, which, if there had been a defeat instead, the nation could scarcely have lived over."[53] The army in the West had done its part to turn back the rebels; now under a new commander with a reputation for hard fighting, the sharpshooters prepared to again take the offensive. Hooker "was now busy getting his troops in proper fighting trim before the campaign opened ... the days were fully occupied in ... target practice—firing by volleys, firing at will, in every position."[54] The new commander had made many changes to increase the overall efficiency and health of the Army of the Potomac. He now outnumbered Lee by more than two to one. Soon he would put his strategy and efforts to the test against Lee on the other side of the Rappahannock.

7

At Their Best: Chancellorsville

Major General Joseph Hooker was conceited, intemperate and immodest, traits that in combination could doom any man's chances in life. Despite these character flaws and a number of indiscretions, Lincoln turned to this man to replace General Burnside as commander of the Army of the Potomac. The president had made his calculations, weighed his alternatives and determined that Joseph Hooker, despite his abundant flaws, was the man for the job. To this point the general had proven himself as an aggressive combat commander. After his appointment, during the long gloomy winter, he showed that he was also a creditable organizer and administrator. Soon he would gather his reorganized and reconstituted army and confidently sally forth in pursuit of Lee and his army.

The new commander had the qualities—he was handsome, intelligent, confident and capable—to corrupt a man with hubris. Born in 1814 in Massachusetts, Hooker was a West Point graduate and Mexican War veteran. Three times he was brevetted for gallantry in Mexico, yet he managed to provoke intense animosity from one of America's all-time greatest generals—Winfield Scott. Hooker revealed his proclivity for indiscretion by conspiring against General Scott and by earning a reputation as a hard drinker and philanderer. With Scott aligned against him, Hooker saw little chance for a career in the Army. He resigned after the Mexican War and took up farming in California. With the Civil War looming on the horizon, Hooker joined the California militia and rose to the rank of colonel, this time quarreling with Henry Halleck, his then commander in the militia. Resigning from the militia, he traveled east to seek a commission in the Army at the outbreak of hostilities. It was President Lincoln who gave Hooker his opportunity by making him a brigadier general of volunteers in spite of General Scott's opposition.[1]

By the time Joseph Hooker had replaced Burnside in command of the Army of the Potomac he was already marked for his perfidy and self-aggrandizement. But more importantly he had earned a reputation for aggression on the battlefield and for urging action from his commanders. During the Seven Days' battles, at 2nd Bull Run and again at Antietam, he had demonstrated admirable fighting spirit, his courage especially evident at Antietam, where he was wounded and carried from the field. To Lincoln he seemed to be the best choice for what was desperately needed—a fighting general.

After assuming command following the "mud march," Hooker implemented several effective changes for the good of the Army of the Potomac. His efforts resulted in better rations, improved sanitation, an improved command structure, and a separate cavalry corps. Hooker also introduced a new bureau to gather military intelligence and a new corps of army scouts. After a few months with Hooker in charge, a New York soldier noted that the camps had never been cleaner and the rations, with the introduction of soft bread, were never better.[2]

During the winter Hooker utilized his intelligence assets to seek a means of striking at Lee without repeating the blunders of his predecessor. In February Lee had dispatched General Longstreet with Hood's and Pickett's divisions to southern Virginia; thereafter, until Longstreet returned, Lee was outnumbered roughly 135,000 to 60,000. Hooker also learned that while the crossings of the Rappahannock near Fredericksburg were strongly defended, the fords farther upriver were not. By the end of April Hooker had devised a plan to get his army across the Rappahannock and away from the formidable Confederate defenses around Fredericksburg, hoping to get at Lee's outnumbered army in open country. On April 27, 1863, Hooker dispatched the V, XI, and XII Corps to cross the river at Kelly's Ford, several miles upstream from the well-guarded fords. He kept Major General John Sedgwick's VI Corps and the I Corps active in the Fredericksburg area and the III Corps temporarily in place at Falmouth to distract attention from the crossing upstream. The plan worked to near perfection; by the morning of the 30th all three corps had crossed the river, and the III Corps was nearing United States Ford on the Rappahannock.[3]

On the afternoon of the 30th the V Corps and XII Corps reached their rendezvous point at Chancellorsville, a few miles west of Fredericksburg, and the XI Corps was not far behind. Hooker's plans had gone off without a hitch. From his Falmouth headquarters Hooker announced General Orders No. 47:

> It is with heartfelt satisfaction the commanding general announces to the army that the operations of the last three days have determined that our enemy must either ingloriously fly, or come out from behind his defenses and give us battle on our own ground, where certain destruction awaits him.
> The operations of the Fifth, Eleventh and Twelfth Corps have been a succession of splendid achievements.
> By command of General Hooker[4]:

Hooker's announcement was in character, and in this case, at least, there was good reason to believe it. Unfortunately, he did absolutely nothing to fulfill his prophecy. His generalship in the ensuing battle was timid, somewhat like what would be expected from George McClellan. Instead of going after the Confederates, he seemingly expected them to "ingloriously fly."

The 2nd U.S.S.S. commenced the Chancellorsville Campaign on the afternoon of April 28, marching from Stoneman's Switch to the Rappahannock below Fredericksburg. This move was apparently part of Hooker's deception to distract attention from the crossing of the three corps at Kelly's Ford. Each man was supplied with sixty rounds and eight days' rations, and two men from each company carried an apparatus for climbing trees. The following afternoon the regiment marched via an indirect route to United States Ford, north of Chancellorsville. This was a very fatiguing march of about twenty miles in full gear. On the morning of May 1, 1863, the sharpshooters crossed the Rappahannock at United States Ford and proceeded down United States Ford Road to the crossroads at Chancellorsville.[5]

That afternoon the sharpshooters heard the distant rumblings of artillery and musket fire from the east. The vanguard of Hooker's army had clashed with Confederates along the Orange Turnpike. Upon report of this action Hooker recalled his forces and assumed a defensive posture around Chancellorsville. He arranged his army to stretch on his left from the Rappahannock to Chancellorsville and on his right along the Orange Turnpike to the west of the intersection of the turnpike and the Orange Plank Road. Meade's V Corps held the left, Couch's II Corps and Slocum's XII Corps hooked around Chancellorsville, Sickles's III Corps was next on the right and Howard's XI Corps held the extreme right.

Hooker's troop dispositions indicate that his priority in positioning his forces was to cover his retreat route rather than deploying for an offensive. Just as his announcement of the 30th stated, he was waiting for the enemy to retreat or to attack him. Hooker certainly could and should have chosen a better place to fight a defensive battle than the tangled, forested region around Chancellorsville locally known as "the Wilderness." The general himself later admitted that he lost his confidence after crossing the Rappahannock.[6] His objective very soon shifted to preventing a defeat rather than seeking a decisive victory, a baffling ratiocination considering he outnumbered Lee two to one. Hooker thusly relinquished the initiative to Lee and waited to react.

Meanwhile Lee reacted by shifting his army from Fredericksburg to Chancellorsville. Only Jubal Early's Division was left behind to block the Federal VI Corps at Fredericksburg. On the evening of May 1, Lee met with Stonewall Jackson to devise a plan for attacking Hooker at Chancellorsville. Jackson proposed a flanking movement to attack the Federal right with his entire corps. Although the plan left Lee with only 14,000 men to face Hooker's 75,000 on the field, Lee gambled that Hooker would not attack. Lee approved the plan. Jackson would march his corps on a day-long twelve-mile march through the thickets in front of Hooker's army. He would mass his corps for an attack on Howard's Federal XI Corps after completing his flanking march.[7]

At sunrise on May 2, 1863, the sharpshooters' corps commander, Major General Daniel Sickles, rode out with General Hooker to inspect the Federal lines to the west of Chancellorsville. From this it is obvious that Hooker intended to wait for Lee to make the next move. On returning to headquarters, Hooker ordered Sickles "to make a reconnaissance in front and to the left of Chancellorsville." The combative Sickles was happy to comply, sending out the 11th Massachusetts and 26th Pennsylvania. "A detachment of Berdan's Sharpshooters, from Whipple's division, accompanied each regiment." The accompanying sharpshooters were apparently from Companies E and K of the 1st U.S.S.S. The remainder of Berdan's two regiments remained in the lines near Chancellorsville that morning.[8]

This reconnaissance encountered Lee's skirmishers and pickets fronting his position east of Chancellorsville. There was some sharp skirmishing during the reconnaissance and differing accounts of the sharpshooters' performance emerged after the battle. According to sharpshooter Charles Stevens years after the battle, the infantry pressed too close to the enemy and suffered "considerable," but the two detachments of sharpshooters actively dodged through the woods and "wonderfully escaped."[9]

However, this story does not match the account from the battle report of Lt. Colonel Porter Tripp of the 11th Massachusetts Infantry. According to Colonel Tripp, the "sharpshooters sent with the regiment shamefully ran away from the enemy's fire," so the colonel was forced to "advance his own men, armed only with smooth-bore Springfield muskets, to take their place."[10] This report was echoed by Colonel William Bliasdell in his report for the 1st Brigade. Bliasdell noted that the sharpshooters were impossible to keep at the front and were censured in "the highest terms" for their conduct during the reconnaissance.[11] The Massachusetts men were armed with Model 1842 Smoothbore Muskets, little better than shotguns, putting them at a great disadvantage as skirmishers. This would explain why the infantry in Stevens's account pressed so closely with the enemy.

This was not the first or only time that the 1st U.S.S.S. drew criticism when operating with infantry. There was an increasing dislike for sharpshooters from both armies as the war progressed. Most mention of the sharpshooters in official reports was favorable, but the Federal Army never fully developed and utilized the sharpshooter concept. It is possible that the unfavorable perception of infantry commanders, unfamiliar with sharpshooter techniques, ultimately hindered the expansion and development of sharpshooter units in the Federal Army.

General Sickles turned his attention from the probe east of Chancellorsville to "reports in quick succession from General Birney, that a column of the enemy was moving along his front to our right." Sickles reported this information to Hooker and also to General Howard, who held the Federal right where the rebel column was headed. At noon Sickles was ordered to "advance cautiously toward the road followed by the enemy, and harass the movement as much as possible." Sickles sent for Berdan's Sharpshooters "to be deployed as skirmishers and as flankers, so as to get all possible knowledge of the enemy's movement and of the approaches to his line of march."[12]

The Confederate column reported by General Birney was from General Jackson's corps marching on the Furnace Road on their way to attack the Federal right. Of course General Hooker only knew that the enemy column was moving away from Chancellorsville. He was left to ponder whether the movement signaled a retreat or an attempt to attack his right. Hooker must have hoped that the advance by Sickles would shed some light on the enemy's intentions.

Berdan's Sharpshooters were utilized in their appropriate role by Sickles, taking the lead in the advance, followed immediately by the 20th Indiana Infantry. The sharpshooters crossed Scott's Run over a makeshift rail bridge and deployed to engage enemy skirmishers. Passing through a dense thicket the sharpshooters began exchanging shots with skirmishers from the 23rd Georgia Infantry. Emerging from the woods the sharpshooters pressed the Georgians through a level field, "the cover being poor, the cedar trees, although numerous, small in size." A company of Georgians took cover at a foundry building where the road made a sharp turn to the south; the ruins of this place are now known on the Chancellorsville National Battlefield as Catharine Furnace.[13]

At this point, according to Colonel Berdan, "I then advanced my right and left, with flankers from the Second Regiment, and kept up so accurate and rapid a fire that the enemy dared not leave the cover of the building. I then ordered my men to cease firing, and called upon the rebels to surrender, upon which they came in, after throwing down their arms and showing a white rag." A major and sixty men from the 23rd Georgia surrendered at Catharine Furnace and were quickly sent to the rear.[14]

Soon Berdan had the sharpshooters moving forward again. It was slow work dodging for cover, drawing fire from the rebels to disclose their position and then forcing them back. At one point during this advance the rebels had a chance to enfilade the left flank of the 2nd U.S.S.S. Captain Dudley Chase of Company A, seeing the danger, directed the line to react to this threat. The captain was hit and mortally wounded at this moment; he died from his wounds on May 8.[15]

The companies by this point were probably spread in a long skirmish line, each man approximately six feet apart and taking advantage of cover while advancing. A portion of the 2nd U.S.S.S. directed their attention to Jackson's wagon train as it passed on the Furnace Road and fired into it. During the advance the sharpshooters overran a disabled enemy artillery caisson, its draft horses being wounded. At a nearby creek the caisson was wrecked and dumped, ammunition and all, into the water.[16]

Colonel Best of the 23rd Georgia stationed about forty men in the Furnace Road to protect the wagon train, and at least two companies from the 14th Tennessee Infantry arrived to assist Best and his Georgians.[17] These troops were assailed by a portion of the 2nd U.S.S.S. Several Confederate infantrymen and two ambulances were captured by men from the 2nd along the road while the 1st U.S.S.S. engaged and pushed back the bulk of the 23rd Georgia.[18]

Soon after the company of Confederates surrendered at the foundry, Colonel Best pulled the remainder of his men, less the forty he left on the road, back to an excavated segment of an unfinished railroad bed, or railroad cut, south of the foundry. Today the area is overgrown with trees and brush, but during the battle the railroad cut was bordered on each side by a wide cleared space. This provided an open field of fire for the Confederates and shelter from return fire. According to Colonel Berdan, "I caused my left to gradually advance, keeping the attention of the enemy by desultory firing while I rapidly pushed forward my right in the woods until I had outflanked them and opened fire."[19]

Colonel Best and his Georgians were charged with keeping the Federals away from Jackson's trains on the Furnace Road, which the unfinished railroad crossed south of Catharine Furnace. Berdan's flanking movement trapped Best and his regiment so quickly that, according to Best, "It was too late to bring out the regiment, except those that escaped after the enemy closed upon us." The sharpshooters' fire so disoriented Best that he thought he was facing at least a full brigade, or as he put it, "I was attacked by a division."[20]

Instead of facing a division of thousands, Best was pinned down by a few hundred sharpshooters strung out in a very thin line on his front. But the sharpshooters poured in an accurate fire that convinced the Confederates that they were surrounded.

A soldier from the 23rd Georgia described the situation from the Confederates' perspective many years after the battle:

> ...we were flanked on both ends of our line. We held them back in front, but our line was too short. Our only chance was to climb an eight- or ten-foot embankment and retreat or go to a Northern prison.... I had divested myself of all my accouterments and felt that I could run a quarter of a mile ... so I climbed the bank in our rear and set out alone for a run of some two hundred and fifty yards to a skirt of timber that would hide me from them. When I had climbed a slight grade and could see the Minie balls strike the ground in front of me, I wished I were back in the cut; but I had started and would not turn back, so I made it to cover without a scratch.[21]

Most of the Georgians remained in the cut or dodged back into it when the bullets struck around them. Colonel Best and a few of his men managed to get away, but the bulk of the 23rd Georgia surrendered at the railroad cut. In his report on May 8, 1863, Colonel Best gave an estimate of his losses in the fighting with Berdan's Sharpshooters:

> As far as I have been able to ascertain, my loss in prisoners was 26 officers and 250 enlisted men. This includes my killed and wounded; how many of either I am unable to state. I only know of my own knowledge that Lieutenant [T.P.] Foster and Lieutenant [R.E.] Lawhorn were badly wounded, and one man killed and several wounded. Most of my officers having been taken, I am unable to give a correct list of the casualties during the time I engaged the enemy at the furnace. I neglected to state that my colors were saved, which I desire to mention in connection with this.[22]

According to Colonel Berdan his two sharpshooter regiments captured 365 Confederates, including nineteen officers, "among whom was the major of the regiment."[23] The exact number of Georgians killed and wounded in the fighting that day will probably never be known. The report given for the regiment could not have included an accounting of those shot during the fighting at the furnace and the railroad cut. From Best's report we know of at least one man killed and several wounded.

Of interest regarding this battle was the involvement of Chaplain Lorenzo Barber of the 2nd U.S.S.S. The good chaplain was a noted marksman. During the fighting around the furnace, Chaplain Barber, according to a few accounts, took a target rifle and joined in the fighting. The term "fighting parson" was by no means unique during the Civil War, but Chaplain Barber more than earned the title with his pluck at Chancellorsville.

Not surprisingly there was some measure of disagreement over who captured the 23rd Georgia that day. At least three regiments laid some claim to the feat. Brigadier General J.H. Hobart Ward, brigade commander of the 20th Indiana, gave credit to that regiment for "capturing nearly the whole of the Twenty-third Georgia Regiment."[24] The 2nd U.S.S.S. had some part in helping force the Georgians to surrender, and it is quite possible that some skirmishers from the 20th Indiana also took part at the railroad cut. However, it seems from most accounts that the Georgians at the railroad cut surrendered to men from the 1st U.S.S.S. and were escorted to the rear by men from that regiment.[25] Colonel Samuel Hayman, who commanded the brigade in action near the railroad cut, gave credit to the sharpshooters for capturing the 23rd Georgia. According to Colonel Hayman, "The sharpshooters understand the true tactics of skirmishers, are possessed of enterprise and courage.... I regard it as one of the best organizations of the volunteer service."[26]

By the time the sharpshooters had swept away the Georgians, Jackson's trains were exiting the area. As General Sickles was preparing to follow up the sharpshooters' success with an attack on the escaping wagons, he was informed that Howard's XI Corps on the Federal right had been routed. The sweeping rebel attack had already reached the rear of Sickles' III Corps and threatened to cut him off from the rest of Hooker's army.

General Sickles recalled his troops, including Berdan's men, sending them back along the same route on which they had advanced shortly after noon. By 7 P.M. the Confederates had pushed the Federal XI Corps almost to Chancellorsville and occupying the ground directly in front of Sickles's troops. Shortly after 9 P.M. Sickles had the leading elements of his corps back to the Hazel Grove vicinity just southwest of the main Federal line around Chancellorsville. Hazel Grove was an important strategic point on the battlefield, separating the wings of Lee's army. Hooker could launch a counterattack from its heights to effectively slice the Confederate army in half. Over the next few hours Sickles's corps went into position to defend Hazel Grove, first with cavalry and artillery and later with infantry.[27]

The weary sharpshooters formed on the extreme left of Sickles's corps backing up the 1st U.S.S.S. The position held by the sharpshooters during the night of May 2 was just behind a small stream, so an attack by the enemy would be slowed by this natural barrier. That night the Confederate advance was checked at Hazel Grove and along the turnpike near Chancellorsville. It was clear to the sharpshooters that the fortunes of war had completely reversed for them — that afternoon they had trapped the enemy, now it seemed that they might be caught in a trap. Sickles's position was tenuous and in danger of being overrun.

After a weary night illuminated by bright moonlight and intermittent flashes of musketry and artillery fire, the sharpshooters waited for the battle to renew on the far left of Sickles's line. About dawn a Confederate foray swept along the stream across from the sharpshooters, but Hooker had ordered Sickles to withdraw to Fairview Heights near Chancellorsville. So the sharpshooters pulled back to a position north of the turnpike and just east of the Chancellor House.

General Stonewall Jackson was severely wounded while making an inspection of the Federal lines after dusk on the 2nd, apparently accidentally by Confederates who mistook his mounted party for Federal cavalry. Major General J.E.B. Stuart, the famous Confederate cavalry commander, assumed command of Jackson's corps and renewed the assault on May 3. As the III Corps evacuated Hazel Grove, the Confederates quickly followed to occupy the high ground. Soon Colonel E. Porter Alexander had thirty cannon in position at Hazel Grove to shell the Federals at Fairview Heights. Very soon thereafter a devastating artillery bombardment presaged a fierce infantry attack along the turnpike just west of Chancellorsville.[28]

7 — At Their Best

The Battle of Chancellorsville had now assumed a familiar routine for the ill-starred Army of the Potomac. Hooker's defensive posture doomed the Federals to a severe pummeling. Lee was in a much more precarious position than Hooker, yet the Federal commander seemed oblivious, reacting as if his army were in extreme peril. Now Lee would go after Hooker like a boxer after a dazed opponent on the ropes. Fortunately for the 2nd U.S.S.S., the worst of the punishment would be inflicted on other portions of the field.

On the morning of May 3, 1863, both of Berdan's regiments spent the morning in advance of Hooker's line, north of the turnpike and Chancellor House and near the road leading to United States Ford. Of the two regiments the 1st U.S.S.S. was closer to the action and suffered the heavier losses. The 2nd U.S.S.S. was positioned by Berdan as a reserve to the right of his other regiment. Still, both regiments were at the front as Stuart's infantry attack struck the Federals.

Throughout the morning the Federals were being pressed into a compact mass surrounding the Chancellor House with the remaining corps of the army holding the roads leading to fords and bridges on the Rappahannock. Around 9 A.M. General Hooker was standing on the porch of the Chancellor House when a rebel shell struck and splintered a porch pillar; a large piece of the shattered pillar stuck the general square on the head, stunning him and rendering him insensible. Trauma from the blow certainly must have affected Hooker as he was recovering, because he soon ordered his army to pull back to a defensive position nearer to the Rappahannock. Whatever fight "Fighting Joe Hooker" had left was snuffed following the incident on the Chancellor porch.

Lee regrouped around Chancellorsville and prepared to launch yet another assault on Hooker's redeployed lines that afternoon. The two days of fighting had jaded the men of both armies, but Lee was determined to press his advantage. During this lull the sharpshooters busily constructed light breastworks for shelter against a renewed attack. As Lee prepared to send his troops against Hooker's makeshift line, he received a message informing him that Sedgwick's VI Corps was attacking at Fredericksburg. Sedgwick's approach from Fredericksburg would leave Lee vulnerable to an attack from the rear, so he dispatched a portion of his force to meet that threat. As the situation developed, Lee sent almost half of his troops away to meet Sedgwick. An attack on Hooker was out of the question. Unfortunately for the Federals, Hooker was in such an apprehensive state of mind that he would not even probe Lee's lines, so no attack was forthcoming.[29]

On May 4 Lee's attention was centered around fighting at Salem Church on the turnpike between Chancellorsville and Fredericksburg. Hooker kept his army behind its new defensive works and waited. That morning the 2nd relieved Berdan's 1st Sharpshooters in front of the III Corps for skirmish and picket line duty. Rebel sharpshooters were very active that morning, picking off artillery gunners and causing numerous casualties in the III Corps lines. Major General Amiel Whipple, the sharpshooters' division commander, stood behind the skirmish line talking with Colonel Berdan when he was apparently hit by a shot fired by a Confederate sharpshooter. Charles Smith of Company B witnessed the incident and remembered years later:

The bullet struck him just above the left hip, passing through his sword-belt and downward to the groin. I stood about three rods from him when he was shot, and saw him fall. A gentleman made his appearance, which was said to be the General's private priest, and the ceremony at that time was a new sight to me. I helped to carry the General to the rear. I think it was a brick house near United States Ford where the General had led us across two or three days before. The General died the first night after his wound.[30]

Colonel Berdan got up a detail of volunteers to chase off the rebel sharpshooters. According to Berdan, "We drove the advanced skirmishers to their rifle-pits, and held the ground gained, so that no more casualties occurred from the enemy's fire."[31]

Hooker's inertia on the 4th is somewhat baffling. Other senior officers were expecting to attack while the enemy was divided. In the past, in a subordinate role, Hooker had criticized General McClellan for his lack of aggression, and for failing to attack Confederate lines separated by the Chickahominy River during the fighting around Richmond in 1862.[32] Now facing a similar situation, Hooker followed the precedent he once strongly denounced. The burden of responsibility clearly deflated Fighting Joe, and he failed the army at that crucial moment of ultimate weighing.

While Hooker awaited his opportunity to retreat, the 2nd U.S.S.S. remained on the skirmish line in the woods in front of the Federal breastworks. Towards evening some firing on the right of the sharpshooters was mistaken for a Confederate attack, and the Federal artillery opened on the sharpshooters before they could pull back from the skirmish line. The 11th New Jersey Infantry was posted behind the 2nd as a support, and, seeing the artillery striking the sharpshooters' position, the 11th opened fire on the sharpshooters too, apparently mistaking them for the enemy. "Shouts and gestures proved of no avail, several men tried to creep back to the Union lines to tell them to stop firing," but the unnerved infantrymen kept firing into the sharpshooters. Finally the 11th New Jersey fell back and the sharpshooters scampered into the Federal lines and took cover. At least five men from the 2nd U.S.S.S. were wounded by friendly fire that evening; Berdan placed the blame on the New Jersey regiment. After the firing ceased the sharpshooters returned to their former position on the skirmish line, finding the enemy had departed. By 10 P.M. the men on the skirmish line were recalled and allowed to rest for the night.[33]

Learning that Sedgwick had been checked at Salem Church, Hooker ordered his entire army to retreat across the Rappahannock. By the morning of May 6, 1863, the Army of the Potomac was safely across the river, and another promising campaign had utterly failed. Much of the army was bitterly disappointed, as one would expect, by the outcome of an offensive once trumpeted by their commander as a sure success. However, it is probable that the sharpshooters did not hold the defeat against Hooker to a great extent and continued to think well of him, especially when compared to General Burnside.

Even without the benefit of comprehensive sources on the subject, it is nevertheless safe to assume that many sharpshooters placed the blame for the defeat at Chancellorsville on the "Dutchmen" of Howard's XI Corps. In fact Sergeant Darius Starr of

Company F gave a fair indication of his comrades' opinion in a letter to his brother dated May 22, 1863. In his letter Starr mentioned that the "Dutchmen" from Major General Carl Schurz's 3rd Division of the XI Corps broke at the first charge of the rebels.[34] A look at the colonels and brigade commanders of Schurz's Division reveals an almost complete roster of German names: Schimmelfennig, Hecker, Braun, Koenig and so forth. General Schurz himself was a German immigrant with political ties to the Republican Party and President Lincoln, and he owed his position as a general to his years as Lincoln's political ally. Thus it was well known that the XI Corps was a "Dutch" or German immigrant outfit.

Further evidence of the sharpshooters' negative opinion of the XI Corps was revealed in an article written by a sharpshooter about the battle, years after the war:

> If it will not be out of order I will say that while on our way to establish the skirmish line that day we passed through the breastworks and protections thrown up by the Eleventh Corps and the remark was often made by some of the boys that we would consider ourselves very fortunate to be attacked by the rebels in such works as those. Indeed they looked impregnable. And I have heard the remark made since by many of my old regiment, that Griffin's old Division of the Fifth Corps, or Birney's old Division of the Third Corps could, in their opinion, repulse Jackson's 20,000 men.[35]

As for the men of the 2nd, they felt that "Sharpshooter stock" was at a premium. One of the sharpshooters noted that General Hooker himself had again praised them, as he had to Colonel Post after Antietam, this time saying that he would have driven the rebels if the rest of the army had fought as well as they did.[36] Indeed, Chancellorsville was an example of the sharpshooters at their best. The 2nd U.S.S.S. suffered two officers and eight men wounded and six men missing, five of the wounded being victims of friendly fire from the 11th New Jersey Infantry.[37] In contrast, the sharpshooters accounted for hundreds of Confederate casualties. Chancellorsville unequivocally demonstrated the value of Berdan's Sharpshooters as skirmishers, scouts and light infantry with a signal success in the capture of the 23rd Georgia Infantry.

8

"Turning the Tide": Gettysburg

The sharpshooters returned to their old camp near Falmouth following the fighting at Chancellorsville, marching through a heavy rain over muddy roads. A sharpshooter remembered that the weary soldiers took "the opportunity to rail at one another jestingly" to relieve their fatigue and disappointment during the return march. They would jokingly mock passing outfits with calls such as, "There's another played out set!" He also remembered with sadness the cheers given by the sharpshooters when the hard-fighting Iron Brigade passed on the route, for it wasn't long before that famous brigade of Westerners was decimated in the forthcoming campaign. There would be a very short interval before the army would again clash with Lee's host in the pivotal campaign of the war.[1]

Chancellorsville is considered by most historians as General Lee's greatest victory, a masterpiece of tactical maneuvering. But the battle did nothing to alter the strategic stalemate in the Eastern Theater. Lee himself realized that nothing of value had been gained by the sanguinary fighting except affording the Confederates with an opportunity to go on the offensive. And that is exactly what Lee wanted.

Confederate secretary of war James Seddon did not agree. The situation at Vicksburg, Mississippi, was going against the Confederates. General Ulysses Grant had won a series of battles and would soon besiege that vital stronghold on the Mississippi River. Secretary Seddon wanted two of Lee's divisions, Hood's and Pickett's, sent to reinforce General Joseph Johnston's army with a view of driving Grant away from Vicksburg. President Jefferson Davis, himself a Mississippian, also believed that Vicksburg should be a priority.[2]

On May 14, 1863, General Lee went to Richmond to present his views to President Davis and his cabinet. More than anything, Robert E. Lee was a Virginian. He wanted the scourge of war removed from his native state. To Lee the situation in Mississippi was uncertain, even with reinforcements from his army. Lee argued for a renewed offensive into the North, a sort of repeat of the Maryland Campaign of September 1862 for basically the same reasons.[3] After Chancellorsville, where he defeated an army twice the size of his own, Lee felt confident that he could succeed with a second invasion of Pennsylvania, this time threatening the region of the North most determined to subdue the Confederacy. A victory or victories on Northern soil would strengthen Northern Democrats calling for a negotiated settlement of the war. Just as important, winning in the North would encourage European powers to recognize the Confederacy and perhaps result in a better supply situation for the Confederacy.

President Davis ultimately had to decide between Lee's persuasive arguments and his own priorities at this crucial point in the war. Lee's status as a proven winner, coupled with his commanding noble bearing, prevailed. By a vote of five to one Lee won approval for his second invasion plan.[4] In effect Davis agreed to seek a significant turn of events to quickly gain the upper hand in the war. His other option would be a vote for a prolonged war; he would have to grind down the will of Northerners and maintain the stalemate in the East. In approving Lee's invasion plan Davis risked the Confederacy's hope of winning a conventional war, but by the same decision he selected the best option for winning the war outright.

As the weeks passed in camp the sharpshooters were occupied with the same routine they had always practiced during lulls between battles: drilling, sick call, reviews, and picket duty along the Rappahannock. Occasionally the sharpshooters would go out miles from camp for picket duty, reporting enemy movements and so forth. The usual camp rumors and politicking for promotion continued in full sway. Nevertheless the men sensed that their time idling at Falmouth wouldn't last as it had the previous summer.

By June 5 General Hooker had indications that the Confederates were moving out of their camps around Fredericksburg. Hooker surmised that the troop movements were "for no other purpose but to enable the enemy to move up the river, with a view to the execution of a movement similar to that of Lee's last year. He must have it in mind to cross the Upper Potomac, or to throw his army between mine and Washington, in case I am correct in my conjecture." Hooker had guessed correctly that Lee had another invasion in mind; but instead of moving to intercept Lee, Hooker wanted to "pitch into his rear" south of the Rappahannock. Lincoln very quickly responded with a message to Hooker, the crux of which advised against crossing the river: "I would not take any risk of being entangled upon the river, like an ox jumped half over a fence and liable to be torn by dogs front and rear, without a fair chance to gore one way or kick the other." The president wanted Hooker to move north to meet Lee before he could cross the Potomac.[5]

Having failed to secure support for his plan to cross the Rappahannock, Hooker informed Halleck on the following day that he was sending his cavalry under Brigadier General Alfred Pleasanton to break up Stuart's cavalry concentrated near Culpeper. Pleasanton carried out this assignment on June 9, resulting in a massive cavalry battle at Brandy Station. After a day-long fight the Federals pulled back across the Rappahannock, having held their own against Stuart's renowned troopers.

On June 10, 1863, General Lee sent General Richard Ewell and his Confederate II Corps into the Shenandoah Valley towards Winchester as the opening phase of his plan to invade Pennsylvania. The cavalry battle at Brandy Station took Stuart's troopers out of the mix for at least a week, but Lee was pressing on nevertheless. Within a week Ewell's troops captured Winchester and several thousand Federal troops. Soon Ewell was on his way to the Pennsylvania border. On June 15, the day Ewell captured Winchester, Lee dispatched Longstreet's I Corps from Culpeper and A.P. Hill's III Corps from Fredericksburg to follow Ewell into Pennsylvania.[6]

At this point Hooker seemed to be out of his element as an army commander. He continued to seek permission to march away from Lee's army, asking the president for permission "to march to Richmond at once," believing he could beat Lee to the Confederate capital. Less than two hours after receiving Hooker's message President Lincoln replied that "Lee's army" and not Richmond should be Hooker's "objective point." Lincoln wanted Hooker to remain on the inside track and to strike Lee "when opportunity offers." Soon Hooker learned of the Confederate movements into the Northern Shenandoah Valley, and he began to shift the Army of the Potomac northward out of necessity.[7]

The 2nd U.S.S.S. broke camp on June 11 as part of Hooker's effort to follow the president's advice in keeping his army on the inside track while following Lee northward. In June both of Berdan's regiments were transferred into the 1st Division of the III Corps as part of Brigadier General John H.H. Ward's 2nd Brigade. Berdan retained command of both regiments as a sort of demi-brigade under Ward's overall command. Hard marching brought the sharpshooters through Catlett's Station to the Manassas and Centerville vicinity by the 15th.

Hooker kept the army spread between Leesburg and Manassas, south of the Potomac, until June 25.[8] On June 24 Homer Stoughton was promoted to lieutenant colonel, and he would serve as commanding officer of the 2nd U.S.S.S. for the following year. Lieutenant Colonel Peteler, whom Stoughton replaced, was discharged on June 23. Stoughton would be the last officer from the 2nd to hold the rank of lieutenant colonel.

With Lee's troops marching through Pennsylvania, Hooker finally moved north to keep the Army of the Potomac between Lee and the District of Columbia. The sharpshooters marched thirty-two miles on June 26 from Gum Springs, Virginia, to Point of Rocks, Maryland, probably the hardest march the regiment ever made in a single day.[9] The next day Hooker, apparently unsettled over having to defend Harpers Ferry while Lee was roaming in Pennsylvania, submitted his resignation from command of the Army of the Potomac. Hooker wrote, "I am unable to comply with this condition with the means at my disposal, and earnestly request that I may at once be relieved from the position I occupy."[10] That same day Hooker's resignation was accepted and Major General George G. Meade was ordered to take command of the Army of the Potomac. By 7 A.M. on June 28 Meade had received his orders and replied to General-in-Chief Halleck that he would accept the "unexpected" assignment and move "towards the Susquehanna." Meade did not attempt to conceal his unprepared and perhaps unqualified condition, writing: "So soon as I can post myself up, I will communicate more in detail."[11]

The new army commander was another unexpected and curious choice by Lincoln. Perhaps the president was looking for a steady hand after Hooker's erratic term as commander. Born in 1815, George Gordon Meade was a West Point graduate and experienced military professional. Tall, gaunt, bookish and irascible, Meade resembled an indignant middle-aged professor, wire-rimmed spectacles sometimes pressed down over his very baggy blue eyes. To his credit Meade had compiled a record of steady competence in the Army. He had served as a brigade, division and corps commander, participating in several major battles with the Army of the Potomac. Seriously wounded at Glendale, he recovered in time to participate in the Battles of Bull Run, Antietam, Fredericksburg and Chancellorsville. To those familiar with the general, his peppery personality was his hallmark.[12]

By evening of his first day in command Meade had studied reports on Confederate movements in Pennsylvania and determined to move his army towards York, Pennsylvania. The following morning Meade sent a report to General-in-Chief Halleck informing him that he was still waiting to react to Lee's movements, and he was concentrating his army in the Emmitsburg and Taneytown area of northern Maryland. Meade intended to keep his army in place to protect Baltimore, or if Lee attempted to cross the Susquehanna River, he would "fall upon his rear and give him battle."[13] The sharpshooters marched about twenty miles on June 29 to near Taneytown and on the 30th camped near Emmitsburg.

Major General George G. Meade, commander of the Army of the Potomac from Gettysburg until the close of the war. Library of Congress Civil War Collection.

On July 1, 1863, the sharpshooters marched through Emmitsburg in a steady rain, the muddy road making the march more difficult and tiring. At about noon Meade sent a message to Halleck to inform him that he was preparing a defensive position near Pipe Creek, "between Middleburg and Manchester," in case Lee decided to attack. That defensive line would not be needed. Within one hour Meade had learned that the Confederates were advancing on Gettysburg. Meade correctly observed, "I expect the battle will begin today."[14]

As the sharpshooters were pitching their tents to camp north of Emmitsburg, the roar of musketry and artillery carried from the intense fighting west of Gettysburg, about eleven miles to the north. Throughout the day on July 1 the Federals were pushed back through the town as both armies concentrated and fed men into the fight. At about 5 P.M. the sharpshooters were ordered to pack up and march toward the sound of the fighting. The regiment bivouacked that night on the battlefield south of Gettysburg just east of the Emmitsburg Road. News of the severe fighting around the town spread

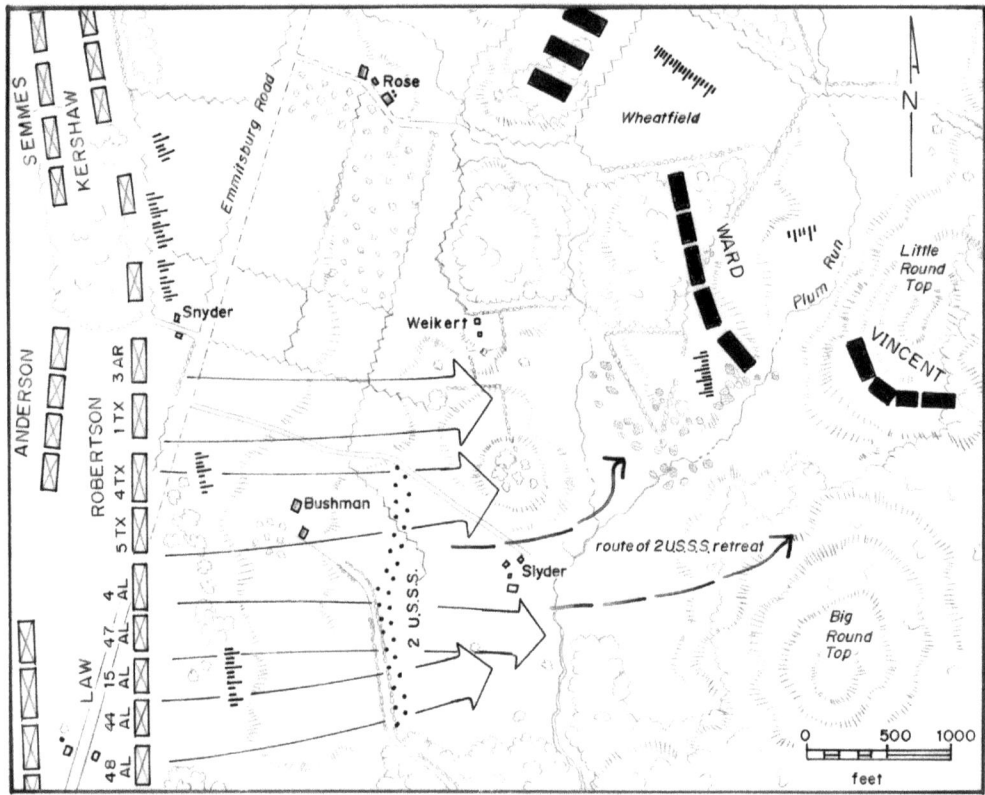

The Battle of Gettysburg, July 2, 1863. Map by John Heiser.

through the army with remarkable speed. Not long after the sharpshooters reached their bivouac they learned that the I Corps had been driven through Gettysburg and General Reynolds had been killed.[15]

On the morning of July 2, the Federals occupied a long curving defensive line formed on the hills and ridges south of Gettysburg. The Federal right was anchored southeast of town on Culp's Hill by the XII Corps. Connecting next on the left was the battered XI Corps on Cemetery Hill just south of Gettysburg. This corps had been shamed at Chancellorsville and on the previous day had again broken and fled through Gettysburg before regrouping south of town. The I Corps occupied the ground just south of the cemetery and east of the Emmitsburg Road, followed on the left by Hancock's II Corps. General Sickles's III Corps occupied the extreme left below the II Corps. Two Federal corps remained: the V Corps was held in reserve along the Baltimore Pike south of Culp's hill, and the VI Corps had not yet reached the battlefield.

The 2nd was awakened before dawn and marched to a position on the extreme left of the Federal army near two large wooded hills known as Little Round Top and Big Round Top. Soon the 2nd was ordered out to watch for approaching Confederates, as Stoughton explained in his report after the battle: "...the colonel [Berdan] commanding instructed me to place my command in a position to cover a ravine near Sugar Loaf hill, which I did by putting Company H on the brow of the hill.... Company D in the ravine near the woods.... Companies A, E, G, and C formed a line perpendicular to the cross-road that intersects with the Emmitsburg pike. Companies B and F I held in reserve."[16] Homer Stoughton signed his report for Gettysburg as "Major Commanding 2nd U.S.S.S." rather than as a lieutenant colonel. His promotion, retroactive to June 24, 1863, had obviously not yet been recognized, so Stoughton was still a major during the Battle of Gettysburg.

As fate would have it, General Lee was preparing to make his main attack on the Federal left against the III Corps. Lee assigned General James Longstreet the task of driving the III Corps northward towards Cemetery Hill. It was several hours before Longstreet could get his corps into position to attack as some of his troops had not even reached the battlefield yet. Meanwhile General Sickles ordered out Colonel Berdan with four companies from the 1st U.S.S.S. supported by the 3rd Maine Infantry to determine whether the Confederates were in force to the east of the Emmitsburg Road. Berdan reported back that indeed the Confederates were there in force. With Berdan's report General Sickles decided to push his troops out to the road. Sickles's redeployment rendered the III Corps vulnerable and left the high ground south of Cemetery Ridge completely undefended. Fortunately for the Federals, Meade ordered Major General George Sykes to move his V Corps from reserve to support Sickles's III Corps.[17]

At about 2 P.M., or shortly before Longstreet attacked the III Corps, General Ward ordered Major Stoughton to advance the 2nd into the open fields southwest of the III Corps. A squad of volunteers went out to the Emmitsburg Road to scout for approaching Confederates at about this time and found none. Corporal Henry Congdon and Private Ira Carr of Company E, volunteers for this scout, apparently got strung out too far from the squad and were captured. Stoughton himself rode out in front of the regiment and spotted enemy skirmishers advancing on the right, so he returned to the line to react to this threat. He then sent his horse to the rear and led the regiment on foot.[18]

Major Homer R. Stoughton faced a situation on July 2, 1863, similar in many ways to what Colonel Best and his 23rd Georgia experienced at Chancellorsville. The situation had been reversed on the 2nd U.S.S.S. Now it was the sharpshooters who stood against overwhelming odds. Soon after Stoughton returned to the sharpshooters' line, Longstreet commenced his attack on the III Corps. Two full Confederate brigades from Hood's Division moved eastward across the Emmitsburg Road and bore down on the thin line of sharpshooters. Stoughton, with approximately 200 riflemen, was facing most of Hood's Division.[19] The northern section of Stoughton's line faced the 4th and 5th Texas. Brigadier General Evander Law's entire brigade, composed of the 4th, 15th, 44th, 47th and 48th Alabama regiments, advanced directly toward the sharpshooters' southern section. The thin line of sharpshooters guarded the left flank of Meade's army; once past Stoughton's line, Hood would be in position to flank the III Corps.

Just before the Alabama brigade stepped off on the attack, Stoughton dispatched a few sharpshooters to harass a Confederate battery positioned directly in front of his line. Then Stoughton saw the butternut-clad Confederates pressing over the ridge near the Emmitsburg Road. One sharpshooter remembered that the enemy regiments made their appearance in mass formation; to him they resembled a mobile plowed field, a large brown patch moving toward the sharpshooters.[20] The crackle of Sharps Rifles commenced soon after Alabamians and Texans stepped into the open fields south of the Peach Orchard. When Law's regiments got within their rifle range of the sharpshooters, they deployed into line of battle. The change of formation greatly widened Law's front, overlapping the sharpshooters' left flank.

Stoughton had no option except to fall back. His line was strung out in skirmish formation for hundreds of yards with no friendly troops supporting on the left or at the rear. Sheltering behind fences, rocks and trees, the sharpshooters peppered the Confederates as they advanced toward the Round Tops. Stoughton described the situation in his report on July 27:

> While they were advancing, the Second Regiment did splendid execution, killing and wounding a great many. One regiment broke three times, and rallied, before it would advance. I held my position until their line of battle was within 100 yards of me and their skirmishers were pushing my right flank, when I ordered my men to fall back, firing as they retired.[21]

The fence on the Slyder Farm where portions of the 2nd U.S.S.S. sheltered on July 2nd, 1863. The Slyder House and Big Round Top are visible in the background.

Before Stoughton ordered a withdrawal, a number of sharpshooters had gathered on the right around the Slyder House and outbuildings east of Big Round Top. Taking cover behind the buildings and a stone wall, the sharpshooters poured a heavy fire into the advancing rebels. Brigadier General J.B. Robertson, commanding the Texas Brigade, mentioned the effect of the sharpshooters' fire in this area: "As we advanced ... we were exposed to a heavy and destructive fire ... from the enemy's sharpshooters from behind numerous rocks, fences, and houses in the field."[22] The effect of the fire from the Slyder House and positions farther east was so galling that the Confederates called it a "perfect hornet's nest."[23] Years after the battle a monument was placed at the Slyder House for the two Vermont companies, E and H, in the 2nd U.S.S.S. A large hornet's nest was sculpted on the face of that monument to commemorate the stinging effect of the sharpshooters on July 2, 1863.

When Major Stoughton gave the order to fall back, the men scampered away from the charging rebels in small detachments or as individuals, the rebels with fixed bayonets less than 100 yards behind. The sharpshooters positioned around the Slyder Farm, including most of Company H and the northern section of the skirmish line, fell back through Devil's Den and the ravine or saddle separating the two Round Tops. Stoughton and the left section of the skirmish line retreated to the base of Big Round Top, their green uniforms blending with the dark green leafy vegetation on the hillside.

Unlike the Georgians captured by the sharpshooters at Chancellorsville, Stoughton's men scattered in small groups, blending with the woods and darting to cover behind trees and boulders. The right section fell back to the stony face of Little Round Top and kept sniping at the advancing Texans and Alabamians, hunkering down behind the plentiful rock outcroppings on the hillside between shots. James Matthews of Company D remembered that some of the ammunition was "poor"; otherwise the sharpshooters would have been even more effective.[24] Civil War–era cartridges were vulnerable to dampness and prone to splitting apart during hard marches or from agitation during combat.

Major Stoughton concealed some of his men along a stone fence on the slope of Big Round Top where they could fire into the advancing Confederates. Colonel William C. Oates led his 15th Alabama Infantry across Plum Run within about 200 yards of the sharpshooters' position. Oates intended to lead his regiment around the face of Big Round Top to the northeast and attack up the valley between the two large hills. The 47th Alabama Infantry followed nearby on the left of Oates's regiment. Oates described the situation in a letter to Stoughton years after the war: "When the right of my regiment approached the first foot of Round Top, we received your fire nearly in flank." The two Alabama regiments continued toward Little Round Top until a second volley from the sharpshooters killed two men and wounded several others, including Lt. Colonel Isaac Feagin of the 15th Alabama.[25]

After the sharpshooters had fired their second volley at the 15th Alabama, Colonel Oates, not knowing how many enemy troops were pouring fire into his regiment, decided to turn and eliminate this threat. Oates explained:

Monument to the Vermont companies of the 2nd U.S.S.S. beside the Slyder House at Gettysburg. A hornet's nest on the monument commemorates the stinging effect of the regiment's fire upon the enemy.

> I then, knowing that it would not do to pass and leave you [Stoughton and the 2nd] on my right and rear gave the command 'Change direction to the right' and swung around far enough to advance on you and the 47th Alabama swung with me. My advance dislodged you, but as you fell back up the ... front of Round Top, you kept up a lively fire on my advance line, which returned it but without much effectiveness, as your men, being trained sharpshooters and skirmishers, kept well under cover, taking advantage of the boulders which line the mountain side. When over half way up, your fire ceased and henceforth to the top I did not see one of your men.[26]

Stoughton and the 2nd evaded the two Alabama regiments with few if any losses before disappearing into the woods. By drawing Oates up Round Top in pursuit, the 2nd U.S.S.S. had performed a great service that they at that time did not realize. While the two Alabama regiments clambered up the steep and rocky face of Round Top, the 20th Maine Infantry was arriving to defend the southern slope of Little Round Top. Part of Colonel Strong Vincent's V Corps brigade dispatched by General Meade to aid the overmatched III Corps, the 20th Maine very probably would not have gotten into position in time to protect Little Round Top had Oates marched to his assigned position instead of chasing the sharpshooters. History has since credited the 20th Maine with saving the battle for the Federals, but without the delay created by the 2nd U.S.S.S. the Confederates likely would have gained the advantage and well might have overrun Little Round Top.

Meanwhile the section of the sharpshooters on the right of the skirmish line had passed through Devil's Den to Little Round Top, closely pressed by Hood's other brigades. These men retreated across Plum Run to the face of Round Top and up the west slope of Little Round Top, where they fell in with the 83rd Pennsylvania as that regiment arrived near the top of the hill. At about this time Adjutant Norton with about a dozen sharpshooters captured twenty-two rebels in the saddle between the Round Tops.[27] These captured men were from the 15th Alabama. Oates had ordered two men from each of his eleven companies to refill canteens for their comrades at a well he had seen during the advance. His men had emptied their canteens during the march to the battlefield that warm July day. Norton's detachment thus deprived Oates of twenty-two men needed for his forthcoming attack on Little Round Top and the water they were bringing to his parched men.[28]

The sharpshooters on Little Round Top held fast behind rocks and boulders, firing at the attacking Texans and Alabamians trying to take the hill. Three times the Confederates charged in a determined effort to outflank the Federal army. Each time a vol-

Modern-day view of the base of Big Round Top from the Devil's Den, an area known as the Slaughter Pen.

ley preceded the attack, bullets striking the rocky hillside and glancing off the granite with a spiteful screech. Few of these shots took effect against the well-concealed sharpshooters, but the Confederates suffered severe losses moving on the attack.[29]

After the sharpshooters disappeared off Round Top, Oates turned his attention to attacking across the ravine separating the two hills. As he moved down the northern slope of Round Top, Oates and his men encountered the 20th Maine just as that regiment was arriving and taking position on Little Round Top. Colonel Joshua Chamberlain of the 20th Maine formed his line and "immediately detached Company B, Captain Morrill commanding," to cover his left flank by extending across the saddle between the two hills in a skirmish line. Soon Morrill's men were joined by about fifteen sharpshooters, probably from the group that retreated over Round Top.[30]

As Oates closed and prepared to engage the 20th Maine, the center of Vincent's line on Little Round Top was attacked. Soon the firing raged along the entire western and southern slopes of the hill, engulfing the hillsides in dense gray smoke. Oates pitched into the 20th Maine with his regiment with aid from the 47th Alabama; for

A photograph of the base of Big Round Top taken while corpses remained unburied on the field. Several bodies are visible in this photograph. Library of Congress Civil War Collection.

nearly an hour the combatants struggled almost continuously, often at close quarters, for possession of the southern slope of Little Round Top.

The fighting intensified and grew more desperate as casualties mounted and ammunition ran out. Neither side was willing to yield until Colonel Chamberlain sensed that it "was imperative to strike," so he "ordered the bayonet."[31] Oates was considering a retreat when the 20th Maine charged. His men were also running low on ammunition, and his regiment was being subjected to fire from front and rear. Chamberlain's Company B and the detail of sharpshooters were firing from behind a stone wall to the rear of the Alabamians, cutting down Oates's men while they were subjected to a heavy frontal fire. At about this time Oates saw that Stoughton's men were again threatening. According to Colonel Oates, the sharpshooters "appeared directly in my rear and opened fire on me ... forcing my thinned ranks to face and fire in both directions, which we could not long endure."[32]

The bayonet charge of the 20th Maine combined with the reappearance of the 2nd U.S.S.S. was more than Oates's fatigued Alabamians could withstand; they turned and ran. A number of Alabamians were taken captive by sharpshooters as they streamed to the rear. Some of the Confederates were immediately captured by the surging 20th Maine; others ran into the saddle between the hills to refuge with other Confederate units. Still others scrambled up the steep, rocky slope of Round Top. Oates and several of his survivors rallied near Round Top's peak and showed enough resolve to check the winded 20th Maine. Chamberlain's weary troops, many out of ammunition, did not push the issue, and soon the 15th Alabama withdrew from Round Top to a position across Plum Run near the Slyder house.[33] The Federals then occupied and held the hill for the rest of the battle.

Among the captured Confederates was Lieutenant Colonel Michael Bulger of the 47th Alabama. As Bulger was somewhat prominent, a controversy arose years after the battle over who actually captured him. William Oates told a dramatic story of Bulger, who was so seriously wounded that he was reported killed, refusing to surrender to a captain. According to Oates, Bulger insisted that he would die before he would surrender to someone of inferior rank, demanding a colonel to accept his sword. Colonel Rice of the 44th New York Infantry, according to Oates, accepted Bulger's sword. Oates apparently wanted to dispute Joshua Chamberlain's claim, years after Gettysburg, that he had captured Bulger. In fact it seems that neither colonel captured Bulger. It was Adjutant Norton of the 2nd who "found Bulger sitting propped against a tree, severely wounded by a ball through the breast, and ... glad to surrender and be taken where he could receive surgical attention, and did so without making any objection." Norton still had Bulger's sword years after the war, the sword "somewhat changed from having passed through the great Chicago fire in 1871."[34]

In the years since the Battle of Gettysburg two Federal regiments, the 20th Maine and the 1st Minnesota, have been singled out by historians for playing a key role in saving the Federals from defeat at Gettysburg. More recently the 20th Maine, perhaps as a result of John Pullen's excellent book about that regiment, has been given much credit for saving the day by its defense of the extreme Federal left flank on Little Round Top.

Confederate dead in the Slaughter Pen at the base of Big Round Top. Library of Congress Civil War Collection.

However, Colonel William Oates believed that the 2nd U.S.S.S. was responsible for his failure to take Little Round Top. Oates recognized the important role of the sharpshooters with the following summary:

> Mine was the largest and best drilled and disciplined regiment in Hood's division. It went in with two field officers, 42 company and staff officers and 644 men with arms in hand, and got out with one field officer, 19 company and staff and 221 efficient men.
>
> The great service which you [Stoughton] and your command [2nd U.S.S.S.] did was, first in changing my direction and in drawing my regiment and the 47th Alabama away from the point of attack. You drew off and delayed this force of over 1,000 men from falling on Vincent and the Union left at the same time of the attack of Law's other three regiments ... but for this service on your part I am confident we would have captured Little Round Top, which would have won the battle for us.... You and your command deserve a monument for turning the tide in favor of the Union cause.[35]

8 — "Turning the Tide"

A view of Confederate dead on the slope of Big Round Top opposite the Devil's Den, an area where the 2nd U.S.S.S. was active on July 2, 1863. Library of Congress Civil War Collection.

July 2 had been another rough day for the Federals at Gettysburg. Sickles's III Corps had been battered and driven back from its deployment along the Emmitsburg Road. Troops from the II and V Corps saved the undersized III Corps from disaster. The Federals had been pressed at several points on the battlefield, but by twilight Meade's army was firmly established on good defensive ground. The VI Corps had arrived that afternoon and waited in reserve east of the Round Tops, further strengthening Meade's hand.

General Lee faced a critical choice that evening. For two days his army had battered the Federals, nearly gaining a decisive advantage on both days. Meade's army was on the defensive, but Confederate attacks on both flanks failed to gain the breakthrough necessary for a victory. This campaign in Pennsylvania was the fulcrum point in the war. Nothing short of decisive victory would justify the risk and cost associated with Lee's invasion of the North. Lee had to choose his next move. He could wait for Meade

This view of a Federal position on Little Round Top looking towards Big Round Top was taken shortly after the fighting. Note the ammunition crate and debris on the ground. Library of Congress.

to attack him, he could move his army to a good defensive position as he had at Antietam, or he could attack yet again. In his previous battles Lee had succeeded by staying on the attack. By July 3 Lee had no tactical surprise left to spring on Meade; he would simply attack Meade's center following a mighty artillery barrage and hope to drive a wedge to split the Federal army apart.

The fighting on July 2 cost the 2nd U.S.S.S. One man had been killed, ten wounded, and fourteen were unaccounted for. Lieutenant D.B. Pettijohn of Company A, one of the missing, had been captured; and three officers, Captains Buxton, McClure and Rowell, were wounded for a total of twenty-eight casualties, counting the missing. Lieutenant Pettijohn would remain a prisoner until the close of the war. After dusk the sharpshooters regrouped and fell in with Ward's Brigade. By morning on July 3 the sharpshooters were with the III Corps north of the Round Tops and just east of the Taneytown Road.[36]

At daylight on July 3, 1863, the sharpshooters awoke to the crash of enemy artillery firing on the left. The men took arms and formed a line, expecting a renewed attack by the enemy. Far off to the right the boom of artillery was followed by a muffled roar as the Confederates under General Edward Johnson attacked Culp's Hill. But the Confederates did not renew their attack on the III Corps or make any significant move on the southern portion of the battlefield. The morning passed relatively uneventfully for the sharpshooters.

At around 11 A.M. the fighting on Culp's Hill sputtered out and a sudden silence pervaded the battlefield with an almost eerie effect. Thick, hot summer air induced torpidity as the soldiers idled and awaited their fate. The sharpshooters probably sensed that the lull was simply a brief respite before their trial by combat resumed. And so it was, as Lee supervised preparations for a stupendous artillery barrage to be followed by a do-or-die ground attack.[37]

James Matthews of Company D recorded in his diary on July 3 that the Confederate bombardment commenced with two shots at about 1 P.M. followed shortly after by the opening of their entire artillery. The Federal artillery quickly replied, and thus commenced the greatest artillery duel Matthews had ever seen.[38] Matthews did not exaggerate. The Confederates had deployed approximately 170 cannon with at least 130 rounds each to fire at the objective of Lee's infantry attack. It was the greatest artillery bombardment in American history up to that day.[39]

Although the seemingly endless rain of exploding shells produced a terrifying spectacle, the massive artillery barrage was relatively ineffective. A heavy cloud of dense white smoke and dust cloaked the lines of both armies as the guns kept up a rapid fire during the opening phase of the bombardment. Most of the Confederate shells passed over the Federal infantry and exploded behind the lines. Men on supply details in the rear felt the full brunt of the shelling. Federal gunners and batteries suffered some losses, however. The Confederate infantry was not so fortunate. Federal return fire also overshot its target, passing over the Confederate batteries and striking the woods behind the artillery where the infantry waited, inflicting about 500 casualties.[40]

During the bombardment Stoughton gathered his men into fours to avoid casualties from enemy artillery fire as he hurried the sharpshooters towards Cemetery Ridge, now the obvious objective of the bombardment and forthcoming attack. As they neared their destination the sharpshooters broke into a run, as though rushing through a gauntlet, to their position behind the 14th Vermont of Stannard's Brigade.

The sharpshooters lay on the ground behind Stannard's Vermont Brigade as the storm of shell and case shot thundered on. Meanwhile a rebel marksman, "a dangerous customer," was making his presence felt while escaping detection. Eli "Bull's Eye" Willard of Company E walked up to General Stannard and remarked, "General, if you'll lend me your glass I guess I'll find that feller." The general agreed and presently Willard located the enemy sharpshooter near a shed by the Emmitsburg Road. Willard then "went in front of a tree near a large boulder, aimed and fired and the troublesome 'feller' caused no further trouble."[41]

Major Stoughton, a Vermont man himself, was standing near General Stannard when a spherical case shot exploded overhead. The exploding projectile rained down iron fragments and lead balls, wounding General Stannard and killing Private George White of Company G. White was yet another example of the high quality composi-

This granite monument commemorates the spot where the New Hampshire companies of Berdan's Sharpshooters faced Pickett's charge on July 3, 1863.

tion of the 2nd U.S.S.S. Before he enlisted in the regiment in 1861, White was a student at Dartmouth College.[42] White was the only man from the 2nd killed at Gettysburg on July 3.

During the afternoon General Birney requested volunteers from the 2nd to drive off a troublesome rebel battery near the Codori House along the Emmitsburg Road. More than enough men volunteered for the assignment, so five men from each of the regiment's eight companies were detailed with an officer to assail the battery. The sharpshooters started toward the battery at a run, but while the artillerymen were switching to canister, the sharpshooters dispersed and found sheltered positions within rifle range of the enemy cannon. Very quickly all the battery horses were shot down or stampeded. Minutes later the artillerymen fired off their canister round and fled, leaving their guns out of action for the afternoon.[43]

At about 3 P.M. the Confederate artillery fire slackened and the Confederate infantry emerged from its concealed waiting area; the most famous attack of the Civil War, Pickett's Charge, was underway. Pickett's Charge was exactly what Meade and the Federals were hoping for: an opportunity to deal Lee's army a crippling blow. The attack was launched across flat, open terrain, and the Federals rained down shot and shell upon the vulnerable advancing Confederates and then pounded them with canister. As Pickett's battered infantrymen neared the Federal lines on Cemetery Ridge, the Federal Infantry opened fire with devastating effect. The sharpshooters were spectators from their position behind the Vermont Brigade. They watched as Pickett's men swept across the open field, their ranks steadily thinning from the effect of the Federal artillery. The attack broke apart a short distance north of the sharpshooters as hundreds of rebels threw down their muskets in surrender, the survivors turning back for their lines.

Captain Abraham Wright remembered the sight of Pickett's defeated men streaming back across the open field that day. As he recalled it, the sharpshooters had opportunity to pick off the fleeing rebels. The terrible slaughter visited upon the rebels apparently seemed sufficient to the sharpshooters. Captain Wright noted that the sharpshooters "did not have much desire just to kill some one," so while some sharpshooters helped gather in prisoners, they did not mercilessly shoot down their beaten foes.[44] The following year, when the situation would be reversed, the rebels would not be so fair-minded.

As the evening shadows lengthened on July 3, Lee knew that his offensive into Pennsylvania was finished. He prepared to return to Virginia. Still hoping Meade would attack, he pulled his army back to the woods along Seminary Ridge to await Meade's next move. The Confederates could still defend against a Federal attack, but further offensive operations were impracticable if not impossible. As the sharpshooters would soon discover, the rebels, though beaten, still could sting.

Having spent the night on Cemetery Ridge, the following day, July 4, the 2nd was sent out to drive rebel skirmishers and sharpshooters away from their proximity to the Federal lines on Cemetery Ridge. Stoughton "was ordered to move forward to the Emmitsburg pike, a few hundred yards to the left of the cemetery," to push the enemy back into the woods along Seminary Ridge.[45] This utilitarian assignment proved costly to the sharpshooters. Soon the object of their mission was effected, but the sharpshooters remained strung out over the open fields for hours, all the while subjected to shots from the Confederate sharpshooters firing from the shelter of their fieldworks in the woods.

The Fourth of July weather was uncharacteristically cool and damp; rain fell in torrents, washing clean the bloody grass and muting the stench of ubiquitous decaying corpses. But the weather didn't favor the sharpshooters lying exposed to enemy fire, hunkered down in any wallow, rut or depression to be found in the open fields. Stoughton's men were disadvantaged and very quickly survival became the primary focus. So they lay in the mud, soaked to the bone, rather than becoming easy targets for the enemy. Orderly Sergeant Josiah Gray of Company D was instantly killed by enemy fire as he sheltered behind a tree. Two other sharpshooters were killed on the 4th, including Corporal James Kent of Company G, and eight others were wounded. Kent had written an interesting account of his part in the Battle of Antietam in a letter the previous year. Finally at around 7:30 P.M. the sharpshooters were relieved from the skirmish line and returned to their brigade.[46]

Evening of the Fourth of July signaled the end of the sharpshooters' combat in the Gettysburg Campaign. History has not taken much notice of their role in the outcome of the battle, with the exception of the writings of Confederate colonel and later Alabama governor William C. Oates. However, their impact on the battle was proportionally very significant. John Pullen, author of a history of the 20th Maine Infantry, also recognized the contribution of the 2nd U.S.S.S. at Gettysburg, calling it "a lesson on the effects of marksmanship." Pullen noted that in addition to helping defeat the 15th Alabama, the sharpshooters caused "significant delays" to Hood's entire initial attack. The 2nd U.S.S.S. proved its value unequivocally at Gettysburg by providing an example of how "well-aimed fire at long distances may have decisive effects on battles."[47] At Gettysburg the 2nd fought in its proper role, not as infantry. The regiment's performance on July 2nd demonstrated the superiority of sharpshooter methods and tactics by altering the battle far more significantly than could be expected.

After dark on the 4th, in the pouring rain, Lee commenced his withdrawal from Pennsylvania. The sharpshooters awoke to a quiet morning on July 5. Meade made no serious attempt to pounce on the retreating Confederates, so the day was spent burying the dead, Meade being very relieved to see the enemy go. While the army delayed at Gettysburg, one of the men from Company D made a representative observation about the inhabitants of Maryland and Pennsylvania. Yankees like this soldier from Maine had long held a distrust and, perhaps, a dislike for foreign immigrants — Germans, who were abundant around Gettysburg, and Irishmen in particular. He noted that the locals were none too anxious to assist the army, apparently preferring to mind their own business. One local man required a deposit of $7.50 for the use of a kettle for boiling beef for the wounded. The man also took $2.00 for helping carry the kettle a short distance to the field hospital. The sharpshooter, of course, resented the perceived ingratitude of the locals, many of whom obviously wished only to be left alone. He noted in his diary that he would henceforth feel free to plunder in Pennsylvania or Maryland.[48] No doubt many others, Federal and Confederate, resented the disinterested, perhaps aloof, stance of Pennsylvania's ethnic inhabitants during the Gettysburg Campaign.

Finally on July 7 the sharpshooters marched away from the battlefield at Gettysburg. Rainy weather made the marching difficult, but it also trapped Lee's army north of the Potomac River in Maryland. Steady rain swelled the Potomac and prevented the Confederates from fording the river on their route to the Shenandoah Valley. Lee's invasion gamble was a complete failure; now a tremendous opportunity to finish the Confederacy awaited Meade and the Army of the Potomac.

9

The Feckless Campaigns

While the sharpshooters were exchanging shots with the rebels along the Emmitsburg Road on the Fourth of July, the Confederates were surrendering their vital stronghold on the Mississippi River at Vicksburg. The days following the Battle of Gettysburg were the most sanguine and propitious of the war for the Federals, until the close of the war. It was a time when the leadership in Meade's army should have been imbued with confidence and urgency to press the beleaguered Confederacy into collapse. Instead the inscrutable kismet of the war ordained just the opposite. The ill-starred Army of the Potomac was doomed to yet again waste an advantage over Lee, and the ineptitude of the army's senior leadership was never more obvious than during the six months following Gettysburg.

The psychology of the army's high command was painfully obvious in General Meade's congratulatory announcement on the afternoon of July 4. Meade incorrectly stated that the enemy at Gettysburg had been "superior in numbers." He further admonished, "Our task is not yet accomplished, and the commanding general looks to the army for greater efforts to drive from our soil every vestige of the presence of the invader." President Lincoln was "a good deal dissatisfied" with Meade's mindset. He notified General-in-Chief Halleck that, in his opinion, Meade intended to "get the enemy across the river again without a further collision." Lincoln fairly expected Meade to immediately attempt to destroy Lee's army before it could escape, as it had following the Battle of Antietam the previous September.[1]

Further evidence of Lincoln's expectations for Meade and his army is found in his message to General Halleck on July 7, 1863: "We have information that Vicksburg surrendered to General Grant on the Fourth of July ... if General Meade can complete his work ... by the literal or substantial destruction of Lee's army, the rebellion will be over." On the following day Halleck sent a message to Meade stressing the importance of striking Lee while opportunity waited: "If Lee's army is so divided by the river, the importance of attacking the part on this side is incalculable. Such an opportunity may never occur again." Halleck continued by assuring Meade that additional forces would be made available should he attack Lee. He closed the message with the following observation: "You will have forces sufficient to render your victory certain. My only fear now is the enemy may escape by crossing the river."[2]

But Meade was in no hurry to press the Confederates. He feared a repeat of Lee's own mistake at Gettysburg. Lee had established a strong line of defense near Hagerstown, Maryland, and Meade had learned of it. Indeed, the Confederates, as a result of Meade's creeping pace, had established a nine-mile-long series of earthworks stretching from near Williamsport to the area around Falling Waters.[3] Wisely, Meade did not wish to "imitate" Lee's example by dashing his army against this strong line. Instead, he hoped to moderate the expectations of President Lincoln or others "who in ignorance of the difficulties to be encountered" were expecting too much of him.[4]

During this period of the president's great anxiety, the sharpshooters marched from Gettysburg to Frederick, Maryland, and on to the area around the Antietam battlefield. It wasn't the sharpshooters, or Meade's soldiers for that matter, who dreaded another battle with Lee. In fact, according to Colonel Stoughton, "The men were zealous to get into a fight with the enemy ... and begged to get up to the Rebel works."[5] The army on the whole was certainly not ignorant of the great opportunity afforded by Lee's retreat to the Potomac, as illustrated by the observations of a Federal colonel at that time: "The demoralization of Lee's army is something awful to witness, and if General Meade would press it hard, fully half of it would certainly be destroyed, or captured. Why he does not press forward is a mystery to us, who can see its hopeless condition."[6]

Finally, with no attack by Meade, Lee's army began crossing the Potomac at Williamsport on the 13th. By evening of the following day the bulk of his army had crossed by pontoon bridge at Falling Waters.[7] All of the urging by the president and the hopes of the ordinary soldiers were in vain. While General Meade's caution is understandable, his failure to press Lee's vulnerable army during its crossing is not. From the distance of time it seems obvious that many lives would ultimately have been spared had Meade shown the determination, fortitude and alacrity required of an apt army commander.

President Lincoln must have felt cursed by the vagaries of his war. He sat down and penned a bitter and angry letter to General Meade on July 14, after having learned of Lee's escape. Lincoln summed up the failures and lapses he perceived in Meade's handling of the situation since Gettysburg and stressed that he did not believe that Meade understood the terrible cost of allowing Lee to escape. He openly questioned how Meade could be expected to ever attack Lee if he could not do so while Lee was trapped with the Potomac at his back. "Your golden opportunity is gone," Lincoln wrote, "and I am distressed immeasurably because of it."[8] After reflection Lincoln never forwarded the letter, simply putting it away instead. Perhaps the president should have sent such a letter a few days earlier; the nation might have been spared much of the terrible cost of the war if he had.

Civil War historian Jeffery Wert observed that Lincoln's assessment of the situation was "deeply flawed."[9] It is true that Lincoln was not present with the army to witness the operations in the field during this period; thus, he could not fully appreciate the difficulty of the task. He did, however, apprehend the magnitude of the situation as it unfolded. The tremendous genius of Abraham Lincoln was wasted at pivotal moments, such as this, during the war. Perhaps Lincoln's true flaw was his reluctance or, perhaps, inability to impose his will when nothing less would answer.

Meade had seen what happened to McClellan after the Battle of Antietam, and he did not repeat that general's blunder. He wisely moved his army to follow the Confederates. He arrived at Berlin, Maryland, with four army corps on July 15. The army's three other corps concentrated at Harpers Ferry. The 2nd U.S.S.S. crossed over the mouth of the Shenandoah at Harpers Ferry on the 17th and marched in the direction of Snicker's Gap as part of Meade's effort to shadow Lee's army.

On July 22 the III Corps was sent into Manassas Gap in the direction of Front Royal to close on Lee's army. While moving through the gap the III Corp clashed with rebels making a stand while their army moved on. The 2nd went in as support for Berdan's other regiment, which suffered several casualties during the action. The 2nd was fortunate to get through the day without losses, being spectators for the most part. A few men from Company D captured six rebels while scouting in the woods.[10] The combat, fought on the mountainsides near Wapping Station, was known thereafter as the Battle of Wapping Heights. Blackberries were in profusion on the mountainside that July. Some of the sharpshooters on the skirmish line took time to pick handfuls of the berries while exchanging shots with the rebels, prompting a foreign officer observing the fight to ponder what kind of men these were to take notice of berries at such a time.[11]

Brigadier General John Henry Hobart Ward and his staff. Ward (seated in the middle), exhibiting his typical dour countenance, was an unpopular brigade commander of the 2nd U.S.S.S. U.S. Army Military History Institute.

Early on the morning of July 23 the sharpshooters marched toward Front Royal, following the Confederates as they withdrew. About three miles from the town orders were given to turn back in the direction of Piedmont, near Manassas Gap, to draw rations. While marching back toward Piedmont, the hungry sharpshooters repeatedly called loudly for hardtack. Brigadier General John Henry Hobart Ward, their troubled division commander, made his appearance at the head of the column. General Ward apparently had a drinking problem to go along with his increasing war fatigue. Still, the general was a veteran soldier from a military family. Ward himself had enlisted in the Army at age eighteen, serving in the Mexican War as a sergeant major. In 1861 he was appointed colonel of the 38th New York. Apparently Ward regarded the chants for food as blatant insubordination and disrespect. Cursing the sharpshooters, he snarled that he would blow hardtack through the next man who called for it. Ward drew his revolver on a man from Company G of the 1st U.S.S.S. and repeated his threat. Hearing the click of rifle hammers cocking, Ward lowered his revolver and rode off, cursing the men angrily. That night the 2nd was ordered to remain under arms after the column halted for half an hour because of the encounter with Ward.[12] The erratic general had now replaced Berdan as a symbol of odium among the sharpshooters.

Around mid-morning on July 24 the sharpshooters marched once again toward Warrenton, Virginia, camping in that vicinity on the 26th. The Gettysburg Campaign now fizzled out with Lee retreating across the Rapidan River and Meade once again occupying the Rappahannock line much like Pope had done the previous summer. The sharpshooters moved down to Sulphur Springs on July 31 and went into camp near the springs, assuming their place on the Rappahannock line.

While President Lincoln was exasperated with Meade's performance, he had no practical option to replace him. It seemed at the time that Meade was indifferent and did not concern himself with retaining his position as army commander. General-in-Chief Halleck set about mollifying Meade with soothing messages, including an assurance that the president was unwilling to have him get into a "general engagement on the impression that we here are pressing him."[13]

Colonel Hiram Berdan left for Washington at about this time. In the previous months Berdan had been seeking authorization to augment his sharpshooter organization, hoping to recruit enough marksmen to form an entire brigade of sharpshooters. As commander of such a brigade Berdan would be a sure candidate for promotion to brigadier general, something he obviously coveted greatly. During the fighting at Wapping Heights, Berdan had even made an effort to be conspicuous; this is something he rarely, if ever, did while bullets were flying.[14] Perhaps the colonel hoped that this appearance at the front would provide a precedent to refute claims of his cowardice. In any case, Berdan went to the trouble of applying for new arms for his proposed brigade of sharpshooters in late July. Berdan asked for Spencer Rifles, a new repeating rifle designed to use brass cartridges.[15]

Colonel Berdan applied for the weapons through Captain D.W. Flagler, Meade's ordnance officer. According to Flagler, Berdan said that he was authorized to raise a brigade of 4,000 sharpshooters to be drawn from eight picked regiments from Meade's army. Officers were to return to the home states of these regiments to recruit men to fill their depleted ranks, telling the recruits that they would be sharpshooters armed with the new Spencer repeaters. Flagler discussed the request with Meade's chief of staff, Andrew Humphreys, who convinced him that the brigade would never be raised. Flagler forwarded this information to General Ripley of the Ordnance Department; the sharpshooters thus never were issued Spencer Rifles.[16]

Hiram Berdan never returned to the sharpshooters. Berdan had learned by August of 1863 that he would not be promoted to brigadier general, and his plan to raise a brigade of sharpshooters was failing. Apparently Berdan abandoned the recruiting effort and obtained a leave of absence for illness or disability. In September Berdan's superior, General Birney, pressed charges against him for neglecting his duties. By October Berdan must have decided to leave the Army, because he sought and received a medical leave of absence for service-connected disability. He remained on medical leave until late December. By then he was eligible for an honorable discharge under stipulations providing for medical discharge to soldiers absent due to illness for more than seventy consecutive days. On January 2, 1864, Berdan was honorably discharged for physical disability.[17]

Without Hiram Berdan the 1st and 2nd U. S. Sharpshooters would, in all likelihood, never have been known to history. He was instrumental in launching the Union's two most famous sharpshooting units and getting them armed with their synergistic Sharps Rifles. Unfortunately, this is as far as the good will for the originator can be carried. He obviously was unqualified for his position as colonel of sharpshooters, and he was obviously more concerned with his personal status than with assuming responsibility. It was the sharpshooters' unfortunate lot to be handicapped by mediocre to poor leadership throughout the war; history will never know the true potential and value of Berdan's two regiments for this reason.

Meanwhile in northern Virginia the shifting vagaries of the war affected the Army of the Potomac. By the summer of 1863 the real momentum in the Federal war effort was in the Western Theater. There the Federal Armies operated deep in Confederate territory, capturing vital strongholds and transportation hubs. The war was being won in the West while Meade and the Army of the Potomac remained mired in a stalemate with Lee's Army of Northern Virginia.

President Lincoln apparently recognized that he was getting proportionally more results in the West and decided to act upon this reality. Lincoln's letter to General-in-Chief Halleck on September 19, 1863, fully explained the president's rationale:

> By General Meade's dispatch to you of yesterday, it appears that he desires your views and those of the Government as to whether he shall advance upon the enemy. I am not prepared to order or even advise an advance in this case, wherein I know so little of the particulars, and wherein he, in the field, thinks the risk is so great and the promise of advantage so small. And yet the case presents [a] matter for very serious consideration in another aspect. These two armies confront each other across a small river, substantially midway between the two capitals, each defending its own capital, and menacing the other. General Meade estimates the enemy's infantry in front of him at not less than 40,000. Suppose we add 50 per cent. to this for

cavalry, artillery, and extra-duty men, stretching as far as Richmond, making the whole force of the enemy 60,000. General Meade, as shown by the returns, has with him, and between him and Washington, of the same classes of well men, over 90,000. Neither can bring the whole of his men into battle, but each can bring as large a percentage in as the other. For a battle, then, General Meade has three men to General Lee's two. Yet, it having been determined that choosing ground and standing on the defensive gives so great advantage that the three cannot safely attack the two, the three are left simply standing on the defensive also. If the enemy's 60,000 are sufficient to keep our 90,000 away from Richmond, why, by the same rule, may not 40,000 of ours keep their 60,000 away from Washington, leaving us 50,000 to put to some other use? Having practically come to the mere defensive, it seems to be no economy at all to employ twice as many men from that object as are needed. With no object, certainly, to mislead myself, I can perceive no fault in this statement, unless we admit we are not the equal of the enemy, man for man. I hope you will consider it.

To avoid misunderstanding, let me say that to attempt to fight the enemy slowly back into his intrenchments at Richmond, and there to capture him, is an idea I have been trying to repudiate for quite a year.... I have constantly desired the Army of the Potomac to make Lee's army, and not Richmond, its objective point. If our army cannot fall upon the enemy and hurt him where he is, it is plain to me it can gain nothing by attempting to follow him over a succession of intrenched lines into a fortified city.

Yours Truly,

A. Lincoln[18]

Confederate President Jefferson Davis had already, in early September, sent two divisions and Lieutenant General James Longstreet to reinforce Bragg's army in Tennessee with hopes of reversing the trend going against the Confederacy in the West. These troops participated in the fierce Battle of Chickamauga in northern Georgia, September 18–20, 1863. Federal forces commanded by Major General William Rosecrans were defeated there and followed to Chattanooga, Tennessee. Bragg's Confederates soon trapped the Federals in Chattanooga, the Tennessee River effectively bottling up Rosecrans' troops. On September 23, President Lincoln, concerned with preventing a disaster at Chattanooga, ordered the immediate transfer of two of Meade's corps to the Western Theater.

The troops selected for transfer from the Army of the Potomac to the West were Major General Oliver O. Howard's XI Corps and Major General Henry Slocum's XII Corps. Howard's corps, known for its high concentration of German-Americans, had been routed at Chancellorsville and badly whipped at Gettysburg. The corps was widely perceived as undependable within the Army of the Potomac; thus, its transfer was not particularly apt to stir regret. Major General Joseph Hooker was rescued from obscurity as commander of the two corps being sent to the West.[19]

The sharpshooters spent about six weeks at Sulphur Springs before breaking camp on September 15 to march to Culpeper. Meade had advanced his line from the Rappahannock to the Rapidan after General Longstreet departed for Tennessee. President Lincoln's decision to also send troops to the West emboldened General Lee to go on the offensive. From September 17 until October 10 the sharpshooters remained in the

Culpeper vicinity. During this period the 1st U.S.S.S. was transferred from Ward's Brigade to Colonel Regis de Trobriand's Third Brigade of the First Division, III Corps.[20] Once again the two regiments of Berdan's Sharpshooters were serving under different brigade commanders.

In early October General Lee initiated an effort to turn Meade's right flank by marching his army to the northwest. Meade, concerned with his supply line and under no pressure to attack Lee, retreated along the Orange & Alexandria Railroad towards Centerville, where he could shelter his army in a strong position. The ensuing ten days of hurried marching was known as the Bristoe Campaign, and, as at Gettysburg, Lee came off with the biggest blunder on his side of the ledger. Leaving the Culpeper area on the morning of the 11th, the sharpshooters joined Meade's retrograde movement towards Centerville. On the 13th the sharpshooters skirmished with rebel cavalry near Auburn, a tiny hamlet east of Warrenton. The 1st Sharpshooters took a more prominent role in this minor affair, charging across a field and driving the enemy out of a wood.[21]

The following day witnessed the most severe fighting of the obscure campaign at Bristoe Station. There Lee's III Corps commanded by Lieutenant General A.P. Hill charged straight into an ambush by the Federal II Corps posted along the railroad. Lee lost around 1,900 men in the one-sided fight and decided to give up his attempt to strike Meade north of the Rappahannock. He pulled back once again to the Rappahannock and, yet again, the stalemate resumed.[22]

Moving a few miles up the railroad to Fairfax Station, the sharpshooters were delighted to see General Daniel Sickles on the 15th. Their former corps commander was received with loud cheering as he rode through the camp in a barouche.[23] At Gettysburg on the second day, Sickles had been severely wounded by artillery fire, which had resulted in amputation of a leg. Having made a speedy recovery, he hobbled among the soldiers with a crutch, reinforcing their admiration for his pluck. But the disabled general would never return to command of his old corps.

Also while at Fairfax Station the sharpshooters were called out to witness the execution of a deserter, the first deserter to be shot from the III Corps. The purpose, of course, of this distasteful performance was to impress upon the soldiers the potential consequence of desertion. The men were drawn up in a hollow square with one side left open for the shooting. A band played a march while the doomed soldier was paraded to his coffin and grave. This deserter made no pathetic cry for mercy or any physical attempt to escape his fate, simply glancing at the ranks lined up to witness his misfortune. A chaplain gave a short prayer and then the deserter was blindfolded and seated on his coffin. Twelve soldiers stepped up to form a firing line and on command fired a volley at about six paces distance. One musket was loaded with a blank cartridge to mitigate the burden of the firing squad; eleven other shots struck their target, toppling the dead condemned man into his coffin. Then the troops were dismissed to return to their camps.[24]

Meade's retreat to the Centerville vicinity drew a puzzled response from Halleck on October 15. The general-in-chief had information that Lee had only about 55,000 troops on hand to confront Meade. Halleck asked,

> Is he [Lee] not trying to bully you, while the mass of the rebel armies are concentrating against Rosecrans? I cannot see it in any other light. Instead of retreating, I think you ought to give him battle. From all information I can get, his force is very much inferior to yours.[25]

President Lincoln also believed that Meade should have attacked rather than retreating from Lee. The president noted that Lee had only followed Meade because he apparently thought that four Federal corps had been sent west. In a message to Halleck, Lincoln noted that "General Meade's apparently avoiding a collision with him had confirmed him in the belief." Lincoln was convinced that Meade should immediately look for an opportunity to strike Lee.[26]

To his credit, Meade immediately focused on the task suggested by Halleck. On October 19 the sharpshooters were rousted out of their blankets by a bugle sounding reveille at 4 A.M. At daybreak the 2nd fell in for a march southward retracing their previous route along the Orange & Alexandria Railroad. The regiment's move was part of Meade's decision to put his forces "in motion" to get at Lee. That evening the sharpshooters camped at Bristoe Station while most of Meade's troops reached Gainesville. Brigadier General Judson Kilpatrick's cavalry division clashed with Stuart's troopers at Buckland Mills during the advance that day. According to Meade, Kilpatrick "extricated himself ... but not without considerable loss."[27]

As his army pushed southward from Bristoe Station, Meade learned that the rebels had completely destroyed the railroad south from that place to the Rappahannock. This was a serious impediment to the Federals. Operating in enemy territory required careful attention to supply routes. General Meade was unwilling to push headlong into Virginia without a secure supply line. The road was so thoroughly destroyed that the next two weeks were required to return it to operable condition. During this period the sharpshooters advanced to Warrenton Junction and camped there.

The two weeks wasted while the railroad was restored were good weather days and could have been put to good use for maneuvering Lee into battle. Favorable weather in Virginia during autumn is something not to be relied upon, as seen from Burnside's "mud march" the previous year. The loss of these weeks proved costly as the campaign unfolded.

On November 2 Meade proposed a movement to cross the Rappahannock at Bank's Ford and Fredericksburg to move against Lee's right flank along that river. President Lincoln could not see the benefit of Meade's plan and Halleck did not support it either. So Meade kept watch on the river crossings for an opportunity to force a passage of the river. By the 5th the general thought he saw an opportunity at Kelly's Ford, but threatening weather induced postponement until November 7.[28]

General Meade's plan for November 7 called for two attempts to force passage of the Rappahannock. Meade directed Major General John Sedgwick to take command of the V and VI Corps and attack the rebel bridgehead on the north bank of the river at Rappahannock Station. The remainder of the army, the I, II, and III Corps, were placed under the command of Major General William French and assigned the task of seizing the river crossing at Kelly's Ford at Kellysville. French was instructed to capture the ford and immediately go to assist Sedgwick, if necessary, at Rappahannock Station. Then French and Sedgwick were to merge and push toward Brandy Station to engage the enemy there. Sedgwick was instructed to march to Kelly's Ford should he fail at Rappahannock Station and join French in the movement to Brandy Station.[29]

The sharpshooters awoke well before dawn on the 7th and took up the march from their camp at Warrenton Station at about daybreak. On this day the 2nd was placed under the command of Brigadier General de Trobriand to lead the assault of the III Corps at Kelly's Ford. The 2nd took "de post of de honor," in the words of the French general commanding the lead elements of the attack. He had substituted the 2nd for his own 17th Maine Infantry for this day's work.[30]

Reaching the ford at about 12:30 P.M., the two sharpshooter regiments assumed two different roles for the attack at the crossing. The 2nd spread out along the wooded bluffs on the northern bank while the 1st deployed in line of battle and prepared to rush across the river. Second Lieutenant Ira Northup of Company C described the fighting from the perspective of the 2nd U.S.S.S. on the bluffs above the rebel rifle pits. This account, written a few days after the fact, is typical of the prosaic descriptions of fighting most soldiers provided in their diaries and letters:

> The 2nd U.S.S.S. had the honor of being the advance guard of the 3d, 2nd and 1st Corps who were to cross the Rappahannock at Kelly's ford. On arriving within about half a mile of the river, the column halted. Gen. Birney having command of the 3d, which was the advance Corps. Our regiment was to advance to the river.... We immediately advanced to the river ... but we had orders not to fire until the 1st Regt. Sharp Shooters, and other troops could get their position on the right of the Ford. The rebels seemed to think we were a small party of dismounted cavalry posting pickets. As the 1st regiment of Sharp Shooters were advancing in line of skirmishers on the right of the Ford, they surprised the rebel pickets, who immediately deployed as skirmishers to defend the "sacred soil" of Virginia, but could not stand the Sharps rifle, which fires so fast and accurate, and immediately fell back across the river to their rifle pits, on which our elevated position and a bend in the river gave us a raking fire, completely covering the opposite bank of the ford. This was the signal for us to try the virtue of the Sharps rifle, which was done with such effect that completely surprised and bewildered them — some skedaddling or lying down in the pits, not daring to show their heads. David H. McCauley, Sergt. our company, waded the river and took one prisoner, who durst not run for our fire; the Adjutant of our regiment stripped off his clothes, swam the river, and, without either arms or clothing, captured another, so completely were they under our fire that they dare not run for fear of being shot by us. We kept the same position until after dark, and until nearly the whole Corps crossed the river, when we were ordered to cross and had the pleasure of crossing on the pontoons with dry feet.[31]

So the Battle of Kelly's Ford was little more than a turkey shoot for the 2nd U.S.S.S. It was, however, more difficult for the 1st U.S.S.S. That regiment had to rush across the rapids just above the ford under fire from the rebels in rifle pits along the south bank of the river. Several men from the 1st were hit during this crossing, but once they made the south bank they were able to find shelter. Sharp and accurate fire from the bluffs across the river, as mentioned by Lieutenant Northup, pinned down the rebel defenders and helped enable the men from the 1st to take the rebel rifle pits. Men from the 1st "charged on them, capturing at this place about 80—'packed in the bottom of the pit like sardines.'" The bulk of the captures along the river at the rifle pits was apparently accomplished by the 1st U.S.S.S.[32]

Confederate major general Robert E. Rodes commanded the forces holding the ford. He reported that his 30th North Carolina Infantry, numbering about 500, attempted to come to the assistance of the men holding the rifle pits, but the Tarheels were "speedily broken and demoralized" by Federal artillery fire as they approached over open ground. Rodes confirmed Northup's version of the fight by mentioning that fire from the opposite bank of the river "had driven" the troops defending the ford to shelter, where they were overwhelmed.[33]

The relative ease of the Federal victory at Kelly's Ford can be attributed to the effective fire of both the sharpshooter regiments and the well-directed fire of the Federal batteries from the north bank. Unfortunately, General French, who was in charge of the operation, did not mention any unit for special praise. However, the two sharpshooter regiments appear to have done the important work in forcing the passage and eliminating the enemy opposition at the ford. French reported taking about 300 prisoners and burying forty enemy dead after the fighting. The 1st U.S.S.S. suffered three killed and sixteen wounded including First Lieutenant C.W. Thorp, the highest casualty total of all units engaged at Kelly's Ford.[34]

General Sedgwick's attack up the river at Rappahannock Station was also a Federal success, although more difficult and costly. Much of the fighting there took place after nightfall, the Confederates being driven across the river with heavy losses. General Meade reported the capture of 1,500 rebels and four cannon at the cost of 300 killed and wounded Federals.[35] With Sedgwick's success the entire army could cross the Rappahannock and concentrate against Lee.

At about sunrise on the following day the 2nd commenced the march to Brandy Station, about six miles to the west. Smoke and fog shrouded the south bank of the river where Sedgwick was to cross, so troops from French's column moved to the railroad near Rappahannock station to ensure the enemy was gone. The Federals then proceeded towards Brandy Station. As the column approached Brandy Station, a rebel cavalry regiment and a battery attempted to hold a hill along the railroad.

A skirmish line composed of infantry failed to dislodge the rebels, so the sharpshooters were called upon to do the job. Lieutenant Ira Northup took part in this action and wrote the following brief account:

> General Birney then sent an aid for our regiment, we being almost a mile back, having had the advance the day before. We came forward at the quick time, and as we passed the General, he said, "I want those chaps drove off yonder hill." It looked to be a big undertaking for our small regiment, however, we had to try, and it was undertaken in earnest. The regiment was deployed ... centering on the railroad, and advanced ... soon overtaking and passing the other [line] of skirmishers, the rebels doing their best with their artillery, it being yet too great a distance for anything else. One shell struck one man ... [McFarland, Company D] joining our left, cutting both his legs off above the knees. Ours being the color company, were the cen-

tre — our position being on either side of the railroad. When within about one hundred yards of the enemy's position, we were ordered to fire as we advanced, which soon caused the rebels to take to their heels, taking their artillery back over the hill by hand, not deeming it prudent to bring up their horses. We drove them from every position which they attempted to hold. After passing about half a mile beyond Brandy Station, there we were ordered to halt, being near a mile in advance of our support. When the support came in sight, the rebels opened [with artillery].... It being nearly night, we remained on the same line as pickets, until a little before daylight, when we were relieved by the gallant 105th Pa. Vol. We were then marched back to the brigade, and the next morning marched to where we now are, and are now in comfortable quarters, made by the hands of the practical soldier ready to move at a moments notice. The Johneys had erected comfortable winter quarters, and, having to leave them this time of year, and at such short notice, will probably cause some hard feelings on their part.[36]

William McFarland of Company D was apparently the only sharpshooter casualty at Brandy Station. He died a few hours after his legs were shot away by a shell.[37] Wounds of that sort, with the loss of multiple limbs, were almost a sure death sentence during the Civil War. Shock and blood loss were nearly impossible to overcome in such cases. It was the first battle for the unfortunate McFarland, who had been on detached duty for several months.

In two days Meade's army had won two battles and inflicted significant losses on the enemy. The Confederates fell back behind the Rapidan River without giving battle. Immediately after the fighting Meade determined that the railroad would have to be repaired before any further advance could be made. But Meade's best opportunity to defeat the Confederates at any time since Gettysburg was immediately after the fighting on the 7th. Lee himself did not want a fight with Meade, admitting that his position near Brandy Station was not "a good one, and I accordingly withdrew on Sunday night to the south bank of the Rapidan, where a battle can be delivered on more favorable terms." Here again Lee was allowed to extricate his army from a bad situation, this time with ease.[38]

The weather was turning cold, so the sharpshooters felt some urgency to build or find some shelter in their camp. A brief snow squall reminded the men that winter was soon on the way. Not knowing how long they would remain at Brandy Station, the soldiers did not go to the trouble of building elaborate quarters; the fortunate ones claimed abandoned rebel huts for shelter. On November 9 the 2nd moved out from the station about a mile to ease the crowding in camps there. In this campaign the common soldiers did not seem to know what to expect regarding further movements, as, indeed, neither did their commander.

By November 13 Meade had made dispositions for his army around Brandy Station. He sent a message to General Halleck indicating that the railroad was repaired as far as Bealton, a few miles up the tracks from Brandy Station. "I should like to visit Washington to-morrow to confer with yourself and the Secretary of War," he wrote. Halleck immediately replied that a consultation would be desirable. So Meade traveled to Washington for a conference, intending to return to headquarters at Brandy Station on the 16th.[39]

After Meade returned to the army, he delayed for nearly another week, when a report from Brigadier General Kilpatrick on the 21st indicated that Lee had only approximately 39,000 troops on hand to confront him. With his army resupplied and the railroad restored and knowing that he outnumbered the enemy by about two to one, Meade at last settled upon a plan to get Lee into a battle on favorable ground. The following is Meade's brief explanation of his plan:

> The plan I decided on was to cross the Rapidan at the lower fords, in three columns, and by a prompt movement seize the plank road and turnpike, advancing rapidly toward Orange Court-House, thus turning the enemy's works, and compelling him to give battle on ground not previously selected or prepared, and I indulged the hope that in the execution of this plan I should be enabled to fall on part of the enemy's forces before he could effect a concentration, and thus so cripple him as to render more certain the success of the final struggle.[40]

In effect Meade hoped to slice Lee's army in two and destroy each half before Lee could react and unite his forces. It was a good plan, but success depended upon prompt and efficient execution. Lee was a deft commander, and his army was mobile and maneuverable. For Meade, the greatest obstacle to success would be slack execution by his subordinates. There would be no margin for error or delay.

Following up on a string of successes at Gettysburg, Rappahannock Station and Kelly's Ford, Meade had good reason to anticipate success with this latest campaign. But a storm on the 23rd, which resulted in a postponement, was a harbinger of what was to come. Meade rescheduled the launch of his campaign for November 26, Thanksgiving Day.

As if preordained, the campaign was fumbled from the outset. Meade selected French's III Corps to lead the advance. Giving General French such an important role was simply poor judgment. The general had a drinking problem which served to hamper his already minimal capacity for command. Civil War historian Jeffry Wert observed that William French was undoubtedly the worst corps commander in Meade's army.[41] It might be just as well to say that French was the army's greatest hindrance. On the 26th the III Corps failed to break camp at sunrise. Sedgwick's VI Corps, following French, was thus clogged on the road waiting on French's corps to strike their tents and take up the march. The army barely managed to get across the river that first day.

The region the Federals had to pass through before getting at Lee was aptly called the Wilderness, an area overgrown with stubby second-growth forest, a very difficult place to maneuver an army. French's tardiness completely threw off Meade's timetable and allowed Lee precious time to react to Meade's advance. By the end of the campaign's first day, Meade had fumbled away much of his opportunity to gain the upper hand in the forthcoming struggle. Worse yet, French would continue to handicap the Federals with a remarkably inept performance.

Meade still held the upper hand, and he issued orders to renew the advance at daylight on the 27th. The 2nd deployed as flankers that day with the III Corps, advancing toward the Orange Turnpike. Tramping and stumbling through the woods and thick underbrush for five miles, the sharpshooters acted as a mobile picket line to protect their division from surprise or ambush while it marched on the roads.[42] In the forenoon General French called a halt and sent a message to headquarters informing Meade that he was waiting for General Warren and the II Corps to link up before moving forward. Once again the hapless French was out of position, foiling Meade's plans. Meade shot back a message directing French to immediately move dead ahead to link up with Warren at Robertson's Tavern, along the turnpike.

At this point General French, who according to reliable evidence was drunk, completely snarled up Meade's plans.[43] After a delay of over three hours, French sent one of his divisions in the wrong direction, where it became engaged with troops from Confederate Major General Edward Johnson's division. This combat escalated until most of French's corps was paralyzed and on the defensive. General Meade detailed French's failures in his post-action report on December 7 as follows:

> I have been thus minute in details of the movements of the Third Corps, because, in my opinion, the unnecessary delay in the progress of this corps, and the failure to attack the enemy as soon as he was encountered, deploying to the left, and allowing the Sixth Corps to pass and continue the line to Warren, was the cause that a junction of the center and right columns was not made early on the morning of the 27th, and was one of the primary causes of the failure of the whole movement.[44]

For their part the 2nd U.S.S.S. went into the fight resulting from their general's ineptitude, which was known as Payne's Farm, forming in line with Ward's Brigade to help repel a Confederate charge against a battery late in the afternoon. The terrain at the battle site was largely wooded with patches of dense brush and cedars. A clearing approximately fifty yards wide allowed for a battery placed near the sharpshooters to get into the action. James Matthews of Company D noted in his diary that the charging rebels were slaughtered by triple loads of canister fired by the battery, but only by hard fighting were the rebels turned back. Bullets seemed to whistle through the sharpshooters from all directions as the rebels charged in a line four brigades long. Much like a furious summer thunderstorm, the intensity of the fighting varied from one portion of the field to another within a few hundred yards' distance. While the 2nd suffered only a few wounded, the 1st U.S.S.S., deployed farther to the left, suffered forty-one casualties.[45]

After nightfall the 2nd lay on their arms in a reserve line of battle. Men from Companies F and H rested beneath a pine tree in the darkness. A shell fired from the Confederate lines struck the trunk of that tree and exploded. The shattered tree fell on New Hampshire and Vermont sharpshooters, wounding four men from Company H and perhaps a few from Company F. This single unfortunate shot accounted for at least half of the eight men reported wounded from the 2nd U.S.S.S. on November 27, 1863.[46]

Meade was prepared to pitch into the Confederates on the morning of November 28, but during the night Lee had pulled his forces back to the west across Mine Run, a creek flowing northward and emptying into the Rapidan. So the sharpshooters marched about two miles to the west and beyond Robertson's Tavern before halting. A cold rainstorm pelted the armies, hampering operations and turning the dirt roads and trails into muddy quagmires. Artillery movement was especially affected by the muddy roads and drenched fields, and thus Meade was unable to position his army to attack until after nightfall on the 28th.

By evening of the 28th Meade had discovered through reconnaissance that he now faced a very hard road against Lee. The Confederate line was firmly set on heights above Mine Run commanding an average of 1,000 yards of cleared sloping ground over which the Federals would have to pass in making an attack. To make matters even worse, the Confederates had already built infantry parapets and artillery emplacements. The enemy was also busily cutting trees for cover and to make abatis to repel an attack. Thus Meade forestalled an attack and instead spent the 29th in searching by reconnaissance for a weak place in Lee's lines.

The 2nd established picket posts along Mine Run on the 29th and exchanged shots with enemy pickets without loss. That day Meade directed General Warren to "feel for the enemy's right flank, and turn him, if practicable." All other corps commanders were instructed to "critically examine" the enemy positions on their front to seek an opening for attack. By nightfall Meade had received reports indicating that Warren and Sedgwick had found a suitable weak spot in Lee's lines. Meade decided to make Warren's front the main focus for an attack on November 30. Meade also received a report encouraging an attack on Lee's left, which he incorporated for part of the VI Corps into his plan for the 30th. Meade's plan called for shifting two divisions from the III Corps to reinforce Warren, which with the Third Division of the VI Corps gave him nearly half of the army's strength for his assault. The remainder VI Corps would also launch an attack from the right flank against Lee's left held by Rodes's and Johnson's Confederate divisions. Meade gave instructions for the I Corps and Birney's III Corps division to advance from his center when the other assaults proved successful. The artillery was scheduled to open at 8 A.M., followed immediately by Warren's attack.[47]

November 30, 1863, dawned bitterly cold along Mine Run, so cold that the sharpshooters, having numbed fingers, resorted to the less reliable spring-fed pellet primers rather than percussion caps to fire their rifles. The 2nd U.S.S.S. had been selected to clear the way for the anticipated attack of the I Corps and Birney's Division, being assigned to a provisional brigade for that purpose. The other troops included were the 1st U.S.S.S., 124th New York, and 3rd Michigan commanded by Colonel Pierce of the Michigan regiment. The anticipation of charging upslope onto a ridge bristling with cannon and lined with infantry waiting behind breastworks was reflected in the gloomy bearing of many, convinced that this would be their last day. A fortunate few had gathered up poultry from a nearby farmstead and prepared for a last meal. At about 8 A.M. Federal artillery opened; the provisional brigade crossed Mine Run over a makeshift bridge and, spread over a line stretching from the I Corps to Warren's right flank, moved towards the enemy-held ridgeline.[48]

During the advance the sharpshooters brushed aside rebel outposts in rifle pits outside the main works. It was here that Lieutenant Colonel Caspar Trepp, commanding the 1st U.S.S.S., was mortally wounded as he was looking out from a captured rifle pit. Trepp was hit in the left temple, the bullet exiting above his right ear. The dying colonel was carried back across the creek by six sharpshooters on a makeshift stretcher of crossed rifles covered with a tent cloth.[49]

That day Chaplain Lorenzo Barber, of the 2nd U.S.S.S., was wounded on the skirmish line. Chaplain Barber was carrying a heavy telescope-equipped target rifle, as he so often had, in his role as a "fighting parson." Some of the sharpshooters asked him to determine the distance across a valley to a rebel battery near a farmhouse. Using his telescope as a range-finder, Barber adjusted his sights for 650 yards and took aim at a razorback hog beside the farmhouse. A loud squeal from the hog confirmed that the chaplain had found the correct range, and within minutes the sharpshooters had adjusted their sights and commenced placing shots on the battery. Shortly afterwards the gunners limbered up and moved out of range. Amid the constant popping and crackling of musket fire, the chaplain was seen falling with a severe leg wound. Barber's career as a chaplain/sniper, and one of the best shots in the army, was finished.[50]

And so was General Meade's battle plan for the day. General Warren had called off the main assault before the artillery had opened fire. The daunting Confederate defenses confronting Warren convinced him that his attack would fail. At about 9 A.M. Meade received a message from Warren explaining, "...I advise against making the attack here — the full light of the sun shows me that I cannot succeed." Fortunately for Meade, he received the message in time to suspend Sedgwick's attack on the Confederate left. Without pressure from Warren's attack, Lee would have been able to easily shuffle troops to repulse Sedgwick. Meade, surely stunned by Warren's change of heart, soon rode to that portion of the field to confer with the man who had just derailed his carefully laid plans.[51]

Warren firmly insisted that he could not make the assault successfully; Meade would have to alter his plans or call off the campaign. After considering his options, Meade decided on the latter. So General Birney sent word for the provisional brigade to fall back across the creek, much to the relief of the sharpshooters. Apparently the Confederates did not even know that a major assault had been called off, and the 2nd was able to get back to their lines north of Mine Run with only three men wounded on the 30th. Among the wounded were Chaplain Barber and William Cummings of Company B.[52]

For the remainder of the day the sharpshooters manned their positions along Mine Run. The Confederates continued to strengthen their works, felling trees and digging in. Again the night was very cold, well below freezing. Men on picket had to take caution for the cold as much as for the enemy. Every half hour the pickets had to be relieved to prevent hypothermia or worse. One soldier recalled that dozing on the picket line in that bitter cold was "the sleep of death."[53]

Meade had already decided not to attempt a large-scale assault on the Mine Run line. By the afternoon of December 1 he was making preparations to withdraw across the Rapidan and march his army back to Brandy Station. He did not feel obliged to attempt a move around Lee's right flank, which would have required him to bring up his supply train and change his main supply route. The cold weather and the possibility of rainy or continued inclement weather was enough to convince Meade to fold his hand. After nightfall on December 1 Meade's army began to slip away from the works along Mine Run. The 2nd left early enough to reach and cross Germanna Ford before daylight.[54] The second of the two feckless campaigns of autumn 1863 was over, as was the season of active campaigning.

Fred Ray, author of a book on Confederate sharpshooters, noted that the Mine Run Campaign was the apogee of the Federal sharpshooters and the start of their decline. Ray opined that Mine Run showed that the Confederate sharpshooter units had reached equilibrium with their Yankee counterparts: that is, they were "fully the equals" of Federal sharpshooters. He pointed to the casualty lists of the 1st and 2nd U.S.S.S. as compared to the losses of Rodes's Confederate sharpshooters during the Mine Run Campaign. Berdan's two sharpshooter regiments suffered more casualties than Rodes's entire division. Indeed, the 1st U.S.S.S. alone suffered forty-seven casualties during the campaign. However, forty-one of these casualties occurred during the fierce charges by Johnson's Division at Payne's Farm and not in sharpshooting duels with Rodes's sharpshooters. Further, the 2nd U.S.S.S. suffered only eleven wounded, eight of these at Payne's Farm against Johnson's men, and about half of these casualties were the result of enemy artillery fire. Thus the casualties of Berdan's Sharpshooters at Mine Run have no relevance as a gauge for a comparison of the abilities of Federal sharpshooters versus their Confederate counterparts.[55]

Even so, Ray was correct in his observation that Berdan's two regiments were on the wane. Most of the original members of the 2nd U.S.S.S. were by this point dead, discharged or departed to other organizations such as the Veteran Reserve Corps. Berdan's departure was a blow to the sharpshooters; he would not be missed for his leadership or tactical expertise but for his organizational skills and the prestige he imparted. The regiment continued to be under strength despite the influx of hundreds of recruits during the course of the war, with large numbers always absent from sickness or other reasons. Still fewer veteran sharpshooters remained in the ranks as the war progressed, and the recruits, being sent directly to the front, did not have the benefit of a training camp and thus were too inexperienced to be effective.

Despite these drawbacks the 2nd U.S.S.S. would continue to contribute significantly to operations in the crucial months to come. A new and final epoch awaited the sharpshooters with the New Year. For the first time a different kind of war awaited, a total, remorseless, consuming war delivered by an apt and obdurate commander.

10

With Ulysses in the Wilderness

A military band awaited the sharpshooters as they crossed the Rapidan early on the morning of December 2. As the regiment reached the north bank, the band struck up the tune "Glad I've Got Out of the Wilderness." One sharpshooter noted in his diary that the tune "was very appropriate." This was the end of the sharpshooters' second foray into the tangled expanse of second-growth forest, and they felt that it was no place for Yankees. Little did they know that within a few months they would again do battle in the detestable region, this time with a new commander.[1]

Arriving back on the 3rd at their former camp near Brandy Station worn and weary from the enervating march out of the Wilderness, the men, after a little rest, set about preparing their camp for a long winter. Winter quarters at Brandy Station were reasonably comfortable and healthy for the time, mud and log huts with tents or split wood for a roof. Most of the regiment spent at least part of that winter on furlough, and some of the fortunate ones managed to get extended leave while the army remained inactive until spring.

For some time the government had been seeking ways to raise men for the Army. Lincoln had issued calls for volunteers, states had been assigned quotas of men to provide, Congress passed the Enrollment or Conscription Act on March 3, 1863, bounties were offered to men willing to enlist, and then finally in the summer of 1863 an actual draft was instituted. Still it remained predominantly a volunteers' war, and retention of veterans became a priority. While the army wintered at Brandy Station, the government offered veterans with at least two years of service an enticement to reenlist. If a large percentage, three-fourths, of a regiment would reenlist for three more years, that regiment would be given a furlough for one month to return home, each man would receive a $400 bounty, and, in some cases, an extended furlough to recruit new men would be part of the deal. The advantage would be that the veterans would remain with their old regiments and comrades as veteran volunteers rather than joining a new outfit or being transferred.[2] The lure of going home for a long visit immediately was also a great enticement: a little touch of heaven in exchange for three more years of misery.

The 1st U.S.S.S. wanted no part of this sugar-coated deal. Perhaps many from this regiment shared the outlook of their former commanding officer Lieutenant Colonel Caspar Trepp. Before his death at Mine Run, Trepp had attempted to resign on five occasions, the last on August 1, 1863. Colonel Berdan had left the regiment at about this time, never to return, yet Trepp still wanted out. In his final letter of resignation Trepp explained that he wished to return to his native Switzerland, and he informed his superiors that he was not even a citizen of the United States. Unfortunately for Trepp the request was denied.[3]

Almost all of the remaining original members of the 2nd U.S.S.S. decided to accept the bounty and furlough offer and reenlisted. Perhaps most were shrewd enough or optimistic enough to figure that the war would end soon after the next national election, one way or another. Taking the cash and trip home made perfect sense if that were the case. On December 21, 1863, those eligible in the 2nd U.S.S.S. reenlisted almost to a man. Of course, only a fraction of the original members remained on the rolls due to attrition: for instance, Company E reenlisted twenty-one and Company H nineteen of the original 100 in each company.[4]

On January 7, 1864, the men who had reenlisted departed from Brandy Station on railroad cars going north. Within one or two days most of the men reached their home states for a much-needed break from the war. According to the *Official Records*, 189 men from the 2nd U.S.S.S. left the Brandy Station encampment under provisions of the reenlistment offer.[5]

While the army wintered at Brandy Station there was good reason for optimism and hope for the New Year among the Federals. General Ulysses S. Grant had lifted the siege of Chattanooga on November 25, 1863. Within a few days General Longstreet abandoned his siege of Knoxville and retreated into eastern Tennessee. Grant now looked for further campaigns to slice apart the Confederacy. Since Grant's victory at Vicksburg, the Mississippi River was firmly and completely under Federal control, and the blockade of Southern seaports was becoming increasingly effective. The views of an Ohio soldier during this period perhaps reflect those of a great many Federal soldiers during the early months of 1864: "Our cause is gaining fast. I have a strong hope that this wicked rebellion will speedily come to a close.... A few more such moves as the Napoleon of the western hemisphere [Grant] has made on them at Chattanooga will bring them to their understanding."[6]

Ulysses S. Grant was now the premier general in the Federal Army. His victories at Fort Donelson, Vicksburg and Chattanooga made him the most accomplished general in the war. Now President Lincoln wanted Grant for supreme command of all Federal armies. On February 24, 1864, Congress approved the reinstatement of the rank of Lieutenant General.[7] Only George Washington had previously held that full rank. Winfield Scott, the only other American Lieutenant General, held the rank by brevet only. By getting the rank approved by Congress, President Lincoln paved the way for Grant to outrank all other generals in the Federal Army, rendering seniority irrelevant.

President Lincoln nominated Ulysses S. Grant for the rank of Lieutenant General on March 1, 1864, and on the following day the Senate confirmed the nomination. Grant was to assume duties as general-in-chief of the Army of the United States henceforth. General Grant departed his headquarters in the West and traveled by train to Washington, where he was to accept his promotion and assignment at a White House reception. On his way east the general met the veterans of Company A, who were returning to the front from furlough, at Pittsburgh, Pennsylvania. By March 9 Grant had received his commission and had attended all the formalities, departing immediately afterwards for Brandy Station by special train.[8]

One of the first changes inaugurated after Grant arrived with the Army of the Potomac affected the command structure of that army. On March 23 the War Department announced that the I and III Corps were to be discontinued and the regiments transferred among the II, V, and VI Corps. As part of the III Corps, the 2nd U.S.S.S. was reassigned to the First Brigade, 3rd Division of the II Corps commanded by Major General David Birney.[9] It was not a popular move with the soldiers of the discontinued corps. But the change was nothing new to the sharpshooters, having been assigned to the I Corps and the Army of Virginia previously. Also the 2nd would remain under the command of General Birney and General Ward; Birney was a good commander for the sharpshooters, having an appreciation for their specialty.

In February the different companies began returning to camp at Brandy Station with their new recruits. The Vermont companies, E and H, split between them eighty-seven new recruits, most having joined in November and December.[10] Many of the companies brought few recruits back. The New Hampshire companies, F and G, gained about twenty new men during the winter and had the lowest enrollment overall in the regiment.[11]

A letter from a new recruit who enlisted on December 11, Private Joseph Barton of Company H, gives some insight into the outlook of the new men who were joining the sharpshooters. Writing to his wife and daughter from Brandy Station on March 30, 1864, Barton expressed his belief that the war would end within a year. Captain Buxton had told Barton that the sharpshooters would be discharged "as soon as peace was declared." Barton assured his wife that enlisting in the sharpshooters was better than joining the Navy, because those in the Navy would be required to serve their entire enlistment regardless of when the war would end. The following is from Barton's hand:

> Within one year I am coming home for they will not want us any longer but them that go into the navey will have to stay their full term of Enlistment ... but we will be discharged just as soon As the war closes I am here for three years but expect to come home within one year for I think the war will close ... them that say into the navey will get their fingers burnt I guess....[12]

The men read in the newspapers a steady stream of reports about Union successes just about everywhere except in northern Virginia. With General Grant taking charge of the Army, many of the sharpshooters shared Barton's belief that the war would end within a year, and so it did, within a year of the commencement of their next campaign. Another new sharpshooter recruit, Private George Jones, also of Company H, mentioned in a letter written in March that most of his comrades believed that the Army of the Potomac would be successful if Grant commanded it.[13] The original sharpshooters were due for discharge in the fall of 1864, but they reenlisted, apparently believing that the war had reached a turning point, and that they were going to win and go home anyway.

Soon after General Grant established his headquarters with the Army of the Potomac, he traveled west by train to Cincinnati for a meeting with Major General

William T. Sherman, the man whom he trusted to carry forth the war in the west. The two generals conferred about strategy for the upcoming spring campaign; there in a hotel in Cincinnati, Grant apparently formulated his plans to destroy the Confederacy by attacking it on all fronts.

General Grant was a much better strategist than his subsequent record in 1864 would indicate. To many, especially in the years just after the war, Grant was a butcher, a man determined to win at any cost while lacking the resourcefulness to win by finesse. More recently, however, Grant has been acknowledged by some historians as perhaps the best general of the Civil War. While my own grandmother, a child of a Union veteran, shared the former view, the later assessment is the more accurate. Almost without fail Grant anticipated the movements and methods required for victory in his campaigns; unfortunately, his subordinates nearly always failed to follow his orders with alacrity and competence. Succinctly, the fault was not with Grant's strategy and tactics, it was with the implementation of these by his subordinates. If Grant had a fault it was in expecting too much from a ponderous army that had never responded agilely and lacked efficient leadership to remedy the defect.

When General Grant formulated his plan to subdue the Confederacy in the spring of 1864, returns from the Federal Army indicated an aggregate strength of 745,000. The Confederate total strength was approximately 303,367. With his great advantage in manpower and resources Grant planned to attack the Confederacy on five independent fronts in concert. As he explained it to General Sherman, his plan for the spring campaign called for the whole army to work together "somewhat towards a common centre." Grant wished to create a synergy of resources, hurling the combined power of the Union in a single enormous effort to finish the war.[14]

Grant's plan for a coordinated spring offensive called for the Army of the Potomac, now consisting of the II, V, and VI Corps and General Burnside's independent IX Corps brought in from Knoxville (totaling 120,000), to operate against Lee's Army of Northern Virginia by attacking across the Rapidan. General Meade would retain command of this army and Grant would accompany and oversee its operations. A movement against Richmond was assigned to Major General Benjamin Butler with the Army of the James (33,000 strong) advancing on the south bank the James River to occupy Richmond or join Grant in a pincer movement against Lee. General Franz Siegel was assigned the task of advancing south into the Shenandoah Valley with a view of capturing Lynchburg, thus cutting a vital railroad center and supply source to Richmond. In the West, General Sherman with 100,000 men was to push into Georgia from Chattanooga and capture Atlanta. Finally Grant intended to capture Mobile, Alabama. For this objective he planned to assemble troops from Major General Nathaniel Banks's army at New Orleans, and with the cooperation of the Navy these troops were to capture Mobile and then proceed into the interior of Alabama. Each of these five campaigns represented a major challenge if undertaken individually. By combining all operations into one enormous offensive Grant was placing a tremendous strain on Confederate resources and greatly enhancing the odds of a Confederate collapse.[15]

In early spring, as the weather improved, the army began drilling with increasing intensity under the watchful eye of their new commander. The new men probably had little opportunity for target practice, but drilling was now "six hours a day, while inspections and reviews were frequent." The veteran sharpshooters "didn't like it ... thought they didn't require it — but they had to stand it, and soon became in good condition for more rough marches and hard fighting." The hard training was indeed strengthening the sharpshooters, as Private Joseph Barton alluded in a letter: "I am well and tuff as a bear My flesh is hard And firm." General Birney held a review involving the sharpshooters, and then on April 22 the sharpshooters took part in a massive review by Grant, Meade and the commander of the II Corps, Major General Winfield Hancock.[16]

At last the sharpshooters broke camp around the last of April and moved into fields south of Brandy Station, camping in tents and makeshift shelters. All surplus camp equipment was taken by the quartermasters. Grant was ready to make his move, and the army waited under marching orders.[17]

As Grant prepared to launch his Overland Campaign that spring, there was a growing tendency for general officers to utilize the sharpshooters as ordinary line infantrymen. Grant himself was no respecter of troop specialties. He was sending cavalrymen and heavy artillerymen to the front as common infantry. By this stage of the war the sharpshooters were increasingly unpopular because of their duty as snipers and their somewhat exalted bearing. Indeed, the sharpshooters seemed to garner preferential treatment and often were not required to perform the usual fatigue duties of ordinary infantrymen. There was naturally a level of resentment from other soldiers who were aware of this special status and treatment.[18] Brigadier General Alexander Hays, the new brigade commander of the 1st U.S.S.S., made it clear that he believed that the sharpshooters were no better shots than ordinary infantrymen; thus, Hays said he would "employ them in ordinary line of battle." Hays felt that the sharpshooters were simply "pets, and not particularly expert with the rifle."[19]

The general's opinion might have held a grain of truth in the spring of 1864. After all, the two depleted sharpshooter regiments had been restocked with raw recruits having little opportunity for intensive training. Nevertheless, in both regiments there remained a cadre of seasoned veterans who were premier marksmen. A detail of such men from the 1st U.S.S.S. convinced General Hays that he was "very much mistaken" about the shooting abilities of Berdan's Sharpshooters, and the general gained a healthy respect for their "efficiency in the use of the rifle."[20] Notwithstanding the good general's opinion shift, there would be a growing tendency to employ the sharpshooters in the role of ordinary infantry, and the casualties for the 2nd U.S.S.S. would reflect this trend in the months ahead.

General Grant launched his spring offensive on May 4, 1864, as planned. The sharpshooters prepared for the movement by limiting their baggage and packing their knapsacks for the campaign on the 3rd, taking up the march from shortly before midnight. The night march was intended to hide the advance from General Lee and thus delay his reaction to it. Grant hoped to get his army across the Rapidan and through the Wilderness before engaging Lee's army. The 2nd U.S.S.S. crossed the Rapidan at

Ely's Ford and by afternoon on the 4th reached the Chancellorsville battlefield. There the regiment camped for the night not far from the site of the Chancellor House.[21]

There are many accounts of the troops passing over the Chancellorsville battlefield on that May evening finding macabre reminders of the fighting that had taken place there the previous year. As they camped that night the sharpshooters found scraps of green uniforms and remnants of their own unique knapsacks on the positions where they had fought the previous May near the burnt-out Chancellor House. Winter rains had washed away the dirt covering bodies of the slain in shallow graves, exposing skulls and skeletons lying among the dried, brown leaves. One sharpshooter mentioned finding bleaching bones in his journal, a haunting reminder of what lay in store for many of them in the days to come.[22] Even a century after the battle moldering leather cartridge boxes, accoutrements, canteens, cartridge box tins and other battle detritus still littered the forest floor in remote portions of the battlefield.

At about daybreak on May 5, the 2nd set out into the Wilderness, passing over the railroad grade where they had helped capture the 23rd Georgia and following the same Furnace Road utilized by Stonewall Jackson during his flank march the previous year. Soon the sharpshooters were deployed as flankers, working their way through the dense thickets and woods to protect the marching column from surprise attack. They stepped off that bright morning as it were through a portal that would usher them into a phantasmagoria of violence and brutality exceeding past experience and present expectation. The fighting, killing, and dying would henceforth increase in frequency and intensity, eroding their resilience, pressing men to the very limit of human endurance.

The day's march would take the sharpshooters into the heart of the Wilderness by the afternoon. It was a forbidding, nightmarish place to fight a battle, a section composed of dense, nearly impenetrable second-growth forest, tangled with scrub oak, cedar, pines, dogwood, and a profusion of brush and bramble. The region was a series of low swells cut with rills and ravines and pocked with cumbering bogs. It had been dubbed the Wilderness long before Civil War soldiers marched through it. Well before the Revolutionary War, German colonists brought in by Governor Spotswood had tried and failed to settle the region. Spotswood then attempted to utilize the area for mining, and the resultant cutting of wood for smelting, mine shoring and road planking consumed much of the original timber. Later the industry fell into disuse, and the forest reclaimed the landscape with the infamous tangle-wood encountered by the soldiers.[23]

Hancock's column followed the Furnace Road to its intersection with the Brock Road and turned left, moving south to the intersection of the Catharpin Road near Todd's Tavern. The sharpshooters arrived at this vicinity well before noon. The plan of the day called for Hancock's II Corps to continue on to Shady Grove Church and then to extend to the right through the thickets towards the Orange Plank Road and Parker's Store.[24]

Very quickly Grant's plans went awry. Grant found that Ewell's Confederate Corps blocked his advance on the Orange Turnpike, and Hill's Corps was pushing beyond Parker's Store on the Plank Road towards the Brock Road crossroads. A battle was

10— With Ulysses in the Wilderness   157

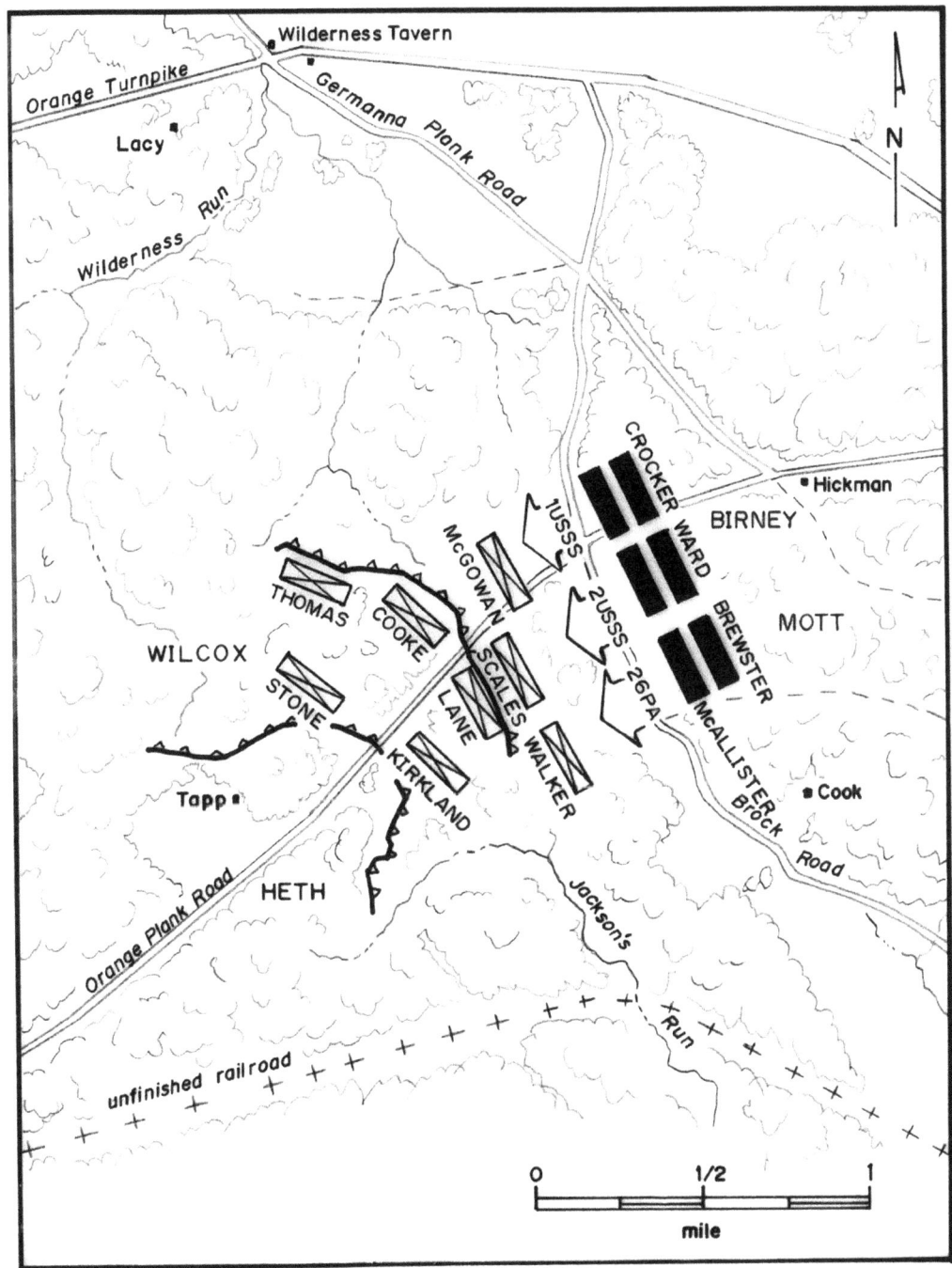

The Battle of the Wilderness, May 5, 1864. Map by John Heiser.

looming in the Wilderness, rapidly building in intensity and violence, a battle Grant had hoped to avoid. Fighting in the dense thickets would deprive the Federals of all of their advantages; thus, Grant had intended to hurry through the Wilderness and engage Lee on more favorable open ground. But when the Confederates challenged on the pathways of the forest, Grant did not hesitate to attack. The impatient general ordered his troops to pitch into the enemy, hoping to overpower with brute force and superior numbers.

Around 11:40 A.M. General Hancock received an order from Meade directing him to proceed to Brock Crossroads; Hancock would, of course, disregard the previous order to march to Shady Grove Church. The general quickly arranged to get his corps moving north on the Brock Road towards the Plank Road intersection with Birney's Division leading the way. Then General Hancock rode ahead with his staff to the crossroads, where he conferred with Brigadier General Getty. Getty's VI Corps division had just arrived to hold the crossroads. Meade sent another message to Hancock directing him to join with Getty and drive back the enemy on the Plank Road toward Parker's Store.[25]

The message directing Hancock to attack in support of Getty was late getting to him; Hancock should have received the message an hour earlier than he did. It mattered little because Birney's troops did not arrive at Brock Crossroads until about 2 P.M. As they arrived, Hancock placed Hays's Brigade south of the Plank Road and Ward's Brigade farther to the left of Hays.[26]

At about 3:45 P.M. a staffer from Meade's headquarters reached General Getty with orders to immediately launch an attack down the Plank Road, assuring Getty that Hancock would follow. Thus, Getty's division was first to attack on the Plank Road, with Colonel Lewis Grant's Vermont Brigade moving forward on the south side of the road and the brigades of Brigadier Generals Eustis and Wheaton moving on the north side. Confronting Getty's men were the brigades of Confederate major general Henry Heth. Along the Plank Road the Confederates "made masterly use" of the terrain; Heth's men were positioned to rain down musket fire on the advancing Federals with the effectiveness of a complete ambush.[27]

Meanwhile General Hancock labored to comply with another directive from General Meade: "The commanding general directs that Getty attack at once, and that you support him with your whole corps, one division on his right and one division on his left, the others in reserve; or such dispositions as you may think proper, but the attack up the plank road must be made at once."[28] As Hancock prepared to follow this order, the Vermonters of Grant's Brigade stumbled into a hurricane of enemy fire and quickly got into serious trouble. Hancock managed to spread his brigades out along the Brock Road for the advance, trying to comply with Meade's instructions as best he could. At about 4:45 P.M. Ward's Brigade, to which the 2nd U.S.S.S. belonged, went forward to assist the Vermonters, moving into the dense thickets and foreboding woods south of the Plank Road.

The 2nd U.S.S.S. stepped off the Brock Road moving west in skirmish formation, the right flank within paces of the Plank Road. Already jaded from their day's march in battle gear with full cartridge boxes, the sharpshooters slowly picked their way through some of the thickest growth in the entire Wilderness. Perspiration stained their green caps and jackets, the dark wet spots presenting a two-tone camouflage contrast. The men strained to navigate through a profusion of thin saplings and waist-high brush amid clusters of giant oaks and pines. The fresh spring leaves spread over the forest in variegated shades of green, completely obscuring vision in every direction.

Immediately after entering the woods it was impossible to maintain even a controlled skirmish line. The roar of thousands of firing muskets emanating from the north and west, and growing louder with each step, indicated their destination. New recruits, in their first combat situation, stumbled along, likely calling out to their nearby veteran comrades with childlike questions: "When will we see 'em? How far do we have to go in here? Will we get out too far to get back?"

After they had moved through the brush for several minutes, a thickening haze of sulfurous gray smoke shrouded them as the clatter of gunfire became deafening. The veterans had been trained to respond to bugle calls on the skirmish line, and now the officers resorted to the buglers to direct the skirmish line in the crowding jungle. Presently the leading edge of their line reached a slight swale; a cluster of willows at the bottom of the declivity indicated a stream or bog — a place to find fresh water to refill their tepid canteens. Incoming bullets clipped through the tree limbs, dropping leaves and twigs on the sharpshooters as they wended their way down the slope towards the stream. Buglers sounded the call to commence firing at will. Near the edge of the stream the vegetation thinned, and there the North Carolina Tar Heels of Brigadier General Alfred Scales's Brigade blasted a thundering volley at the green-coats. Instantly the sharpshooters dove for cover in the brush and behind trees, and the Tar Heels, firing from the high ground west of the creek, overshot them, the bullets tearing into the brush and tree limbs with little effect.[29]

Having served their function as skirmishers by finding the enemy, the sharpshooters apparently held their line while other regiments from Ward's Brigade passed through their sector. The fighting shifted away and intensified with a resounding thunder echoing through the forest; fortunately for the 2nd, it was somebody else's fight. Now part of Ward's second line, the sharpshooters were put to work building breastworks and entrenching as best they could on the root-choked forest floor. For the balance of the afternoon the 2nd remained as a support for Ward's advanced regiments.[30]

Later in the evening, as the fighting was subsiding, General Birney asked for volunteers from the 2nd to bring in a Parrott Gun that had been abandoned and was in possession of some rebels. Captain Norton of Company E responded with several men from the regiment. These men charged down the Plank Road, driving the enemy away and recapturing the cannon. A harness was removed from the dead battery horses and was brought in along with the gun to the Federal lines, as the sharpshooters reveled in their accomplishment.[31]

The fighting sputtered out as darkness set in. It had been a terrible day for the Federals; Lee had again stymied the Army of the Potomac. Separated by a wide expanse of nearly impenetrable forest, the heaviest fighting had occurred on the two thoroughfares traversing the Wilderness, the Orange Turnpike and the Orange Plank Road. On both of the roads Grant had piled in troops in an attempt to destroy his divided enemy, and in both locations the Confederates had dug in and utilized the terrain effectively to punish the attackers. The Federal lines had extended out into the Wilderness, weakening the impact of the poorly coordinated assaults.

Nevertheless, General Grant remained optimistic; in his previous important victories at Shiloh and Chattanooga he had won with perseverance, staying on the offensive when other, lesser generals might have withdrawn. Grant decided after dark to renew the attacks at dawn. He would concentrate the major effort along the Plank Road, intending to destroy A.P. Hill's III Corps, which was already teetering on collapse. Lieutenant General James Longstreet had returned with the Confederate I Corps from eastern Tennessee, but he was yet to reach the battlefield. The plan for May 6 called for Hancock to advance his II Corps along the Plank Road at dawn; three divisions from the newly arrived IX Corps would assist along with Wadsworth's V Corps division. The massive assaulting force would heavily outnumber Hill's battered corps. Grant's plan called for the remainder of Warren's V Corp and Sedgwick's VI Corps to renew the fighting around the Orange Turnpike farther north in the Wilderness to occupy the enemy and prevent Lee from shifting troops to help Hill.[32]

As the first streaks of predawn light erased the stars from the clear eastern horizon, the slumbering sharpshooters were awakened by the clatter of musket fire. Some of the men were boiling coffee for their breakfast as the order to fall in interrupted their chore. The regiment had lain on its arms all night behind their makeshift breastwork bisecting the Plank Road west of Brock Crossroads. In quick order after they awakened, the sharpshooters spread out on both sides of the road and stepped out into the thicket to engage Hill's jittery rebels. The 2nd was at the very apex of Hancock's attack, the spearhead of the day's planned offensive.

There was no call for skirmishing for this massive attack; the enemy's position was already developed. So shortly after 5 A.M., and after the regiment had driven in the rebel pickets, as they neared the main enemy line crossing the road, the men closed ranks, shifting into a condensed line of battle.

According to the late Civil War regimental historian Warren Wilkinson, a great many officers leading in the attack that morning already had resorted to "Dutch courage" to fortify themselves for the terrible day awaiting them. Commissary whiskey was apparently guzzled by officers in the predawn hours; a veritable "epidemic" of imbibing visited the army.[33] One of the new recruits from Company H alleged, in a letter after the battle, that Colonel Stoughton himself was "half crazed with intoxication" that morning. By implication the colonel was drunk when he ordered the regiment to charge as it neared the main rebel line along the Plank Road.[34]

The soldier's impression of Stoughton cannot be confirmed, but, in any case, the sharpshooters charged in line of battle, just like the infantry, that terrible May morning in the Wilderness. Hill's Confederates quickly crumbled facing the Federal onslaught; nevertheless, sharpshooters began to fall from rebel bullets as they advanced along the road. At first the Confederate line seemed to evaporate as Hancock's men poured through the gaps left by the men filtering to the rear.[35] The sharpshooters worked their way through the dense foliage, keeping up a constant cheer and firing at the few rebels who stood in their way.

After over an hour of forging their way through Hill's Corps, the sharpshooters began to encounter stiffening opposition. Although they did not know it, Longstreet had arrived on the field to reinforce Hill just after 6 A.M. By around 7 A.M. rebels from Kershaw's division of Longstreet's Corps were confronting the sharpshooters, shoring up the rebel line and greatly increasing the volume of fire directed at the them.[36] According to a sharpshooter from Company H, the 2nd held "without yielding an inch" until relieved by an infantry regiment. Already several men had been killed and wounded, including the kindly Captain Albert Buxton of Company H, who died that day as his shattered leg was being amputated.[37]

Although the 2nd had been relieved and had pulled back from the front, overshooting bullets still hummed and snapped through the foliage around them. Waiting to replenish their ammunition supply, the sharpshooters took shelter as best they could behind stout trees and logs. After a brief rest the men refilled their cartridge boxes, and soon the regiment was put back in line facing Kershaw's attack.

There is little to draw upon in the *Official Records* about the regiment's part in the fight on May 6, and the accounts of various other sources cannot adequately untangle the exact chronology of the chaotic fighting of that day. What is evident from the letters and diaries of men from the 2nd is that the regiment went into the fight in line of battle and essentially remained at the front until Hancock's attack dissolved around them. In the thick underbrush and dense thickets, shrouded in billowing clouds of smoke, it was nearly impossible for either side to gauge the strength of their enemy except by the volume of incoming fire. The 2nd simply spent the morning rapidly working their Sharps Rifles, pouring fire into the counterattacking rebels until, again, their ammunition was running low. Their superior firepower probably held the rebels in check on their front better than that of adjacent Federal units; by mid-morning the regiment was holding an exposed position far to the front of Hancock's corps.

Shortly after 11 A.M. the Confederates sprung a complete surprise on Hancock's left flank. Lee's chief engineer had found a hidden path leading through the forest along an unfinished railroad bed; this path enabled General Longstreet to send four brigades undetected into position to attack Birney's troops from behind. When the attack commenced, the rebels emerged from the railroad bed and sliced through the Federal brigades on the extreme left of Hancock's line. The attacking rebels must have appeared as apparitions lofting up from the forest floor to the stunned Federals, as the attack severely rattled them. McAllister's Brigade was hit from behind before it could turn to meet the attack, and very quickly the brigade collapsed and headed for the Brock Road.[38]

The four Confederate brigades continued to slice through Birney's division; this, coupled with increased pressure from Kershaw, completely unraveled the Federal line. At some point, as the 2nd stood facing Kershaw's men, rebel bullets began whizzing in from the flank and rear; these rebels, likely from the attacking force that routed McAllister's troops, had managed to outflank the sharpshooters. The 2nd, nearly out of ammunition, fell back to the slight breastworks bisecting the road where the regiment had spent the previous night, "closely followed by the enemy." During this retreat Private George Jones, a new recruit from Company H, was shot and killed instantly as he attempted to help mortally wounded Corporal Lewis Pike escape.[39] Jones was one of dozens of inexperienced recruits in the regiment cut down that dreadful day.

Just how long the 2nd remained at this line is uncertain. According to Corporal Wyman White of Company F, the regiment remained here until after 3 P.M.[40] By early afternoon the Confederate attack had stalled, and Hancock's troops were regrouping behind breastworks lining the Brock Road. General Longstreet was severely wounded before he could reorganize his scattered command and resume his attack; thus, there was a lull lasting a few hours along the Plank Road. General Lee prepared for a decisive attack against the Brock Road line during this lull.

According to White's account the sharpshooters were behind this advanced line of slight breastworks when Lee hurled perhaps as many as fifteen brigades at the Federal line on the Brock Road. The sharpshooters heard the menacing racket of thousands of rebels stomping through the thickets approaching their flimsy line, the crackle of breaking limbs and crushed leaves plainly audible. There was a clatter of musket fire as the Federal pickets tumbled out of the woods and into their lines. The sharpshooters opened fire when the rebel skirmishers appeared and kept up a rapid fire as the enemy battle line closed on their position. Heavy lines of rebel infantry unleashed thundering volleys but did not rush the breastwork. After holding firm with their fast-shooting breechloaders, the sharpshooters were forced back to the main II Corp line along the Brock Road when the overpowering rebel advance overlapped their flanks.[41]

Just as the rebels were overrunning the sharpshooters' advanced line, General Ward yet again demonstrated erratic behavior. Within a week charges would be filed against him for misbehavior and intoxication in the presence of the enemy. Corporal White mentioned that Ward had just sent his horse to the rear when the rebels attacked. Two Federal cannon with caissons were parked in the road adjacent to the sharpshooters' breastwork. Rather than retreating with his troops, General Ward, according to White's account, clambered onto one of the caissons and ordered the artillerymen to immediately drive him to the rear. Apparently the general was rumored to have abandoned his men for the rest of the afternoon, returning after nightfall to resume command of his brigade. Ward was not well liked by Berdan's Sharpshooters, if for no other reason than his threat to shoot men for repeatedly calling out for hardtack in his presence during a march. Ward remained in command of his brigade, which included the 2nd, until May 12. Although he had a proven record as brigade commander, he was honorably discharged on July 18, 1864. Even with the urging of prominent backers he was unable to get reinstated or to even obtain a trial. Perhaps Ward had chosen the wrong soldiers to offend.[42]

As General Ward made his escape in a cloud of dust, the sharpshooters dashed for the shelter of the main line of breastworks parallel to the Brock Road. At about 4:15 P.M. Lee unleashed his main attack with troops combined from the Confederate I and III Corps. As the rebels approached the main Federal line they exchanged volleys with the defenders, this time at a disadvantage as the Federals were protected by log breastworks. Soon a brush fire flared up and blew into the breastworks, igniting the logs and spreading flames along the works. Leaping flames and billowing smoke caused the defenders to recoil and allowed the rebels to approach the works. But the rebels could not exploit the breach because of a fierce Federal counterattack. Corporal White's account of the battle indicated that the sharpshooters took part in this counterattack, helping drive the Confederates away from the Brock Road line. Within an hour the fighting along the Brock Road had fizzled out, and the Confederates abandoned any further attempt at an offensive on that sector.[43]

The fighting continued on the northern sector of the battlefield until darkness drowned it. After the attack on the Brock Crossroads, Lee focused his attention on attacking the Federal VI Corps, which was done with some success. By nightfall of May 6 the battle was finished for all intents and purposes. Nevertheless, the troops endured one of the most horrific nights of the war in the dismal Wilderness. Moans and cries from the multitude of wounded wafted through the thickets until smoldering brush fires engulfed the immobile ones, then terrible screams resounded as the flames killed them. The popping of exploding dropped paper cartridges and ammunition on the burning dead and wounded kept up a chilling clatter for hours into the night.[44]

Casualties in the Federal Army were staggering, especially considering that artillery played almost no role in the fighting. Out of a total of 17,666 Federal casualties, 2,246 were killed in action, the third highest total of the war. Confederate losses were not fully reported, and estimates vary, but the figure of 11,000 in total seems probable.[45] The 2nd U.S.S.S. lost heavily: one officer and fifteen men killed, two officers and forty-seven men wounded and one officer and ten men missing or captured. Several of the wounded later died, perhaps as many as ten.[46]

Not surprisingly, a large percentage of the casualties in the 2nd U.S.S.S. were new recruits. The two Vermont companies, E and H, suffered about half of the total casualties of the regiment. Those two companies had the highest number of recruits in the entire regiment.[47] Two obvious reasons account for the large percentage of casualties among the recruits. First, the new men had very little training and no combat experience; the veterans now knew how to use cover in any situation. Second, the new men would have wanted to prove their courage, making them more likely to take chances veterans would avoid.

The great disparity in casualties between the Federals and Confederates at this battle was the start of a trend that would continue for most of the war in northern Virginia. The usually cautious and plodding General Meade was forced, by the presence of General Grant, to launch large-scale attacks for the first time since he assumed command of the Army of the Potomac. These attacks were met by strong, well-concealed fieldworks. In almost all of the combat the two sides exchanged fire at close range; the side that opened fire first held a huge advantage. The Confederates often opened fire from concealed positions on higher ground. Another factor in the high Federal casualties was the effective flank attack by Longstreet's Corps on the 6th. Here the Confederates penetrated the Federal left flank undetected and unleashed a devastating enfilading fire. By this stage of the war Grant should have realized the futility of assailing breastworks, but his success at Chattanooga must have convinced him that the enemy could yet be driven from works. In any case, he would continue to rely on the attack for the duration of the war.

Early on the morning of May 7, General Grant ordered Meade to make "all preparations during the day for a night march, to take position at Spotsylvania." Grant had decided to move south in order to place his army between Lee and Richmond, the most effective and direct means of forcing Lee into another battle elsewhere.[48] Hancock's corps would remain on the battlefield to confront Lee until the rest of the army was on the road. So the 2nd U.S.S.S. spent May 7 in the breastworks along the Brock Road or, in the case of a few, skirmishing and scouting to keep track of the enemy.

On that day the 1st U.S.S.S. went out on the Plank Road to engage the rebels and lost several men. After the fighting the two sides "began to amuse themselves" by firing ramrods from dropped muskets lying about the field. The spinning ramrods whirred and hissed through the air, making a noise similar to an arcing shell. Each side roared with laughter with each shot. Many years after the battle some twisted ramrods were found along the Plank Road strangely bent and encrusted with rust. A photograph of the ramrods appears in a book covering the Battle of the Wilderness published in the 1980s. The caption explains that the ramrods had been mistakenly left in the barrel and then fired or had been fired by spontaneous ignition in hot gun barrels. It seems more likely that jesting sharpshooters and rebels actually fired the now rusted relics on that day long ago.[49]

Although the 2nd remained in the trenches on the Wilderness battlefield as darkness set in on the night of the 7th, Grant had decided there would be no turning back and no waiting for Lee to take the initiative. Until Grant took command, other commanders—Burnside, Hooker and Meade—had always pulled back after the fighting went against them in this part of Virginia. In Grant, President Lincoln had finally found a general who would not step back, one who could be depended upon to fight an inevitable war of attrition. The 2nd, or what was left of it, and its new recruits would now follow Grant through a continuous series of large-scale battles in the weeks and months to come, the fighting reaching a frequency, intensity and ferocity unimagined.

11

A Plethora of War: Spotsylvania to Cold Harbor

General Grant had made the crucial decision to move by his left flank rather than retreating back across the Rapidan, a decision that set him apart and eventually led to victory. The army began its move to Spotsylvania Courthouse near dusk, Grant hoping to cloak his movement by the cover of darkness. Warren's V Corps moved south on the Brock Road starting around 8:30 P.M.; the VI and IX Corps marched back to Chancellorsville and then turned south. Hancock's II Corps, to which the 2nd was assigned, would closely follow Warren south on the Brock Road to Todd's Tavern. The sharpshooters waited on the Brock Road long after nightfall, snoozing in darkness as Warren's troops trudged past in a dense cloud of road dust.[1]

Lee soon discerned Grant's intention to seize the roads around Spotsylvania Courthouse, and he knew that Grant would have the advantage if he did, so it became a footrace between the contending armies to get there first. The sharpshooters with Hancock's corps got a late start as a result of waiting on Warren's troops, but the II Corps managed to reach Todd's Tavern as ordered by Grant. Once there Hancock established a defensive position to guard the army's rear while Warren pushed ahead, attempting to beat the Confederates to Spotsylvania. Although the Confederates had a more difficult route, they still got there first and quickly prepared to hold Laurel Hill, at the fork of Brock Road and Block House Road, just northwest of Spotsylvania Courthouse. Warren's V Corps pushed ahead on the 8th and unsuccessfully attempted to drive off rebels from the Confederate I Corps at Laurel Hill. Warren's attack that day was part of the opening phase of a tumultuous series of sanguinary battles known to history as Spotsylvania.

Towards evening on May 8, Confederate major general Wade Hampton's dismounted cavalry drove in Hancock's pickets and attacked the II Corps works at Todd's Tavern. The 2nd U.S.S.S. took part in the fighting against Hampton's men that evening.[2] Hampton's attack was soon repulsed; the Federals spent the night ensconced behind their works. The real fighting on May 8 was at Laurel Hill, and Warren's inability to seize Spotsylvania would soon impel both armies into a seemingly endless nightmare of horrific trench warfare battles, the sort Grant had hoped to avoid.

On May 9 the two armies continued to concentrate northwest of the courthouse around the Spindle Farm and east of the Brock Road around the McCoull House. The troops on both sides immediately began burrowing in; henceforth in the war it would be the custom to throw up breastworks whenever a halt was called within the proximity of the enemy.

By noon on the 9th General Hancock had sent both regiments of sharpshooters about two miles south of Todd's Tavern near Tinder's Mill on the Po River. There some of the Vermont sharpshooters were dispatched to drive off Confederate signalmen across the river. The Vermonters, probably from the 1st U.S.S.S., worked under General Hancock's intent observation. Rebel signalmen were working from an improvised station about 1,500 yards' distance from the Federals. Because the flip-up sights on the Sharps Rifles could adjust to a maximum range of 1,000 yards, the sharpshooters improvised by carving sticks and fitting them on the sights to adjust for the greater distance. A staff officer with field glasses observed the effect of shots fired by the Vermonters, who could only make out signal flags without the benefit of a telescope. After a few adjustments the sharpshooters found the correct elevation by trying different lengths of sticks attached to their fixed sights. Several sharpshooters cut sticks to conform to the necessary elevation and then opened on the signalmen. With bullets whizzing around their station, the rebels quickly moved away and ceased their signaling. Through improvisation the sharpshooters had made effective use of their rifles at extreme maximum range, without the advantage of heavier powder loads.[3]

While the 2nd stood by near Tinder's Mill, Grant, Hancock and Meade met near the Tally House a short distance to the east. The generals spied an enemy wagon train trundling along on Shady Grove Church Road in the distance across the Po River. Soon the 1st Rhode Island Battery opened fire on the train and drew counterbattery fire from a Confederate horse artillery battery. A sharpshooter from Company G took note of the firing and jotted down in his diary for May 9 that two men were killed in the Rhode Island battery.[4]

Although the generals had initially focused their attention on the rebel wagon train, Grant saw an opportunity to strike a blow against Lee. Soon Hancock began sending his corps across the river on makeshift pontoon bridges. General Grant had determined to send the II Corps against the Confederate left to drive the enemy off the Laurel Hill line. Birney's division crossed on an old mill race at Tinder's Mill. By 7 P.M. Hancock's three divisions were across the Po and on their way towards the Confederate I Corps defenses on the Laurel Hill line. Late in the afternoon the 2nd U.S.S.S. held a position on the right flank of Barlow's troops along the Shady Grove Church Road due south of Tinder's Mill.[5]

Grant's idea had great potential to turn the tide of battle in his favor, but Hancock moved ploddingly and found the river a greater obstacle than anticipated. By 10 P.M. Hancock still had not reached the left flank of the Laurel Hill line. Hancock grew skittish about advancing further after the onset of darkness. He sent a message to Meade explaining that the river was too deep to cross, that he would have to cross over on a single bridge and that "the darkness and thick woods near the stream caused great confusion and risk of firing into our men." He asked for Meade to decide whether he should continue the advance that night. Meade replied by directing that "the column move forward again at daylight."[6]

On the morning of May 10, 1864, General Hancock found that his task of assaulting the Confederate I Corps from the Po River vicinity had grown much more daunting. Lee had stripped troops from his III Corps on the opposite side of his line to confront Hancock. Upon learning of the presence of rebel reinforcements on Hancock's front, Grant reasoned that Lee must have weakened his line elsewhere, perhaps on Laurel Hill. Therefore, Grant decided to abandon the offensive by Hancock along the Po River and attack Laurel Hill with troops from Hancock's II Corps and Warren's V Corps. Grant scheduled the assault for 5 P.M.[7]

Grant was the first Federal general in the east to fully comprehend that he held a significant strength advantage over Lee. He introduced a virtually fearless war of constant offensive maneuver against Lee. Unfortunately, the senior leadership of the Army of the Potomac was unready for Grant's methods. General McClellan had set the tone of fighting Lee with caution and trepidation; subsequent commanders had followed that example. Now as Grant engaged Lee in this 1864 Overland Campaign, he had to surmount the fears and wariness of his torpid subordinates. The fighting on May 10 demonstrated well the command inefficiency plaguing Grant throughout the summer campaign.

Of the series of frontal attacks against the Laurel Hill line on May 10, the most impressive of these involved Ward's Brigade, to which the sharpshooters belonged. The exact role of the sharpshooters in Ward's attack on May 10 remains somewhat unclear. The *Official Records* shed little light on their involvement, and other accounts hardly mention them. From sharpshooter accounts it seems that the 2nd participated in Ward's attack in at least a supporting role, perhaps providing suppressing fire if not actually taking part in the charge itself.

What is known is that Ward's attack commenced at about 7 P.M., the brigade advancing in a stacked column of eight regiments led by the 86th New York. The object of the attack was a redoubt manned by the Richmond Howitzers and the Texas Brigade composed of the 3rd Arkansas, 1st, 4th and 5th Texas. Ward was struck in the temple by a shell fragment just before the attack was launched. Colonel Egan of the 40th New York helped Ward clean the wound and placed a handkerchief over it. Ward remained on the field during the attack.[8]

Once inside the redoubt the leading regiments in the attack only remained there for about ten minutes before being driven back out by a blizzard of bullets and canister. Other regiments in the attacking column were still approaching the fort when heavy fire from other areas of the rebel line shook them and they turned back. At the point when the situation seemed hopeless, the Federals broke and ran for the cover of the woods where the attack had commenced. Enraged rebels showed no mercy and shot down many of Ward's men as they tried to escape, a complete departure from the behavior of the sharpshooters after Pickett's Charge at Gettysburg.[9]

Colonel Stoughton was shot while leading the 2nd during Ward's attack, the bullet "breaking two ribs" and causing other injuries. Stoughton left the field because of his wounds and did not return to the regiment for over a month. As fate would have it, he would have no further impact on the 2nd, serving with the regiment for less than one day thereafter.[10]

Though ultimately unsuccessful, Ward's attack showed great promise and might have altered the outcome of the battle had it been properly supported. Another attack by Colonel Emory Upton with troops from the VI Corps on the east sector of the battlefield at about the same time garnered much more attention and accolades. Upton's attack was also unsuccessful because of the same lack of support. In both attacks the Federals did not stop to fire during their charge, and in both cases the attackers broke through the enemy works. Ultimately Ward's attack by his single brigade was the most successful made on Laurel Hill, although Warren and his V Corps made numerous assaults during the battle.[11]

After Ward's attack the sharpshooters returned to their lines near the Jones Farm, a short distance north of the Po and west of Brock Road. For the remainder of the evening the enemy artillery kept up a brisk shelling to discourage any further attacks before nightfall. During the night both sides improved their fieldworks and the Confederates extended their earthworks farther to the west beyond the Po River.[12]

Early the next morning the sharpshooters, both regiments, were called out to counter rebel sharpshooters ranging from the woods in the no-man's-land between the lines. By this point in the war the Confederate sharpshooters were armed with accurate Enfield Rifles and Enfield Rifle Muskets, and a select few even carried Whitworth Rifles. The Whitworth guns were more than a match for the Sharps carried by most of Berdan's Sharpshooters at long-range shooting. Most of the 1st U.S.S.S. carved out shallow rifle pits in the sandy soil on the Jones Farm and exchanged long-range fire with Confederate marksmen. A long Federal skirmish line consisting of several regiments fronted the length of the Federal works to guard against a surprise Confederate attack.

Corporal Wyman White of Company F remembered the day spent dueling with rebel snipers years after the war as the "hardest proposition" the 2nd had ever faced. White went out into the woods between the lines to eliminate a rebel sharpshooter who had killed three Federal pickets. He was on his own, free to roam the area between the lines in search of prey. It was extremely dangerous duty, and men who were killed or shot and left to die would likely be listed as missing with little chance that their fate would ever be known to their families. Corporal White picked his way through a wood, dodging from tree to tree until he drew fire from the rebel sharpshooter. He readied his Sharps Rifle using the pellet primer system and waited to draw fire once again. Then he held out his cap and drew fire. Immediately White fired six shots in rapid succession into the limbs of a large pine tree where he had seen smoke and the rebel's form. White waited for return fire and then moved back into the fieldworks; there was no further trouble from the dangerous rebel on that picket line that day. By this stage of the war this type of duty was becoming routine for the sharpshooters of both armies. Unlike earlier in the war, the Confederates now had a corps of capable, well-armed sharpshooters to challenge men from the 2nd. Henceforth the sharpshooters would face the dual danger of stalking enemy killers and charging enemy breastworks, their duties growing more demanding and dangerous than frontline infantry.[13]

Rain pelted down on the sharpshooters as they lay in their shallow rifle pits, making the day even more miserable. The men were subjected to random enemy shots if they attempted to rise from their muddy cover holes; the rebels, better sheltered in the woods, held the advantage. Private John F. Kennedy, a new recruit and a Scotsman, one of the few foreigners in Company F, was mortally wounded on the 11th.[14]

General Grant had been favorably impressed with the success of Ward's and Upton's assaults on the rebel trenches the previous day. He was confident that a repeat of Upton's assault at the same location would succeed if adequately supported. Thus, on the 11th General Grant directed Meade to move Hancock's II Corps from the Laurel Hill vicinity to the opposite corner of the battlefield. Grant planned to launch the II Corps against the relatively weak Confederate fieldworks on the eastern sector of the battlefield known as the Mule Shoe. The Mule Shoe was a horseshoe-shaped bulge in the rebel lines manned by troops from Ewell's Confederate II Corps. Upton's attack the previous evening had punched through the works here, and Grant believed that a repeat performance by the large Federal II Corps would quite possibly sweep the enemy corps away.[15]

The sharpshooters were called in from their scrap with the rebel snipers towards evening on the 11th, expecting a chance to eat a cooked meal, even if it was only fried pork. The men had spent the day with only hard crackers to munch while enduring drenching downpours and enemy fire. Having spent the last seven days exposed to enemy fire, and having had three days of fierce battle, the men were desperately weary. Poor rations and water drawn from streams in fields plagued with rotting corpses and excrement from the hosts subjected them to an additional menace. More than a few no doubt suffered from diarrhea and related illnesses.

Grant was pressing on; he would push his army to the extreme limit, knowing the enemy was equally afflicted by the enervating campaign. Although Meade was annoyed by the constant stream of orders from Grant, the commander's orders for the flank march were executed after dark. The soldiers were instructed to secure their gear, canteens and cups and to march in complete silence to conceal their movement from the enemy. The sharpshooters followed Hancock's other two divisions over slick, muddy lanes and roads in the inky darkness, all the while pounded by a heavy rain. It was a terrible ordeal, perhaps the worst yet of the war for the exhausted warriors, stumbling through the rain-soaked woods, the cold, numbing rain alone keeping them awake. Finally after 2 A.M. the column reached the staging area for the forthcoming attack near the Brown House, about a half mile north of their objective. Nearly 20,000 Union troops gathered under the cloak of darkness in the soggy woods and fields in preparation for one of the largest frontal assaults of the war.[16]

Once again the 2nd U.S.S.S. would lead the assault. As usual, they would be the point men, first in the fight. The sharpshooters spread out in front of Ward's brigade and Birney's whole division. On their right the 1st U.S.S.S. was in a similar skirmish line, and the 66th New York extended on their left. At about 4:30 A.M. the rain had let up, and a misty fog shrouded the woods as the first rays of light broke the eastern horizon. A few minutes passed, then the order to advance spread down the ranks and the sharpshooters were off.

The 2nd U.S.S.S. was under orders not to fire; every regiment was to hold its fire

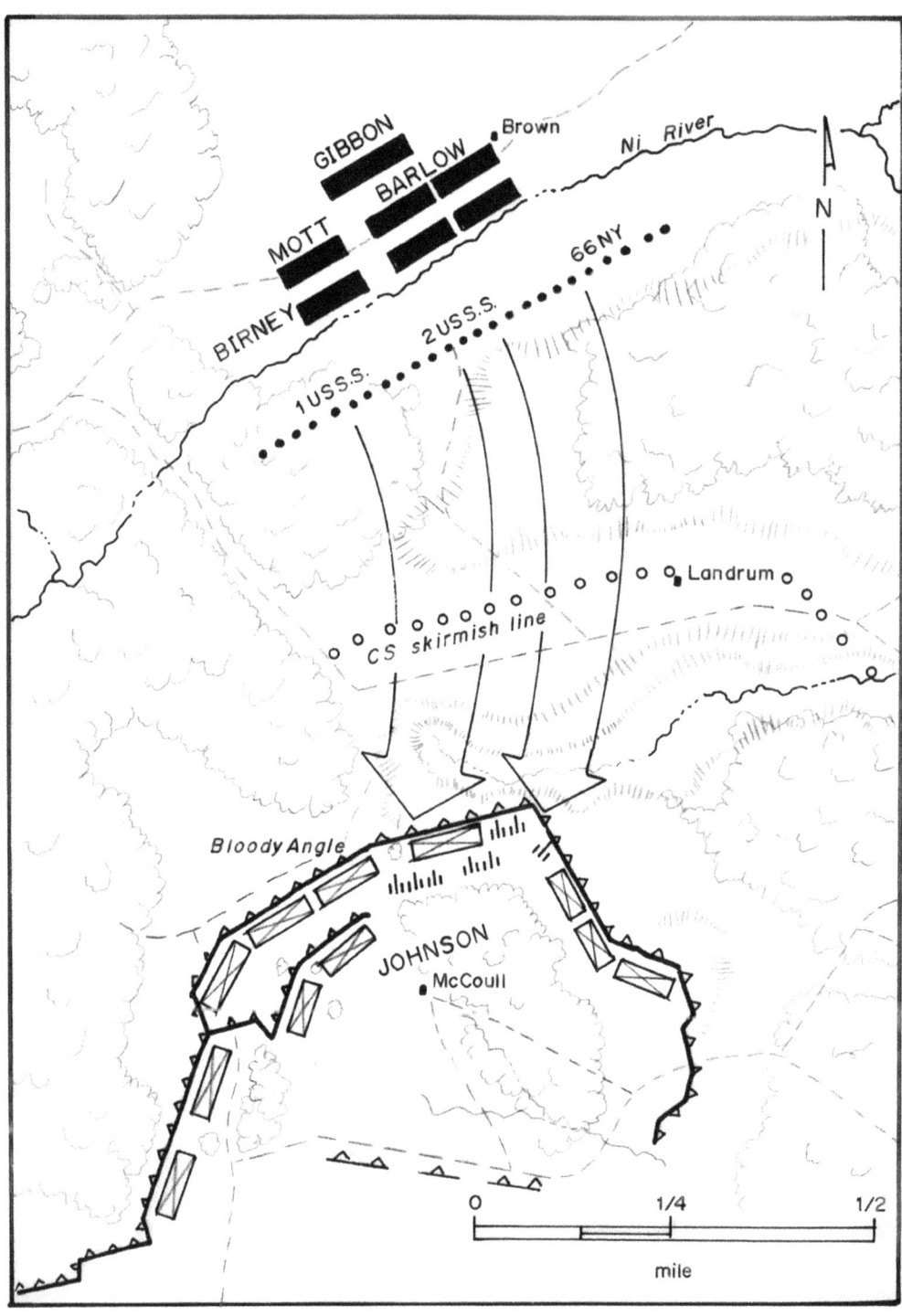

The Battle of Spotsylvania Courthouse, May 12, 1864. Map by John Heiser.

until reaching the main rebel lines at the Mule Shoe salient. The sharpshooters rushed through the trees to the edge of a cleared field; ahead in the dim morning light was the apex of the Mule Shoe. A few rebel pickets managed some scattered shots, but most were stunned by the tide of blue-clad Federals rushing through their outposts, which were quickly overrun.

On the sharpshooters ran, followed by Ward's other eight regiments. About halfway across the 200 yards of cleared space the Federals descended into a swale and then up a slight slope to the rebel works. Brigadier General de Trobriand, who filed the battle report for Ward's Brigade, mentioned that "some thoughtless person raised a shout, and the whole line immediately took it up" as the men rushed to the enemy works. A fierce hand-to-hand fight ensued as the rebels fought desperately to hold the flood of Federals behind their earth and log walls. "Nevertheless, the charge was successful, and the first line was taken with a large number of prisoners, and the troops, inspired with success, rushed forward to the second line of the enemy's works."[17]

After breaching the Confederate works, the Federals pursued fleeing rebels to the second line of works. In fighting their way over the breastworks the Federal brigades lost all unit cohesion. Soon the Federal II Corps became a jumbled mass of disordered regiments, fighting more as a mob than an army. The 2nd U.S.S.S., like the other sharpshooter regiment, was probably "mixed in promiscuously with the other troops" fighting inside the Mule Shoe.[18]

Of course General Lee did not panic. He rode to the sound of the fighting and soon had reinforcements on the way from the far left of his line. Brigadier General John B. Gordon pulled troops from the west side of the salient to blunt the attack at the second line south of the McCoull House, and the situation stabilized for the Confederates. By the time Gordon had checked the Federals, Hancock's men had already captured twenty cannon, 3200 men and two generals, along with dozens of enemy colors.[19]

At about 6 A.M. troops from the Federal VI Corps attacked just west of the apex of the Mule Shoe but were unable to produce a decisive breakthrough. Each side had rushed more troops into the melee as the Confederates desperately sought to drive the Federals out of their works. Hancock's troops hunkered down in the enemy trenches to meet Lee's counterattacks. One sharpshooter counted five rebel charges during the day. The fighting took on a character of brutality and horror of incredible magnitude. It was, in the words of a sharpshooter, "a bloody carnival." Troops on both sides kept up a constant close-range fire, as did the artillery. Ammunition was continually brought up by pack mules carrying 3,000 rounds per delivery.[20]

The fighting continued for hours in this fashion on the Mule Shoe front. Heavy downpours resumed, turning the bare dirt earthworks into a muddy quagmire. Men were literally spattered with mud head to toe during the fighting. The wounded were often smothered in the standing water and viscous mud after falling, then pressed down into the soft mud as others fell or stepped upon them. A continuous hail of bullets literally tore fallen men to pieces, arms, heads, and torsos being blown apart. Brigadier General Lewis Grant described the scene as the two sides clashed along the captured fieldworks:

It was emphatically a hand-to-hand fight. Scores were shot down within a few feet of the death-dealing muskets. A breast-work of logs and earth separated the combatants. Our men would reach over the breast-works and discharge their muskets in the very face of the enemy. Some men clubbed their muskets and in some instances used clubs and rails.... In this way the brigade was engaged for about eight hours.... The sight the next day was repulsive and sickening.... Some of the wounded were almost entirely buried by the dead bodies of their companions that had fallen upon them. Many of the dead were horribly mangled....[21]

General Ward, brigade commander for the 2nd, encountered General Birney during the confused melee shortly after the initial breakthrough. Ward was repeating his erratic behavior in much the same manner as what had occurred during the confused fighting in the Wilderness the previous week. Seen running toward the rear, Ward explained that he was trying to retrieve his horse. Birney gave Ward a mount from one of his staffers and sent him back to his men. Before long Ward was acting completely irrational, and General Birney became convinced that Ward was very intoxicated. Birney had little recourse but to send Ward to the rear in arrest. This day marked the end of Ward's involvement with the sharpshooters.[22]

Grant remained determined to finish the Confederates and believed he would. More attacks were ordered on all fronts that morning as the Federal commander-in-chief expected a breakthrough. It wasn't to be. None of the attacks found a soft spot. The Confederates, behind their fieldworks, simply added to the long Federal casualty list. The pandemonium continued in the Mule Shoe until well after dark when finally the shooting sputtered out. During the night Lee pulled his men back from the Mule Shoe into a new line stretching across its base. Lee had been shoved back a little but the stalemate continued.

There simply had never been anything quite like the dreadful pandemonium of the Mule Shoe to this point in the Civil War. Part of that line is still known as the Bloody Angle to this day. In the Smithsonian Institution in Washington, D.C., there is displayed a stump from a twenty-two-inch-thick oak tree recovered near the Bloody Angle. That

Brigadier General John H.H. Ward strikes an unpretentious, perhaps natural pose in this wartime photograph. Library of Congress Civil War Collection.

A modern replica of the dirt and earth fieldworks utilized by the Confederates at Spotsylvania Courthouse.

oak was cut down by the incredible volume of random musket fire on that front. And it was not the only such indicator of the ferocity of Spotsylvania; the entire disputed area around the Mule Shoe was so chewed and churned by musket and artillery fire that even the grass was cut low. The battlefield remains today as a monument to the incredible determination and pluck demonstrated by Civil War soldiers.

On May 13 both of the exhausted armies finally got a relative day of rest as Grant needed to gather intelligence following the extensive fighting on the 12th. Some of the sharpshooters probably assisted with burial details, witnessing the nauseating spectacle of horrors within the Mule Shoe. Others took part in probing the enemy picket lines to develop the strength and location of enemy resistance. While driving in the rebel pickets on the 13th, Sergeant G.S. Scribner of Company H and three others were wounded.[23] Overall the day was something of a reprieve compared to the cataclysmic 12th of May.

Over the next few days Grant tried to maneuver to advantage against Lee but without success. From the 14th to the 18th of May portions of the 2nd U.S.S.S. were in action as skirmishers and snipers at various points on the lines. Several men were killed and wounded in these little personal battles on the days between the major assaults at Spotsylvania. Grant attempted one final heavy assault on May 18, sending Neil's 2nd

Division of the VI Corps and two divisions from the II Corps, the 1st and 2nd, on another forlorn attack through the Mule Shoe. Within a few hours after dawn the Confederates had checked the attack and commenced blasting the stalled Federals with a devastating artillery bombardment. Before 9 A.M. Meade called off the slaughter, and the Federals retreated out of the Mule Shoe deathtrap yet again.[24]

After the disaster on the 18th Grant finally realized that the Confederates were simply posted too strongly behind earthworks around Spotsylvania to be dislodged. Thus it was General Lee who initiated the last offensive of the campaign by sending his II Corps on a reconnaissance in force against the Federal right flank on May 19. The Confederates ran into a new division of green heavy artillery regiments fresh from the Washington defenses. Grant had ordered the men to be transferred to the Army of the Potomac to serve as infantry. The new division was assigned to Brigadier General Robert Tyler as the 4th Division of Hancock's II Corps. The heavy artillery regiments were organized with extra companies and contained far more soldiers than the veteran regiments already serving in the corps; in fact, Tyler's five heavy artillery regiments actually outnumbered the Confederate II Corps that day. One of Tyler's regiments brought nearly 1,800 into the fight.[25] To the veterans in the field just one heavy artillery regiment seemed to equal in numbers an entire brigade of veteran regiments.

Confederate Lieutenant General Richard Ewell, commanding Lee's reconnaissance in force, quickly discerned that he was facing inexperienced troops. For one thing, the heavy artillerymen were wearing clean uniforms with brightly polished brass belt plates, having spent their time in Washington, where appearance counted for something. The new men were derisively called "paper collar" or "bandbox" soldiers by the veterans in the field. Ewell decided to pitch into these nascent infantrymen as if they were just so many militiamen. To his unpleasant surprise the newcomers fought back with spirit and gallantry. Soon a fierce engagement raged on the Harris and Alsop farms east of the Ni River on Grant's far right flank.[26]

Not surprisingly, Tyler's new division was soon in need of help. General Hancock sent Birney's Division to the Harris Farm, and troops from the V Corps were also dispatched to reinforce Tyler's hard-pressed regiments. One of the sharpshooters remembered watching the inexperienced 7th New York Heavy Artillery Regiment advance during the battle. The green New Yorkers fought as if on parade, taking care to ensure that their lines were straight and simply standing in ranks when firing without taking cover. Other veterans from Birney's Division were also baffled by the fighting methods of the heavy artillerymen. One veteran observed that the novices thought it was cowardly to lie down in face of the enemy, so they stood in ranks and suffered hundreds of unnecessary casualties while the veterans took cover and lost few men.[27]

By nightfall, however, Ewell was quite ready to pull back; the inexperienced heavy artillerymen had fought hard, and with Federal reinforcements arriving Ewell was in serious trouble. In fact, Grant missed his best opportunity yet to deal a crushing blow to a large portion of Lee's army outside of its trenches. With better cooperation and coordination Grant could have blocked Ewell's retreat and then crushed his corps. Even with the aggressive Grant in command, the unwieldy Army of the Potomac yet again proved incapable of exploiting an obvious tactical advantage. As it was, Ewell's corps managed to retreat under the cover of a very black night, returning to its original lines by around midnight.[28]

When the fighting erupted on the morning of May 19, Grant was already planning to move on by his left flank to skirt Lee's trenches and move closer to the enemy capital. On the night of May 20 he put a new plan into motion by dispatching Hancock's II Corps on a night march around the Confederates' right flank. Hancock's corps set out that night for Milford Station. Grant intended to seize the crossings of the North Anna River, one of most formidable defensive positions between Spotsylvania and Richmond.[29]

Hancock's departure on the 20th marked the end of the Spotsylvania Campaign. Confederate losses for the campaign exceeded 10,000. Total Federal casualties during the series of battles at Spotsylvania were the second heaviest of the war. Only Gettysburg counted more. The Federals suffered a staggering 18,399 casualties, of which 2,275 were killed. The 2nd U.S.S.S. reported twelve killed, thirty-eight wounded and three missing for a total of fifty-three casualties. At least seven of the wounded sharpshooters later died from their wounds, making a total of nineteen 2nd U.S.S.S. deaths resulting from the fighting at Spotsylvania.[30]

Grant still hoped to engage Lee while on the road to the North Anna in open country, before the rebels could dig in. There he could effectively utilize his artillery and take full advantage of his superior numbers. Hoping to tempt Lee into an ill-advised attack outside the security of fortifications, Grant sent Hancock marching well in front of the rest of the army, as if on an independent mission. Grant risked having the II Corps—and the sharpshooters—gobbled up before he could pitch into Lee with the rest of his corps. But Lee ignored the opportunity to smash Hancock's corps; instead he chose to concentrate his army at the strong defensive position below the North Anna River.[31]

As Lee concentrated along the North Anna, Grant pondered his options. He could continue on to the North Anna line and look for a weak point to attack. His second option, favored by General Meade, called for bypassing Lee's new line and making for the Pamunkey River and on to Richmond. Grant chose to follow Lee to the North Anna. His choice reflected his preference for the attack, but Grant had ample reasons for pressing Lee. He felt constrained to seek an immediate success for political reasons, and he continued to misjudge the condition of Lee's army. His experience at Chattanooga, where his army drove the Confederates from a very formidable line, and the fact that Lee had declined to attack his scattered forces convinced him that he still could shorten the war by assailing the enemy.[32] For now—and the remainder of the war—he would look for the opportunity to strike. Maneuver would be his second and less favored alternative.

On May 23 the Federal corps arrived at the North Anna and deployed as follows: Warren's V Corps on the Federal right, south of the river at the Jericho Mills Crossing; Wright's VI Corps north of the river, backing up Warren; Burnside's IX Corps at Ox Ford, north of the river; Hancock's II Corps on the Federal left along the Telegraph

Road, north of the river above the Chesterfield Bridge.³³ By late afternoon, after Warren's troops had crossed the river and as Hancock approached the Chesterfield Bridge, fighting erupted. Around 4 P.M. troops from the II Corps encountered a fieldwork just north of the Chesterfield Bridge on the west side of the road. The fieldwork, called Henagan's Redoubt, was manned by troops from Colonel John Henagan's South Carolina brigade. The 2nd U.S.S.S. deployed into a skirmish line and probed the approach to the bridge. Soon the sharpshooters were engaged in a sharp exchange of fire with rebel skirmishers and sharpshooters. A Confederate sharpshooter firing a Whitworth Rifle from the redoubt was particularly dangerous. Private Luther Crane of Company G was mortally wounded, the bullet striking his side and passing through his entire body. Perhaps Crane was hit by the sniper firing the Whitworth, as the bullet retained considerable energy for a long-range shot.³⁴

Hancock unleashed his artillery to silence the rebel batteries across the river, and by 6 P.M. he was ready to attack Henagan's Redoubt. Hancock selected two of Birney's brigades: the 1st, commanded by Colonel Thomas Eagan (who had replaced the disgraced Brigadier J.H.H. Ward); and 2nd, commanded by Colonel B.R. Pierce. The 2nd U.S.S.S. raced up a gentle slope towards the redoubt in a skirmish line, leading Eagan's attack. Charging through heavy musket and cannon fire, and pelted by a rainstorm, the 2nd led their brigade into the rebel works. Birney's two brigades soon overwhelmed the redoubt and drove the South Carolinians from their works and across the river.³⁵

While the charge at the Chesterfield Bridge was a complete success for Hancock, and well worth the cost in his opinion, it proved deadly to the depleted 2nd. Several men were hit, and at least five in addition to Private Crane were killed or mortally wounded on May 23. Among the mortally wounded was Private Joseph Barton of Company H. A new recruit, Barton had joined the regiment at Brandy Station before the campaign commenced. He had written to his wife from Brandy Station to persuade her that his choice to join the sharpshooters was indeed wise. Expecting to be home within a year upon the defeat of the Confederacy, he would instead die in August from his wounds.³⁶

Fighting also raged on Warren's front, south of the river on the Federal right. Confederates from Hill's III Corps attacked Cutler's 4th Division, including the remnant of the famous Iron Brigade, and drove them back before being checked. Warren's troops constructed fieldworks south of the river and held their ground for the night. Darkness closed out the fighting on both fronts.³⁷

At about 8 A.M. on the following morning Hancock sent the 20th Indiana across the Chesterfield Bridge under covering fire from division artillery. Both of Berdan's Sharpshooter regiments rushed over the bridge shortly afterwards. The three regiments spread out into a skirmish line and overran the rebel pickets. They continued on hurriedly to the Fox home and outbuildings, about 400 yards south of the bridge. General Hancock then sent his divisions across the river to secure a bridgehead on the south bank. Soon he had his men digging earthworks on both sides of the Telegraph Road.³⁸

Around 3 P.M. Hancock, intending to develop the enemy lines, sent Symth's 1st

Division brigade into a thick wood to probe the Confederate works. Fighting exceeded expectations, and before nightfall Hancock had committed most of Gibbon's 2nd Division to the combat. Gibbon's men breached the enemy works in the dense wood, but the Confederates counterattacked. Although the fighting continued until well after dark, nothing significant was gained from it. Other meaningless fighting broke out on the 24th when troops from Ledlie's IX Corps brigade made an unauthorized attack on Lee's stronghold near Ox Ford. Ledlie was apparently drunk, and he made the worst of an already hopeless assault. Scores of his men were cut down without any advantage or gain. The fighting on the 24th finally ended in the inky darkness without altering the standoff along the North Anna line.[39]

On the morning of the 25th Grant remained unsure of the configuration of Lee's defensive line south of the river. Grant needed more details from Warren's sector before making his next move. Thus the V Corps was sent forward to test the Confederate III Corps lines along the Virginia Central Railroad west of the Telegraph Road and south of the river. Hancock continued to probe the Confederate lines on his sector. The 2nd took part in this work as Companies C and G were ordered to move forward and harass the enemy lines. A sharpshooter from Company G recorded in his diary on the 25th that he and his comrades crawled on their hands and knees as individuals until within rifle range of the Confederate works. Using their tin cups and case knives, the sharpshooters dug rifle pits to shelter themselves from enemy fire. The two companies then assailed the Confederate artillery with an effective harassing fire and often shouted taunts at the rebels throughout the day.[40]

Private Henry Campbell of Company H, which remained in the rear on the 25th, spent part of the day writing a letter to his cousin Anna. Campbell noted that the firing was brisk on the skirmish line. He also mentioned that one of the "skedadlers" who had never taken part in any battle just "came up" and was being ridiculed by the others. Like any regiment the sharpshooters had a few deadbeats and malingerers, men who managed to keep out of harm's way. Campbell's letter also gives some indication of the regiment's morale after twenty days of continuous combat and movement without rest. He referred to the ordeal as "what tries mens souls," but he pointed to the fact that "the rebs have to work as hard as we do." Campbell admitted that the Federals were losing more men than the enemy because they had to continually attack breastworks, but he indicated that the sharpshooters remained "very confident" and still did their best. His letter gave no indication of deep discouragement or pessimism.[41]

By the morning of May 26, 1864, General Grant had realized that he had no further business at the North Anna. However, he, like Private Campbell, remained optimistic about the prospects for ultimate victory over Lee. Grant expressed his confidence in a letter to General Halleck on the 26th. He admitted that attacking at the North Anna "would cause a slaughter of our men that even success would not justify." So Grant decided to again move around Lee's right, explaining that moving around Lee's left would require the army to cross three streams in succession, "all of them presenting considerable obstacles to the movement of an army." The fighting at the North Anna had convinced Grant that victory was assured:

Lee's army is really whipped. The prisoners we now take show it, and the action of his army shows it unmistakably. A battle with them outside of intrenchments cannot be had. Our men feel that they have gained the *morale* over the enemy and attack with confidence. I may be mistaken, but I feel that our success over Lee's army is already insured.[42]

Grant's army began withdrawing from the North Anna line after dark on the 26th. Well before dawn on the 27th the Federals were on the north bank of the river and on their way to again outflank the Confederates. Grant managed to disengage without bringing on an attack while his army was vulnerable.[43]

The next combat action involving the 2nd occurred on May 30 and 31 along Totopotomoy Creek. General Lee quickly reacted to Grant's shift from the North Anna by establishing a new defensive line south of Totopotomoy Creek, a narrow stream less than ten miles northeast of the Richmond defenses. Grant's ultimate objective remained to get Lee's army into a battle in open country and then destroy it, so finding Lee entrenched behind yet another natural barrier was vexing. Nevertheless, he had to determine the strength of this new line.[44] Probes of the Totopotomoy line involved the sharpshooters on the 30th and 31st.

On the 30th two companies from the 2nd U.S.S.S. skirmished while others erected breastworks north of Totopotomoy Creek. The next day saw the 2nd engaged in yet another rush against rebel earthworks. William Humphrey mentioned this charge in his postwar account of Company E. According to Humphrey, "We were told by General Grant, in person, to go across the creek, if we had to surrender when we got there, but we did not surrender, we took ... [137 prisoners] and held the works that night." A diary entry from a soldier in Company D indicated that the regiment charged shortly after 9 A.M. in a skirmish line and captured the Confederate works on its front. According to the sharpshooter's diary entry, thirteen men from the regiment were wounded during the fighting that day. Private Horatio P. Bruce of Company E, one of those wounded, died on June 21 from his wounds.[45]

While the sharpshooters battled along the Totopotomoy, Grant was focusing his attention on a dusty road junction a few miles north of the Chickahominy River called Cold Harbor. The place amounted to nothing more than an old tavern situated at an obscure crossroads. Having already been the scene of a battle during McClellan's Richmond Campaign in 1862, the place once again assumed a status and notoriety it otherwise never would have garnered. To Grant and Lee the road intersection was a vital key to their battle strategy. For Grant the place was important because one road leading to Cold Harbor connected to White House Landing, his supply base on the Pamunkey River. Another road led south across the Chickahominy, providing a route to the strategically important James River and Petersburg area. Grant could also utilize the crossroads to get around Lee's flank and force a confrontation outside of the Richmond defenses. Lee, on the other hand, needed to seize Cold Harbor to deny Grant's strategic options.[46]

Both Grant and Lee sent cavalry forces to secure the Cold Harbor crossroads; thus, on May 31 a cavalry struggle over possession of the junction initiated one of the most terrible battles of the Civil War. Major General Phillip Sheridan led a Federal cavalry attack at Cold Harbor that drove the rebels back and then managed to hold the crossroads until VI Corps infantry reinforcements arrived. Grant had ordered up the XVIII Corps from Butler's force at Bermuda Hundred, south of Richmond along the James River, and these troops also arrived to reinforce Sheridan on June 1. After the infantry reinforcements arrived at the crossroads, Grant ordered an attack. Unfortunately for the Federal infantry, Confederates from Anderson's I Corps had also reached the battlefield and had time to dig in and prepare. Attacks by the two Federal corps going in against fieldworks made minimal gains at a high cost in casualties. As the fighting sputtered out at dusk on June 1, both army commanders shifted their forces to renew the fighting around Cold Harbor.[47]

Grant and Meade saw an opportunity to strike a decisive blow with Hancock's II Corps attacking in concert with the other forces already in place at Cold Harbor. Hancock's corps would have to make a difficult night march from the Federal right to be in place for the planned attack by dawn of June 2. Meade sent the following instructions to Hancock at 11 P.M. on June 1: "On reaching Cold Harbor you will take position on the left of the Sixth Corps and at once attack the enemy, endeavoring to turn his right flank and interpose between him and the Chickahominy. If practicable you will detach a force to the Chickahominy and endeavor to secure possession of a crossing-place." So the sharpshooters pulled out of their entrenchments around midnight and took their place in Hancock's column.[48]

Hancock's night march resulted in yet another example of the just plain bad luck that plagued the Army of the Potomac during most of the war. Although the marching distance was only about nine miles, part of the corps took the wrong route. Marching through clouds of dense dust during an oppressively hot and black night, the lead elements of the II Corps did not reach Cold Harbor until after 6 A.M. By the time Hancock's troops were in position to fight, it was too late and the men were too exhausted to be effective.[49]

Lee also shifted his troops to Cold Harbor, but although they marched along interior lines of shorter distance, Lee's forces arrived just in time to confront Hancock's corps. If the II Corps had not been delayed, the outcome of the Battle of Cold Harbor might well have been dramatically altered in favor of Grant. Had the Federals secured the route across the Chickahominy, Lee might have ultimately been forced to attack them in open country, something Grant had sought since the beginning of the Overland Campaign.[50]

With Hancock's corps arriving late, Grant had no choice except to reschedule the attack. June 2 was lost to the Federals, but Lee's troops took advantage of the extra time to construct strong earthworks along the low ridges where the Federals would attack. These were perhaps the most skillfully constructed fieldworks yet seen in the war. A newspaper correspondent who later examined the works called them a "labyrinth" of redundant lines designed to cover and enfilade every approach. The rebel artillery was also cleverly positioned within the works to sweep the front and flanks of attackers with crossfire. Viewing the works from a distance, the Federals did not perceive that they were any more formidable than what they had seen at Spotsylvania. But the forthcoming attack would exact a terrible toll of Federal casualties at an unprecedented rate.[51]

Once again, as many had done before the scheduled assault at Mine Run, Federal soldiers wrote their names and addresses on pieces of paper and pinned them on the backs of their coats so that their corpses could be identified. Nothing more need be said about the expectations of the men of Hancock's II Corps. Well before dawn on June 3, 1864, Bugler George Gracey of the 2nd New York Heavy Artillery moved to the front of the II Corps to sound the charge. He had been specially selected by Hancock himself for the duty because of his eloquent and inspiring musical talent. At around 4:30 A.M. Gracey's bugle echoed the call to charge. Two of Hancock's divisions stepped out of their trenches and moved across open fields towards the imperceptible enemy works. Meade also sent his other corps forward on all sectors of the battlefield that morning, the troops on the northern sector attacking to occupy the Confederates while the main assault was made by the II and VI Corps to the south.[52]

General Winfield S. Hancock and his division commanders near Cold Harbor. Left to right: Brigadier Francis Barlow, Major General Winfield S. Hancock, Major General David Bell Birney, and Brigadier General John Gibbon. General Birney was divisional commander over the 2nd U.S.S.S. during the Overland Campaign. Library of Congress Civil War Collection.

June 3, 1864, was a tragic day for the United States Army. Somehow Grant's order to go forward with this delayed attack at Cold Harbor has been remembered since as one of the most flawed command decisions of the war. Perhaps it is because Grant himself admitted that he regretted it. There were many other equally futile and bloody assaults ordered by Grant before and afterwards, but the Cold Harbor assault remains best remembered for its wantonness. The final effect was to beat the last bit of dash out of Hancock's corps.

On Hancock's front Gibbon's 2nd Division went forward on the right and Barlow's 1st Division charged on the left. Hancock kept Birney's 3rd Division as a support behind Barlow. Thus, in this battle the 2nd U.S.S.S. was fortunate to escape yet another costly sacrificial charge. All along the Confederate lines the attacks were repelled with ease, the Federal II and XVIII Corps suffering heavy losses. Directly in front of the sharpshooters Barlow's troops made the only significant Federal breakthrough along a lightly defended sunken road that had been turned into a bog by recent rains. Scores of rebels and three cannon were captured, but Lee had posted a reserve nearby and the Confederates counterattacked. Barlow's men were driven back with heavy losses; they then took cover in captured rifle pits or dug in with bayonets on a slight rise a short distance from the recaptured works.[53]

Gibbon and Barlow had seen their divisions so badly battered during the attack that neither commander requested support from Birney's division. So the 2nd U.S.S.S. waited in the II Corps trenches while the fighting fizzled on their front. By 10 A.M. Meade had decided to shift Birney's troops to the north to support Warren's V Corps on the Federal right. Moving Birney's division away deprived Hancock of the catalyst that might have enabled him to turn the tide of the battle in favor of the Federals. Had Birney promptly reinforced Barlow at the sunken road, the day might have been turned into a "Union celebration" instead of yet another doleful disappointment.[54]

As it was, the massive Federal attack at Cold Harbor produced only a sickening day of horror and carnage for Meade's army. An unprecedented 3,500 Federals fell within one hour of the start of the attack, a killing and maiming rate that probably surpassed all other battles of the Civil War. A great many surviving Federals were pinned down near the Confederate trenches after the sun rose with the rebels mercilessly shooting any man that moved. One Federal officer reported that the Confederates even intentionally shot exposed wounded men lying between the lines.[55]

By afternoon the 2nd had moved to a supporting position near the V Corps. The worst of the bloodletting was over and the regiment had been fortunate to miss it. Many of the sharpshooters probably did not even know the extent of the carnage that day. After spending the night in support of Warren's corps, Birney's troops marched back on June 4 to their previous position with the II Corps.[56]

For the next week portions of the 2nd U.S.S.S. were sent out for sharpshooting duty at various points along the Federal lines. After the massive assault on the 3rd, the Federals settled into a defensive stance for several days. During this period the sniping intensified to a level surpassing anything yet seen during the long campaign. Civil War writer Ernest Furgurson observed that at Cold Harbor the opposing lines were dug so close together and the targets were so plentiful that "the trained sniper may have been more intensively employed and more feared than anywhere else in the war."[57]

As they had occasionally done during previous battles, some of the sharpshooters managed a truce with their rebel counterparts while on sharpshooting duty. On June 5 Companies C and G were out on the firing line, and even after Private Daniel Smith of Company G was severely wounded the two sides agreed in the afternoon to a ceasefire. Then, after doing their best during the day to kill each other, men from each side met between the lines to exchange coffee for tobacco. They also buried a dead horse that had afflicted both sides with its disgusting stench. The truce was repeated on the 7th, but roaming snipers continued to pick off the unwary and unfortunate of both armies.[58]

Already unpopular before the Overland Campaign, sharpshooters, Union and Confederate, were by now widely and intensely disliked in both armies. Reports of men killed by sharpshooters while answering Mother Nature's call were particularly infuriating to soldiers. One Federal artilleryman noted that for ordinary infantrymen such killing was a *taboo*, but sharpshooting "brutes" constantly ignored the convention of showing mercy at such times. The artilleryman admitted that he hated all sharpshooters and "was always glad to see them killed."[59]

As these incidents of virtual murder multiplied and the war grew increasingly brutal, sharpshooters in both armies perhaps feared that they would eventually receive no quarter if captured. There is at least some evidence to this effect. Park Service historian and Civil War author Chris Calkins noted that when he worked at Appomattox National Battlefield several years ago a Confederate sniper's Whitworth Rifle was uncovered on that battlefield. The rifle, found with a handful of Whitworth bullets, had apparently been smashed against a tree and discarded so that the man who carried it would not be identified as a sniper when Lee's army surrendered.[60]

Even the sharpshooters themselves were occasional victims of random sniper shootings and sharpshooting duels. On June 9, thirty men from Company D reported to General Barlow for service as sharpshooters at different points along the lines. James F. Sally of that company was killed, shot through the head that day. Bugler Carmillus T. Warner was killed in camp on June 11 by a rebel sharpshooter, and Private James Millet of Company A was killed in action on June 10th. In addition to these three men killed, the 2nd U.S.S.S had six men wounded (two mortally) and three were reported missing during the fighting at Cold Harbor.[61]

As in all the previous battles of this campaign, Grant had failed to defeat Lee at Cold Harbor. Federal losses were far greater than the Confederates' and nothing had been gained by the horrendous casualties. But Grant was not even remotely close to repeating the mistakes of his predecessors. He was looking ahead to the next battle and the next objective, looking for the key to victory. While the 2nd plied their sharpshooting on the far left flank at Cold Harbor, Grant was implementing the boldest and riskiest plan of the campaign, if not the war.

Grant still held a great advantage over Lee despite the outcome of Cold Harbor. In the Shenandoah Valley a Federal force under Major General David Hunter had won an important victory at Piedmont and was moving towards the strategically important city of Lynchburg, Virginia. Lee dispatched Lieutenant General Jubal Early on June 11 with the Confederate II Corps to confront Hunter and defend Lynchburg. Grant now planned to again skirt past Lee's right flank, this time with decisive effect. He would swing to his left, cross the tidal James River and have his army in position to capture Petersburg, Virginia, a vital railroad transportation hub. If the Federals could capture and hold Petersburg, the Confederate capital at nearby Richmond would inevitably fall, and very soon.[62]

Under Grant's leadership, the coming of spring had induced a plethora of war. In the Army of the Potomac alone, the over 50,000 casualties suffered since May equaled about half of the total in that army since the start of the war.[63] Even so, Grant wisely remained committed to the offensive on all fronts. Sherman's campaign to capture Atlanta was progressing slowly but steadily. With the presidential election coming in the fall, Grant understood that his position depended upon immediate progress towards ultimate victory. His decision to move across the James to Petersburg held great potential, but it was also fraught with great peril. Grant had taken great risks previously, especially during the Vicksburg Campaign. The upcoming weeks would mark another pivotal point in the war.

12

Winning the Hard Way: Petersburg

By the early morning hours of June 13, 1864, the 2nd U.S.S.S. was on the march to the James with Hancock's II Corps. Grant had managed to catch his adversary by surprise, getting completely out of the Cold Harbor lines and to the James River crossings before Lee could react. Grant's greatest concern had been that the Confederates would anticipate his plan and strike while his army was strung out during the march to the James. The sharpshooters camped within a mile of the James that night, and like the rest of Grant's forces, they would cross the river without having to fight Lee to do it.[1]

On the morning of the 14th the sharpshooters embarked on a transport to cross the James. The ship steamed downriver a few miles to a channel and turned about, landing the regiment almost directly across the river from where it embarked. The V and IX Corps crossed the river on a 2,100-foot-long pontoon bridge near Windmill Point. Smith's XVIII Corps had steamed from White House Landing to the south bank of the James near Petersburg. The movement from Cold Harbor to Petersburg was a signal success.[2]

June 15 was a day of tremendous opportunity for the Federals. Major General William Smith led a force composed of his XVIII Corps, a division of United States Colored Troops (U.S.C.T.) and a division of cavalry to the outskirts of Petersburg. Defending Petersburg that morning was a force of only about 2,200 men under command of General P.G.T. Beauregard.[3] Grant's last flanking maneuver had worked to near perfection, giving the Federal commander-in-chief an opportunity to shorten the war by months. With a great superiority in numbers, Smith was in position to capture Petersburg the easy way before Lee could get his forces in place to man its defenses.

From this distance in time it seems obvious that General Smith should have appreciated the fact that he had an opportunity to save tens of thousands of lives. The general surely understood that if he failed to breach the lightly held works around Petersburg that day, the Confederates would strongly reinforce Petersburg and soon. Smith should have attacked the weak Petersburg line without delay. Instead, he approached the rebel lines cautiously, conducting "interminable reconnaissances." He was in position to attack, and could have succeeded, around 1:30 P.M., but after delays it was about 7 P.M. before he ordered an attack. Smith's troops easily overran the Confederate fortifications on his front before dark, but with the capture of the city at hand, Smith called a halt. He later explained that he thought that he had already captured the key positions defending the city and thus further attacks could wait.[4]

Around dusk Hancock and his II Corps arrived at the site of the captured works completely fatigued from the day-long march from the river. At Smith's request the II Corps relieved the U.S.C.T. in the captured works. The sharpshooters with Birney's division held the left near captured Battery No. 11. Although famished and intensely weary, the II Corps men wanted to push on to capture Petersburg that night. One soldier recalled that the moon was bright and conditions perfect for a night attack.[5] So obvious was it that the city could be captured with ease that a sharpshooter noted in his diary on the 15th that only the "faltering" of the officers prevented the capture of Petersburg that night. The sharpshooter's remarkable diary entry gives an indication of how quickly accurate information circulated during a battle. From his notes, written that night, it is obvious that even the enlisted men were aware that Lee would bring in reinforcements before morning.[6]

Major General Hancock assumed command of all Federal forces on the Petersburg front on the morning of June 16. Meade was yet to arrive so Hancock as the senior officer present was in charge temporarily. General Grant wanted a strong reconnaissance to test the new rebel lines; Hancock ordered a probe to find a weak spot in the defenses in preparation for a general assault to follow later. General Birney's 3rd Division furnished the troops, and as fate would have it, Eagan's 1st Brigade, to which the 2nd U.S.S.S. belonged, was selected to do the job.[7]

Early in the morning the sharpshooters went out to locate the new enemy positions. Eagan then formed his brigade for an attack in a belt of cut timber just to the left of the Prince George Court House Road. Eagan led three of his regiments forward that morning: the 17th Maine, 20th Indiana and 40th New York. The sharpshooters and the remainder of Eagan's brigade supported the attack under intense artillery fire. The initial attack was driven back with heavy losses, as an entire Confederate brigade had arrived just in time to reinforce the militiamen holding the works. Eagan regrouped and went forward again, this time capturing Battery No. 12. In both of Eagan's attacks, the 40th New York did little except seek "refuge" from the heavy enemy fire. The attacking regiments suffered numerous casualties; Eagan himself was severely wounded and was later replaced by Colonel Henry J. Madill.[8]

The day passed for the sharpshooters with little activity, and so it was for most of the Federals under Hancock. This lack of initiative enabled General Beauregard to reinforce and strengthen his defensive lines. Around 6 P.M., after General Meade had arrived, the attacks were renewed against the now much stronger Confederate lines. At the end of the day the attacking II Corps had captured a few more Confederate fortifications but made limited progress. Sharpshooter William Green recorded in his diary that eighteen men from the 2nd were wounded along with Captain Abraham Wright of Company A. Private Green noted that the regiment remained in its original position during the attack, apparently providing suppressing fire for the attacking brigades. According to Green the enemy shellfire and canister was as intense as he had yet seen during the war.[9] By nightfall on June 16 it was obvious that Grant's brilliant movement across the James had been largely wasted. Petersburg would now have to be won the hard way.

During the following two days, Grant attempted to batter his way through the reinforced Confederate trenches before Petersburg with even more headlong assaults. In a way, Grant was lured into a repeat of his dismal failures of the Overland Campaign by limited successes won on June 16 and 17. The inevitable result was yet another 10,000 casualties and yet another stalemate. During the Petersburg assaults the 2nd U.S.S.S. was "employed in almost constant skirmishing in the attempts to carry the place by direct assault." Apparently the sharpshooters did not charge the trenches in the manner that created enormous casualty lists at Petersburg.[10]

However, Madill's Brigade, to which the 2nd U.S.S.S. belonged, took part in an assault on June 18 that cost the 1st Maine Heavy Artillery, fighting as infantry, the highest casualty total of any regiment in a single battle during the entire war. Attacking to the left of the Mainers, Madill's men were also hit hard "and retreated behind a sheltering barn." The Maine heavy artillerymen continued on without support and were simply cut to pieces in an open field near the Hare House. In only ten minutes the 1st Maine suffered 632 men killed and wounded out of approximately 875 men who made the attack. A diary entry written by Sergeant George Coffin of Company D mentioned that the 2nd had charged earlier in the day across an oat field and had operated as sharpshooters against a rebel battery. Coffin's entry seems to indicate that the sharpshooters missed the horrifying attack that demolished the 1st Maine, instead returning to Madill's brigade from sharpshooting duty after dark. Another sharpshooter mentioned the 1st Maine Heavy Artillery in his diary entry for June 18, noting that the Mainers suffered very heavy casualties and their dead and wounded remained isolated between the lines beyond reach of assistance.[11]

After four days of brutal but ineffective fighting around Petersburg, General Grant called off the offensive operations. His brilliantly executed plan to capture that vital city had failed on the morning of June 16, 1864. The subsequent series of attacks upon the Confederate trenches served only to compact the enemy lines. On June 20 Grant sent a message to Major General Benjamin Butler informing him that he intended to initiate an effort to "cut the enemy's lines of communication south." That evening Grant also informed Butler, "I have determined to try to envelope Petersburg."[12] Grant was reluctantly preparing for what he had sincerely hoped to avoid: a siege of Petersburg.

Before shifting fully into siege operations, Grant made one more attempt to entice Lee out into the open. Two railroads remained open to supply Petersburg and Richmond, the Southside Railroad and the Weldon Railroad. Grant hoped to lure the Confederates out of their Petersburg defenses by sending forces to destroy or at least threaten these roads. On June 21 General Meade dispatched the II Corps, temporarily commanded by Major General David Birney, and the VI Corps to raid the Weldon Railroad. The two corps were to "inflict as much damage as possible" and then return to Federal lines near Ream's Station, a few miles south of Petersburg on the Weldon Railroad.[13]

Early on the morning of June 21, 1864, Lieutenant Colonel Homer Stoughton returned to the regiment and resumed command. Stoughton had just arrived at the front from medical leave for the wound he suffered during the fighting at Spotsylvania. That morning the 2nd joined the flank movement against the Weldon Railroad, marching with the II Corps. At about 3 P.M. the 2nd U.S.S.S. was ordered to the front to act as an advance guard for the corps. The sharpshooters, already weary from the hard march, nevertheless hurried almost at a run to get into position. Colonel Stoughton later described the situation:

> ...the second regiment ... was put to the front to encounter the described squadron of Fitz Hugh Lee's cavalry. Colonel McDougal, who commanded the brigade [having already reported to Brigadier General Barlow, this would be the 3rd Brigade of the 1st Division, II Corps], and to whom I reported, sent our regiment in and we soon found ourselves largely outnumbered, and reported to Colonel McDougal, when he replied, "go on, there is nothing in your front," so I pushed on.[14]

The sharpshooters advanced straight into a trap sprung by the Confederate cavalry and were soon nearly surrounded. Colonel Stoughton thought he heard support coming up, and "in attempting to adjust and join the line, fell into the hands of the Second N.C. cavalry, dismounted." Captain Murry of Company F was also captured in the action, for the second time during the war. Most of the regiment, however, managed to escape by scrambling back to the main Federal position. Men from Company H captured the colonel and a lieutenant from the North Carolina cavalry regiment to somewhat offset the losses of the day.[15]

On the following day, June 22, the II and VI Corps moved westward from the Jerusalem Plank Road towards the Weldon Railroad as intended by General Grant. Moving through thick woods, the two corps became separated, creating a gap that effectively isolated each corps. Lieutenant General A.P. Hill's Confederate III Corps moved out of its Petersburg trenches undetected and attacked the VI Corps, driving it back. Hill's Confederates then took advantage of the gap between the two Federal corps to strike the II Corps ferociously. The II Corps gave way and retreated back to the Jerusalem Plank Road, losing 1,700 men captured.[16]

The 2nd U.S.S.S. also had several men captured that day when a portion of Barlow's 1st Division was outflanked by the Confederates. Early that morning the 2nd was sent forward in a skirmish line through

Lieutenant Colonel Homer R. Stoughton. He commanded the 2nd U.S.S.S. following Colonel Post's resignation. Stoughton was captured in June 1864, and although he was apparently well liked by the sharpshooters, he was mustered out after being released by the Confederates. Library of Congress Civil War Collection.

a thick wood, halting at the edge of a cleared field. Observing a large enemy cavalry force, the 2nd remained undetected in the woods for some time. Later a force of Federal infantry coming up to relieve the sharpshooters was seen by the rebel cavalry. The cavalry mounted and split into three bands. One portion remained in the field while two bands disappeared into the woods and worked their way around both flanks of the sharpshooters' position. Part of the cavalry attacked across the open field, receiving fire from the sharpshooters. While pulling back from the cavalry charge, the sharpshooters were assailed on both flanks by rebels demanding their surrender. Heavily outnumbered and outflanked, most of the sharpshooters ran a gauntlet of fire through the woods in a dash for the rear. Some of the men, perhaps as many as twenty-five, were overrun and taken prisoner. The regiment regrouped behind a breastwork with their brigade and waited for the Confederates to follow, but the cavalrymen made no attempt to attack the breastwork and made off with their prisoners.[17]

The 2nd U.S.S.S. turned in its poorest performance of the war during the Weldon Railroad expedition. Colonel Stoughton and Captain Murry had been captured and four officers had been wounded since June 16: Major Rowell, shot through a leg on the 17th, Captain Abraham Wright of Company A on the 18th, Lieutenant John Law of Company E also on the 18th, and Lieutenant William Newell of Company H on the 21st. Not enough officers remained with the regiment to provide an officer to command each company. On the 22nd, for instance, Sergeant Walter Smith assumed command of Company H. With a captain commanding and the command structure in flux, the regiment was fortunate to escape an even greater debacle on June 22.[18]

When the fighting was over for the II Corps on the Weldon Railroad expedition, little had been accomplished except to control more of the area west of the Jerusalem Plank Road. Grant immediately put his troops to work digging trenches and forts to extend his line towards the railroad. The Federals needed earthworks to secure their lines so that Grant could shift his forces for a flanking movement or another raid. The Confederates, already badly outnumbered, had to extend their lines and stretch their thin forces to match the Federals. During the weeks of June and July the sharpshooters returned to the Petersburg trenches and stood picket and fatigue duty. Sometimes the sharpshooters withheld firing at the rebel pickets for the obvious purpose of making life bearable while awaiting the next battle.[19] While these informal picket truces somewhat lessened the tension briefly, they also ultimately must have made duty at Petersburg more dangerous. Men on picket or doing duty on the front lines never knew when an outbreak of firing would commence, catching the incautious unaware or unprepared.

For a few days after Colonel Stoughton went missing, he was rumored to have been killed. One of the sharpshooters reported seeing the colonel killed on the 21st. A captured Petersburg newspaper settled the issue with a paragraph about captured Yankees. Information about captured sharpshooters probably appeared in more than one newspaper article. An article mentioned Colonel Stoughton and Captain Murry by name, so the sharpshooters knew that the two officers were prisoners. Descriptions of the captured sharpshooters were anything but flattering. They were called murderers, foreigners, prowling hounds, uncouth Yankees and the like. Although the Confederates utilized snipers, probably more vicious than the sharpshooters themselves, the newspaper called for no quarter for the green-clad captured Yankees.[20]

Casualties for the period covering June 15–30 were totaled and the tally for the 2nd U.S.S.S. showed six killed, thirty-eight wounded and twenty-eight missing. Since the Battle of the Wilderness the 2nd had suffered 235 casualties. By June 26 only 149 men and three officers were present with the regiment.[21] With the difficulty of finding qualified recruits for the sharpshooters, few replacements were forthcoming. Continuing attrition from combat casualties and disease would cause the numbers to dwindle until finally the regiment would be disbanded before the war's end.

For the 2nd U.S.S.S. the month of July was passed manning the pickax and the picket line. Grant always sought ways to keep his soldiers occupied as a means of avoiding discipline problems from idle, bored troops. For miles around the outskirts of Petersburg the Army of the Potomac dug trenches and constructed earthen forts. The weather was unusually hot and dry for Virginia that July, so the pale, powdery, moon-like soil of that region wafted clouds of dust as each shovelful was turned by the diggers. By late July the two armies had turned the Petersburg vicinity into a strange landscape of burrows and dirt piles amid devastated pine groves.

Amid all this burrowing Grant concealed a mining operation with a view of blasting a hole through the Confederate lines. The unlikely undertaking ultimately proved practicable. A regiment of Pennsylvania coal miners managed to dig a tunnel from their lines to a point underneath a Confederate redoubt. The plan called for filling two branching galleries with kegs of black powder with enough blasting power to create a gap in the rebel line. General Burnside's IX Corps would immediately attack in the chaos following the blast.[22]

With the mining operation nearing completion, Grant decided it was time to "make a demonstration on the north side of the James River, having for its real object the destruction of the railroad on that side." On July 25 he informed General Meade that he could "direct the loading of the mine in front of the Ninth Corps." Grant hoped that the expedition against the railroads north of the river would "cause such a weakening of the enemy at Petersburg as to make an attack there possible, in which case you would want to spring Burnside's mine." Thus Grant intended to draw Confederate forces away from Petersburg with a diversion north of the James River, then attack Petersburg at the site of the mine explosion.[23]

General Grant selected the II Corps and two divisions of cavalry for the "demonstration" north of the James. General Meade issued orders for the II Corps to "proceed to the upper bridge at Deep Bottom, crossing the James at this bridge and moving from thence to Chaffin's farm." So as the day waned on July 26, the 2nd U.S.S.S. left its camp near Petersburg and marched all night to the crossing at Deep Bottom. During the night-long march the route took the sharpshooters through a dense pine forest so dark that torches were left burning at intervals to light the way for the weary columns. By dawn of the 27th the sharpshooters had reached their destination on the north bank of the James. The corps marched a distance of over eighteen miles that night, and a great many straggled or simply lay down along the road to sleep, later hurrying to catch the slowly moving columns before dawn.[24]

Major General David Birney was reassigned to command of the X Corps, Army of the James, on July 23, 1864; thus, Brigadier General Gershom Mott assumed command of the Third Division, II Corps, to which the 2nd U.S.S.S. belonged during the movement to the James. Mott's division was held in reserve during the morning's action involving the II Corps. Hancock's lead units encountered strong opposition along Bailey's Creek by midday, and it soon became apparent that Lee had prepared to meet Grant's latest move north of the James. During the afternoon the sharpshooters were sent to the right of Hancock's line to skirmish and guard that flank. The regiment had no recorded casualties during the Deep Bottom operation.[25]

By evening of the following day Grant had realized that the II Corps would not accomplish much at Deep Bottom. He informed General Halleck that the mission was a failure, but he still hoped it would prove worthwhile: "We have failed in what I had hoped to accomplish — that is, to surprise the enemy, and get to their roads with the cavalry near to Richmond and destroy them out to South Anna. I am yet in hopes of turning this diversion to account, so as to yield greater results than if the first object had been accomplished." Grant wanted to spring the mine explosion the next day, July 29, but General Meade demurred, explaining that he needed to recall Hancock's troops before the attack could be made. Meade instead scheduled the mine explosion and attack for dawn of the 30th. After dark on the 28th the sharpshooters began their return march to Petersburg, again marching through the night to the XVIII Corps lines near Petersburg.[26]

On the evening of July 29 the 2nd U.S.S.S., as part of Brigadier General de Trobriand's 1st Brigade, relieved Turner's Division of the X Corps in the Petersburg trenches near the Hare House.[27] The sharpshooters were in this position when the mine was detonated at 4:40 A.M. the following morning and remained there throughout the day to silence enemy artillery on their front. At this they succeeded, being complemented by General de Trobriand.[28] Unfortunately for the Federals the assault at the mine explosion, known as the Battle of the Crater, proved to be perhaps the greatest fiasco of the war.

Grant showed his frustration and disappointment in a note to Meade on August 1, calling the affair a "miserable failure." According to Grant, "So fair an opportunity will probably never occur again for carrying fortifications. Preparations were good ... so far as I could see, subsequent to the explosion of the mine, shows that almost without loss the crest beyond the mine could have been carried. This would have given us Petersburg with all of its artillery and a large part of the garrison beyond."[29] As it was, Burnside's troops suffered heavy casualties and gained nothing. The Confederates simply dug a new defensive line behind the breach created by the mine explosion.

There were no official reports of casualties for the 2nd U.S.S.S. for the Battle of the Crater; however, at least one man was shot that day. Private Reuben F. Carter of Company G was wounded during the mine explosion on July 30. A letter from one of his comrades mentioned that Carter was shot through the jaw, the tongue being nearly shot away. Carter had been previously wounded at Antietam and had recovered. He again recovered and served with the regiment until the end.[30]

For the following several days a relative calm prevailed where the sharpshooters stood duty. No casualties were reported for the regiment during this period. Then on Friday, August 12, 1864, General Grant initiated another of his efforts to get at Lee north of the James River. Grant fought the war like a determined boxer, jabbing here, and then throwing a hook closely followed by yet another punch from a different angle. Grant was quite unlike any of his predecessors. He was never content to wait for his opponent to make the next move; instead, he continually looked for an opening to strike a blow, seldom looking to counterpunch.

Grant decided to send General Hancock once again to Deep Bottom for a repeat of the "demonstration" carried out there in late July. This time Grant believed that Lee had weakened his forces at Petersburg to reinforce General Early in the Shenandoah Valley, and by feinting north of the James he hoped to entice Lee to further weaken his defenses to counter Hancock at Deep Bottom. Grant believed that if Hancock's feint proved successful he would easily capture Petersburg this time.[31]

For their part, the sharpshooters marched to City Point, where they embarked on transports, getting underway down the James River after dark. Grant wanted this movement kept secret, even from his own men. Meade's chief of staff, Major General A.A. Humphreys, informed Hancock that "every arrangement and effort must be made to conceal the destination of the corps from the officers and troops, artillery and trains, and from the enemy. The idea will be held out that the Second Corps is going to Washington." The sharpshooters thought they were going to Maryland when they embarked on the transports.[32]

Hancock's movement resulted in the Second Battle of Deep Bottom and severe fighting around Fussell's Mill. About all that was accomplished by the operation was the recall of a Confederate cavalry division headed for Early's army in the Shenandoah Valley, this at the cost of 2,901 Federal casualties.[33] The 2nd U.S.S.S. escaped without any casualties, being fortunate to miss the heavy fighting. The regiment helped capture a four-gun Confederate battery, however. Being relieved from picket duty on the night of the 18th, the regiment crossed the James and Appomattox Rivers via pontoon bridges and arrived at Petersburg the following morning. At Petersburg the sharpshooters' brigade relieved Potter's IX Corps division in the trenches so that those troops could take part in another movement against the Weldon Railroad.[34]

Again Grant had formulated a good strategic plan with great potential, and yet again his subordinates failed to carry it out successfully. In the past, when he commanded forces in the West, Grant had benefited from satisfactory performances by most of his subordinates, General William T. Sherman among them. Here in the East, Grant was foundering. For one thing, Grant was now in charge of all Federal operations as commander-in-chief, and his duties prevented him from overseeing each operation in detail. But the onus for the repeated failures should be laid at the feet of the Army of the Potomac's corps commanders themselves, for they performed in such a hapless manner that fate seemed aligned against them. It is a testament to the tremendous fortitude of the sharpshooters and soldiers of that army that they continued to keep the faith and fight on after so many botched battles and campaigns.

The 2nd U.S.S.S. remained in the trenches during the defeat of Hancock's divisions at Ream's Station on August 25, 1864.[35] The regiment's next combat action was an attack on the rebel rifle pits near the location known as the Chimneys along the Jerusalem Plank Road on the night of September 9 and the following day. General Mott gave the following description of the sharpshooters' part in the attack:

> Instructions were given to Lieutenant-Colonel Meikel to strike at a rush with the Twentieth Indiana Volunteers the enemy's line half way between the Chimneys and the point where our main line was to connect with the old one; to double up and carry on the right all the rifle-pits up to the plank road and establish his line there, reversing the old pits, &c., while the Second U.S. Sharpshooters would perfect the connection between the captured pits and the old line, the enemy to be driven with the bayonet, and without unnecessary firing.[36]

The attack was carried out with the utmost secrecy, each sharpshooter carrying only a rifle, ammunition, a canteen and a shovel. After the moon went down and darkness fell, a shot signaled the attack. Passing over the crest of a slight swell, the sharpshooters could clearly see by the enemy campfires that the pickets were completely unaware of what was about to befall them. The Federals rushed into the enemy rifle pits almost completely unopposed and immediately took most of the Confederates prisoner. Nearly seventy Confederates were captured by the sharpshooters alone. Once the rifle pits were secured and the rebels driven out, the Federals immediately set to work with shovels to reversing the rifle pits as ordered. The regiment apparently lost only one man wounded in the attack.[37]

Expecting to be relieved at dawn, instead the sharpshooters spent the day under a hot fire without rations; relief could not be sent in until darkness covered the approach. For a while the shooting ceased by mutual agreement, but it flared up and intensified throughout the day. After nightfall the sharpshooters were finally relieved, and back in camp they ate for the first time in twenty-four hours.[38]

That night Private William Matteson, a new recruit in Company C, was killed in the camp by an enemy shot. Captain Ira Northup of Company C mentioned the death and its circumstances in a letter to his wife written on September 11. According to the captain, after dark Matteson was killed by a ball that "struck him in the right temple causing death in a short time." Matteson "never spoke after being hit." Northup admitted to his wife that the sharpshooters "on both sides keep up a hot fire, the balls Whistles around a good deal." Indeed, the firing was quite intense on the 11th; several sharpshooters were struck by spent bullets that day. Continuing his letter, Northup mentioned that the unfortunate Matteson left a wife and "quite a large family to morn" his loss in Pennsylvania. The incident was a tragedy that might never have happened. Northup mentioned that the rebel pickets wanted to stop the constant firing, "but the boys say their officers wont let them."[39]

The sharpshooters remained in the Petersburg lines throughout September. In late September, General Grant determined that it was yet again time for another major offensive on both sides of the James River. This time he would utilize troops from the Army of the James to attack the Confederate New Market line near Deep Bottom and Chaffin's Bluff on the north bank of the James. The object was to capture the Confederate capital at Richmond, but Grant knew that at the very least the attacks would force Lee to draw troops from the defense of Petersburg to meet this threat. Grant was prepared to strike hard for the remaining railroad supplying Petersburg, the Southside Railroad, as soon as Lee dispatched troops to defend Richmond.[40]

Attacks by troops from the Army of the James met with some success north of the James, causing alarm in the Confederate capital. As Grant anticipated, Lee weakened his Petersburg defenses to deal with the threat to Richmond, so Grant dispatched Major General G.K. Warren with two of his V Corps divisions, Major General John G. Parke with two IX Corps divisions, and some cavalry commanded by Brigadier General David Gregg, to go after the Southside Railroad. Warren made some progress from the area around Poplar Springs Church south of Petersburg, but General Parke was stopped and repulsed before he could reach the Boydton Plank Road to move against the railroad. The seemingly ubiquitous Confederates threw two divisions at the Federals and fighting intensified around Peebles's Farm. General Meade wanted a further advance from Peebles's Farm as Grant had anticipated, so he called upon General Hancock to supply a division from his II Corps still in the Petersburg trenches. Thus by the morning of October 1, the fighting south of Petersburg would also involve the II Corps.[41]

In his last battle Hancock had suffered an embarrassing defeat at Ream's Station. He probably wanted to avoid a similar showing by the reinforcements he was asked to forward to Peebles's Farm. Thus he selected the 3rd Division of his corps, to which the sharpshooters belonged, to answer the call. These troops had not been involved in the poor showing by Hancock's corps at Ream's Station, being instead in the Petersburg lines. Civil War historian Richard Sommers observed that at this phase of the war the 3rd Division was the strongest and best-led division in the II Corps. According to Sommers, the division's brigade commanders "formed the best team of senior commanders then available to the II Corps." Sommers also noted of the 3rd Division, "Its men fought hard because they were the sole guardians of a proud tradition." Nearly all of its regiments had belonged at some point to the now defunct III Corps, and they "still strove to live up" to the proud fighting record of that old corps.[42]

Major General Gershom Mott loaded his 3rd Division onto cars beginning at about 1 P.M. "at two points, viz: Hancock's Station and near the trestle bridge. There were three trains and each train made three trips." The first of his troops reported to General Parke at about 2:30 P.M. and the rear of his division arrived by 5 P.M. from the Petersburg lines. Mott's movement of the sharpshooters and the 3rd Division was an historical first. It was probably the first time in world military history that a commander moved troops by railroad from a quiet sector of a battlefield to an active sector in the midst of a battle. Nevertheless, by the time Mott's troops reached the front it was nearly dark. It would be the following morning, Sunday, October 2, 1864, before the sharpshooters would advance at Peebles's Farm.[43]

It was after 8 A.M. on October 2 when General Mott commenced an advance in conjunction with General Wilcox's Division of the IX Corps. The 2nd U.S.S.S. was deployed as flankers on the left of the advancing Federal line. The sharpshooters drove back the Confederate skirmishers for over a mile, where Mott's troops overran a lightly defended line of fieldworks. Mott continued his advance for another mile, the sharpshooters again driving back the enemy skirmishers. According to Mott, a stronger line of works manned by infantry and artillery here stopped his advance. Sharpshooter William Greene of Company G described the encounter that day in a letter, mentioning that the rebel artillery sent solid shot rapidly down the sharpshooters' line; this artillery fire helped check Mott's advance. After skirmishing for a while General Mott attempted an attack on the Confederate fieldworks at about 3 P.M. This attack was almost immediately recalled by order of General Meade. By Mott's account, "...General Meade did not wish me to run any great risk, but to take up a line and intrench. The attacking column was immediately recalled." Private Greene explained it slightly differently. As he described it, "the Johnnys" were going to make things hot for the Federals if they continued the advance, so the Federals fell back and dug in.[44]

The sharpshooters held the left flank of the Federal line around the Clements place after Mott pulled back to Peebles's Farm. Neither side was willing to renew the attacks after October 2, so the sharpshooters and Mott's other troops spent the following three days in the same location. Mott reported that his division supplied large details "to work at the forts building near the Clements house, Smith's house, and the Poplar Springs Church." The sharpshooters did not escape this fatigue work as they often did in the past. Work details spent the three very hard days cutting trees, digging trenches and helping construct new earth and log forts.[45]

Most of the fighting was over before Mott arrived at Peebles's Farm, thus the V Corps and IX Corps suffered nearly all of the 2,950 Federal casualties resulting from the four days of combat south of Petersburg. A large portion of these losses were men from the IX Corps captured early in the fighting. The sharpshooters' casualties totaled three wounded. Although the offensive did not accomplish its intended result, it did meet with limited success. The Federals broke through a portion of the Confederate lines defending the approach to the Southside Railroad. By seizing Peebles's Farm, Grant controlled key road junctions to move westward, and by extending the Federal siege lines to Hatcher's Run the Federals forced Lee to stretch his defending forces even thinner in response.[46]

The sharpshooters were back in their old camp by evening of October 6. For the following three weeks the sharpshooters remained there, probably anticipating a long stay with the colder weather approaching. Over the next few weeks the sharpshooters performed their usual siege warfare duties, taking their turn at picket duty alternating with the other regiments. Private David Bolster, a recruit who had just mustered in during late August, was killed while on picket duty on October 18. On a few days the Confederates shelled their camp thoroughly, but few, if any, casualties resulted. Perhaps the most noteworthy happening during this period was a reported attempt by the enemy to mine their way beneath nearby Fort Sedgwick. The Federals attempted to locate the supposed mine shaft by countermining, but there was not a repeat of the mine explosion of July 30.[47]

In September and October the Federals scored decisive victories in the Atlanta and Shenandoah Valley campaigns. These victories were crucial in helping Lincoln regain support for the war and his reelection. But at Petersburg and Richmond the stalemate continued. Grant had been unable to produce a decisive breakthrough after several disappointing efforts, yet clearly he held the upper hand. Each successive offensive increased the pressure on the Petersburg defenders. In late October, Grant sought another opportunity to capture the last remaining rail supply line to Petersburg.

This latest offensive against the Southside Railroad called for 40,000 Federal troops to move west of the forts and fieldworks near Peebles's Farm, cross Hatcher's Run and march northwest to the Southside Railroad. The strike force was composed of portions of the II, V and IX Corps and 3,000 cavalry.[48] Overall, the offensive amounted to a continuation of the fighting around Peebles's Farm earlier in October.

On Monday, October 24, 1864, "pursuant to orders from headquarters," Mott's 3rd Division was relieved and withdrawn from the front at Petersburg in preparation for the offensive. Two days later the division marched to Globe Tavern along the Weldon Railroad and camped for the night. The sharpshooters were awakened shortly after 2 A.M. on October 27 and began marching about 3:30 A.M. to the Vaughn Road. Turning south on the Vaughn Road, the division continued to the Cummings place. There Mott's division closed up and massed in preparation to cross Hatcher's Run.[49]

At 8 A.M. the sharpshooters and de Trobriand's Brigade crossed Hatcher's Run, following Eagan's 2nd Division. According to General Mott, immediately after crossing the run he sent out the 73rd New York and the 2nd U.S.S.S. "as skirmishers to drive the enemy out of a corn-field where it was reported they were throwing up some works to delay our advance, which they had no difficulty in doing. The column then advanced through a wood road to Dabney's Mill, where the road intersected another on which the Second Division was lying."[50]

By 12:30 P.M. the 1st Brigade had reached the intersection of the Boydton Plank Road and White Oak Road near Hatcher's Run. Unfortunately, the V Corps troops had not kept pace, so a gap of over one mile separated the two Federal corps. General Meade ordered Hancock to wait for the V Corps to catch up and to extend to his right. Hours passed and still the two corps failed to link up, so Hancock was ordered to hold his ground until nightfall and then pull back to safer ground. While Hancock waited, Confederate Lieutenant General A.P. Hill attacked with two divisions. Hancock's lead division under Brigadier General Thomas Eagan was hit hard and nearly cut off by late afternoon. While Eagan's Division and Mott's 3rd Brigade battled Hill's Confederates, the sharpshooters and Mott's 1st Brigade were attacked on the Federal left.[51]

Late in the afternoon the sharpshooters were called to the front to face the Confederate attack along with the 73rd, 86th, and 124th New York infantry regiments. The sharpshooters formed a line behind a Virginia rail fence as the rebels, by Mott's account, attacked vigorously. One sharpshooter noted in his diary that it was "hot work" and there was no place to take cover or dodge enemy fire. Although the day's fighting was not remembered as a prominent battle, it was one of the severest firefights the sharpshooters faced during the war.[52]

The Confederate attacks by Hill's infantry and Hampton's cavalry were repulsed by Hancock's two divisions. At 10 P.M. Mott's Division began withdrawing from the Boydton Plank Road towards Globe Tavern. The fighting around Hatcher's Run was over for the time being; Grant was again thwarted in his attempt to close the Southside Railroad, this time with the loss of 1,758 casualties. Losses for the 2nd U.S.S.S. were two killed and ten wounded.[53]

Strangely, all of the regiment's casualties were in the two Vermont companies, E and H. Again it was the new recruits who died. Privates Joseph Bradley and Charles Cilley, both of whom had mustered in the previous month, were killed along the rail fence during the battle. Captain Churchill and Lieutenant Beach of Company H were both wounded early in the fighting while on the skirmish line. Captain Churchill later died of his wounds.[54]

On October 29 the sharpshooters were positioned around the Chieves House near the Jerusalem Plank Road to support the Federal lines in that vicinity. General Hancock was pleased with the performance of his two divisions at Hatcher's Run, despite the outcome of the offensive. He expressed his gratitude for their brave conduct and for their capture of nearly 1,000 enemy troops.[55]

On the following day the Confederates managed to infiltrate the lines of Miles's Division of the II Corps, capturing numerous prisoners. On November 4, perhaps expecting further trouble from the Confederates, the sharpshooters were moved to the breastworks near Battery 22, lining the works with other regiments from their brigade. The men were required to wear their accouterments and keep their rifles at hand all night "till one hour before daybreak," when the entire brigade was to take arms. On the following night the Confederates indeed attacked Mott's picket-line, capturing several rifle pits from the Federals. The Confederates were driven out after a stubborn fight that lasted most of the night. Grant expected further trouble because the presidential election was scheduled for November 8, and the general anticipated that the Confederates might attempt to attack while the soldiers were voting.[56]

As the sharpshooters prepared to cast their votes for president on Tuesday, November 8, 1864, the war had changed dramatically on virtually every front except Petersburg. Major General William T. Sherman had captured Atlanta, Georgia, and he was preparing to commence his march through Georgia to the sea. In the Shenandoah Valley Major General Phillip Sheridan had soundly defeated the Confederates at Cedar Creek the previous month. Sheridan's victory wrested the Valley permanently from Confederate control, cutting off important food supplies from Lee's army and eliminating further threats of a northern incursion by rebel forces. Even in the distant Trans-Mississippi the Confederates were in retreat as Confederate General Sterling Price was driven out of Missouri and Kansas and into Texas in late October. Just two months previously it had seemed that President Lincoln had no chance for reelection. Lincoln himself realized that without a significant victory or improvement in the war situation he was doomed to lose.⁵⁷ It was the Federal successes elsewhere besides Petersburg that had turned Lincoln's fortunes around by Election Day.

As for the 2nd U.S.S.S. itself, the regiment cast eighty-seven votes for Lincoln and twenty for George McClellan. Lincoln also won a solid majority of the votes cast by the Army of the Potomac, and he won reelection by a huge majority of electoral votes in the loyal states. Being composed of companies from several states, the most likely source of McClellan votes in the 2nd U.S.S.S. was from the two New Hampshire companies. New Hampshire's own Franklin Pierce was a Democrat elected president in 1852. In New Hampshire McClellan drew 47.4 percent of the presidential vote. The 5th New Hampshire Infantry, also in the II Corps, voted a majority for McClellan. Company D of Maine was probably the most likely company in the regiment to strongly support Lincoln.⁵⁸

Lincoln's reelection had dashed the Confederacy's last hope for victory or at least a favorable settlement of the war. Having failed to obtain foreign recognition and assistance, the rebels had held out hope for Northern intervention at the ballot box. Now the end was increasingly obvious to all except the quixotic irreconcilables of the South. Confederate currency, a truly accurate indicator of public confidence, fell dramatically against the gold dollar after the election. By December the exchange rate was thirty-eight Confederate bills to one gold dollar.⁵⁹

For the sharpshooters the end of their organization was at hand too. Neither of Hiram Berdan's regiments would remain intact until the end of the war. Like the Army of the Potomac's now defunct I and III Corps, Berdan's sharpshooter organization would be broken up and absorbed into other units, passing into history without the tribute of the final victory parade celebrated at the war's conclusion.

Epilogue

For the rest of November the sharpshooters manned their trenches on the Petersburg front. It was now routine duty, so much so that the 3rd Division itinerary stated that nothing of importance occurred in November following the election. But the always-hazardous picket duty continued unabated with the sharpshooters taking shifts every night or on alternating days and nights. Boxes of clothing arrived by train and were distributed to accommodate the increasingly cold weather. A large portion of the regiment was absent from wounds or illness, probably requiring the remaining sharpshooters to stand more frequent duty than would otherwise be necessary.[1]

On November 26, 1864, Major General Winfield Scott Hancock relinquished command of the II Corps to Major General A.A. Humphreys, Meade's chief of staff. Hancock had been the most renowned and yet most tortured corps commander in the Army. The following is from General Orders No. 44 pertaining to Hancock's farewell statement to his troops:

> ...previous to entering upon another field of duty, in accordance with instructions I transfer the command of this corps to Maj. Gen. A.A. Humphreys, U.S. Volunteers. I desire at parting with you to express the regret I feel at the necessity which calls for our separation.... The story of the Second Corps will live in history, and its officers and men will be ascribed the honor of having served their country with unsurpassed fidelity and courage. Conscious that whatever military honor has fallen to me during my association with the Second Corps has been won by the gallantry of the officers and soldiers I have commanded, I feel that in parting from them I am severing the strongest ties of my military life.[2]

In late November the sharpshooters and their II Corps comrades were relieved from their trenches by the IX Corps and marched to the IX Corps's former position on the extreme left of the Federal lines. The corps was preparing for the final operation of the year, another raid against the Weldon Railroad. After a few days the sharpshooters set out with the corps marching south on the Jerusalem Plank Road to the Nottoway River, several miles south of Petersburg in Sussex County.[3]

Chaplain Lorenzo Barber of the 2nd U.S.S.S. submitted the report for the 3rd Division giving an account of the destruction of the Weldon Railroad during December 7–12, 1864. His report was incorporated into the *Official Records*. Chaplain Barber served as a true "fighting parson" with the sharpshooters, often carrying a target rifle into battle, until he was wounded in action during the Mine Run Campaign. According to Barber's report the division marched on the 8th to Jarratt's Station on the Weldon Railroad and camped there for the night.[4]

At daylight on December 9 the men marched along the railroad to different locations by brigade and commenced destroying the railroad. Chaplain Barber gave the following description of how the track was destroyed:

> ...the division was drawn up in line, facing the road, and stacked arms on its bank. The rails were so bolted together at the ends as to make a continuous rail, rendering the destruction of the track very difficult. Each brigade, under the immediate supervision of the brigade commander, took hold of the rails and ties on one side, and the entire track — a whole brigade front at once — was turned up on the ends of the ties on the side opposite, as if by magic. While held in this position, the ties were knocked off and piled up on the bed of the road, making a narrow top, the rails broken apart and laid across the stack of ties, the center of the rail resting at the apex of the pile. The pile was then set on fire.... The heat of the burning ties, with the weight of the ends of the rails, caused them to bend into nearly the shape of a semicircle, and rendered them unfit for further use.[5]

After destroying about fifteen miles of track and bridges, the raiding party began the march back to Petersburg on December 10. A winter storm had blown in during the night with heavy freezing rain that coated the trees and roads with ice. Although Lee's troops did not leave Petersburg to oppose the raid, enemy guerrillas killed stragglers along the route, in some cases the dead were found stripped and mutilated. "Until these outrages were discovered but little destruction of private property had occurred, but now the burning of buildings commenced, in retaliation, and nearly every building, including the Sussex courthouse, for miles, was given to the flames." While the burning had little impact on the Petersburg siege, the destruction of the Weldon Railroad seriously impaired the already strained supply situation in Lee's army.[6]

By the afternoon of Monday, December 12, the division had reached its assigned bivouac near Fort Siebert between the Vaughan and Halifax roads. The camp was well south of the Confederate lines, making it a more favorable place for a winter camp. Over the next two months the weather turned colder and more inclement than usual for a Virginia winter. Offensive operations came to a halt in the bitter weather. The sharpshooters returned to a camp routine and resumed limited drilling in late December.[7]

The end of the 1st U.S.S.S. as an organization came on December 31, 1864, when the remaining recruits and veterans of Berdan's first sharpshooter regiment, excepting those from Michigan, were consolidated with the 2nd U.S.S.S. Most of the remaining men of the 1st had been discharged between August and September when their enlistments expired; very few had reenlisted. The Michiganders were transferred to the 5th Michigan Infantry rather than to the 2nd U.S.S.S. Company F of the 1st was a Vermont company, and like the Vermont companies of the 2nd, it had the largest number of recruits in its regiment. Thirty-two men from that company were transferred into Company E of the 2nd U.S.S.S.[8]

While the fighting was in hiatus around Petersburg, the Federal armies in the West continued to win battles and capture Confederate territory. During the month of January, while the weather precluded offensive operations, both sides considered the possibility of a negotiated end to the war. By mid–January, Confederate President Jefferson

Davis had agreed to a peace conference seeking terms for ending the war. The month of January passed without major fighting around Petersburg while the peace talks were considered. A peace conference was actually held on a steamer in Hampton Roads on February 3 between President Lincoln and Confederate Vice President Alexander Stephens and two other Confederate commissioners. The conference was a failure as Lincoln was in position to demand immediate surrender from the Confederates, and they were not ready to comply.[9]

On the day after the failed peace conference, General Grant resumed offensive operations around Petersburg. Grant hoped to keep the Confederates corralled at Petersburg and ultimately force their surrender, much like his victory at Vicksburg in 1863. Unlike at Vicksburg, Grant here did not have his enemies completely hemmed in; he needed to keep the Confederates occupied so that they could not slip away. On February 5 Grant sent out a cavalry division to disrupt and capture Confederate supply trains believed to be moving on the Boydton Plank Road near Dinwiddie Court House. The V Corps was dispatched to support the cavalry, and the 2nd and 3rd divisions of the II Corps moved to threaten Confederate lines near Hatcher's Run to prevent the Confederates from concentrating against the raiding forces on the Boydton Plank Road.[10]

General Lee responded, of course, to the Federal movements, which he thought could be a threat to his last rail supply line. At 7 A.M. on Sunday, February 5, 1865, the 2nd U.S.S.S. went into combat for the last time. Brigadier General de Trobriand "deployed the Second U.S. Sharpshooters, Major Doughty commanding, as skirmishers, in front and right of the enemy's works, so as to keep his attention engaged by a threatening advance." De Trobriand led two regiments across Hatcher's Run while the sharpshooters distracted the Confederates and soon forced a passage for the rest of the division to follow.[11]

Apparently the last casualties suffered by the 2nd occurred during this opening phase of its involvement in the Battle of Hatcher's Run, as indicated in a letter written by Private Henry Lesslie of Company E: "...the S.S. was used as skirmishers, after firing a few rounds we drove the Reb's from their line of works. I don't know how many we killed of them, they killed one and wounded 2 in this Regt." In this, its last fight, the 2nd U.S.S.S. again charged breastworks, something the regiment had always held to be the duty of infantrymen rather than sharpshooters.[12]

Private Lesslie noted that the regiment "was not in the hardest of the fight." He was again correct as the Confederates attacked Colonel McAllister's 3rd Brigade that day and not the sharpshooters' position. As for the 2nd U.S.S.S., the regiment "skirmished till afternoon and then went on picket and staid till morn," according to Lesslie. General de Trobriand's report agrees: "I remained in that position during the afternoon of the 5th and most of the night."[13]

On the following afternoon severe fighting erupted between the Federal V Corps and three Confederate divisions. Again the sharpshooters were not involved in the heavy fighting. Instead, the sharpshooters took part in a reconnaissance with General de Trobriand and three of his other regiments: the 20th Indiana, 17th Maine and 1st Maine Heavy Artillery. After sending out his skirmishers in advance for some distance, the

Sharpshooter stationery. This envelope was sent by Private Henry Lesslie of Company E. Note the target motif on the upper left portion of the envelope. U.S. Army Military History Institute.

Confederate entrenchments were encountered, which consisted of a manned redoubt with two cannon. After developing the Confederate position, de Trobriand withdrew his force to its previous position. In the evening the brigade was ordered to go to the assistance of the V Corps, but the before the movement could be completed, de Trobriand was informed by General Meade that his services were not needed any more, and he could take his "brigade back."[14]

That night a severe storm of sleet, snow and freezing rain blew in and drenched the soldiers. Private Lesslie noted that he got "a good soaking." When morning came the frozen woods were thickly covered with icicles and the men shivered from a fierce north wind. But the fighting was over, over forever for the 2nd U.S.S.S.[15]

After the battle the Federals extended their earthworks to the southwest, stretching for nearly another three miles to where the Vaughn Road crossed Hatcher's Run. The sharpshooters remained on the field until February 13, building earthworks and forts and standing picket duty.[16] As previously noted, the sharpshooters lost one man killed and two wounded at Hatcher's Run, although the official casualty report for the 2nd U.S.S.S. listed men three wounded and none killed.[17]

Brigade commander Regis de Trobriand complimented the sharpshooters in his report for this their final battle:

> During these operations the Second U.S. Sharpshooters, under command of Maj. J. Ed. Doughty, has done good service. This regiment being about to be broken up, and this being probably its last engagement as a distinct organization, I take this opportunity of acknowledging its good and efficient services on this as on many other occasions during the campaigns of 1863 and 1864 when it was under my command.[18]

By February 14 the sharpshooters were back in their winter quarters awaiting their transfer to other regiments in the Army of the Potomac. On February 3, just before the Battle of Hatcher's Run, news of the impending breakup had reached the men. Now late in the war, following Lincoln's reelection, the Army began consolidating worn and depleted regiments and remnants of regiments whose veterans had been discharged. Not surprisingly, the sharpshooters were greatly displeased with the involuntary dissolution of their proud regiment. One sharpshooter observed that news of the breakup "made most of the boys feel pretty sober." He also observed that although the news came on February 3, the generals "could not be satisfied to give up the S.S. with out one more fight," referring to the Battle of Hatcher's Run.[19]

There were two obvious reasons why the sharpshooters were disgusted with the Army's decision to dissolve their regiment. First, each man had been required to qualify for service in the regiment and had joined for service in their state company belonging to the United States Sharpshooters. Second, the men had enlisted to serve specifically as sharpshooters and now were being sent to serve in infantry regiments. But there was little to be done about it; General Grant had been utilizing cavalrymen and heavy artillerymen to fight as infantry for months, so, of course, he could do the same with sharpshooters. For its part, the Army was careful to transfer all of the sharpshooter companies to regiments hailing from the same states where the sharpshooters enlisted. Company A consolidated with the 1st Minnesota Infantry Battalion, Company B with the 5th Michigan Infantry, Company C with the 105th Pennsylvania Infantry, Company D with the 17th Maine Infantry, Companies E and H with the 4th Vermont Infantry, and Companies F and G with the 5th New Hampshire Infantry.[20]

Brigadier General Regis de Trobriand. As the final brigade commander of the 2nd U.S.S.S., he issued a fitting farewell when the regiment was disbanded. Library of Congress Civil War Collection.

All of the regiments accepting the sharpshooters belonged to the II Corps except the 4th Vermont Infantry, which belonged to the VI Corps. It seems that the Army chose regiments with an established record for hard fighting to receive the transferred sharpshooters. The 5th New Hampshire Infantry, for example, was not only known as a reliable regiment, it was also known for suffering the greatest loss in battle of any infantry regiment in the Federal service.[21]

On February 16, 1865, as the end was approaching for the 2nd U.S.S.S., Brigadier General Regis de Trobriand gave a final tribute to the regiment with General Orders No. 12:

> The U.S. sharpshooters (including the First and Second consolidated battalions), being about to be broken up as a distinct organization, in compliance with orders from the War Department, the brigadier general commanding division will not take leave of them without acknowledging their good and efficient service during about three years' service in the field. The U.S. sharpshooters leave behind a glorious record in the Army of the Potomac, since the first operations against Yorktown in 1862, up to the last movement of the army on Hatcher's Run, and few are the battles or engagements where they did not make their mark. The brigadier general commanding, who had them under his command during most of the campaigns of 1863

and 1864, would be the last to forget their brave deeds during that period, and he feels assured that in the different organizations to which they are to belong, severally, officers and men will show themselves worthy of their old reputation. With them the past answers for the future.[22]

From the diary of sharpshooter James Matthews it seems that the last few days of the life of the 2nd U.S.S.S. were passed in camp preparing for the transfers. Matthews mentioned playing ball on Saturday, February 18, and on the following day orders were received for the completed regimental papers. Matthews, who had enlisted as a private in the autumn of 1861, was now regimental adjutant. On Monday, February 20, 1865, Matthews recorded that the regiment held a dress parade in the morning and formed into a hollow square, the traditional defense to face a cavalry charge. A farewell was read to the green-clad sharpshooters forming the hollow square.[23] The following address from Major James E. Doughty, commanding officer of the 2nd U.S.S.S., was found in the regimental record book, verbatim[24]:

> Head Quarters 2d U.S.S.S.
> In the Field Near Petersburg Virginia,
> February 20, 1865
>
> Regimental Orders)
>)
> No 10)
>
> In obedience to S.O. No 47. C.S. (U.S.) War Department and S.O. No 42. Head Quarters 2d Army Corps the command is promulgated, and the moment has arrived which completes the disruption of this Regiment as a distinct body and assigns the different companies of the several states to the Regimental organizations of those States to which they will repair this date
>
> This regretted movement having culminated and the adieus about to be bidden, *Officers* and *Men* your commanding officer feels at liberty to throw aside the restraint of Official Position and expresses himself as one of you. And to give vent to those feelings and sympathies nurtured and matured by long association through all the vicissitudes of the numerous campaigns executed by the armies to which we have been attached for the past three years. These feelings peculiarly allying all soldiers so closely together from contact with and taking part in the scenes and acts of such a war as that in which we are engaged.
>
> Henceforth different paths are to be pursued and we are no longer to strive and wrestle together. Maine companies with Minnesota. Vermont with New Hampshire. New York with Michigan and Wisconsin with Pennsylvania in this conflict for the common cause. Your commanding officer at this time would pay proper tribute to your merits earned under most adverse circumstances. Your honorable career and standing is well attested by many officers of superior grade. Among which is the General Officer commanding the Division whose Order No 12 you have just heard. And when in addition the commanding officer considers your worth and personal attributes which his long and intimate connection with you has taught him to appreciate and admire and which has lead you on in securing the good name you have, which is your just due. He feels that no confidence is misplaced. Which anticipates from you a continuance of your past character and a surety is given of what you[r] future course will be.
>
> Comrades with the knowledge of your honor and character in the past well won.

> Your commanding officer is assured that no further voucher can be required. That the standard you have established by accreditted labor you will never fall below. This is your last parade as the Second United States Sharp Shooters with earnest wishes for your personal welfare and an early return to your families and friends; with the meed of a soldiers honor upon you Your commanding officer bids you *farewell*
>
>   By Order
>   J E Doughty (signature)
>   Major 2*d* U.S.S.S.
>   Comm'd'g Regt
>
> J.M. Matthews (signature)
> Adjutant

And so the seal of history was affixed upon the Second United States Sharpshooters. The Vermont men were well "received by their comrades in arms of the Fourth" Vermont Infantry. Such was probably the case overall with the other companies. No doubt there was some friction after the move coming from both parties involved. In all likelihood there was a degree of resentment on the part of the sharpshooters in taking orders from their new superiors. In one case, Norris Smith, formerly a Lieutenant of Company G, was reduced to the ranks after his transfer to the 5th New Hampshire, perhaps an indication of such friction. Nevertheless, a good many former sharpshooters served on with their new regiments throughout the Appomattox Campaign and until the summer of 1865, when most Federal regiments mustered out of the service.[25]

In summation, the 2nd U.S.S.S. should be remembered as the quintessential pan–Yankee regiment with three salient qualities — proficiency, pragmatism and patriotism. The sharpshooters' proficiency as skirmishers and expert riflemen is unchallenged. From their enlistment the sharpshooters believed they served a specific function in the service: they were not the type of soldier to seek opportunities to demonstrate bravery. And their function in battle, usually fighting on the skirmish line or as snipers, often kept their individual acts of bravery far from the eyes of their reporting brigade and division commanders. Thus the regiment was seldom mentioned for gallantry in official reports. Finally, the regiment demonstrated its patriotism in the purest way possible: by reenlisting almost to a man during the winter of 1863 when the outcome of the war was still far from certain.

History will never know the full impact of the 2nd U.S.S.S., because the regiment suffered needless, excessive losses, was not particularly well led, and was not utilized to its maximum potential. Like the aged Federal chief of ordnance General James Ripley, the Federal leadership failed to grasp the unique quality and immense potential of the regiment. Every effort should have been made to husband this valuable resource; instead, the regiment was situated in an unhealthy camp during its training phase and was repeatedly sent into action without regard to potential losses. General Grant's personal order to the regiment at Totopotomoy Creek to charge across the creek, even if it cost the regiment every man, serves as a good example of the overall disregard of Army command for this highly valuable unit.[26]

As was the case with most Civil War regiments, deaths from disease took a heavy toll on the regiment. But the most telling losses in the regiment were the men discharged for disability. Company E, for example, lost sixty-one enlisted men to discharge for disability; and a number of men were lost because of transfer to the Veteran Reserve Corps, a branch of the Army for men unfit to perform regular duty.[27]

Some of the sharpshooters who availed themselves of discharge for disability returned to the Army in other regiments. Private John A. Huff of Company B, for instance, was a good example of this pattern. Soon after obtaining a disability discharge, Huff joined a Michigan cavalry regiment and became famous for killing the renowned Confederate cavalry commander Major General J.E.B. Stuart at the Battle of Yellow Tavern, May 11, 1864.

Captain James Deering Fessenden of Company D left the regiment in September 1862 and moved on to higher station. The captain, a son of Maine senator William Pitt Fessenden, eventually became the highest-ranking former member of the regiment. After leaving the sharpshooters, Fessenden organized the first African American regiment in Federal service. Before the war was over he had reached the rank of brevet major general of volunteers.[28]

In his exhaustive study of Civil War Federal regiments William F. Fox gave high praise to Berdan's Sharpshooters, noting that they were the best known regiments in the Army. Fox noted that the regiments were composed of men with a high level of intelligence and physical qualification. According to Fox the regiments had no equal as skirmishers and doubtlessly killed more rebels than any other Federal regiment. But the best compliment paid to the 2nd United States Sharpshooters came from the rebels themselves. First Lieutenant William H. Humphrey of Company E recalled this fact years after the war when he wrote, "We get praise from a source that but few get theirs from; ours comes from the enemy, they knew us well. Often the enemy has been heard to sing out, 'Look out, there are those devils with big hats and short guns!'"[29]

Appendix: Roster

The following roster is from the original Descriptive Book of the Second Regiment, U.S. Sharpshooters, now stored in the National Archives. All of the original entries were handwritten in ink by more than one person; therefore, the quality and legibility of the entries vary. Names from the original book were checked against other existing rosters, and in some cases the spellings differ. The names, ages, state or country of birth and occupations of the enlisted men of the Second United States Sharpshooters are here recorded in their original order. In the book the names were usually in alphabetical order, but often names were added out of sequence or without regard to alphabetical order. Descriptive information of some men was left blank in the original book; this accounts for most the names on this roster without descriptive information; a — means that the information was missing, and a ? means that the writing was illegible. Also, the names of recruits who joined in 1862, 1863 and 1864 in companies B, D, E and G were recorded on separate pages of the book after the original roster was completed. For this roster I have followed the sequence as recorded in the Descriptive Book of the Second Regiment rather than rearranging the names in alphabetical order.

Company A

Name	*Age*	*Birth Place*	*Occupation*
Sergeants			
Abraham Wright 1st	29	PA	carpenter
Edward Jackson	24	OH	laborer
Levanson Rogers	33	NY	farmer
Samuel Hancock	31	PA	"
George Cummings	29	—	druggist
Corporals			
Uriah Penny 1st	24	ME	wheelwright
Owen Evans	36	IN	farmer
Abraham Howe	25	NY	engineer
Joseph Walker	32	ME	lumberman
John Veeder	38	IL	farmer
David Craig	25	ME	cabinet maker
William Collins	23	MA	carpenter
Charles Rees 8th	22	NY	farmer
Isaac Mosier	35	ME	"
Francis Little	29	NH	?
John Young	28	PA	farmer

Name	Age	Birth Place	Occupation
Charles Ackley	24	NY	blacksmith
Albert Little	27	NH	teamster
Asa Caldwell	23	MI	hunter
George McKellup	35	NY	farmer
Henry Page	21	—	hunter
John Doulon	21	MA	farmer
John Bugbee	21	ME	"
George James	21	NY	"
James Hawes	28	"	?
Augustus Hall	30	—	—
George Slocum	27	NY	?
Aldritt, Edwin	21	England	farmer
Blockner, John	26	Germany	blacksmith
Bell, Lucius	19	WI	farmer
Babcock, John	24	MA	"
George Black	24	NY	millwright
Crippen, Robert	30	"	lumberman
Charles, Edward	22	Canada	farmer
Cooper, Christian	24	PA	"
Carpenter, Rives	27	ME	"
Charlton, Richard	18	NY	"
Dolson, John	19	IL	"
Dickey, Joseph	23	NY	"
Dunsmore, Irving	18	ME	"
Frederick, Sylvester	21	NY	"
Horton, John	21	England	"
Hartford, Elder	23	PA	mason
Haynes, Alfred	30	NY	farmer
Hershberger, Martin	25	PA	"
Hamlet, Albert	26	MA	"
Hamlet, Benjamin	21	IL	"
Hank, Gilbert	21	OH	"
Heald, Daniel	38	PA	laborer
Jacobs, Elias	30	VA	farmer
Jones, Daniel	19	NH	mechanic
Jones, Oliver	37	IL	farmer
Kerr, James	22	PA	millman
Kerr, William	18	"	farmer
Livingston, Alex	21	WI	hunter
Millet, James	26	ME	"
McGaffey, Henry	18	"	farmer
Moriarty, Eugene	18	MA	"
Mason, William	22	IL	"
Miracle, Abraham	34	NY	trader
Mixler, Horace	20	MA	weaver
Newman, Charles	27	Germany	farmer
O'Neal, Henry	18	Ireland	"
Pierce, Joseph	27	MA	carpenter
Powers, James	24	OH	farmer
Pickard, Daniel	24	"	"
Pettyjohn, Dyer	25	"	"
Prescott, Lawrence	24	MN	"
Parmenter, Silas	26	NY	"
Rees, Thos	24	"	"

Name	Age	Birth Place	Occupation
Reese, Samuel	18	"	"
Rand, Julian	29	VT	hunter
Storrs, Francis	21	NY	farmer
Storrs, Orin	28	"	"
Smith, Anson	24	"	butcher
Sarver, Wm.	32	PA	engineer
Seamons, W.	30	RI	farmer
Saxton, W.	34	NJ	butcher
Stacy, W.	21	MA	farmer
Sampson, Henry	23	"	mason
Seward, Watson	20	NY	farmer
Samson, Edward	25	Canada	"
Scoville, Everett	26	NY	"
Thompson, Terrance	18	"	"
Wales, James	—	—	—
Wheaton, Willard	41	NY	builder
Walker, John	21	OH	hunter
White, Jacob	31	PA	farmer
Benj. Kelley	20	OH	"
J. Bertram	—	—	—
A. Doughty	—	—	—
W. Bailey	—	—	—
A. Corwin	24	NY	carpenter
Kerr, John	36	—	—

Company B

Name	Age	Birth Place	Occupation
Austin, Calvin	22	MI	mechanic
Barnes, Newton	18	"	farmer
Benson, Royal	40	VT	"
Adams, Edward	22	MI	"
Bolton, Enos	20	NY	"
Beers, Henry	21	"	"
Bartlett, Emerson	19	"	"
Bigelow, Henry	30	"	mechanic
Bigelow, Francis	29	"	farmer
Jeremiah Brown	22	OH	"
Blanchard, Llewellyn	19	ME	"
Cummings, William	24	NY	"
Cronkhite, Charles	18	"	"
Childs, Irwin	22	OH	"
Cramer, Dora	44	PA	lawyer
Childs, Simon	24	NY	farmer
Hulsapple, Albert	19	"	"
Church, Menzer	32	"	carpenter
Clark, Rufus	22	"	farmer
Coshun, Joshua	23	"	"
Dana, Henry	19	MI	"
Denny, William	22	NY	gunsmith
Darrin, Walter	18	"	blacksmith
Elder, Joseph	20	OH	mechanic
Fisher, Baswell	21	"	farmer

Name	Age	Birth Place	Occupation
Fitts, Welton	27	"	"
Fifield, John	18	MI	"
Orrin Case	—	—	—
Goodhue, Benjamin	22	MI	farmer
Gallup, Jerry	23	NY	teamster
Graham, Wm.	33	VT	farmer
Hunt, Joseph	18	MI	"
Hazleton, George	18	"	"
Howe, Jedediah	26	NY	"
Haskill, A.	22	"	"
Huff, John	42	"	mechanic
Johnson, James	34	"	farmer
Lewis, George	18	MI	"
Loree, William	25	NY	mechanic
Leslie, Nelson	26	NH	farmer
Lindsley, Silas	44	NY	mason
Lawrence, George	26	"	miller
Maltby, Chauncey	28	"	farmer
Morton, George	21	"	"
Morton, Delos	24	MI	"
Morrow, Henry	20	NY	miller
Milo Moore	20	"	farmer
McCord, Samuel	22	"	mechanic
Mascho, George	23	MI	farmer
Nicholas, Ransom	27	NY	"
Norton, Morris	26	"	mechanic
Northup, Alanson	18	OH	farmer
Nixon, Edwin	18	MI	"
Nixon, Robert	23	Canada	"
Oakes, Oscar	20	MI	"
Phelps, Martin	45	NY	"
Potter, Nelson	25	MI	mechanic
Piersons, Sylnanus	21	"	farmer
Preston, Theodore	23	"	"
Skinner, John	27	VT	"
Sherwood, William	18	NY	"
Smith, George	29	MI	"
Smith, Charles	23	NY	mechanic
Shovan, Frank	23	MI	"
Tuttle, Chas.	23	NY	"
Tuttle, James	20	Canada	"
Tuttle, George	19	"	farmer
Tremble, Stephen	29	MI	"
Vanhorn, George	19	NY	"
Warfle, Richard	33	MI	"
Woodman, George	21	NY	"
Waggoner, David	18	MI	"
Washburn, Benjamin	25	NY	"
Ward, Ulysus	33	"	builder
Wood, Chas.	27	MI	farmer
Willcox, Joseph	20	"	"
Willcox, Wm.	21	NY	"
Whitmore, Monroe	39	"	"
Niles, William	21	"	"

Appendix

Name	Age	Birth Place	Occupation
Sergeants			
Aldolphus Guest 1st	22	NY	clerk
George Morton	27	NY	farmer
Asa Shattuck	54	NH	mechanic
Charles Foot	19	VT	farmer
David Gibbs	33	NY	mechanic
Corporals			
Elias Landers 1st	18	NY	farmer
Charles Bennett	20	MI	student
Wm. Washburn	20	NY	mechanic
John Hunt	23	MI	farmer
Henry Parker	22	NY	"
Henry Ballard	22	OH	"
William Ostrom	22	NY	"
William Howard 8th	23	"	clerk
Otto Hammonds	32	Germany?	farmer
Orlando Wheelock	21	MI	"
William Bell	19	OH	"
William Bruce	23	England	"
George Cole	18	MI	"
Charles Foster	28	NY	"
Althouse, John	29	"	"
Buel, Frederick	18	OH	"
Beach, Cyrus	28	NY	"
Baker, Oscar	18	OH	painter
Bigelow, Gilbert	18	MI	farmer
Bohnet, John	22	Germany	"
Cory, Judson	21	MI	"
Curtis, Henry	27	England	"
Davis, Miron	21	MI	"
Daniels, Almeron	46	NY	"
Ellis, Daniel	18	England	"
Ellis, John	22	"	mechanic
Ellis, Thomas	20	"	butcher
Ellison, Hiram	18	NY	farmer
Foster, Seymour	18	MI	clerk
Fishell, Michael	34	NY	farmer
Granbuer, William	21	Germany	"
Goodrich, William	17	MI	"
Goodhue, Benjamin	24	"	"
Helwig, Conrad	18	Germany	"
Hunt, Charles	36	NY	banker
Hawkins, Thomas	38	"	farmer

Company C

Name	Age	Birth Place	Occupation
Abbott, Jared	19	NY	hunter
Berm, Bannister	15	PA	farmer
Boak, George	26	"	"
Foreat, William	—	—	—
Brown, Joseph	21	PA	farmer

Name	Age	Birth Place	Occupation
Callen, John	19	"	lumberman
Carey, John	29	"	hunter
Chilson, Eli	24	"	farmer
Chilson, Rufus	20	"	"
Coals, Russel	40	"	"
Corey, Benjamin	25	NY	merchant
Crandall, George	20	PA	farmer
Crow, Michael	23	"	lumberman
Dickerson, William	20	"	farmer
Dickus, Danl.	—	—	—
Dimmock, Chauncey	18	PA	farmer
Dinkle, George	34	"	?
Daniel Easterbrook	25	"	farmer
Fall, Henry	18	NY	?
Farnsworth, Ulysses	26	PA	farmer
Farmaner, Horace	26	"	laborer
Gere, John	34	IN	"
Luvingmeg, J.	—	—	—
Hosley, Henry	26	PA	farmer
Houghlrailing, Jos.	28	NY	hunter?
Howard, Samuel	30	"	nailer?
Hoyt, John	36	"	hunter
Hull, Samuel	39	England	merchant
Jacox, Leroy	28	PA	laborer
Jacox, William	23	"	"
Lattimer, Samuel	28	"	lumberman
Law, James	37	OH	laborer
Lehy, William	22	Ireland	lumberman
Lewis, Samuel	39	NY	"
Long, Thomas	21	PA	hunter
Lyle, Isaac	31	"	lumberman
Lytle, William	19	"	hunter
McCauley, David	25	NY	bricklayer
McCullough, William	52	PA	gunsmith
McMurray, John	35	"	carpenter
Miller, Isaac	35	"	farmer
Mott, John	28	NY	laborer
Multins, John	35	"	"
Nearman, Andrew	21	"	blacksmith
Northup, Ira	2 —	"	laborer
Pearsall, John	20	PA	blacksmith
Pringle, Julius	25	NY	laborer
Quick, Joseph	21	"	farmer
Quinn, John	35	Ireland	laborer
Riddle, Edgar	21	NY	painter
Rumberger, Franklin	19	PA	laborer
Sanders, Albert	24	NY	"
Sanders, George	25	"	"
Scott, Benjamin	33	"	lumberman
Scott, Lyman	21	"	"
Sharkaw, Michael	26	Canada	laborer
Stewart, George	20	NY	"
Studor, Anthony	24	"	"
Thompson, Wesley	19	PA	"

Name	Age	Birth Place	Occupation
Vanover, Levi	17	NY	"
Warren, Horrace	34	"	gunsmith
Warren, Hiram	28	"	laborer
Warren, Robert	24	"	"
Williams, Samuel	26	"	"
Zimwalt, John	20	Germany	"
Ryan, Americus	21	NY	"
Black, David	19	PA	"
Johnson, Obadiah	24	"	farmer
Pease, Ashbol	21	"	carpenter
Pease, Laitus	21	"	farmer
Perkins, Russel	24	NY	laborer
Peters, Frederick	23	"	farmer
Willard, Martin	21	"	laborer

Company D

Name	Age	Birth Place	Occupation
Sergeants			
Lorenzo Hall	22?	ME	seaman
Albion Morey	33	"	blacksmith
Stephen Barker	24	"	farmer
Asa Conary	35	"	joiner
George Nash	25	"	lumberman
Corporals			
James Stephens	24	"	caulker
Edwin Morse	24	"	farmer
William McFarland	32	"	lumberman
Maxey Hamlin	21	"	farmer
Brigham Edgley	26	"	"
Wilson Woodard	30	"	mill man
Daniel Cummings	28	"	carpenter
Josiah Gray	24	"	farmer
Warren Ladd	43	"	"
Allen, John	30	"	mill man
Bartlett, Sanford	18	"	seaman
Barton, Benjamin	18	"	farmer
Brickford, Albert	22	"	"
Bird, James	21	England	clerk
Boynton, Richard	23	ME	farmer
Bradbury, James	26	"	"
Brown, Henry	28	Germany	seaman
Chandler, Rubin	21	ME	"
Clark, Lemuel	18	"	farmer
Coffin, Fred	25	"	joiner
Coffin, George	22	"	lumberman
Coffin, Hilliard	18	"	scholar
Crockett, Edgar	23	"	seaman
Crowley, Walter	18	"	"
Davis, Luther	21	"	lumberman
Dow, Joseph	38	"	ship?
Dunbar, Oscar	19	"	farmer

Name	Age	Birth Place	Occupation
Eaton, Daniel	20	"	"
Emerson, Charles	18	"	"
Emerson, Stillman	27	"	seaman
Evans, Stephen	21	"	blacksmith
Farnsworth, Alonzo	21	"	lumberman
Fuller, James	19	"	farmer
Gray, Ezra	20	"	farmer
Hall, Nelson	19	"	seaman
Hall, Rufus	22	"	"
Henderson, Thomas	31	"	"
Hodgdon, Elisha	19	"	farmer
Doyle, James	25	"	"
Hopkins, Martin	22	"	blacksmith
Hussey, John	24	"	teamster
Hutchins, Abel	18	"	farmer
Johnson, Charles	18	"	"
Jordon, John	21	"	mechanic
Knowlton, John	18	"	farmer
Ladd, Francis	22	"	stone mason
Leighton, George	25	"	seaman
Leighton, James	20	"	farmer
Lyman, Joseph	26	"	lumberman
Maddocks, Nelson	29	"	"
Mains, Leonaard	18	"	mill man
Matthews, James	21	"	printer
McKinzie, William	—	"	—
McLaine, Simon	26	"	lumber?
McNaughton, George	36	Scotland	farmer
Merrill, Thomas	—	ME	shoemaker
Moore, Wyatt	36	"	blacksmith
Morse, Argill	21	"	farmer
Newhall, Andrew	18	"	c —?
Osgood, James	28	"	farmer
Place, Charles	30	"	"
Pratt, Frank	20	"	lumberman
Richardson, George	20	"	farmer
Roberts, George	27	"	mill?
Rounds, George	27	"	clerk
Sally, James	19	"	farmer
Scofield, Samuel	22	"	teamster
Small, Leonard	21	"	farmer
Smith, Charles	19	"	"
Smith, William	20	"	"
Steele, William	18	"	"
Sullivan, John	26	Ireland	"
Trask, Charles	18	ME	"
Tucker, Arthur	23	"	lumber
Tucker, Fred	22	"	"
Tucker, Washington	23	"	"
Twombly, Andrew	32	"	"
Wade, John	32	"	seaman
Ward, Silas	24	"	millerman?
White, Charles	20	"	farmer
Wilson, John	24	"	"

Name	Age	Birth Place	Occupation
Young, William	26	"	"
Riggs, Franklin	41	"	teamster
Hall, John	19	"	druggist
Bessy, Charles	31	"	butcher
Bridgham, Charles	21	"	physician
Buck, Llewellyn	21	"	farmer
Teague, Charles	28	"	mechanic
Hamlin, Roscoe	21	"	farmer
Coffin, Lucins	22	"	photographer
Crockett, A.	29	"	seaman
Conant, W.	18	"	sailmaker
Bragg, Barziler	32	"	laborer
Pendleton, James	33	"	joiner
Thompson, Edwin	36	Canada	farmer
Wentworth, Charles	32	ME	seaman
Newall, Roderick	18	"	farmer
Jameson, John	20	"	"
Boynton, Samuel	44	"	?
Hall, Lorenzo	42	"	?
Haley, John	24	"	farmer
Crisswell, Robert	44	MA	laborer
Bickford, Henry	18	ME	farmer
Decovin, Joseph	20	"	"
Eaton, Daniel	19	"	"
Esancy, John	—	—	—
Foster, Sanford	22	Me	farmer
Gordon, Byron	18	"	"
Hannigan, David	21	Ireland	?
Hamilton, Cyrus	27	ME	mechanic
Hartford, Stephan	22	"	farmer
Keenan, John	20	Ireland	machinist

Company E

Name	Age	Birth Place	Occupation
Abby, Osmond	21	VT	carpenter
Bain, Charles	22	"	?
Brown, Willard	19	"	farmer
Bruce, Horatio	20	"	"
Carr, Ira	20	"	?maker
Coolidge, John	20	"	farmer
Coolidge, Daniel	29	"	"
Cook, William	18	"	"
Coburn, Oscar	21	MA	carpenter
Culver, Harry	24	VT	farmer
Davis, Dan	21	"	"
Dunton, George	20	"	"
Freeman, Garry	21	"	"
Gilman, Joseph	21	"	"
Hart, Willis	38	"	blacksmith
Hinckly, Elijah	21	NY	shoemaker
Hastings, Charles	19	MA	blacksmith
Hill, Thomas	22	VT	carpenter

Name	Age	Birth Place	Occupation
Hodge, Holden	23	"	wheelwright
Halthorn, Edward	23	"	farmer
Humphrey, William	23	"	"
Howard, Silas	20	NY	"
Howard, Thomas	22	"	"
Holmes, Charles	18	VT	"
Jefts, Rosalvo	22	"	"
Joslyn, Edwin	17	"	"
Kemp, Milton	20	NH	"
Keith, George	22	VT	"
Keith, Charles	21	"	"
Lamson, George	18	"	"
Latimer, Willson	34	NY	carpenter
Lewis, Luke	22	VT	farmer
Licklin, Samuel	23	"	shoemaker
Martin, Burnap	26	"	farmer
McClellan, Byron	18	"	"
Minet, Exes	23	"	"
Morey, Joel	22	Canada	blacksmith
Moshier, Henry	18	VT	farmer
Markham, Samuel	18	"	"
Page, Charles	21	"	carpenter
Parris, John	20	"	farmer
Partridge, Edward	37	"	carpenter
Pike, Preston	20	"	"
Powell, Elijah	26	—	—
Proctor, Oscar	19	VT	farmer
Rand, Preston	32	"	"
Richardson, Burton	19	"	"
Sanborn, Asa	18	"	"
Scott, William	26	"	wheelwright
Shephard, John	26	"	farmer
Smith, Bowman	24	"	sawyer
Smith, Willard	18	"	farmer
Squier, Daniel	26	"	"
Squier, Willard	18	"	"
Stockwell, Arthur	22	"	"
Stockwell, Elbridge	22	NY	artist
Swan, Henry	21	VT	farmer
Tarbell, James	18	"	"
Terill, Delevan	21	"	"
Thompson, Henry	21	"	"
Thompson, William	27	MA	"
Trask, Joseph	20	"	"
Turner, Charles	24	VT	?
Wills, Liman	23	NY	painter
West, Henry	21	VT	sailmaker
White, Alonso	41	"	stonecutter
Whitman, Shepard	23	NH	farmer
Willis, Orin	18	VT	stone mason
Willard, Eli	18	VT	farmer
York, Albert	29	NH	"
Tilson, William	18	VT	"
Brown, Alfred	20	"	"

Name	Age	Birth Place	Occupation
Culver, Daniel	22	—	—
Farman, George	21	NH	farmer
Holbrook, Manlius	18	VT	"
Hill, Caleb	24	"	"
Martin, Richard	22	"	steward
Ruck, Alphonso	20	"	farmer
Whitley, Edward	44	"	mason
Hill, Franklin	21	"	farmer
Morris, George	33	"	"
Davies, John	27	"	salesman
Sergeants			
Seymore Norton	20	"	student
John Law	38	"	carpenter
William Perkins	21	"	student
Thomas Tarbell	27	"	engineer
William Strong	25	"	"
Corporals			
James Parker	33	"	shoemaker
Addison Benedict	21	"	student
Henry Church	23	"	blacksmith
James Newton	18	"	farmer
Prescott Thompson	24	"	"
Ames Smith	27	MA	wheelwright
John Howard	28	NH	stone mason
Harrison Holden	36	VT	carpenter
Congdon, Henry	24	"	farmer
Smith, Montillion	36	NY	"
Gibbs, James	22	VT	painter
Culver, Albert	25	"	farmer
Adams, George	22	"	"
Albee, Vietts	23	"	blacksmith
Atwood, Edward	18	"	farmer
Blanchard, Henry	25	"	laborer
Bennett, Daniel	21	MA	mechanic
Brown, George	23	VT	farmer
Collins, John	38	"	stonecutter
Clay, George	21	NY	farmer
Daggett, James	24	VT	teamster
Edgerton, Andrew	31	"	farmer
Foster, James	37	VT	"
Fairbanks, Charles	18	"	"
Fairbanks, Alfred	19	"	"
Howes, David	32	NY	carpenter
Hathorn, William	40	VT	farmer
Hathorn, Horace	44	"	"
Joiner, George	25	"	"

Company F

Name	Age	Birth Place	Occupation
Abbott, Ames	23	NH	spring maker
Applin, Charles	22	"	mechanic

Name	Age	Birth Place	Occupation
Alexander, Thomas	25	"	joiner
Barnard, Alonzo	20	"	farmer
Beard, William	20	"	student
Boydton, James	33	"	painter
Bent, James	26	MA	farmer
Bowen, William	22	NH	Sythemaker?
Barnes, George	21	"	stonemason
Bamford, Leone	21	MA	manufacturer
Boice, Henry	21	NH	farmer
Brown, Lemeuel	26	"	mechanic
Baker, Hazel	27	CT	janitor
Bankes, Charles	40	NH	farmer
Bixby, Asa	21	NH	"
Boyce, Warren	10	"	mechanic
Batchelder, Abby	22	"	shoemaker
Caldwell, Horace	30	"	farmer
Chadwick, Edwin	21	"	student
Currier, Hazen	24	"	shoemaker
Clough, Jeremiah	32	"	farmer
Cilby, Joseph	18	"	"
Chase, Daniel	44	MA	"
Collins, George	21	VT	machinist
Collins, Marvin	18	NH	mechanic
Day, George	18	"	farmer
Dodge, Julian	19	"	"
Durgin, Stephen	36	—	—
Everest, Joseph	44	NH	farmer
Farnum, Isaac	23	"	carpenter
Farnum, Cyrus	18	"	farmer
Frachum, Orin	23	"	"
Foristull, Charles	20	"	"
Fletcher, Oliver	23	"	"
Gitchel, Samuel	24	"	"
Griggs, Azel	24	"	"
Gould, William	18	"	"
Goodrich, William	19	MA	"
Horne, Charles	23	NH	cooper
Hadley, Francis	19	"	student
Hadley, Sylvester	23	"	—
Hoffman, John	19	NY	moulder
Hunt, Lucius	20	NH	mechanic
Jameson, Daniel	23	"	farmer
Jillson, Anson	21	"	mechanic
Jackson, Oliver	25	"	farmer
Kimball, John	22	"	machinist
Leighton, Jerome	23	"	farmer
Lamprey, George	25	"	joiner
Dane, George	23	"	blacksmith
Murry, Samuel	20	"	student
Moore, Horace	34	VT	shoemaker
Moody, John	18	NH	farmer
Mathes, Henry	35	England	?
McVicar, Alexander	38	Canada	carpenter
Mills, Frank	18	NH	farmer

Appendix

Name	Age	Birth Place	Occupation
Morse, Nathan	35	"	mechanic
Muzzey, Hiram	18	"	farmer
Myer, Frederick	25	Germany	painter
Mills, Joseph	27	NH	farmer
Marsh, John	23	"	"
Page, John	20	"	"
Paul, Nelson	30	"	"
Quimby, Moses	23	"	"
Richard, Henry	24	"	carpenter
Reynolds, Hooser	41	ME	blacksmith
Reynolds, William	33	"	?
Robinson, John	22	NH	farmer
Rollins, Carlton	36	"	"
Speed, Lemond	24	"	stonecutter
Speed, William	28	"	stonemason
Scott, William	24	VT	moulder
Starr, Darius	19	CT	student
Strickland, William	26	MA	syth?
Sanborn, Alfred	21	NH	farmer
Severans, William	28	"	"
Sanborn, Henry	24	"	"
Thompson, Joseph	18	"	student
Thayer, Charles	37	"	farmer
Towne, James	21	"	carpenter
Tenney, Silas	22	"	farmer
Upton, Charles	25	MA	mechanic
Van Valin, Daniel	25	NY	book agent?
West, Orin	29	NH	shoemaker
Whittier, Charles	18	"	student
Whipple, Edwin	22	"	farmer
White, Lyman	21	"	mechanic
Withington, William	20	MA	"
Wilson, Charles	19	NII	farmer
Walker, Ruel	27	"	"
Weatherbee, Frank	28	NY	station
Davis, Solon	—	—	—
Buckingham, D.	22	OH	farmer
Sexton Williams	32	KY	horticulturalist?
Clark, Lewis	24	VA	mechanic
Fox, Charles	31	NY	?
German, Thomas	18	MA	butcher
Kennedy, John	18	Scotland	painter
Hayward, Alvin	19	NH	butcher
Simons, James	18	"	farmer
Manchester, John	18	"	"
Wood, William	21	"	"
Brown, John	18	"	?
Longee, Walter	18	"	farmer

Company G

Name	Age	Birth Place	Occupation
Aiken, Josiah	20	NH	farmer
Ames, John	21	"	"

Name	Age	Birth Place	Occupation
Blake, Christopher	21	ME	student
Bland, Joseph	34	England	lumberman
Burge, Frederick	25	NH	farmer
Brown, Samuel	20	MA	"
Blake, Ira	26	NH	"
Crane, Luther	21	"	"
Carr, Frank	20	"	"
Carter, Reuben	21	"	"
Colby, Henry	20	"	mechanic
Collins, William	27	"	harness maker
Drew, Andrew	32	"	stone cutter
Dudley, Charles	21	"	farmer
Dow, Dura	18	"	shoe maker
Eastman, Frank	16	"	musician
Edgerly, Calvin	24	"	stone cutter
Edwards, William	44	"	mechanic
Ellis, Thomas	18	"	farmer
Foster, Jeremiah	20	"	student
Fletcher, Augustus	23	VT	Hass?
Foss, Alfred	23	NH	shoe cutt?
Fletcher, Warren	23	"	farmer
Gamsby, Harvey	24	"	bridge builder
Greene, William	18	"	student
Graham, Benjamin	34	"	carpenter
Gilman, James	19	"	farmer
Hodgkins, Frank	21	"	"
Hodge, Joseph	20	"	"
Hanson, Elijah	26	"	carpenter
Hastings, Ames	33	"	blacksmith
Hopkins, Chas.	24	ME	farmer
Hubbard, Stimson	22	"	machinist
Hoyt, Lewis	32	NH	"
Holt, Albian	35	"	cook
Jackson, Chas.	33	"	shoemaker
Keach, James	23	NY	farmer
Kenney, Horace	20	NH	"
Kay, Charles	23	"	"
Langley, George	18	"	"
Law, Joseph	25	VT	"
Lovejoy, John	21	ME	"
Moores, William	19	NH	"
Moulton, True	19	"	"
Morrow, William	20	"	"
Martin, Ezra	22	VT	"
Morse, Horace	23	NH	"
McCrillis, George	36	"	"
Moore, Admo	20	MA	clerk
Osgood, Ruel	35	NH	farmer
Porter, Jerome	18	"	student
Pilbro, John	27	England	farmer
Perkins, Uriah	25	NH	shoemaker
Quimby, Chas.	20	"	farmer
Redfield, Henry	21	ME	railroader
Shephard, George	29	NH	teamster

Appendix

Name	Age	Birth Place	Occupation
Smith, Norris	27	"	farmer
Smith, Daniel	22	"	"
Stevens, Chas.	26	ME	mechanic
Sischo, William	42	NH	teamster
Stevens, Charles F.	22	"	farmer
Steele, Allen	18	"	"
Smith, Dustin	40	"	"
Sanborn, Freeman	35	ME	"
Sanborn, John	25	NH	?
Scales, George	21	"	carpenter
True, Warren	24	MI	"
True, Augustus	18	NH	musician
Thomas, Job	22	"	shoemaker
Thomas, William	19	"	farmer
Twombly, Robert	19	"	"
Taylor, Henry	20	MA	shoemaker
Wiggins, Isiah	21	NH	mechanic
Winn, Joseph	33	NH	farmer
White, Geo.	21	NH	student
Whitten, Thomas	44	"	carpenter
Batchelder, Nathan'l	23	"	"
Roundy, George	37	"	mechanic
Sergeants			
John Thompson	26	"	?
Howard Smith	23	"	engineer
Geo. Marden	22	"	mechanic?
Albert Fisher	22	"	machinist
Davis Sargent	22	—	—
Corporals			
Joseph Sanborn	40	—	shoemaker
Elbridge Moore	26	—	farmer
Abner Colby	31	NH	machinist
David Gibson	35	—	mans?
Zeb. Twitchell	31	—	—
James Webster	24	—	—
Edward Folsome	22	—	—
James Kent	23	NH	wheelwright
Enlisted in 1862:			
Clifford, Joseph	26	"	farmer
Irving, John	23	"	shoemaker
Ingalls, Andrew	31	"	carpenter
Kimball, William	27	"	book keeper
Longer, John	23	"	farmer
Palmer, James	28	ME	"
Railey, John	19	MA	"
Tillotson, Center	28	VT	"
Bernice Scales	19	NH	"
Blood, George	18	"	"
Blood, Alonzo	18	"	"
Blood, Andrew	29	"	"
Cross, King	32	"	"
Floyd, Joseph	44	"	shoemaker
Hackett, Warren	18	"	brickmaker
Marston, David	18	"	carpenter

Company H

Name	Age	Birth Place	Occupation
Abbott, Curtis	21	VT	student
Alexander, Caleb	42	"	farmer
Averill, Philetus	34	"	carpenter
Ayers, John	19	"	farmer
Barry, George	26	NY	private
Benson, William	22	VT	clerk
Bliss, Wartsill	30	MA	student
Bond, Charles	18	VT	"
Britton, George	21	"	mechanic
Brockway, John	19	"	farmer
Brophy, Harvey	27	"	mechanic
Bulloch, David	18	"	farmer
Burlingame, Zelotes	42	"	mechanic
Butterfield, Abner	29	"	farmer
Campbell, Henry	20	"	"
Clark, James	18	"	"
Clark, Lewis,	22	"	mechanic
Cressy, Everett	23	MA	farmer
Cressy, George	21	"	"
Cressy, Martin	25	"	"
Davis, Noyes	27	NH	carpenter
Diamond, George	18	VT	mechanic
Dix, Hosea	36	"	farmer
Elmer, Edward	41	"	R.R. Employ
Emerson, Gary	16	"	farmer
Emerson, Orange	23	"	"
Everleth, Henry	18	MA	"
Giddings, Benjamin	19	VT	student
Goodenough, Ezra	37	"	mechanic
Harrington, Elisha	26	NY	farmer
Howard, Alfred	41	VT	carpenter
Howard, Charles	18	"	farmer
Henry Houghton	21	"	"
Hyde, Charles	22	"	student
Johnson, Edwin	19	"	farmer
Kendall, George	30	MA	peddler
King, William	22	VT	student
Kendall, Merrill	25	"	dentist
Mason, Almon	21	"	mechanic
May, George	21	CT	farmer
Miller, Allen	27	NH	mechanic
Miller, George	25	"	"
McGrath, John	19	Ireland	farmer
Monroe, Atherton	44	MA	mechanic
Mullet, Chas.	20	VT	farmer
Newall, Lucius	20	MA	mechanic
Ober, Joseph	19	"	"
Ober, Henry	19	"	"
Paris, Jared	22	VT	farmer
Patterson, Haynes	21	"	mechanic
Peabody, Ariel	23	MA	farmer
Phelps, George	23	"	"

Name	Age	Birth Place	Occupation
Pike, Lewis	23	VT	"
Prindle, Albert	23	"	jeweler
Putnam, William	22	"	artist
Rawson, Harrison	19	"	peddler
Rawson, Kimball	21	"	carpenter
Richardson, George	22	"	"
Robbins, George	37	"	farmer
Rawson, Riley	22	"	carpenter
Scribner, Grove	20	"	farmer
Smith, Henry	27	NH	mechanic
Stevens, Edward	31	MA	farmer
Stewart, Harvey	22	VT	"
Strong, Sylvester	21	"	"
Strow, William	25	"	U.S. Navy
Town, William	23	"	farmer
Tower, George	18	"	"
Tyler, Chas.	26	"	mechanic
Witt, Lucien	18	NH	farmer
Willis, Daniel	23	VT	"
White, Chas.	22	"	carpenter
White, Ebon	18	MA	farmer
White, William	18	VT	"
Worden, Herbert	18	"	"
Wyman, Loring	37	NH	farmer
York, George	32	VT	"
Warren, George	28	WI	"
Ramsey, Francis	23	NH	mechanic
Barnes, Daniel	22	MA	farmer
Keeler, Willis	18	VT	"

Buglers

Robinson, Chas.	25	"	mechanic
Warner, Camilles	19	"	farmer

Wagoner

Stephins, Joel	45	"	"

Sergeants

Newell, William	—	—	—
Smith, Walter	—	—	—
Churchill, Wm.	—	—	—
Clark, Frederick	—	—	—
Chipman, Tobey	—	—	—

Corporals

Albert Burgess	—	—	—
Northrop, Ezekiel	—	—	—
Fairfield, Alvah	—	—	—
Holland, Albert	—	—	—
Shattuck, Wm.	—	—	—
Giddings, Henry	—	—	—
Stevens, Warren	—	—	—
Potter, Preserved	—	—	—

Enlisted in 1862:

Rodolphus Allen	19	VT	farmer
Chas. Smith	—	—	—

1864
Company B

Name	Age	Birth Place	Occupation
Hawkins, Luther	28	MI	farmer
Hardy, Emory	43	CT	"
Hagerty, Elias	23	MI	"
Hunt, John	33	"	butcher
Hill, Jefferson	18	NY	farmer
Lane, Hiram	23	OH	"
Lane, William	40	"	shoemaker
Lyon, Francis	21	MI	farmer
Morrow, Charles	—	"	"
Parke, James	18	"	"
Piper, Thomas	18	NY	shoemaker
Roe, John	18	"	farmer
Slaght, Chauncy	18	"	"
Sabin, Marcus	40	"	"
Stroble, Jacob	21	Germany	"
Thompson, John	22	NJ	"
Touse, James	18	Canada	?
Tyler, Stephen	44	NY	farmer
Warfle, Richard	24	MI	"
Willoughby, Samuel	35	Canada	"
Willoughby, William	34	NY	"
Wolfe, Christian	30	Germany	brewer
Wolfe, Jacob	23	"	clerk
Von Wie, Abram	18	NY	farmer

1864
Company D

Name	Age	Birth Place	Occupation
Murphy, Michael	18	Canada	laborer
O'Donnell, John	20	Ireland	"
Rodgers, John	22	Canada	farmer
Robinson, Robert	22	"	laborer
Sidlinger, Hilton	19	ME	blacksmith
Ward, David	24	"	farmer
Witham, George	18	"	"
Wentworth, Tristan	28	"	"
Burgess, John	18	"	"
Doe, William	39	"	"
Stanwood, Franklin	18	"	"
Hunter, Henry	38	"	sailmaker?
Early, Patrick	—	—	—
Hadley, T.	28	ME	farmer
Harden, Russell	19	"	"
Knight, Johnas	37	"	machinist
Kelley, Jonathan	22	"	farmer
Landers, James	23	Ireland	"
Lee, William	44	Scotland	shoemaker

Name	Age	Birth Place	Occupation
Murch, Jepthen	20	ME	peddler
Plemmar, Gnoberg	21	"	laborer
Richardson, Isaac	37	"	butcher
Spencer, Joseph	33	"	farmer
Tabor, W.	23	"	"
Taylor, John	22	Germany	botanist?
Welch, John	27	Canada	carpenter
Conner, John	25	"	tin smith?
Thayer, John	45	ME	farmer
Hunt, Wilson	25	Canada	"
Ball, Joseph	18	ME	seaman
Teague, Rufus	40	"	farmer

1862
Company E

Name	Age	Birth Place	Occupation
Longley, Rensellear	30	VT	farmer
Rice, Edward	21	MA	mechanic
Quimby, John	18	VT	farmer
Rounds, Isaac	25	NY	"
Rollins, Ledrell	18	VT	"
Munsel, John	19	"	laborer
Severance, Luther	25	NY	mechanic
Newell, Luther	26	NH	"
Thompson, D.	36	VT	"
Wallace, Franklin	43	NH	farmer
Walker, Alvin	28	VT	"
Packard, Albert	18	"	"
Pinney, Edson	29	"	"
Sawyer, David	44	"	mechanic?
Sawyer, Edwin	18	"	mechanic
Sawyer, Charles	19	"	farmer
Gates, George	25	"	carpenter
Bailey, James	42	" deserter	"
Wheeler, Horace	34	" deserter	farmer
Lavelly, Victor	20	"	"
Packard, Philander	43	"	"

Enlisted in 1863:

Name	Age	Birth Place	Occupation
Packard, Alanson	41	"	"
Davis, Martin	18	"	laborer
Robinson, Wallace	19	"	farmer Enl. 2/'64
Spicer, Addison	22	"	" "
Bowen, James	25	"	"
Clay, Smith	18	NY	"
Foster, William	22	ME	"
Foster, Lyman	44	SC	"
Fairbanks, Charles	18	VT	"
Goodenough, Charles	28	"	"
Hodges, Sylvester	21	"	"
Hinkson, Calvin	18	"	"
Ladd, Seneca	21	"	" Enl. 1/'64

Name	Age	Birth Place	Occupation
Langworthy, Sanford	35	"	"
Livermore, George	18	MA	"
Leach, N.	21	VT	"
Leach, Welcome	27	"	"
Newton, John	19	"	"
Shippey, Azra	40	"	"
Tarbell, Abner	25	"	"
Whitcomb, Silas	40	NH	"
Wing, Lemuel	18	VT	"
Durkee, Tracy	20	"	"
Darling, Aquila	18	"	" Enl. 1/'64
Chase, Walter	21	"	"
Cutts, Tilton	32	NH	"
Fleury, Thomas	39	Canada	carpenter Enl. 1/'64
Law, John Jr.	18	VT	farmer
Law, James	20	"	"
McGetrick, Felix	17	"	" Enl. 1/'64
Willey, George	25	"	"
White, Wallace	20	"	fiddler?
Abbott, Abial	27	"	hunter
George Doty	26	NY	farmer
Edgerton, Hiram	40	VT	"
Eldred, Henry	26	NY	"
Elkins, Thomas	28	VT	"
Green, Samuel	36	"	"
Headle, David	41	"	"
Headle, Levi	18	"	laborer
Howard, Suel	35	"	farmer
Leach, James	41	"	"
White, Rufus	44	"	laborer

1864
Company G

Name	Age	Birth Place	Occupation
Osgood, Charles	18	NH	farmer
Reed, Isaac	25	MA deserter	?
Riley, John	19	"	mechanic?

Chapter Notes

Chapter 1

1. H.S. Fuller, "Narrowly Escaped Prison," *Confederate Veteran*, November 1918, p. 473.
2. "The 23rd Georgia," *National Tribune*, 10 July 1884, p. 7.
3. Stephen W. Sears, *Chancellorsville* (New York: Houghton Mifflin, 1996), p. 254.
4. Douglas Mastraino, "Alvin York: View From the Other Side," *Military History*, September 2006, pp. 28–29.
5. William C. Davis, *First Blood: Fort Sumter to Bull Run* (Alexandria, VA: Time-Life Books, 1983), p. 13.
6. Frederick H. Dyer, *A Compendium of the War of the Rebellion* (Des Moines, IA: Dyer Publishing, 1908), III.
7. Davis, pp. 15–17.
8. Frederick Phisterer, *Statistical Record of the Armies of the United States* (New York: The Blue & The Gray Press), p. 4.
9. *The New York Times*, 1 May 1861, p. 4.
10. William Y.W. Ripley, *Vermont Riflemen in the War for the Union, 1861 to 1865: A History of Company F First United States Sharpshooters* (Rutland, VT: Tuttle, 1883), pp. 3–5.
11. Henry Woodhead, ed., *Echoes of Glory* (Alexandria, VA: Time-Life Books, 1991), p. 296.
12. Harold L. Peterson, *The Treasury of the Gun* (New York: Golden Press, 1962), p. 140.
13. Gene Gurney, *A Pictorial History of the United States Army* (New York: Crown, 1966), p. 27.
14. Kevin Phillips, *The Cousins' Wars: Religion, Politics, & the Triumph of Anglo-America* (New York: Basic Books, 1999), p. 576.
15. James Webb, *Born Fighting: How the Scotch-Irish Shaped America* (New York: Broadway Books, 2004), p. 171.
16. Peterson, p. 144.
17. "The Sharpshooters," *The New York Times*, 2 June 1861, p. 3.
18. Kenneth S. Katta, "Conflicts in Command: An Analysis of Leadership in the Berdan Sharpshooters in the Civil War," *Military Collector and Historian*, Summer 2001, p. 54.
19. *The New York Times*, 2 June 1861, p. 3.
20. R.R. Palmer & Joel Colton, *A History of the Modern World*, 5th ed. (New York: Alfred A. Knopf, 1978), p. 78.
21. Roy M. Marcot, *Civil War Chief of Sharpshooters Hiram Berdan, Military Commander and Firearms Inventor* (Irvine, CA: Heritage Press, 1989), p. 23.
22. U.S. War Department, *The War of the Rebellion: A Compilation of the Official Records of the Union and Confederate Armies* (Washington, D.C.: U.S. Government Printing Office, 1880–1901), Series III/ I, p. 270; hereafter cited as OR. All references are to Series I unless otherwise noted.
23. *The New York Times*, 28 June 1861.
24. Robert Hunt Rhodes, ed., *All for the Union: The Civil War Diary and Letters of Elisha Hunt Rhodes* (New York: Orion Books, 1985), p. 13.
25. "Sharp-Shooting Regiments," *The New York Times*, 17 July 1861, p. 4.
26. Rudolph Aschmann, *Memoirs of a Swiss Officer in the American Civil War*, ed. Heinz K. Meier (Bern, Switzerland: Herbert Lang, 1972), p. 9.
27. "Col. Berdan's Sharpshooters," *The New York Times*, 7 August 1861, p. 1.
28. "Sharp-shooters," *The New York Times*, 17 September 1861, p. 1.
29. Phillips, pp. 447 and 450.
30. Ibid., p. 133.
31. Charles Powers Smith, *Yankees and God* (New York: Hermitage House, 1954), p. 3.
32. Ibid., p. 5.
33. Michael Lind, *What Lincoln Believed* (New York: Doubleday, 2005), p. 303.
34. Phillips, pp. 27–28.
35. Marcot, p. 34.
36. *The Rutland Daily Herald*, 10 August 1861, p. 2.
37. "The Sharpshooters," *The Rutland Daily Herald*, 12 August 1861, p. 2.
38. Edward B. Quinter Collection, *Correspondence of Wisconsin Volunteers* II, 56, copy from Manassas National Battlefield Park Library.
39. OR, Series III/II, p. 644.
40. Minnesota Board of Commissioners, *Minnesota in the Civil and Indian Wars 1861–1865* (St. Paul, MN: Pioneer Press, 1890), p. 507.
41. *The Rutland Daily Herald*, 26 November 1861.
42. Marcot, p. 34.
43. William F. Fox, *Regimental Losses in the American Civil War 1861–1865* (Albany, NY: Albany Publishing, 1889), p. 62.
44. Alan T. Nolan, *The Iron Brigade: A Military History* (Indianapolis: Indiana University Press, 1994), p. 32.
45. Muster and Descriptive Rolls, 2nd United States Sharpshooters, National Archives, Washington, D.C.; Augustus D. Ayling, *Revised Register of the Soldiers and Sailors of New Hampshire in the War of the Rebellion 1861–1865* (Concord, NH: Ira Evans, Public Printer, 1895), p. 985.
46. Theodore S. Peck, ed., *Revised Roster of Vermont Volunteers and Lists of Vermonters who Served in the Army and Navy of the United States* (Montpelier, VT), p. 605; copy from Antietam National Battlefield Library.

Chapter 2

1. Wyman S. White, *The Civil War Diary of Wyman White First Sergeant of Company F, 2nd United States Sharpshooter Regiment, 1861–1865*, ed. Russell C. White (Baltimore: Butternut & Blue, 1991), p.18.
2. Robert V. Bruce, *Lincoln and the Tools of War* (Indianapolis: Bobbs-Merrill, 1956), p.111.
3. Ibid.
4. Woodhead, pp. 24–26.
5. Ibid.; David Nevin, *The Road to Shiloh: Early Battles in the West* (Alexandria, VA: Time-Life Books, 1983), pp. 50–51.
6. Hiram Berdan to Secretary Simon Cameron, October 22, 1861, Letter, copy on p. 30, Regimental Record Book, 1st U.S. Sharpshooters, National Archives, Washington, D.C.
7. Orders, Regimental Record Book, 2nd U.S. Sharpshooters, National Archives, Washington, D.C.
8. White, pp. 24–25.
9. Ibid.
10. *Letters From a Sharpshooter: The Civil War Letters of Private William B. Greene, Co. G 2nd United States Sharpshooters (Berdan's) Army of the Potomac 1861–1865*, transcribed by William Hastings (Belleville, WI: Historic Publications, 1993), p 63.
11. C.A. Stevens, *Berdan's United States Sharpshooters in the Army of the Potomac 1861–1865* (Dayton, OH: Morningside Bookstore, 1984), p. 11.
12. Wiley Sword, *Sharpshooter: Hiram Berdan, His Famous Sharpshooters and Their Sharps Rifles* (Lincoln, RI: Andrew Mowbray, 1988), pp. 68–71.
13. Ibid.
14. Ibid.
15. *The New York Times*, 26 December 1861, p. 1.
16. "Letter From Washington," *The Rutland Daily Herald*, 17 December 1861.
17. Phillips, pp. 371–372.
18. James Mero Matthews, *Soldiers in Green: The Civil War Diaries of James Mero Matthews 2nd U.S. Sharpshooters*, ed. Peter Dalton (Sandy Point, ME: Richardson Civil War Round Table, 2002), p. 28.
19. "A Weapon for the Sharpshooters: Three Perspectives," Library Collection, Gettysburg National Military Park.
20. Matthews, pp. 29–30.
21. *National Tribune*, 17 January 1907.
22. Matthews, pp. 28–31.
23. Lt. Colonel William Ripley, March 8, 1862, Letter, copy from Gettysburg National Military Park Library.
24. Regimental Record Book, 2nd U.S. Sharpshooters.
25. Matthews, p. 28.
26. Caspar Trepp to Colonel Hiram Berdan, Letter, Regimental Record Book, 1st U.S. Sharpshooters.
27. Ibid.
28. Matthews, pp. 16, 25, 30.
29. Stevens, p. 10.
30. Charles N. Race, "Story of Mr. Lincoln at Target Practice," *Confederate Veteran*, August 1909, p. 374.
31. Brent Nosworthy, *The Bloody Crucible of Courage: Fighting Methods and Combat Experience of the Civil War* (New York: Carroll & Graf, 2003), pp. 34–35.
32. W. Reid McKee & M.E. Mason, Jr., *Civil War Projectiles II: Small Arms & Field Artillery* (Mechanicsville, VA: Rapidan Press, 1980), p. 10.
33. Ibid., p. 159.
34. Nosworthy, pp. 32–33.
35. Woodhead, p. 44.
36. Winston O. Smith, *The Sharps Rifle: Its History, Development and Operation* (New York: William Morrow, 1943), pp. 88–89.
37. John J. Pullen, *The Twentieth Maine: A Volunteer Regiment in the Civil War* (Philadelphia and New York: J.B. Lippincott, 1957), pp. 38–39.
38. Sword, p. 37.
39. OR, V, pp. 108–109.
40. Ibid., p. 717.
41. Marcus Woodcock, *A Southern Boy in Blue*, ed. Kennedy W. Noe (Knoxville: University of Tennessee Press, 1996), p. 249.
42. Peck, p. 608.
43. "A Weapon," p. 2.
44. Colonel Hiram Berdan to J.C. Palmer, March 6, 1862, letter, Regimental Record Book, 1st U.S. Sharpshooters.
45. Lt. Colonel William Y.W. Ripley to his wife, March 18, 1862, letter, copy from Gettysburg National Military Park Library.
46. Lt. Colonel William Y.W. Ripley to his wife, March 19, 1862, letter, copy from Gettysburg National Military Park Library.
47. *Letters From A Sharpshooter*, p. 70.
48. Jeffery D. Wert, *The Sword of Lincoln: The Army of the Potomac* (New York: Simon and Schuster Paperbacks, 2005), p. 19.
49. Darius Starr, September 8, 1863, letter, copy from Gettysburg National Military Park Library.
50. Gerald L. Earley, *I Belonged to the 116th: A Narrative of the 116th Ohio Volunteer Infantry During the Civil War* (Bowie, MD: Heritage Books, 2004), p. 37.
51. Stevens, p. vii.
52. "Sharpshooting in Lee's Army," *Confederate Veteran* 3 (1895): p. 98.
53. Katta, p. 53.
54. Matthews, p. 41.

Chapter 3

1. Stephen W. Sears, *To the Gates of Richmond: The Peninsula Campaign* (New York: Ticknor & Fields, 1992), p.11; Ronald H. Bailey, *Forward to Richmond: McClellan's Peninsular Campaign* (Alexandria, VA: Time-Life Books, 1983), p.63.
2. Dyer, I, pp. 280–312.
3. Bailey, *Richmond*, p. 96.
4. Peck, p. 606.
5. Wert, *Sword*, p. 3.
6. Warren Wilkinson, *Mother, May You Never See the Sights I Have Seen: The Fifty-Seventh Massachusetts Veteran Volunteers in the Army of the Potomac, 1864–1865* (New York: Harper & Row, 1990), pp. 44–45.
7. *Letters From A Sharpshooter*, p. 100.
8. Dyer, I, p. 347.
9. *Letters From A Sharpshooter*, p. 100.
10. Minnesota, *Minnesota in the Civil and Indian Wars*, p. 507.

11. *Letters From A Sharpshooter*, p. 100.
12. Ibid., p. 101.
13. Ibid.
14. Ibid., p. 104.
15. Nolan, p. 46.
16. *Letters From A Sharpshooter*, p. 104.
17. Bailey, *Richmond*, p. 100.
18. "Exploits of Berdan's Sharpshooters," *The New York Times*, 12 April 1862, p. 1.
19. Bailey, *Richmond*, p. 100.
20. *Letters From A Sharpshooter*, p. 104.
21. Stephen W. Sears, ed., *The Civil War Papers of George B. McClellan: Selected Correspondence, 1860–1865* (New York: Ticknor & Fields, 1989), p. 231.
22. *Letters From A Sharpshooter*, p. 105.
23. Ezra Warner, *Generals in Blue: Lives of the Union Commanders* (Baton Rouge: Louisiana State University Press, 1964), p. 12.
24. Stevens, p. 162.
25. OR, XII/1, p. 431.
26. White, p. 59.
27. Stevens, p. 161.
28. OR, XII/1, p. 430.
29. White, pp. 60–61.
30. OR, XII/1, p. 436.
31. *Minnesota in the Civil and Indian Wars*, p. 507.
32. Fox, p. 117.
33. White, p. 61.
34. James R. Furqueron, "The Best Hated Man in the Army, Part II: The Remarkable Career of William Babcock Hazen," *North & South* 4, no. 5 (June 2001): pp. 75–76.
35. Stephen Ambrose, *Crazy Horse and Custer: The Parallel Lives of Two American Warriors* (New York: Anchor Books, 1996), p. 205.
36. S.E. Chandler, "In the Thick of It," *National Tribune*, 17 October 1895, p. 1.

Chapter 4

1. Nolan, p. 47.
2. *Letters From A Sharpshooter*, pp. 108–109.
3. Nolan, P. 50.
4. Roy P. Basler, ed., *The Collected Works of Abraham Lincoln* (New Brunswick, NJ: Rutgers University Press, 1953), pp. 208–209.
5. *The New York Times*, 27 April 1861, p. 1.
6. Sword, p. 78.
7. Nolan, p. 55.
8. Basler, p. 232.
9. *Letters From A Sharpshooter*, p. 117.
10. Minnesota, *Minnesota in the Civil and Indian Wars*, p. 507.
11. Basler, p. 232.
12. Champ Clark, *Decoying the Yanks: Jackson's Valley Campaign* (Alexandria, VA: Time-Life Books, 1984), p. 114–115.
13. Basler, p. 235–236.
14. Ibid., pp. 232–233.
15. Matthews, p. 59.
16. Sword, p. 90.
17. Earley, p. 146.
18. Matthews, p. 59.
19. Sword, p. 78.
20. Matthews, p. 59.
21. OR, XII/3, p. 279.
22. Nolan, p. 56.
23. OR, XII/3, pp. 300–301.
24. Matthews, p. 54.
25. OR, XII/3, p. 300.
26. *Letters From A Sharpshooter*, p. 119.
27. Ibid.
28. Matthews, p. 59–60.
29. Stevens, p. 163.
30. *Letters From A Sharpshooter*, p. 119.
31. Matthews, p. 60.
32. OR, XII/3, pp. 318, 324.
33. *Letters From A Sharpshooter*, p. 123.
34. Matthews, p. 64.
35. Earl J. Coates and Dean S. Thomas, *An Introduction to Civil War Small Arms* (Gettysburg, PA: Thomas Publications, 1990), pp. 31, 92.
36. Matthews, p. 64.
37. Marcot, p. 55.
38. *Penn Yan Chronicle*, 6 November 1862, copy from service file of Hiram Berdan, Richmond National Battlefield files.
39. Dyer, p. 349.
40. Wert, *Sword*, pp. 121, 127.
41. OR, XII/3, p. 492.
42. Ibid., p. 504.
43. OR, XII/2, p. 106.
44. Time-Life, ed., *Lee Takes Command: From Seven Days to Second Bull Run* (Alexandria, VA: Time-Life Books, 1984), p. 98.
45. OR, XII/2, p. 106.
46. *Letters From A Sharpshooter*, p. 134.
47. OR, XII/2, p. 106.
48. OR, XI/3, p. 343.
49. Warner, pp. 216–217.
50. Wert, *Sword*, p. 127.
51. Nolan, pp. 64–65.
52. Stevens, p. 106.
53. *Letters From A Sharpshooter*, p. 140.
54. Nolan, p. 53.
55. Robert K. Krick, "Cedar Mountain," in *The Civil War Battlefield Guide*, ed. Frances H. Kennedy (Boston: Houghton Mifflin, 1990), p. 71.
56. OR, XII/3,
57. Ibid., p. 560.
58. *Letters From A Sharpshooter*, p. 142.
59. Nolan, p. 70.
60. Stevens, p. 168.
61. Peck, p. 621.
62. Stevens, p. 168.
63. Ibid., p. 169.
64. John J. Hennessy, *Return to Bull Run: The Campaign and Battle of Second Manassas* (New York: Simon and Schuster, 1993), p. 68.
65. Minnesota, *Minnesota in the Civil and Indian Wars*, p. 511; Ayling, p. 979.
66. Hennessy, *Return to Bull Run*, pp. 108–109.
67. Chandler, p. 2.
68. Stevens, pp. 170–171.
69. Matthews, p. 79.
70. Peck, p. 623.
71. *Letters from A Sharpshooter*, p. 146.
72. Matthews, p. 79.

73. Hennessy, *Return to Bull Run*, pp. 116–117.
74. Ibid., pp. 138–143 & pp. 162–163.
75. Nolan, pp. 78–79.
76. Ibid., pp. 77–80.
77. Stevens, p. 178.
78. *Lee Takes Command*, p. 139.
79. Matthews, p. 80.
80. Stevens, p. 178.
81. Hennessy, *Return to Bull Run*, pp. 190–192.
82. Ibid., pp. 192–193.
83. Ibid., pp. 194–200.
84. Ibid., p. 236.
85. John Hennessy, "Second Manassas," in *The Civil War Battlefield Guide*, ed. Frances H. Kennedy (Boston: Houghton Mifflin, 1990), p. 76.
86. Hennessy, *Return to Bull Run*, pp. 290–300.
87. OR, XII/2, pp. 367–368.
88. G.G. Benedict, *Vermont in the Civil War: A History of the Part Taken by the Vermont Soldiers and Sailors in the War for the Union, 1861–1865* (Burlington, VT: Free Press Association, 1888), II, pp. 758–759.
89. Hennessy, "Second Manassas," pp. 290–300.
90. Stevens, pp. 181–182.
91. OR, XII/2, p. 254.
92. Minnesota, *Minnesota in the Civil and Indian Wars*, pp. 511–512; *Revised Roster*, p. 978; Benedict, p. 759.
93. Stevens, p. 182.
94. *Lee Takes Command*, p. 152.
95. Nolan, pp. 104–105.
96. John Hennessy, "Historical Report on the Troop Movements for the Second Battle of Manassas, August 28 Through August 30, 1862," U.S. Department of the Interior National Park Service Denver Service Center Northeast Team, 1985, copy from Manassas National Battlefield Park.
97. OR, XII/2, p. 810.
98. Ibid.
99. Ibid.
100. *Lee Takes Command*, p. 154.
101. Quinter Collection, II, 83.
102. Terry Jones, *Lee's Tigers: The Louisiana Infantry in the Army of Northern Virginia* (Baton Rouge: Louisiana State University Press, 1987), p. 125.
103. Nolan, pp. 106–109.
104. Stevens, p. 188.
105. White, p. 87.
106. E.A. Wilson, "Second Bull Run," *National Tribune*, 19 October 1905.
107. Wert, *Sword*, pp. 135–136.
108. Peck, p. 606.
109. OR, XII/2, pp. 344–346.
110. *Lee Takes Command*, pp. 166–167.
111. Stevens, pp. 188–189.
112. White, p. 90.

Chapter 5

1. Wert, *Sword*, p. 139.
2. Ronald H. Bailey, *The Bloodiest Day* (Alexandria, VA: Time-Life Books, 1984), pp. 8–10.
3. Ibid., p. 15.
4. Dyer, p. 284.
5. Nolan, p. 118; OR, XIX/1, pp. 42–43.
6. Stephen W. Sears, *Landscape Turned Red: The Battle of Antietam* (New Haven, CT: Ticknor & Fields, 1983), pp. 117–120.
7. Ibid.
8. Ibid., pp. 122–129.
9. Bailey, *The Bloodiest Day*, p. 45.
10. Ibid. p. 47.
11. OR, XIX/1, p. 51.
12. Matthews, p. 86.
13. OR, XIX/1, p. 220.
14. Matthews, p. 86.
15. Sword, pp. 82–86.
16. Fred L. Ray, "On the Skirmish Line in Virginia," *North & South* 9, no. 6, p. 47.
17. Matthews, p. 86.
18. Peck, p. 608.
19. Bailey, *The Bloodiest Day*, p. 52.
20. Sears, *Landscape*, p. 119.
21. OR, XIX/1, p. 220.
22. Ibid., pp. 184–185.
23. Ibid., p. 187.
24. Bailey, *The Bloodiest Day*, p. 55.
25. Matthews, p. 86.
26. James S. Kent to his mother, September 22, 1862, letter, copy from Antietam National Battlefield Library.
27. Sears, *Landscape*, p. 161.
28. OR, XIX/1, p. 30.
29. OR, XIX/2, p. 307.
30. OR, XIX/1, p. 30.
31. John M. Priest, *Antietam: The Soldiers' Battle* (New York: Oxford University Press, 1989), p. 11.
32. Edwin H. Chadwick to his friends, September 25, 1862, letter, copy from Antietam National Battlefield Library.
33. Matthews, p. 87.
34. Chadwick.
35. OR, XIX/1, p. 218.
36. Nolan, pp. 135–137.
37. Ibid., p. 138.
38. OR, XIX/1, p. 218.
39. William H. Humphrey to John Gould, March 23, 1893, letter, Dartmouth College Library, copy from Antietam National Battlefield Library.
40. Chadwick.
41. William H. Humphrey to John Gould, March 9, 1893, letter, Dartmouth College Library, copy from Antietam National Battlefield Library.
42. Nolan, p. 138.
43. Jeffery D. Wert, *A Brotherhood of Valor: The Common Soldiers of the Stonewall Brigade, C.S.A., and the Iron Brigade, U.S.A.* (New York: Simon and Schuster, 1999), p. 181.
44. OR, XIX.1, p. 233.
45. James M. McPherson, *Crossroads of Freedom: Antietam* (New York: Oxford University Press, 2002), pp. 117–118.
46. Humphrey, March 23, 1893, Letter.
47. OR, XIX/1, p. 233.
48. William H. Humphrey to John Gould, March 24, 1893, letter, Dartmouth College Library, copy from Antietam National Battlefield Library.
49. Humphrey, March 23, 1893, Letter.
50. Kent.

51. Chadwick.
52. Humphrey, March 9, 1893, Letter; Chadwick.
53. Ibid.
54. Chadwick.
55. Jones, pp. 131–133.
56. Humphrey, March 24, 1893, Letter.
57. Chadwick.
58. Kent.
59. Priest, *Antietam*, p. 323.
60. Chadwick.
61. Kent.
62. Nolan, p. 141.
63. Humphrey, March 23, 1893, Letter.
64. Kent.
65. Priest, *Antietam*, p. 62.
66. OR, XIX/1, p. 218.
67. Ibid., p. 234.
68. Bailey, *The Bloodiest Day*, p. 150.
69. Stevens, p. 202.
70. Priest, pp. 327–328.
71. Humphrey, March 23, 1893, Letter.
72. OR, XIX/1, p. 189.
73. *Letters From A Sharpshooter*, p. 152; Matthews, p. 87.
74. Chadwick; Kent.
75. OR, XIX/1, p. 234.
76. Priest, *Antietam*, p. 336.
77. Bailey, *The Bloodiest Day*, p. 151.
78. Chadwick.
79. Ibid.
80. Bailey, *The Bloodiest Day*, p. 151.
81. Benjamin Calef to Mr. Parmelee, September 19, 1862, letter, copy from Antietam National Battlefield Library.
82. Carl Sandburg, *Abraham Lincoln: The Prairie Years and the War Years, One Volume Edition* (New York: Galahad Books, 1993), p. 345.
83. Chadwick.
84. Wert, *Brotherhood*, p. 190.
85. Stevens, p. 211.
86. OR, XIX/2, p. 342.
87. Sandburg, pp. 323–324.
88. OR, XIX/2, p. 485.
89. Ibid., p. 496.
90. Sandburg, p. 326.

Chapter 6

1. Bailey, *The Bloodiest Day*, p. 168.
2. William K. Goolrick, *Rebels Resurgent* (Alexandria, VA: Time-Life Books, 1985), pp. 24–27.
3. Ibid.
4. Edward J. Stackpole, *The Fredericksburg Campaign* (Harrisburg, PA: Military Service Publishing, 1957), p. 56.
5. Wert, *Sword*, p. 180.
6. Stackpole, p. 53.
7. Nolan, p. 171.
8. Stackpole, pp. 78–79.
9. Matthews, p. 89.
10. Peck, p. 608.
11. White, p. 106.
12. Stevens, pp. 214–215.
13. Colonel Henry A.V. Post to the 2nd U.S. Sharpshooters, November 18, 1862, letter, Regimental Record Book, 2nd U.S. Sharpshooters.
14. Stackpole, pp. 116, 122.
15. Wert, *Sword*, p. 208.
16. White, p. 110; Stackpole, pp. 121–122.
17. Goolrick, p. 56.
18. Francis Augustin O'Reilly, *The Fredericksburg Campaign: Winter War on the Rappahannock* (Baton Rouge: Louisiana State University Press, 2006), p. 59.
19. Goolrick, p. 57.
20. Nolan, p. 180.
21. OR, XXI, p. 461.
22. Ibid., p. 462.
23. White, pp. 111–112.
24. Nolan, p. 181.
25. White, p. 112.
26. Nolan, p. 183.
27. OR, XXI, p. 137.
28. Ibid., p. 464.
29. Stevens, p. 223.
30. White, p. 114.
31. OR, XXI, p. 464.
32. Ibid., p. 474.
33. Matthews, p. 111.
34. Stackpole, pp. 239–241; Nolan, p. 189.
35. OR, XXI, p. 900; Goolrick, pp. 93–94.
36. OR, XXI, p. 945.
37. Ibid., p. 954.
38. Ibid., p. 973.
39. "Sharpshooting in Lee's Army."
40. Benedict, p. 763.
41. Goolrick, p. 95; Stevens, p. 230.
42. Thomas F. Wildes, *Record of the One Hundred and Sixteenth Regiment Ohio Infantry Volunteers in the War of the Rebellion* (Sandusky, OH: I.F. Mack & Bro., 1884), p. 47.
43. James McPherson, *What They Fought For* (Baton Rouge: Louisiana State University Press, 1994), p. 57.
44. Phillips, p. 422.
45. Ibid., pp. 359, 422.
46. Stevens, p. 242.
47. Marcot, pp. 64–67.
48. Sword, p. 22.
49. General Order No. 79, Regimental Record Book, 1st U.S. Sharpshooters.
50. Stevens, p. 243.
51. Goolrick, p. 102; Nolan, pp. 206–207.
52. Stevens, pp. 232–235.
53. James Street, Jr., *The Struggle for Tennessee: Tupelo to Stones River* (Alexandria, VA: Time-Life Books, 1985), p. 142.
54. Stevens, p. 254.

Chapter 7

1. Goolrick, pp. 98–99.
2. Ibid., pp. 102–104.
3. Ibid., pp. 118–120; Wert, *Sword*, pp. 232–234.
4. OR, XXV/1, p. 171.
5. Stevens, pp. 245–246.
6. Goolrick, pp. 125–126.
7. Ibid., pp. 126–128.

8. OR, XXV/1, pp. 385–386.
9. Stevens, p. 248.
10. OR, XXV/1, p. 454.
11. Ibid., p. 452.
12. Ibid., p. 386.
13. Stevens, pp. 248–249.
14. OR, XXV/1, p. 502; Stevens, p. 249.
15. Stevens, p. 249.
16. Ibid., p. 250.
17. OR, XXV/1, pp. 934, 980.
18. W.H. Proctor, "Stonewall Jackson and Berdan's Sharpshooters," *National Tribune*, 8 May 1884, p. 7.
19. OR, XXV/1, p. 502.
20. Ibid., p. 980.
21. Fuller, p. 473.
22. OR, XXV/1, p. 380.
23. Ibid., p. 502.
24. Ibid., p. 430.
25. Simon Van Akin, Jr., "Who Captured the 23rd GA," *National Tribune*, 20 October 1889.
26. OR, XXV/1, p. 432.
27. Goolrick, pp. 140–141.
28. Ibid., pp. 142–143.
29. Goolrick, pp. 151–156.
30. Charles W. Smith, "General Whipple's Death," *National Tribune*, 6 August 1885.
31. OR, XXV/1, p. 503.
32. Wert, *Sword*, p. 124.
33. OR, XXV/1, p. 503; Benedict, pp. 764–765.
34. Darius Starr, letter excerpt from *The Green Gazette* 5, no. 5 (September-October 1993). Copy from Fredericksburg and Spotsylvania National Military Park Library.
35. Van Akin.
36. Starr, Excerpt.
37. OR, XXV/1, p. 180.

Chapter 8

1. Stevens, pp. 277–278.
2. Clifford Dowdey, *A History of the Confederacy: 1832–1865* (New York: Barnes & Noble Books, 1992), p. 260.
3. Champ Clark, *Gettysburg: The Confederate High Tide* (Alexandria, VA: Time-Life Books, 1985), pp. 13–14.
4. Ibid.
5. OR, XXVII/1, pp. 34–35.
6. Clark, *Gettysburg*, pp. 22–25.
7. OR, XXVII/1, pp. 34–35.
8. Clark, *Gettysburg*, p. 34.
9. Benedict, p. 765.
10. OR, XXVII/1, p. 60.
11. Ibid., pp. 61–62.
12. John Bowman, ed., *The Civil War Almanac* (New York: World Almanac Publications, Bison Books, 1993), p. 359.
13. OR, XXVII/1, pp. 65–67.
14. Ibid., pp. 70–71.
15. Matthews, p. 160.
16. OR, XXVII/1, p. 518.
17. Clark, *Gettysburg*, pp. 66–72.
18. OR, XXVII/1, p. 518; Benedict, p. 766.
19. Benedict, p. 765.
20. White, p. 164.
21. OR, XXVII/1, p. 519.
22. OR, XXVII/2, p. 404.
23. Stevens, p. 329.
24. Matthews, p. 160.
25. "Vermont Sharpshooters: A Confederate Officer Testifies to Their Great Service," *The Rutland Weekly Herald*, 27 December 1888.
26. Ibid.
27. OR, XXVII/1, p. 519.
28. Glenn W. LaFantasie, *Gettysburg Requiem: The Life and Lost Causes of Confederate Colonel William C. Oates* (New York: Oxford University Press, 2006), p. 86.
29. White, pp. 165–167.
30. OR, XXVII/1, pp. 623–625.
31. Ibid.
32. "Vermont Sharpshooters."
33. LaFantasie, pp. 104–107.
34. Benedict, p. 768; LaFantasie, pp. 376–377, Note 40.
35. "Vermont Sharpshooters."
36. OR, XXXVII/1, p. 519; Stevens, p. 345.
37. Clark, *Gettysburg*, pp. 126–133.
38. Matthews, p. 161.
39. Clark, *Gettysburg*, p. 129.
40. Ibid., p. 136.
41. Stevens, pp. 336–337.
42. Ibid.
43. Ibid.
44. A. Wright, *National Tribune*, 18 February 1909, p. 7.
45. OR, XXVII/1, p. 519.
46. Matthews, pp. 163–164; OR, XXVII/1, p. 519.
47. John J. Pullen, "Effects of Marksmanship — A Lesson From Gettysburg," *Gettysburg Magazine*, January 1990, pp. 59–60.
48. Matthews, p. 165.

Chapter 9

1. OR, XXVII/3, pp. 519, 567.
2. OR, XXVII/1, pp. 83, 85.
3. Clark, *Gettysburg*, p. 152.
4. OR, XXVII/1, p. 84.
5. Peck, p. 607.
6. Earley, p. 53.
7. Clark, *Gettysburg*, pp. 156–157.
8. Paul M. Angle and Earl Schenck Meyers, ed., *The Living Lincoln* (New York: Barnes & Noble, 1992), pp. 563–564.
9. Wert, *Sword*, p. 309.
10. Matthews, p. 170.
11. Stevens, pp. 349–350.
12. Warner, pp. 537–538; Matthews, pp. 170–171; Stevens, p. 428.
13. Stevens, p. 352; OR, XXVII/1, pp. 104–105.
14. Matthews, p. 170.
15. Marcot, p. 141.
16. Ibid.
17. Ibid., p. 98.
18. OR, XXIX/2, pp. 207–208.

19. OR, XXIX/1, pp. 147–151.
20. Stevens, p. 354.
21. Ibid., p. 360.
22. Gregory Jaynes, *The Killing Ground* (Alexandria, VA: Time-Life Books, 1986), p. 28.
23. Stevens, p. 362.
24. Ibid., pp. 362–363.
25. OR, XXIX/2, p. 328.
26. Ibid., p. 332.
27. Stevens, p. 364; ORXXIX/1, p. 10.
28. OR, XXIX/2, pp. 409, 412, 423–424.
29. OR, XXIX/1, p. 11; OR, XXIX/2, pp. 424–426.
30. Stevens, pp. 366–367; Matthews, p. 192.
31. Ira J. Northup, "Army Correspondence From the Sharpshooters," *Brookfield (Pennsylvania) Republican,* 9 December 1863, p. 1.
32. Stevens, pp. 270–271.
33. OR, XXIX/1, p. 632.
34. Ibid., pp. 556, 632.
35. OR, XXIX/2, p. 435.
36. Northup, "Correspondence."
37. Matthews, p. 195.
38. OR, XXIX/2, p. 435; OR, XXIX/1, p. 611.
39. OR, XXIX/2, pp. 449, 460.
40. OR, XXIX/1, p. 14.
41. Wert, *Sword,* p. 320.
42. Matthews, p. 198.
43. Wert, *Sword,* p. 320.
44. OR, XXIX/1, p. 15.
45. Matthews, p. 198; Stevens, pp. 379–380.
46. Ibid.; Benedict, p. 769.
47. OR, XXIX/1, pp. 16–17.
48. Matthews, pp. 199–200; OR, XXIX/1, p. 751.
49. Aschmann, p. 133.
50. Stevens, p. 388.
51. OR, XXIX/1, p. 17.
52. Matthews, p. 200; OR, XXIX/1, p. 752.
53. Jaynes, p. 31.
54. Matthews, pp. 200–201; or, XXIX/1, P. 18.
55. Ray, pp. 49–50; Stevens, pp. 379–380; OR, XXIX/1, p. 681.

Chapter 10

1. Matthews, p. 201.
2. Stevens, p. 394; Wert, *Sword,* pp. 322–324.
3. Ibid.; Marcot, p. 99.
4. Benedict, p. 770.
5. OR, XXXIII, p. 358.
6. Earley, pp. 59–60.
7. Bowman, p. 185.
8. Ibid., pp. 187–188; Minnesota, *Minnesota in the Civil and Indian Wars,* p. 509.
9. Dyer, I, pp. 291–292.
10. Benedict, p. 770.
11. Fox, p. 419.
12. Joseph Barton to his wife, March 30, 1864, letter, copy from the United States Army Military History Institute; hereafter cited as USAMHI.
13. George Jones, March 1864, letter, copy from Fredericksburg and Spotsylvania National Battlefield Park Library.
14. Edward Steere, *The Wilderness Campaign* (Harrisonburg, PA: Stackpole, 1960), p. 16; Ulysses S. Grant, *Memoirs and Selected Letters* (New York: Literary Classics, 1990), p. 26.
15. Steere, p. 16.
16. Stevens, p. 398; Barton.
17. Stevens, p. 398.
18. Sword, p. 56.
19. Stevens, p. 394.
20. Ibid.
21. OR, XXXIII, p. 1017; Steere, pp. 29–37; Stevens, p. 460.
22. Stevens, p. 400; George A. Marden, May 6–8, 1864, Journal, copy from Fredericksburg and Spotsylvania National Military Park Library.
23. Noah Andre Trudeau, "The Wilderness," in *The Civil War Battlefield Guide,* ed. Frances H. Kennedy (Boston: Houghton Mifflin, 1990), p. 203.
24. Steere, p. 64.
25. Ibid., pp. 136, 186.
26. Robert Garth Scott, *Into the Wilderness With the Army of the Potomac* (Bloomington: Indiana University Press, 1985), pp. 70–71.
27. Gordon C. Rhea, *The Battle of the Wilderness May 5–6, 1864* (Baton Rouge: Louisiana State University Press, 1994), pp. 191–193.
28. OR, XXXVI/2, p. 410.
29. John Michael Priest, *Nowhere to Run: The Wilderness, May 4th & 5th, 1864* (Shippensburg, PA: White Mane Publishing, 1995), p. 188.
30. Ibid., p. 193.
31. Stevens, p. 403; *Letters From A Sharpshooter,* p. 201.
32. Jaynes, pp. 73–74.
33. Wilkinson, p. 68.
34. Thomas T. Prentiss to Hiram Jones, June 9, 1864, letter, copy from Fredericksburg and Spotsylvania National Military Park Library.
35. Rhea, *Wilderness,* p. 286.
36. Ibid., pp. 309–310.
37. Prentiss; Benedict, pp. 770–771.
38. Jaynes, p. 78.
39. White, p. 229; Prentiss.
40. White, p. 229.
41. Ibid., pp. 229–232; Stevens, pp. 422–423.
42. White, p. 232; Warner, p. 538.
43. Rhea, *Wilderness,* pp. 392–397; White, pp. 229–231.
44. Jaynes, pp. 80–81.
45. OR, XXVI/2, p. 133; Rhea, *Wilderness,* p. 440; Fox, p. 541.
46. OR, XXVI/1, p. 122; Fox, p. 419.
47. Benedict, p. 770.
48. OR, XXXVI/2, p. 481; Gordon C. Rhea, *The Battles of Spotsylvania Courthouse and the Road to Yellow Tavern* (Baton Rouge: Louisiana State University Press, 1997), p. 13.
49. Aschmann, p. 152; Jaynes, pp. 70–71.

Chapter 11

1. OR, XXXVI/2, p. 484.
2. Benedict, p. 771; Rhea, *Spotsylvania,* p. 80.
3. Stevens, p. 417.

4. *Letters From A Sharpshooter*, p. 203; Rhea, *Spotsylvania*, p. 110.
5. Rhea, *Spotsylvania*, p. 111; Battlefield Map, Spotsylvania, Fredericksburg and Spotsylvania National Military Park.
6. OR, XXXVI/2, pp. 567–568.
7. Gregory A. Mertz, "General Gouverneur K. Warren and the Fighting at Laurel Hill During the Battle of Spotsylvania Courthouse, May 1864," *Blue & Gray*, Summer 2004, p. 49.
8. Rhea, *Spotsylvania*, pp. 179–181; Mertz, p. 51.
9. Rhea, *Spotsylvania*, pp. 180–181.
10. Peck, p. 607.
11. Rhea, *Spotsylvania*, p. 181; Mertz, p. 51.
12. White, p. 234.
13. Ibid., pp. 234–237.
14. Ayling, p. 979.
15. Rhea, *Spotsylvania*, pp. 215–217.
16. Ibid., pp. 221–224.
17. OR, XXXVI/1, p. 470.
18. Stevens, p.425.
19. Jaynes, pp. 98–100.
20. Stevens, pp. 425–426; Jaynes, p. 102.
21. OR, XXXVI/1, p. 704.
22. Rhea, *Spotsylvania*, pp. 243–244.
23. Benedict, p. 771.
24. Gordon C. Rhea, *To the North Anna River: Grant and Lee, May 13–25, 1864* (Baton Rouge: Louisiana State University Press, 2000), pp. 139–152.
25. Ibid., p. 188.
26. Ibid., pp. 167–181; Jaynes, pp. 125–125.
27. White, pp. 245–247; Rhea, *North Anna*, pp. 181–183.
28. Rhea, *North Anna*, pp. 186–188,
29. Jaynes, pp. 130–131.
30. Ibid.; Fox, pp. 419, 541; OR, XXXVI/1, p. 139.
31. Jaynes, pp. 131–132.
32. Rhea, *North Anna*, pp. 260–261.
33. Ibid., p. 295.
34. Jaynes, p. 133; *Letters From A Sharpshooter*, pp. 211–213; Rhea, *North Anna*, pp. 300–302.
35. Jaynes, p. 133.
36. Benedict, p. 771; Barton.
37. Jaynes, pp. 133–135.
38. Rhea, *North Anna*, pp. 330–332.
39. Jaynes, pp. 136–137.
40. *Letters From A Sharpshooter*, pp. 211–213.
41. H.S. Campbell to his cousin, May 25, 1864, letter, Perkins Library, Duke University, copy from Richmond National Battlefield Park.
42. OR, XXXVI/1, p. 9.
43. Rhea, *North Anna*, p. 367.
44. Earnest B. Furgurson, *Not War But Murder: Cold Harbor 1864* (New York: Vintage Books, 2000), pp. 60–63.
45. Peck, pp. 609 & 612; Matthews, p. 299.
46. Furgurson, p. 78.
47. Jaynes, pp. 151–154.
48. OR, XXXVI/3, p. 441.
49. Furgurson, pp. 122–123.
50. Ibid., p. 124.
51. Jaynes, pp. 156, 165.
52. Furgurson, pp. 134–135, 139–142.
53. Jaynes, pp. 158–160.
54. Furgurson, p. 159.
55. Wert, *Sword*, p. 365.
56. Matthews, p. 300.
57. Furgurson, p. 172.
58. *Letters From A Sharpshooter*, p. 218.
59. Furgurson, p. 195.
60. Notes from Chris Calkins, January 8, 2007.
61. Matthews, p. 300; *Letters From A Sharpshooter*, p. 220; Minnesota, *Minnesota in the Civil and Indian Wars*, p. 511; OR, XXXVI/1, p. 168; Ayling, p. 979.
62. William C. Davis, *Death in the Trenches Grant At Petersburg* (Alexandria, VA: Time-Life Books, 1986), pp. 18–19.
63. Jaynes, p. 169.

Chapter 12

1. Furgurson, pp. 249–252; *Letters From A Sharpshooter*, p. 220.
2. Ibid.
3. Davis, *Death*, pp. 34–41.
4. Ibid., pp. 41–43.
5. Thomas J. Howe, *The Petersburg Campaign: Wasted Valor* (Lynchburg, VA: H.E. Howard, 1988), pp. 35–36.
6. *Letters From A Sharpshooter*, p. 220.
7. Davis, *Death*, p. 45.
8. Howe, pp. 44–46.
9. Howe, p, 46; Davis, *Death*, p. 45; *Letters From A Sharpshooter*, p. 221.
10. Davis, *Death*, p. 53; Benedict, p. 771.
11. Howe, pp. 130–131; Matthews, p. 301; *Letters From A Sharpshooter*, p. 221.
12. OR, XL/2, pp. 257–258.
13. Chris Calkins, "The Battle of Weldon Railroad (or Globe Tavern) August 18–19, 1864," *Blue & Gray*, Winter 2007, p. 7.
14. *Letters From A Sharpshooter*, p. 226; Peck, p. 607.
15. Peck, p. 607; Benedict, p. 772.
16. Davis, *Death*, p. 56.
17. *Letters From A Sharpshooter*, pp. 226–228.
18. Ayling, p. 981; Minnesota, *Minnesota in the Civil and Indian Wars*, p. 511; Benedict, pp. 771–772.
19. Calkins, p. 8; Davis, *Death*, pp. 64–65; Stevens, p. 472; *Letters From A Sharpshooter*, pp. 230–231.
20. Aschmann, p. 170; *Letters From A Sharpshooter*, p. 226.
21. OR, XXXVI/1, pp. 121, 139, 155, 168, XL/1, p. 221; *Letters From A Sharpshooter*, p. 227.
22. Davis, *Death*, pp. 65–72.
23. OR, XL/3, pp. 437–438.
24. Ibid., p. 443; Stevens, p. 437.
25. Warner, p. 34; Stevens, p. 474.
26. OR, XL/3, pp. 551–554; *Letters From A Sharpshooter*, p. 240.
27. OR, XL/1, p. 393.
28. Stevens, p. 479.
29. OR, XL/1, p. 134.
30. OR, XL/1, p. 253; *Letters From A Sharpshooter*, p. 243; Ayling, p. 977.
31. Bryce A. Suderow, "Nothing But a Miracle Could Save Us: Second Battle of Deep Bottom, Vir-

ginia, August 14–20, 1864," *North & South* 4, no. 2, p. 12.
32. OR, XLII/2, p. 131; *Letters From A Sharpshooter*, p. 246.
33. Suderow, p. 31.
34. OR, XLII/1, p. 358.
35. Ibid., p. 51.
36. Ibid., p. 342.
37. *Letters From A Sharpshooter*, pp. 254–255.
38. Matthews, p. 255.
39. Ibid.; Ira J. Northup to his wife, September 11, 1864, letter, copy from USAMHI.
40. Davis, *Death*, pp. 138–139.
41. Ibid., pp. 150–152.
42. Richard J. Sommers, *Richmond Redeemed: The Siege of Petersburg* (Garden City, NY: Doubleday, 1981), pp. 361–362.
43. OR, XLII/1, p. 344; Sommers, pp. 365–369.
44. OR, XLII/1, pp. 344–345; *Letters From A Sharpshooter*, p. 260.
45. OR, XLII/1, 345.
46. Sommers, pp. 416–417, 478–479.
47. Matthews, pp. 260–261; Peck, p. 612; Stevens, pp. 497–498.
48. Davis, *Death*, p. 154.
49. OR, XLII/1, p. 346.
50. Ibid.
51. Davis, *Death*, p. 156.
52. OR, XLII/1, p. 346; Matthews, p. 261.
53. OR, XLII/1, pp. 158, 160, 346.
54. Peck, pp. 612, 618; Benedict, p. 773.
55. OR, XLII/3, pp. 431, 509.
56. Ibid., pp. 437, 510, 528, 551.
57. Suderow, p. 31
58. OR, XLII/3, p. 560; Wert, *Sword*. P. 391; Phillips, p. 419.
59. Dowdey, p. 359.

Epilogue

1. OR, XLII/1, p. 50; Matthews, p. 263; Benedict, p. 773.
2. OR, XLII/3, p. 714.
3. OR, XLII/1, p. 50.
4. Ibid., p. 355.
5. Ibid., pp. 355–356.
6. Ibid.; Wert, *Sword*, p. 394.
7. OR, XLII/1, p. 351; Wert, *Sword*, p. 394; Matthews, pp. 268–269.
8. Stevens, p. 494; Peck, p. 610.
9. Dowdey, pp. 378–382.
10. Jerry Korn, *Pursuit to Appomattox: The Last Battles* (Alexandria, VA: Time-Life Books, 1987), pp. 26–27.
11. OR, XLVI, pp. 226–227.
12. Henry Lesslie to his mother, February 14, 1865, letter, copy from USAMHI.
13. Ibid.; OR, XLVI/1, p. 227.
14. Korn, p. 30; OR, XLVI, p. 227.
15. Korn, p. 31; Lesslie.
16. Ibid.
17. OR, XLVI/1, p. 64.
18. Ibid., p. 228.
19. Lesslie.
20. Dyer, III, p. 1717; Benedict, p. 774.
21. Fox, p. 139.
22. OR, XLVI/2, p. 568.
23. Matthews, p. 278.
24. Regimental Record Book, 2nd U.S. Sharpshooters.
25. Benedict, p. 619; Ayling, p. 981.
26. Benedict, p. 609.
27. Ibid., p. 775.
28. Warner, pp. 153–154.
29. Fox, p. 419; Benedict, p. 610.

Bibliography

Ambrose, Stephen E. *Crazy Horse and Custer: The Parallel Lives of Two American Warriors*. New York: Anchor Books, 1996.

Angle, Paul M., and Earl Schenck Meyers, ed. *The Living Lincoln*. New York: Barnes & Noble, 1992.

Aschmann, Rudolph. *Memoirs of a Swiss Officer in the American Civil War*. Ed. Heinz K. Meier. Bern, Switzerland: Herbert Lang, 1972.

Ayling, Augustus D. *Revised Register of the Soldiers and Sailors of New Hampshire in the War of the Rebellion 1861–1865*. Concord, NH: Ira Evans, Public Printer, 1895.

Bailey, Ronald H. *The Bloodiest Day*. Alexandria, VA: Time-Life Books, 1984.

_____. *Forward to Richmond: McClellan's Peninsular Campaign*. Alexandria, VA: Time-Life Books, 1983.

Barton, Joseph. Letter to his wife, March 30, 1864.

Basler, Roy P., ed. *The Collected Works of Abraham Lincoln*. New Brunswick, NJ: Rutgers University Press, 1953.

Benedict, G.G. *Vermont in the Civil War: A History of the Part Taken by the Vermont Soldiers and Sailors in the War for the Union, 1861–1865*. Burlington, VA: Free Press Association, 1888.

Berdan, Hiram. Letter to Secretary Simon Cameron, October 22, 1861.

_____. Letter to J.C. Palmer, March 6, 1862.

Bowman, John, ed. *The Civil War Almanac*. New York: World Almanac Publications, Bison Books, 1983.

Bruce, Robert V. *Lincoln and the Tools of War*. Reprint. Indianapolis: Bobbs-Merrill, 1956.

Calef, Benjamin. Letter to Mr. Parmelee, September 19, 1862.

Calkins, Chris. "The Battle of Weldon Railroad (or Globe Tavern), August 18–19, 1864." *Blue & Gray*, Winter 2007.

Campbell, H.S. Letter to his cousin, May 25, 1864.

Chadwick, Edwin H. Letter to his friends, September 25, 1862.

Chandler, S.E. "In the Thick of It." *National Tribune*, 17 October 1895, p. 1.

Clark, Champ. *Decoying the Yanks: Jackson's Valley Campaign*. Alexandria, VA: Time-Life Books, 1984.

_____. *Gettysburg: The Confederate High Tide*. Alexandria, VA: Time-Life Books, 1985.

Coates, Earl J., and Dean S. Thomas. *An Introduction to Civil War Small Arms*. Gettysburg, PA: Thomas Publications, 1990.

"Col. Berdan's Sharpshooters." *New York Times*, 7 August 1861, p. 4.

Davis, William C. *Death in the Trenches*. Alexandria, VA: Time-Life Books, 1986.

_____. *First Blood: Fort Sumter to Bull Run*. Alexandria, VA: Time-Life Books, 1983.

Dowdey, Clifford. *A History of the Confederacy: 1832–1865*. New York: Barnes & Noble Books, 1992.

Dyer, Frederick H. *A Compendium of the War of the Rebellion*. 3 vols. Des Moines, IA: Dyer Publishing, 1908.

Earley, Gerald L. *I Belonged to the 116th: A Narrative of the 116th Ohio Volunteer Infantry during the Civil War*. Bowie, MD: Heritage Books, 2004.

"Exploits of Berdan's Sharpshooters." *New York Times*, 12 April 1862, p. 1.

Fox, William F. *Regimental Losses in the American Civil War 1861–1865*. Albany: Albany Publishing, 1889.

Fuller, H.S. "Narrowly Escaped Prison." *Confederate Veteran*, November 1918, p. 473.

Furgurson, Earnest B. *Not War But Murder: Cold Harbor 1864*. New York: Vintage Books, 2000.

Furqueron, James R. "The Best Hated Man in the Army, Part II: The Remarkable Career of William Babcock Hazen." *North & South* 4, no. 5 (June 2001): pp. 75–76.

Goolrick, William K. *Rebels Resurgent*. Alexandria, VA: Time-Life Books, 1985.

Grant, Ulysses S. *Memoirs and Selected Letters*. New York: Literary Classics, 1990.

Gurney, Gene. *A Pictorial History of the United States Army*. New York: Crown, 1966.

Hennessy, John. "Historical Report on the Troop Movements for the Second Battle of Manassas, August 28 through August 30, 1862." U.S.

Department of the Interior National Park Service Denver Service Center Northeast Team, 1985.

_____. *Return to Bull Run: The Campaign and Battle of Second Manassas.* New York: Simon and Schuster, 1993.

_____. "Second Manassas." In *The Civil War Battlefield Guide.* Ed. Frances H. Kennedy. Boston: Houghton Mifflin, 1990.

Howe, Thomas J. *The Petersburg Campaign: Wasted Valor.* Lynchburg, VA: H.E. Howard, 1988.

Humphrey, William H. Letter to John Gould, March 9, 1893.

_____. Letter to John Gould, March 23, 1893.

_____. Letter to John Gould, March 24, 1893.

Hunt, Roger D., and Jack R. Brown. *Brevet Brigadier Generals in Blue.* Gaithersburg, MD: Ole Soldier Books, 1990.

Jaynes, Gregory. *The Killing Ground.* Alexandria, VA: Time-Life Books, 1986.

Jones, George. Letter, March 1864.

Jones, Terry. *Lee's Tigers: The Louisiana Infantry in the Army of Northern Virginia.* Baton Rouge: Louisiana State University Press, 1987.

Katta, Kenneth S. "Conflicts in Command: An Analysis of Leadership in the Berdan Sharpshooters in the Civil War." *Military Collector and Historian,* Summer 2001, p. 54.

Kent, James S. Letter to his mother, September 22, 1862.

Korn, Jerry. *Pursuit to Appomattox: The Last Battles.* Alexandria, VA: Time-Life Books, 1987.

Krick, Robert K. "Cedar Mountain." In *The Civil War Battlefield Guide.* Ed. Frances H. Kennedy. Boston: Houghton Mifflin, 1990.

LaFantasie, Glenn W. *Gettysburg Requiem: The Life and Lost Causes of Confederate Colonel William C. Oates.* New York: Oxford University Press, 2006.

Lee Takes Command: From Seven Days to Second Bull Run. Alexandria, VA: Time-Life Books, 1984.

Lesslie, Henry. Letter to his mother, February 14, 1865.

"Letter From Washington." *Rutland Daily Herald,* 17 December 1861, p. 2.

Letters from a Sharpshooter: The Civil War Letters of Private William B. Greene, Co. G 2nd United States Sharpshooters (Berdan's) Army of the Potomac 1861–1865. Transcribed by William H. Hastings. Belleville, WI: Historic Publications, 1993.

Lind, Michael. *What Lincoln Believed.* New York: Doubleday, 2005.

Marcot, Roy M. *Civil War Chief of Sharpshooters Hiram Berdan, Military Commander and Firearms Inventor.* Irvine, CA: Heritage Press, 1989.

Marden, George A. Journal, May 6–8, 1864. Copy from Fredericksburg and Spotsylvania National Military Park Library.

Mastraino, Douglas. "Alvin York: View from the Other Side." *Military History,* September 2006.

Matthews, James Mero. *Soldiers in Green: The Civil War Diaries of James Mero Matthews, 2nd U.S. Sharpshooters.* Ed. Peter Dalton. Sandy Point, ME: Richardson Civil War Round Table, 2002.

McKee, W. Reid, and M.E. Mason, Jr. *Civil War Projectiles II: Small Arms and Field Artillery.* Mechanicsville, VA: Rapidan Press, 1980.

McPherson, James M. *Crossroads of Freedom: Antietam.* New York: Oxford University Press, 2002.

_____. *What They Fought For.* Baton Rouge: Louisiana State University, 1994.

Mertz, Gregory A. "General Gouverneur K. Warren and the Fighting at Laurel Hill During the Battle of Spotsylvania Courthouse, May 1864." *Blue & Gray,* Summer 2004.

Minnesota Board of Commissioners. *Minnesota in the Civil and Indian Wars 1861–1865.* St. Paul, MN: Pioneer Press, 1890.

Muster and Descriptive Rolls, 2nd United States Sharpshooters. National Archives, Washington, D.C.

National Tribune, 17 January 1907.

Nevin, David. *The Road to Shiloh: Early Battles in the West.* Alexandria, VA: Time-Life Books, 1983.

New York Times, 27 April 1861, p. 1.

New York Times, 1 May 1861, p. 4.

New York Times, 2 June 1861, p. 3.

New York Times, 28 June 1861.

New York Times, 26 December 1861, p. 1.

Nolan, Alan T. *The Iron Brigade: A Military History.* Indianapolis: Indiana University Press, 1994.

Northup, Ira James. "Army Correspondence from the Sharpshooters." *Brookfield (Pennsylvania) Republican,* 9 December 1863, p. 1.

_____. Letter to his wife, September 11, 1864.

Nosworthy, Brent. *The Bloody Crucible of Courage: Fighting Methods and Combat Experience in the Civil War.* New York: Carroll & Graf, 2003.

O'Reilly, Francis Augustin. *The Fredericksburg Campaign: Winter War on the Rappahannock.* Baton Rouge: Louisiana State University Press, 2006.

Palmer, R.R., and Joel Colton. *A History of the Modern World.* 5th ed. New York: Alfred A. Knopf, 1978.

Peck, Theodore S. *Revised Roster of Vermont Volunteers and Lists of Vermonters who Served in the*

Army and Navy of the United States. Press of the Watchman Publishing, Montpelier, VT.

Penn Yan Chronicle, 6 November 1862.

Peterson, Harold L. *The Treasury of the Gun.* New York: Golden Press, 1962.

Phillips, Kevin. *The Cousins' Wars: Religion, Politics & The Triumph of Anglo-America.* New York: Basic Books, 1999.

Phisterer, Frederick. *Statistical Record of the Armies of the United States.* New York: Blue & The Gray Press.

Post, Henry A. Letter to the 2nd U.S. Sharpshooters, November 18, 1862.

Prentiss, Thomas T. Letter to Hiram Jones, June 9, 1864.

Priest, John Michael. *Nowhere to Run: The Wilderness, May 4th & 5th, 1864.* Shippensburg, PA: White Mane Publishing, 1995.

_____. *Antietam: The Soldiers' Battle.* New York: Oxford University Press, 1989.

Proctor, W.H. "Stonewall Jackson and Berdan's Sharpshooters." *National Tribune,* 8 May 1884, p. 7.

Pullen, John J. "Effects of Marksmanship — A Lesson From Gettysburg." *Gettysburg Magazine,* January 1990.

_____. *The Twentieth Maine A Volunteer Regiment in the Civil War.* Philadelphia and New York: J.B. Lippincott, 1957.

Quinter, Edward B. Collection. *Correspondence of Wisconsin Volunteers* II, 56.

Race, Charles M. "Story of Mr. Lincoln at Target Practice." *Confederate Veteran,* August 1909, p. 374.

Ray, Fred L. "On the Skirmish Line in Virginia." *North & South* 9, no. 6, p. 47.

Regimental Record Book, 1st U.S. Sharpshooters, National Archives, Washington, D.C.

Regimental Record Book, 2nd U.S. Sharpshooters, National Archives, Washington, D.C.

Rhea, Gordon C. *The Battle of the Wilderness, May 5–6, 1864.* Baton Rouge: Louisiana State University Press, 1994.

_____. *The Battles for Spotsylvania Courthouse and the Road to Yellow Tavern.* Baton Rouge: Louisiana State University Press, 1997.

_____. *To the North Anna River: Grant and Lee, May 13–25, 1864.* Baton Rouge: Louisiana State University Press, 2000.

Rhodes, Robert Hunt, ed. *All for the Union: The Civil War Diary and Letters of Elisha Hunt Rhodes.* New York: Orion Books, 1985.

Ripley, William Y.W. Letter, March 8, 1862.

_____. Letter to his wife, March 18, 1862.

_____. Letter to his wife, March 19, 1862.

_____. *Vermont Riflemen in the War for the Union, 1861 to 1865: A History of Company F First United States Sharpshooters.* Rutland, VT: Tuttle, 1883.

Rutland Daily Herald. 10 August 1861, p. 2.

Rutland Daily Herald. 26 November 1861.

Sandburg, Carl. *Abraham Lincoln: The Prairie Years and the War Years, One Volume Edition.* New York: Galahad Books, 1993.

Scott, Robert Garth. *Into the Wilderness With the Army of the Potomac.* Bloomington: Indiana University Press, 1985.

Sears, Stephen W. *Chancellorsville.* New York: Houghton Mifflin, 1996.

_____, ed. *The Civil War Papers of George B. McClellan: Selected Correspondence, 1860–1865.* New York: Ticknor & Fields, 1989.

_____. *Landscape Turned Red: The Battle of Antietam.* New Haven, CT: Ticknor & Fields, 1983.

_____. *To the Gates of Richmond: The Peninsula Campaign.* New York: Ticknor & Fields, 1992.

"The Sharpshooters." *New York Times,* 2 June 1861, p. 3.

"The Sharpshooters." *Rutland Daily Herald,* 12 August 1861, p. 12.

"Sharp-shooters." *New York Times,* 17 September 1861, p.1.

"Sharpshooting in Lee's Army." *Confederate Veteran* 3 (1895): p. 98.

"Sharp-Shooting Regiments." *New York Times,* 17 July 1861, p. 4.

Smith, Charles Powers. *Yankees and God.* New York: Hermitage House, 1954.

Smith, Charles W. "General Whipple's Death." *National Tribune,* 6 August 1885.

Smith, Winston O. *The Sharps Rifle: Its History, Development and Operation.* New York: William Morrow, 1943.

Sommers, Richard J. *Richmond Redeemed: The Siege of Petersburg.* Garden City, NY: Doubleday, 1981.

Stackpole, Edward J. *The Fredericksburg Campaign.* Harrisburg, PA: Military Service Publishing, 1957.

Starr, Darius. Letter excerpt. *The Green Gazette* 5, no. 5 (September–October 1993).

_____. Letter, September 8, 1863.

Steere, Edward. *The Wilderness Campaign.* Harrisonburg, PA: Stackpole, 1960.

Stevens, C.A. *Berdan's United States Sharpshooters in the Army of the Potomac, 1861–1865.* Dayton, OH: Morningside Bookshop, 1984.

Street, James, Jr. *The Struggle for Tennessee Tupelo to Stones River.* Alexandria, VA: Time-Life Books, 1985.

Suderow, Bryce A. "Nothing But a Miracle Could

Save Us: Second Battle of Deep Bottom, Virginia, August 14–20, 1864." *North & South* 4, no. 2.
Sword, Wiley. *Sharpshooter: Hiram Berdan, His Famous Sharpshooters and Their Sharps Rifles.* Lincoln, RI: Andrew Mowbray, 1988.
"The 23rd Georgia." *National Tribune,* 10 July 1884, p. 7.
Trepp, Caspar. Letter to Colonel Hiram Berdan, copy from 1st U.S. Sharpshooters Regimental Record Book.
Trudeau, Noah Andre. "The Wilderness." In *The Civil War Battlefield Guide.* Ed. Frances H. Kennedy. Boston: Houghton Mifflin, 1990.
U.S. War Department. *The War of the Rebellion: A Compilation of the Official Records of the Union and Confederate Armies.* 128 vols. Washington, D.C.: U.S. Government Printing Office, 1880–1901.
Van Akin, Simon, Jr. "Who Captured the 23rd GA." *National Tribune,* 20 October 1889.
"Vermont Sharpshooters: A Confederate Officer Testifies to Their Great Service." *Rutland Daily Herald,* 27 December 1888.
Warner, Ezra J. *Generals in Blue: Lives of the Union Commanders.* Baton Rouge: University of Louisiana Press, 1964.
"A Weapon for the Sharpshooters: Three Perspectives." Gettysburg National Military Park Library.
Webb, James. *Born Fighting: How the Scotch-Irish Shaped America.* New York: Broadway Books, 1999.
Wert, Jeffery D. *A Brotherhood of Valor: Common Soldiers of the Stonewall Brigade, C.S.A., and the Iron Brigade, U.S.A.* New York: Simon and Schuster, 1999.
_____. *The Sword of Lincoln: The Army of the Potomac.* New York: Simon and Schuster Paperbacks, 2005.
White, Wyman S. *The Civil War Diary of Wyman White: First Sergeant of Company F 2nd United States Sharpshooter Regiment, 1861–1865.* Ed. Russell C. White. Baltimore: Butternut & Blue, 1991.
Wildes, Thomas F. *Record of the One Hundred and Sixteenth Regiment in the War of the Rebellion.* Sandusky, OH: I.F. Mack & Bro., 1884.
Wilkinson, Warren. *Mother, May You Never See the Sights I Have Seen: The Fifty-Seventh Massachusetts Veteran Volunteers in the Army of the Potomac, 1864–1865.* New York: Harper & Row, 1990.
Wilson, E.A. "Second Bull Run." *National Tribune,* 19 October 1905.
Woodcock, Marcus. *A Southern Boy in Blue.* Ed. Kenneth W. Noe. Knoxville: University of Tennessee Press, 1996.
Woodhead, Henry, ed. *Echoes of Glory.* Alexandria, VA: Time-Life Books, 1991.
Wright, A. *National Tribune.* 18 February 1909, p. 7.

Index

Abbott, Pvt. Amos 46
Alabama 154
Alabama troops: Infantry (4th) 121; (15th) 121, 123–125, 127 134; (44th) 121; (47th) 121, 124, 126, 128; (48th) 121
Alexander, Col. E. Porter 112
Alexandria, VA 35, 68–69
Alsop Farm 174
Antietam, Battle of 87–88, 90–91, 93–94, 106, 115, 129, 133, 135–136, 190
Antietam Creek 76–77
Applin, Pvt. Charles 46
Appomattox Campaign 204
Appomattox River 191
Arkansas troops: Infantry (3rd) 167
Army of Northern Virginia 70–71, 92, 101, 139, 154, 178
Army of Virginia 35, 55–56, 70, 153
Army of the James 190, 193
Army of the Potomac 34–35, 70–72, 91–94, 96, 102, 105–106, 112, 114, 118–119, 134–135, 139–140, 153–154, 159, 163, 167, 174, 179, 183, 189, 191, 197, 201–202
Aschmann, Capt. Rudolph 10–11
Atlanta Campaign 195
Atlanta, GA 154, 183, 196
Auburn, VA 141
Augur, Maj. Gen. Christopher C. 35, 41–42

Bailey's Creek 190
Bank's Ford 100–101, 142
Barber, Chap. Lorenzo 111, 149, 198–199
Barlow, Maj. Gen. Francis 180–182, 187
Barney, Maj. Andrew 66–67
Bartlett, Sanford 51–52
Barton, Pvt. Joseph 153, 155, 176
Battery B, 4th U.S. Artillery 35, 42–43, 78, 86
Battery No. 11 185
Battery No. 12 185
Battery No. 22 196
Bayard, Brig. Gen. George 94
Beach, Lt. Edgar A. 196
Beard, Pvt. William 46

Beauregard, Gen. P.G.T. 184–185
Berdan, Col. Hiram 1, 7–14, 16–26, 29–31, 34, 38, 48, 50, 54–55, 65, 101, 103–104, 109–110, 113–114, 120–121, 138–139
Berlin, MD 137
Bermuda Hundred 179
Bernard House 97
Best, Col. Emory F. 5, 110, 121
Big Round Top 120–121, 123–130
Birney, Maj. Gen. David B. 109, 131, 143–144, 149, 153, 155, 159, 172, 180, 186, 190
Blair, Francis P., Jr. 11
Bliasdell, Col. William 109
Bloody Angle 172
Bolster, Pvt. David 194
Boonsboro, MD 71–72, 76
Bradley, Pvt. Joseph 196
Bragg, Lt. Gen. Braxton 70
Brandy Station 143–145, 149, 151–155, 176
Brandy Station, Battle of 117
Bristoe Station 38–39, 141–142
Brooks, Brig. Gen. W.T.H. 102
Brooks' Brigade 28
Brooks Station 96
Brown House 169
Bruce, Pvt. Horatio 178
Brunow, Scott 14
Buck, Pvt. Llewellyn 23–24
Buckingham, Brig. Gen. Catharinus 93
Buckland Mills 142
Bulger, Lt. Col. Michael 127
Burnside, Maj. Gen. Ambrose E. 93–97, 99–104, 106, 164
Butler, Maj. Gen. Benjamin 154, 186
Buxton, Capt. Albert 130, 153, 161

Caldwell, Capt. Henry 15, 58
Caldwell, Sgt. Horace 46
Calef, Q.M. Benjamin 89
Calkins, Chris 182
Cameron, Sec. Simon 9, 18–19
Campbell, Pvt. Henry 177
Carr, Pvt. Ira 121
Carter, Pvt. Reuben F. 190
Catharine Furnace 109–111
Catlett's Station 39–40, 50–51, 118

Cedar Creek, Battle of 196
Cedar Mountain, Battle of 58
Cemetery Hill 120–121
Cemetery Ridge 121, 131, 133
Centerville, VA 34, 37, 62–63, 118, 141
Chadwick, Sgt. Edwin H. 77–78, 84, 86, 88–89
Chaffin's Bluff 193
Chaffin's farm 189
Chamberlain, Maj. Gen. Joshua 126–127
Chancellor House 112–113, 156
Chancellorsville 5, 107–109, 112–113, 156, 165
Chancellorsville, Battle of 112, 114–116, 120–121, 123, 140
Chantilly, Battle of 68
Chase, Capt. Dudley 110
Chase, Sec. Salmon P. 46
Chattanooga, Battle of 152, 160, 164, 175
Chattanooga, TN 140, 154
Chesterfield Bridge 176
Chickahominy River 114, 178–179
Chickamauga, Battle of 140
Chickasaw Bluffs, Battle of 102
Churchill, Capt. William 196
Cilley, Pvt. Charles 196
Cincinnati, Ohio 153–154
City Point, VA 191
Clay, Corp. George A. 99
Clements house 194
Cochrane, Brig. Gen. John 102
Codori House 131
Coffin, Sgt. George 186
Cold Harbor 178–179, 184
Cold Harbor, Battle of 179, 181–182
Collins, Corp. William T. 59
Colt Revolving Rifles 20–21, 23–25, 29–30, 36, 42, 46–47, 50–52
Congdon, Corp. Henry 121
Connecticut troops: 14th Infantry 88
Cooper, Sgt. Preston 59
Cox, Brig. Gen. Jacob 72
Crampton's Gap 72, 74
Crane, Pvt. Luther 176
Crater, Battle of 190
Culpeper, VA 140–141
Culp's Hill 120, 131

241

Cummings, Corp. William 149
Cummings house 195

Dabney's Mill 195
Davis, Pres. Jefferson 13, 25, 96, 116–117, 140, 200
Dawes, Maj. Rufus 98
Deep Bottom 189–191, 193
Deep Bottom, Second Battle of 191
de Trobriand, Brig. Gen. P.R. 141, 143, 171, 190, 200–202
Devil's Den 123, 125, 129
Dewey, Capt. John 15
Dinwiddie Court House 200
Doubleday, Brig. Gen. Abner 74, 77, 80, 87, 97, 99
Doughty, Maj. James E. 65, 200–202, 203–204

Early, Lt. Gen. Jubal A. 183, 191
Egan, Maj. Gen. Thomas W. 167, 176, 185
Eighteenth Corps 179, 181, 184, 190
Eleventh Corps 94, 107–108, 112, 114–115, 120, 140
Ely's Ford 156
Emmitsburg, MD 119
Enfield Rifle Muskets 168
Enfield Rifles 168
Ewell, Lt. Gen. Richard 48, 50, 117, 174

Fairfax Courthouse 37
Fairfax Station 141
Fairview Heights 112
Falling Waters 136
Falmouth, VA 41–45, 48, 50, 52, 55–58, 95–96, 101, 104, 107, 116–117
Farnum, Pvt. Cyrus 46
Farnum, Pvt. Isaac 46
Feagin, Lt. Col. Isaac 123
Ferrero, Maj. Gen. Edward 102
Fessenden, Maj. Gen. James D. 15, 23, 205
Fessenden, Sen. William Pitt 23–24, 205
Field, Brig. Gen. Charles 42
Fifth Corps 35, 107, 120–121, 124, 129, 142, 153–154, 160, 165, 167–168, 175, 177, 181, 184, 194–195, 200–201
First Corps 35–36, 38, 71–73, 77, 86, 94, 97, 107, 120, 143, 148, 153, 179, 197
First Corps, Army of Northern Virginia 117, 160, 162, 165–166
First United States Sharpshooters 2, 6, 10–11, 14, 27–28, 31, 35, 39, 47, 53, 66–67, 89, 101, 103–104, 108–113, 121, 138–139, 141, 143–144, 147–149, 151, 155, 164, 166, 168–170, 176, 199

Flagler, Capt. D.W. 138–139
Fort Donelson, Battle of 152
Fort Sedgwick 194
Fort Siebert 199
Fort Sumter 33
Fort Ward 36
Fortress Monroe 34–35
Foster, Lt. T.P. 111
Fourth Corps 35
Fox home 176
Fox, William F. 205
Fox's Gap 72–73
Franklin, Maj. Gen. William 40, 72, 74, 94, 97, 102
Fraser, Gen. Simon 7
Frederick, MD 71–72, 136
Fredericksburg, VA 37, 40, 42, 46, 48, 96, 100, 102, 107–108, 113, 142
French, Maj. Gen. William 142–143, 146–147
Front Royal, VA 52, 137–138
Furgurson, Ernest 181
Fussell's Mill, Battle of 191

Gaines's Mill, Battle of 53–54
Georgia 154, 196
Georgia troops: 23rd Infantry 5–6, 109–111, 115, 121, 123, 156
Germanna Ford 150
Getty, Brig. Gen. George W. 158
Gettysburg, Battle of 120–121, 127, 134–136, 140–141, 145–146, 175
Gettysburg, PA 35, 119–120, 124, 129, 134, 136
Gibbon, Maj. Gen. John 35, 42, 55–56, 62, 78–80, 86, 180–181
Gilbert, Maj. Edwin 66
Glendale, Battle of 119
Globe Tavern 195–196
Gordon, Maj. Gen. John B. 171
Gracey, Bugl. George 180
Graham, Pvt. Benjamin 65
Grant, Brig. Gen. Lewis 158, 171
Grant, Maj. Gen. Ulysses S. 33, 102, 116, 135, 152–156, 158, 160, 163–167, 169, 172–175, 177–179, 182–193, 195–196, 200, 202
Gray, Sgt. Josiah 133
Greater New England 2, 12–13
Green, Pvt. William 39, 47, 185, 194
Gregg, Brig. Gen. David 193
Grigsby, Col. Andrew 79
Groveton, VA 62
Gum Springs, VA 118

Hadley, Pvt. Sylvester 59
Hagerstown, MD 71, 135
Halleck, Maj. Gen. Henry 56, 70, 76, 91, 106, 117–119, 135, 138–139, 141–142, 145, 177, 190
Hampton, Maj. Gen. Wade 165

Hampton Roads 200
Hancock, Maj. Gen. Winfield S. 70, 155, 158, 160, 166–167, 174–177, 179–181, 185, 191, 193, 195–196, 198
Hancock's Station 193
Hanger, Gen. George 8
Hanover Courthouse, Battle of 54
Hare House 186, 190
Harpers Ferry 6, 48, 71–72, 74, 76, 94, 118, 137
Harris Farm 174
Harrison, Pres. William Henry 55
Hart, Capt. Gilbert 15
Hatch, Brig. Gen. John P. 57–58, 61–66, 73–75
Hatcher's Run 194–196, 200–201
Hatcher's Run, Battle of 200–202
Hayman, Col. Samuel 112
Haymarket, VA 52
Hays, Brig. Gen. Alexander 155
Hazel Grove 112
Head, Pvt. Truman or "California Joe" 17–18, 39, 47
Heintzelman, Brig. Gen. Samuel 34, 71
Henagan's Redoubt 176
Hennessy, John 63
Heth, Maj. Gen. Henry 158
Hill, Lt. Gen. A.P. 31, 141, 160–161, 195
Hill, Lt. Gen. Daniel H. 72–73
Hood, Lt. Gen. John B. 80, 121
Hooker, Maj. Gen. Joseph 70–71, 77–78, 80, 86–87, 93–94, 102, 104–109, 112–115, 118, 140, 164
Howard, Maj. Gen. Oliver O. 109
Howard, Corp. Wilber 24
Huff, Pvt. John A. 205
Huguenots 9
Humphrey, Lt. William 74–75, 82, 86, 178, 205
Humphreys, Maj. Gen. Andrew A. 139, 191, 198
Hunt, Gen. Henry 7
Hunter, Maj. Gen. David 182

Illinois 103
Indiana 103
Indiana troops: Infantry (19th) 42; (27th) 71; (20th) 109, 111, 176, 185, 192, 200

Jackson, Lt. Gen. Thomas "Stonewall" 5, 47–48, 50, 52–53, 58, 61–65, 67–68, 74, 77, 97, 108, 112, 156
Jacobs, Pvt. Charles M. 65
James River 55, 154, 178, 183–184, 189–191, 193

Jarratt's Station 198
Jericho Mills Crossing 175
Johnson, Maj. Gen. Edward 131, 147
Jones, Pvt. George 153, 162
Jones, Brig. Gen. John R. 77
Jones, Pvt. Oliver 41
Jones, Sgt. William 1
Jones Farm 168

Kansas 2, 196
Keith, Pvt. Charles E. 65
Kelly's Ford 107, 142–143
Kelly's Ford, Battle of 143–144, 146
Kennedy, Pvt. John F. 169
Kent, Corp. James 77, 84, 133
Kerr, Pvt. William 82–83
Kershaw, Maj. Gen. Joseph 161
Keyes, Maj. Gen. Erasmus D. 34
Kilpatrick, Maj. Gen. Judson 35, 41, 146
King, Brig. Gen. Rufus 50–52, 55, 61, 63
Kings Mountain, Battle of 7
Knoxville, TN 152, 154

Lamprey, Pvt. Joseph 104
Laurel Hill 165–169
Law, Lt. John 188
Lawhorn, Lt. R.E. 111
Lawton, Brig. Gen. Alexander 77–78
Lee, Gen. Robert E. 48, 55, 57, 59–61, 68. 70–72, 74, 76–77, 87–90, 92, 95–97, 100, 105–108, 113, 116–119, 121, 129–131, 133–136, 138, 140–142, 144–147, 155, 159–160, 162–167, 171–172, 174–175, 177–179, 182–184, 186, 190–192, 193–194, 200
Leesburg, VA 118
Leslie, Pvt. Henry 200–201
Lincoln, Pres. Abraham 6–7, 9, 20, 25–26, 33–36, 40, 46–48, 56–57, 68, 70, 91, 93–94, 97, 100–103, 105–106, 117–118, 135–136, 138–140, 142, 152, 195–197, 200
Little Round Top 120, 123–130
Longstreet, Lt. Gen. James 61, 67–68, 71–72, 74, 107, 121, 140, 152, 160–162
Louisiana troops: 9th Infantry 84
Lynchburg, VA 154, 183

Madill, Col. Henry J. 185
Maine 12, 15
Maine troops: Heavy Artillery: (1st) 186, 200; Infantry: (3rd) 121; (17th) 143, 185, 200, 202; (20th) 124–127, 134
Malvern Hill, Battle of 53–55

Manassas Gap 137–138
Manassas, VA 34, 62, 118
Marcy, Capt. R.B. 20
Maryland 191
Massachusetts troops: Infantry: (11th) 108
Matteson, Pvt. William 192
Matthews, Adjt. James M. 74–75, 123, 131, 147, 203–204
McAllister, Col. Robert 200
McCauley, Sgt. David H. 143
McClellan, Major Gen. George B. 20–22, 24, 29–30, 33–35, 39–40, 45–46, 52–53, 55–58, 68, 70–76, 87–94, 96, 107, 114, 136, 167, 197
McClure, Capt. Jacob 130
McCoull House 165, 171
McDougal, Col. 187
McDowell, Maj. Gen. Irvin 34, 37, 40, 42, 46–48, 50–53, 60–61, 63–64, 68
McFarland, Pvt. William 144–145
McPherson, James 80
McPherson, Capt. Wm. 15
Meade, Maj. Gen. George G. 73, 77, 118, 129–130, 132–136, 138–142, 145–149, 154–155, 158, 163–164, 166, 169, 175, 179–180, 184–186, 189–190, 193–195, 201
Meikel, Lt. Col. 192
Michigan 12, 15
Michigan troops: Infantry (3rd) 148; (5th) 202; (24th) 42, 98
Milford Station 175
Miller, Pvt. James 182
Mine Run 147–150
Mine Run, Battle of 150–151, 180, 198
Minnesota 12, 14–15, 95
Minnesota troops: Infantry (1st) 127; (1st Battalion) 202
Mississippi 116
Mississippi River 33, 55, 102, 116, 135, 152
Mississippi troops: Infantry (18th) 97
Missouri 196
Mobile, AL 154
Model 1842 Muskets 109
Morrill, Capt. 126
Mott, Maj. Gen. Gershom 190, 192–195
Mule Shoe, the 169, 171–174
Murphy, Tim 7
Murry, Capt. Samuel F. 57, 95, 187–188

New Hampshire 15, 197
New Hampshire troops: Infantry (5th) 197, 202, 204
New Jersey troops: Infantry (11th) 114–115

New Market, VA 38
New Orleans, LA 154
New York troops: Heavy Artillery (2nd) 180; (7th) 174; Infantry (14th Brooklyn or 84th) 38, 40, 50–51, 66; (21st) 73–74; (22nd) 40, 66, 73; (24th) 40, 59, 65–66; (25th) 66; (30th) 40, 52, 66; (35th) 73; (38th) 138; (40th) 167; (44th) 127, 185; (66th) 169–170; (73rd) 195; (86th) 167, 195; (124th) 148, 195
Newell, Lt. William 188
Newton, Maj. Gen. John 102
Ni River 174
Ninth Corps 72, 77, 93, 154, 160, 175, 184, 189, 191, 194–195, 198
North Anna River 175, 177–178
North Carolina troops: Cavalry (2nd) 187; Infantry (30th) 144
Northern Democrats 116
Northup, Capt. Ira 143–144, 192
Norton, Adjt. S.F. 125, 127, 159

Oates, Col. William C. 123–128, 134
Ohio 6, 70, 103
Orange Court House, VA 56, 146
Ox Ford 175, 177

Palmer, J.C. 29–30, 48–49
Pamunkey River 175, 178
Parke, Maj. Gen. John G. 193
Parker's Store 156, 158
Parmelee, Adjt. Lewis C. 63, 82–83, 89
Parrott Gun, recaptured 159
Patrick, Brig. Gen. Marsena 73
Patuxent River 37
Peebles's Farm 193, 195
Payne's Farm, Battle of 147, 150
Pennsylvania 6, 12, 15, 72, 118–119, 133–134, 192
Pennsylvania troops: Infantry (10th Reserves) 97; (13th "Bucktails") 74–75; (26th) 108; (48th) 189; (83rd) 125; (105th) 145, 202
Peteler, Lt. Col. Francis 15, 41–42, 56, 58–59, 64, 95, 118
Petersburg, VA 178, 183–186, 188–189, 191–200
Pettijohn, Lt. D.B. 130
Phelps, Col. Walter 73, 80, 87, 99
Piedmont, Battle of 183
Pierce, Col. B.R. 176
Pierce, Pres. Franklin 197
Pike, Corp. Lewis 162
Pipe Creek 119
Pittsburgh, PA 152
Pleasanton, Maj. Gen. Alfred 117

Plum Run 123, 125, 127
Po River 166–168
Point of Rocks, MD 118
Pope, Maj. Gen. John 55, 57–58, 60–65, 67–68, 138
Poplar Springs Church 193–194
Port Hudson, LA 33
Porter, Maj. Gen. Fitz-John 46, 53, 67–68
Post, Col. Henry A.V. 15, 24, 28, 60, 62, 64–65, 68, 73–75, 80–82, 94–95, 115
Potomac River 35–37, 71, 76, 89, 92, 117, 134–136
Price, Maj. Gen. Sterling 196
Pullen, John 127, 134

Rapidan River 138, 140, 145–147, 149–151, 154–155, 165
Rappahannock River 34, 37, 40, 42, 45, 58, 60–61, 95–97, 99–101, 104–105, 107–108, 113–114, 117, 141–143
Rappahannock Station, Battle of 144, 146
Rappahannock Station, VA 58–59, 98, 142–143
Ray, Fred 150
Ream's Station 186
Ream's Station, Battle of 192–193
Rector Station 51
Reno, Maj. Gen. Jesse 72
Reynolds, Maj. Gen. John 94; killed 120
Rhode Island troops: Artillery (1st Battery) 166; Infantry (2nd) 10
Rhodes, Col. Elisha H. 10
Rice, Col. 127
Richards, Sgt. Henry 65
Richmond Howitzers 167
Richmond, VA 29, 32–36, 45, 47, 52, 55, 93, 96, 114, 116, 118, 140, 154, 164, 175, 178, 183, 186, 190, 193, 195
Ripley, Brig. Gen. James Wolfe 18–23, 48, 139, 204
Ripley, Col. William Y.W. 7, 30, 54
Robertson, Brig. Gen. J.B. 123
Robertson's Tavern 147
Rodes, Brig. Gen. Robert 73–74, 144
Rogers, Col. William 100
Rosecrans, Maj. Gen. William 105, 140, 142
Rowell, Maj. Edward T. 130, 188
Rowland, Maj. W.S. 9, 11–12, 24–25

Salem Church, Battle of 113–114
Sally, Pvt. James F. 182
Schurz, Maj. Gen. Carl 115
Scott, Lt. Gen. Winfield 9, 18, 106, 152

Scribner, Sgt. G.S. 173
Second Corps 34–35, 77, 108, 120, 129, 141–143, 153–156, 160–162, 165–167, 169, 171, 175–176, 179–181, 184–187, 189–191, 193, 195, 197–198, 200, 202
Second Corps, Army of Northern Virginia 117, 169, 174, 183
Second United States Sharpshooters 2, 6, 12, 14–16, 18–20, 23, 25, 31, 35–36, 38, 40, 45, 47, 50, 52–53, 55, 71, 89, 94–96, 101–104, 116–119, 135–142, 144–146, 150–153, 155–156, 164–165, 189–193, 205; Antietam 77–88; camp illnesses 27–28; Chancellorsville 107–108, 110–115; Cold Harbor 179–182; dissolved 202–204; Fredericksburg 97–100; Gettysburg 120–125, 127–134; Hatcher's Run, 1st 195–196; Hatcher's Run, 2nd 200–201; Kelly's Ford 143–144; Mine Run 148–150; North Anna 176–177; Payne's Farm 147, 150; Peebles' Farm 194; Petersburg Assault 184–186; reconnaissance to Orange Court House 56; Second Bull Run 62–68; skirmish at Falmouth 41–43; skirmish at Sulphur Springs 60–61; skirmishes at Rappahannock Station 57–59; South Mountain 73–76; Spotsylvania 166–175; Totopotomoy Creek 178; voting 197; Weldon Railroad 187–188; Weldon Railroad Raid 198–199; Wilderness 157–163
Seddon, Sec. James 116
Sedgwick, Maj. Gen. John 113–114, 142–144, 148–149
Seminary Ridge 133
Shady Grove Church 156, 158
Sharps Rifles 2–3, 17–25, 26–27, 29–31, 44, 47–53, 74, 77, 82, 122, 143, 148, 161–162, 166, 168
Sharpsburg, MD 76–77, 87, 89–90, 92, 94–95
Shenandoah Valley Campaign 195
Sheridan, Maj. Gen. Phillip 178, 196
Sherman, Maj. Gen. William T. 102, 154, 191, 196
Shiloh, Battle of 160
Shoup, Sgt. Maj. Samuel 58
Sickles, Maj. Gen. Daniel 108–109, 112, 121, 141
Sigel, Maj. Gen. Franz 154
Sixth Corps 35, 94, 97, 107, 113, 120, 129, 142, 146–148, 154, 158, 160, 163, 165, 168, 171,
174–175, 179–180, 186–187, 202
Slaughter Pen 127
Slyder Farm 123, 127
Smith, Pvt. Charles 113
Smith, Pvt. Daniel 182
Smith, Lt. Norris 204
Smith, Sgt. Walter 188
Smith, Maj. Gen. William F. 97, 102, 184
Smith's house 194
Snicker's Gap 137
Sommers, Richard 193
South Anna River 190
South Mountain 71–76
Spead, Pvt. Leonard 46
Spead, Pvt. William 46
Spencer Repeating Rifles 21–22, 138–139
Spindle Farm 165
Spotsylvania Campaign 175
Spotsylvania Court House 164–165, 174–175
Spotsylvania Court House, Battle of 170, 173, 175, 180, 186
Springfield Rifle Muskets as arms for sharpshooters 11, 18
Stannard, Maj. Gen. George J. 131
Stanton, Sec. Edwin M. 25, 46, 93
Starke, Brig. Gen. William E. 84
Starr, Pvt. Darius 29, 114–115
Stephens, V. Pres. Alexander 200
Stevens, Capt. Charles 20, 104, 108
Stevens, Corp. Warren 59
Stewart, Capt. 43
Stewart, Lt. James 78
Stoneman's Switch 101–103, 107
Stones River, Battle of 105
Storrs, Pvt. Francis 65
Stoughton, Lt. Col. Homer 15, 35, 68, 88, 94–95, 100, 120–124, 128, 131, 133, 136, 160, 186; captured 187–188; promoted to Lt. Col. 118; wounded 167
Stuart, Capt. Andrew 15
Stuart, Maj. Gen. J.E.B. 112, 205
Sturgis, Brig. Gen. Samuel D. 102
Sullivan, Col. Timothy 61
Sulphur Springs, VA 58, 60–61, 138, 140
Sumner, Sen. Charles 103
Sumner, Maj. Gen. Edwin V. 34, 94
Susquehanna River 118–119
Sussex County, VA 198
Sykes, Maj. Gen. George 72, 121

Talley House 166
Taneytown, MD 119
Tennessee 140, 152, 160

Tennessee River 140
Tennessee troops: Infantry (14th) 110
Tenth Corps 190
Texas 196
Texas troops: Infantry (1st) 86, 167; (4th) 121, 167; (5th) 121, 167
Third Corps 34–35, 104, 107–108, 112–113, 118, 120–121, 124, 129–131, 137, 141–143, 146–148, 153, 193, 197
Third Corps, Army of Northern Virginia 117, 141, 160, 162, 167, 176–177, 187
Third Corps, Army of Virginia 55, 71
Thompson, Lt. John 89
Thoroughfare Gap 51–52
Thorp, Lt. C.W. 144
Tinder's Mill 166
Todd's Tavern 156, 165–166
Totopotomoy Creek 178, 204
Trepp, Lt. Col. Caspar 10–11, 24–25, 103, 148–149, 151–152
Tripler, Surg. C.S. 28
Tripp, Lt. Col. Porter 109
Tucker, Pvt. Washington 77
Turner's Gap 72–76
Twelfth Corps 72, 77, 86, 94, 107–108, 120, 140
Twenty-fourth Corps 35
Twombly, Pvt. Robert 84
Tyler, Brig. Gen. Robert 174

United States Ford 100, 107–108, 114
United States Navy 153–154
Upton, Maj. Gen. Emory 168

Vermont 14–15
Vermont troops: Infantry 4th 202, 204; 14th 131
Virginia 189
Vicksburg, Battle of 152, 200
Vicksburg Campaign 183
Vicksburg, MS 33, 102, 116, 135
Vincent, Col. Strong 124, 128
Virginia troops: Cavalry: (9th) 41; Infantry: (40th) 41

Wapping Heights, Battle of 137–138
Wapping Station 137
Ward, Brig. Gen. John H.H. 111, 118, 121, 137–138, 153, 162, 167, 172, 176
Warner, Bugl. Carmillus 182
Warren, Maj. Gen. Gouverneur K. 147–149, 165, 168, 193
Warrenton, VA 50, 92–95, 138, 141
Washington, Gen. George 7, 40, 76, 152
Washington, D.C. 15, 30, 33–37, 45, 68, 70, 95, 100–102, 117–118, 138, 140, 145, 152, 172, 191
Wert, Jeffery D. 35, 136, 146

Wheaton, Pvt. Willard 41
Whipple, Maj. Gen. Amiel 113–114
White, Pvt. George 131–132
White, Corp. Wyman 162, 168
White House Landing 178, 184
White Plains, VA 50–51
Whitworth cannon 99
Whitworth Rifles 168, 176, 181
Wilderness, Battle of 157–158, 164
Wilkinson, Warren 160
Willard, Pvt. Eli 131
Williams, Brig. Gen. Alpheus 72
Williamsport, MD 136
Willis, Pvt. Daniel 60
Winchester, Battle of 49
Winchester, VA 117
Windmill Point 184
Wisconsin 12
Wisconsin troops: Infantry (2nd) 42, 56, 78; (6th) 42, 50, 78–79; (7th) 42
Wright, Capt. Abraham 133, 185, 188

Yellow Tavern, Battle of 205
York, Corp. Alvin 6
York, PA 119
Yorktown, VA 39, 47, 202